ALSO BY ELI SAGAN

Cannibalism: Human Aggression and Cultural Form

*The Lust to Annihilate: A Psychoanalytic Study
of Violence in Ancient Greek Culture*

AT THE DAWN OF TYRANNY

AT THE DAWN
OF TYRANNY

*The Origins of Individualism,
Political Oppression,
and the State*

ELI SAGAN

ALFRED A. KNOPF NEW YORK 1985

Copyright © 1985 by Eli Sagan
All rights reserved under International and Pan-American
Copyright Conventions. Published in the United States by
Alfred A. Knopf, Inc., New York, and simultaneously in
Canada by Random House of Canada Limited, Toronto.
Distributed by Random House, Inc., New York.

Owing to limitations of space,
all acknowledgments for permission to
reprint previously published material and to
reproduce illustrations can be found on page 421.

Library of Congress Cataloging in Publication Data

Sagan, Eli.
At the dawn of tyranny.

Bibliography: p.
1. Political anthropology   2. Social classes.
3. Ethnology—Polynesia.   4. Ganda (African people)—
Politics and government.   I. Title.
GN492.6.S23 1985   303.3   84-48736
ISBN 0-394-53922-2

Manufactured in the United States of America
FIRST EDITION

*This book is dedicated to the memory of Otto Isakower,
who gave me—among other gifts—a profound respect for the
ambiguity that exists between the psyche and society.*

Contents

Acknowledgments   ix

Cherubino and the Countess   xi

An Introduction   xv

I ANCIENT BUGANDA AND ITS TRANSFORMATION

1   The Pearl of Africa   3

2   The Life and Times of Prime Minister Mukasa, Part I   10

3   The Life and Times of Prime Minister Mukasa, Part II   19

4   The Blood of the Martyrs, Part I: Mutesa   27

5   The Blood of the Martyrs, Part II: Mwanga   33

6   The Life and Times of Prime Minister Mukasa, Part III   49

II ANCIENT POLYNESIA: TONGA, TAHITI, HAWAII

7   The Beauties of Tonga   59

8   The Enchanted Isles   62

9   The Arioi Society   69

10   Finow, Father and Son   78

11   "The Taboos Are at an End. . . . The Gods Are a Lie"   90

III O BRAVE NEW WORLD

12   O Brave New World . . .   97

13   'Ban 'Ban, Ca-Caliban   112

14 . . . That Has Such People In't!   135
15 Of Drums, of Cruelty, and Pissing on the King   150
16 Sing Muse: Of Bards, Jesters, Riddles, and the Birth of the
    Theatre   166
17 The Heroic Age   184
18 The Slaughter of the Innocents   196
19 Male Homosexuality and Male Bisexuality   204
20 Gambling, Prostitution, Exhibitionism, and Adultery
    Games   211

IV THE KINSHIP SYSTEM, THE STATE,
AND THE BEGINNINGS OF TYRANNY

21 From Kinship to the State; from Band Society to Complex
    Society   225
22 The Transformation of the Kinship System   243
23 "He Who Never Travels Praises His Mother's Cooking"   252
24 The Kabaka and the Clans   261
25 On Tyranny   277

V THE STATE AS A WORK OF ART

26 Chieftainship   301
27 Kingship: The Dream of Omnipotence   319
28 Kingship: The Failure of Omnipotence   331

VI PSYCHE AND SOCIETY

29 Toward a Theory of Social and Cultural Development   347
30 Drives, Needs, and Symbolic Transformation   367

    Notes   385
    Bibliography   397
    Index   407

Acknowledgments

Burton Raffel championed this book from the very beginning. Without his sustained enthusiasm it is doubtful whether it would have been published in its present form.

Robert Bellah has provided me, for the last twenty-five years, with a reality against which I could test my ideas and my work.

Lloyd deMause, Alan Dundes, Edmund Leites, and Miriam Sagan read every word of this work in manuscript, and each made valuable suggestions for its improvement.

John Rowe, of Northwestern University, who knows more about the Baganda than I ever shall, was enormously generous to me, giving advice, criticism, and unpublished works by Buganda historians. Marcia Wright, of Columbia University, helped steer me to important contemporary work on African history. Elizabeth Widenmann, of the Columbia University Library, shared with me her knowledge of African bibliography.

Reading the work of Irving Goldman and meeting with him first excited me about Polynesian history. It was his suggestion that I include Tahiti as well as Hawaii among my typical societies. Marion Kelly, Douglas Oliver, Sherry Ortner, and Marshall Sahlins generously provided me with unpublished work about Polynesia.

Joanne Nussbaum has been a near-perfect typist.

Sarah Blackburn made an important and difficult decision about this book which the fullness of time has vindicated.

It is a pleasure to thank Ann Close, who is the kind of person not supposed to exist anymore—an editor who cares greatly for style and has the time to expend on its infinite improvement.

Susannah Sagan—not unexpectedly—was called upon to provide the right help at the right moment during the final processing of this book.

Frimi Sagan has lived with this book since 1975. She has provided enormous encouragement and support to an author who, at some risk, had decided to go where he had never been before.

Cherubino and the Countess

What follows is a matter of fact, not of fiction; a matter of history, not of legend.

Princess Luwedde was the niece of Mutesa, king of Buganda (1856–84). She had been given as a wife to Prime Minister Mukasa by Mutesa as a reward for the minister's good services. They had two children together.[1]

One day, as was the custom with female members of the royal family, Princess Luwedde paid a visit to Princess Zansanze, a senior member of the family. Luwedde found the company being entertained by Kalemba, a comely youth, who was amusing those assembled with music on the harp. The youth, his youth, the harp, his singing were all too much for the only-too-human princess, "Prime Minister's wife that she was," and she became dangerously infatuated with Kalemba, regarding him as the most charming young man she had ever seen.

Knowing nothing of puritan restraint, Princess Luwedde confessed her need and desire to Princess Zansanze, who assured her cousin that arrangements would be made for the lovers to meet in private. We are not told of Kalemba's feelings, but presumably he could not refuse such an offer from a woman of high rank, and he must have known beforehand the risks and rewards of such beautiful singing and harp playing.

Several days later, Princess Zansanze, with seven other women, and with the youth Kalemba dressed as a woman, all proceeded to the house of Princess Luwedde, in the prime minister's compound. Each of the visitors carried a parcel of food, that being the public purpose of the visit. Overjoyed at the success of the stratagem, Lady Mukasa sequestered Kalemba in her hut, announced to the prime minister that she had entered into her "periods," and wished to be excused from her wifely night duties. Mukasa, having no reason to suspect the princess, busied himself with matters of state and consoled himself with another of his wives, while Kalemba and Luwedde spent several days obliterating the distinction between day and night.

Getting Kalemba out of the prime minister's enclosure proved more difficult than getting him in. The conspirators developed the plan of setting fire to Mukasa's house at night, with the expectation that in the ensuing confusion Kalemba could slip out to safety. Luwedde herself set the brand, and the anticipated rush and excitement followed. However, one of the prime minister's followers suggested that the gates be kept locked so that the perpetrator of the arson would be trapped and found. Kalemba stayed carefully concealed in Luwedde's house, but the problem of his escape remained unsolved.

Luwedde decided that the only way to get Kalemba out unnoticed was to use the same stratagem, in reverse, that was used to get him in. Accordingly, she sent one of her young female servants to Zansanze to make arrangements, using as an excuse the need to give her the news of the fire in the prime minister's compound.

Mukasa himself was sitting in his audience hall, playing the role of "little king" to those who were dependent upon him, when he spied Nnamukundi, the female messenger, returning from Zansanze's after having delivered Luwedde's message. We don't know why the prime minister's suspicions should have been aroused; possibly the fire had so unsettled him that he suspected treachery everywhere. In any case, he questioned the young girl, refused to believe her when she recited the contrived story to explain her errand, threatened to beat her if she did not declare the truth, and elicited from her the complete saga of Kalemba and Luwedde.

An immediate search was ordered. Luwedde's house was pulled down. After most of the grass had been removed, the harpist was found hiding under the last thin layer. Both Kalemba and Luwedde were brought before the prime minister, who was surrounded by followers sure to assent to whatever judgment he gave.

Lady Mukasa confessed her fault, asserting that she had been helpless in the face of the youth's exceptional beauty, and asked for mercy. Kalemba, however, struck the arrogant pose of the conqueror who has himself been conquered. He asserted that he had been perfectly aware of the risks he had hazarded and was prepared to take the consequences.

Kalemba's arrogance infuriated Mukasa. He ordered the youth's head cut off and given to Luwedde. His blood was to be smeared all over her head and dress. There was no court in which to appeal such a verdict from the prime minister. His executioners carried out the sentence.

In the royal city of Buganda there was no way to keep such news from the king, and Mutesa immediately knew of it. He sent Kaddu, one of his principal governors, to Mukasa, demanding that the princess be sent to him so that the king could punish her himself. The prime minister was so caught up in his own cruelty that at first he insisted Luwedde carry her lover's head with her when she went to Mutesa. But his subordinates and advisers cautioned him against this, and since no one remains a king's prime minister for fifteen years without having a large share of wisdom, Mukasa relented and let their judgment prevail over his fury.

Smeared all over with her lover's blood, the princess was led by Kaddu into the presence of Mutesa, who was furious that Mukasa had not sent the couple to him for punishment after having found them guilty. What did the prime minister mean by such an action, Mutesa mused aloud. It was an act of rebellion against the king. Was Mukasa planning to remove Mutesa and usurp the throne?

In part, Mutesa was acting. All prime ministers were of common, not royal, blood. Never in the history of Buganda had a prime minister usurped the throne. This was Mutesa's way of letting Mukasa know there should be a limit to the prime minister's power and arrogance.

Mukasa swallowed his anger. Advised again by his followers, he sent gifts to the king, together with his deepest apologies. The king sent Mukasa a message of pardon.

We hear no more of the Princess Luwedde.

An Introduction

When John Hanning Speke in 1862, and Henry Morton Stanley in 1875, entered the ancient kingdom of Buganda at the northwest corner of Lake Victoria in East Africa, each of them found what he had been looking for: Speke correctly conjectured, and Stanley confirmed, that Lake Victoria was the source of the Nile. What they also found there, eight hundred miles inside "darkest Africa," was an extraordinary and fascinating society, a society that had evolved independently of more "advanced" cultures into a complex, sophisticated kingdom. Lacking any written language, which for us has become the hallmark of civilization, Buganda had nevertheless developed an amazing variety of social and cultural institutions that we are accustomed to regard as compatible only with a culture capable of the written word. An authoritarian monarch, heading an aristocratic social structure of governors, subgovernors, sub-subgovernors, and thousands of petty bureaucrats, ruled a million people. Politics was as sophisticated and complex as that of any nineteenth-century English borough. A complete legal system, consisting of a hierarchy of courts to which one could appeal, was in place. Specialization of labor had proceeded to the extent that many people no longer worked the land but made their living as tax collectors, army officers, bards, drummers, fishermen, house builders, and executioners of the thousands sent each year to their death as human sacrifices. The stratification of society along economic and political lines had reached such a degree that it is not inappropriate to speak of social classes. The English explorers soon learned that in this sophisticated society they could no longer condescend to black Africans.

The contrast between this ancient kingdom and the tribal societies that Stanley and Speke had passed through on their way to Buganda was palpable. In these tribes there was no government as we understand the term—no police, no courts, no jails; no governors, no kings, no tax collectors. They lacked schools, standing armies, an organized priesthood, and any extensive division of labor. They exhibited no social classes, no stratification of society. In sharp distinction to the kingdom of Buganda, the tribal societies supported no political tyranny. There was no state.

Since the days of Stanley's explorations we have learned an enormous amount about tribal, primitive societies through the field of anthropology. We know that such societies, though lacking a state, did not live in social chaos. The kinship system—a highly structured sense of family—was the primary mechanism of social control in primitive society, and it did its job so well that there was no need for the intricate machinery of government that is essential for our (nonkinship) society. The height of political power in a primitive society rested in a lineage or village head, but these leaders had no real ability to enforce their will; all their functions were loose, flexible, and unstructured. The lineage or village head acted as a nonauthoritarian leader of a family—endless conversation, not raw power, was the means to whatever control existed.

Similarly, custom and the power of custom, reinforced by the inexorable pressure of the kin, maintained order. There was no law as we understand the term. This does not mean that a delinquent individual was free to thieve, rape, or murder. Punishment for such crimes was as swift and as certain as in any society, but the instrument of punishment was always the kin of the victim. Murder, for instance, was avenged by the victim's kin, either on the perpetrator himself or on someone of *his* kin. The kin always shared in the psychological victimization felt by the injured party. What we would call a crime against society was conceived as a crime against the kin.

In primitive society there was no stratification along economic lines, no social class. Though there were a few positions of prestige, these did not carry the capacity to oppress others. The notion that adult men should oppress other adult men in the same society was unknown. Tyranny of men over women and older people over younger ones (sexual and generational tyranny) did exist, and varied greatly in degree and quality from one culture to another. Primitive society was "egalitarian" only for adult males.

The absence of a complex division of labor meant that primitive society lacked a standing army or professional officers. Wars, of which there were plenty, were fought by almost every adult male when the time came. Killing, raiding for cattle or slaves, shoving others off a certain piece of territory—all this was an important part of social life in most primitive societies, but there was no conquest of other peoples, no ruling over another group that was allowed to stay on its land. Primitive peoples who did not "rule" themselves, in our sense of the word, certainly could not conceive how to rule others.

There were two important attitudes in which primitive societies differed sharply from nonliterate kingdoms like that of ancient Buganda. First, the primitive stance vis-à-vis acts of what we would call "individuality" was cool, if not downright hostile. The man who tried to set himself above other men, in either a political, a sacred, or an economic way was treated with animus. Second, the sacred life in primitive society leaned very far toward magic. The gods were of little concern to most primitive societies, priests hardly existed, and there was no organized priesthood. The characteristic functionary in the sacred world was the shaman, who was essentially a worker of magic. Witchcraft, not a moralistic religion, made the world go round.

The life that Speke and Stanley found in ancient Buganda was far different from that in a primitive society. And yet Buganda and other African monarchies were not like the societies we have come to call archaic civilizations—the literate, sophisticated, variegated empires of ancient Mesopotamia, Egypt, India, China, Mexico, and Peru. Archaic civilization represented a degree of social evolution vastly more complex than primitive society. To be transported from the relatively simple primitive world to the archaic—to fourth- and fifth-dynasty Egypt or to the great flowering of society under Sargon or Hammurabi in Mesopotamia—is to arrive not only on another continent but almost on a different earth. Everything that seems to us "missing," "lacking," "absent" in primitive society is vibrantly alive—for good or for ill—in the archaic. An authoritarian king rules a society of several million people; he is capable even of empire: conquering, subduing, and ruling alien peoples. The monarch reigns from the top of a vast bureaucratic, aristocratic, oppressive pyramidal societal structure: courtiers, governors, subgovernors, tax collectors, judges, police, jailers. The whole complex network that we call "government" is fully formed. A hereditary aristocracy lords it over common people. The world has become full of rich and poor, oppressors and oppressed, tyrannical politics and occasional faint cries for justice. A vast priestly organization, in the service of powerful gods, plays a crucial role in the religious and political life of the society and demonstrates the vague beginnings of a conscious moral life.

When we read Stanley's and Speke's descriptions of ancient Buganda, we immediately begin to wonder what kind of society this was. What stage of social evolution had it reached in its independent way? What evolutionary relationship did such a stage of society have to the primitive and the archaic? Neither Stanley nor Speke—nor the culture in which they lived—possessed the theoretical sophistication that would have been required to think about various stages in the evolution of society. The theoretical structure that would help answer such questions—and is, indeed, responsible for their even being asked—has been over a hundred years in the making.

The years 1850 to 1950 witnessed the beginnings of the new fields of anthropology and archaeology and saw them grow to full maturity. The revelation of the worlds of primitive peoples and the great archaic civilizations of Egypt, Mesopotamia, and the Aegean enabled the historical imagination to make a quantum leap. Previous to that, history—which is really people's sense of the past—began only in biblical times and in classical Greece and Rome. Anthropology and archaeology added a million years to human history.

As the worlds of the Zuñi, the Nuer, the Bushman, the Kwakiutl, the Australian aborigine, and the Trobriand Islander became part of the imagination of people who were thinking about the nature of human culture; as the history, literature, law, and art of the Sumerians, Babylonians, Assyrians, Egyptians, Minoans, and Mycenaeans became readily available, some students of world history and culture, especially in England, began to inquire how these newly discovered regions related to the earliest cultures previously known, those of Israel, Greece, and Rome. In the last years of the nineteenth century and the first years of the twentieth, British anthropologists, biblical scholars, and classicists—people like Frazer, Cornford, Robertson-Smith, Gilbert Murray—began to construct an evolutionary, or a developmental, schema of human cultural history that postulated a continuous line of development from primitive to archaic civilization to classical and biblical times. The work was sketchy and incomplete, and it remained so when, in the 1920s, evolutionary and developmental thinking in cultural matters went almost entirely out of intellectual fashion. For the next forty years, except for Marxist historians, who were, and are, committed to a developmental view of society, only a few lonely souls pursued this course of thought. Among others, there were Julian Steward in anthropology, the sociologist Talcott Parsons, the classicist E. R. Dodds, and the archaeologist Henri Frankfort.

Two works resulting from these efforts—Henri Frankfort's book *The Intellectual Adventure of Ancient Man*,[1] published in 1946, and an essay by Robert Bellah (who began his career as a student of Parsons) entitled "Religious Evolution,"[2] published in 1964—support an evolutionary-developmental view of history and culture. Both see such development as proceeding through certain definite stages, and both conceive of the first two stages as primitive society and archaic civilization.

When I began thinking about this problem, it seemed to me that such a situation was impossible. If one imagined a typical primitive society, like the Zuñi or like the Nuer on the White Nile, and then one evoked the great kingdoms of archaic civilization, it seemed impossible that any culture could have gone from Nuer to early dynastic Egypt in one jump. No matter what kind of revolutionary change society has been capable of, so much cultural ground could not have been traversed in only one cultural revolution. There must have been, I felt, a stage of society between the primitive and the archaic, a stage that put an end to primitive society and that led, by reasonable revolutionary change, to the beginnings of archaic civilization.

Once I decided to look for such a stage, it proved remarkably easy to find. The traditional societies of East, West, and South Africa and of Polynesia provided literally dozens of examples of centralized, hierarchical, tyrannical (but nonliterate) states operating at a high stage of development during the eighteenth and nineteenth centuries: Benin, Dahomey, Zulu, Bunyoro, Buganda, Hawaii, Tahiti, Tonga. These states ceased to exist only as a result of contact with European and American societies. The state of Buganda, where one centralized monarch ruled a million people with the aid of nearly fifty thousand civil servants, collected taxes on an organized basis, put thirty thousand soldiers into the field, and presided over a complex hierarchical society, was no primitive society, even though it lacked a written language. Directly contrary, states such as ancient Buganda were the end process of one of the most important, most difficult, most revolutionary cultural changes ever accomplished—the radical and permanent transformation of primitive society and culture. It was in such ancient kingdoms that the state as we know it first made its appearance on earth. That early dynastic Egypt evolved out of a society that resembled ancient Buganda, and not out of a primitive society, seems a most reasonable hypothesis.

After immersing myself in the vast historical data on nonliterate kingdoms, I quickly discovered that many scholars, almost all of them with anthropological training (e.g., Fried, Service, Claessen),[3] have been working on the problems of the early evolution of society from a theoretical point of view for the past thirty years. I have learned much from these scholars, though my approach to social evolution differs radically from theirs.

I call the stage of social and cultural development represented by such ancient kingdoms as Buganda and Hawaii "complex society," because the word "primitive," when used in a scientifically accurate way not intended to degrade people, means "simple." Primitive societies *were* simple compared with the complex societies that developed out of them. If we continue to use "primitive" to describe simple, tribal, kinship societies, it seems appropriate to designate as "complex" all forms of society that existed between primitive society and archaic civilization. The central purpose of this book is to describe, to evoke, and to analyze complex society.

As always happens in such circumstances, once a particular form has been isolated, it in turn becomes capable of further analysis. Complex society itself seems to develop through three distinct stages: chieftainship, early monarchy, and complex monarchy, chieftainship being the first stage of complex society to emerge out of the primitive matrix. Both stages of monarchy, taken together, I have called "advanced complex society," and these societies are the true subject of this book, although I will spend time on chieftainships as well.

The great accomplishment of complex society was the creation of nonkinship forms of social cohesion. Loyalty to the king and fear of his power to oppress are forms that go beyond kinship. So close was the connection between the breakdown of the kinship system and the rise of the state that, in my view, the state may be defined as that form of society in which nonkinship forms of social cohesion are as important as kinship forms. Why only a tyrannical monarch had the power to overthrow the kinship system is one of the fundamental questions raised in this book.

The demise of the kinship system and the erection of nonkinship political forms was by no means a calm and rational process. Leaving the security of the kin, which may have been one of the most difficult tasks human beings have ever set themselves, was a separation fraught with anxiety, and a heightening of anxiety always brings an acceleration of aggression. Any society caught in a situation of increasing anxiety will look for aggressive outlets as a defense against that dread. It is remarkable to discover how many *identical* means various complex societies resorted to in the attempt to deal with the anxiety brought on by the breakdown of the kinship system. The resemblance between the various complex societies we know of is striking.

It is the similarity of cultural and social forms that legitimizes the concept that these societies belonged to a particular and unique stage of human social development. For example, *every* advanced complex society had a centralized monarchy, a political bureaucracy, the systematic collection of taxes, an organized priesthood, and a hierarchically ordered social system. These institutions, which have been so important in human history, have their origins in this stage of social development, not in the archaic. Further, within all complex societies, we find developed, rich cultures, full of imaginative and differentiated cultural forms. The individuality that we prize so highly, which did not exist in primitive society, had its beginnings in the complex. Epic poetry, fairy tale, professional bards, and the theatre originated here. Again, what is so striking is that *all* advanced complex societies partook of these pleasures.

Even in regard to certain minor but important cultural forms one is struck over and over again by the fact that cultures halfway around the globe from one another should have differentiated themselves from their primitive antecedents in exactly the same ways. Male homosexuality and bisexuality played an important role in most advanced complex societies. Royal incest, in which the king marries his half- or full sister, was a widespread ritual form. Prostitution, adultery games, sexual exhibitionism, and compulsive gambling made their first, but not their last, appearance on the cultural scene in these same societies.

One of the great delights in the study of complex society is the discovery that the people themselves were some of the most attractive, from the human point of view, of any who have graced this earth. When one is reading descriptions of those who lived in ancient Buganda or ancient Polynesia, images of the Italian Renaissance or Athens in the fifth century B.C. come to mind in the attempt to find a people as energetic, expansive, as full of the possibilities and complexities of human existence. From Captain Cook in the Pacific to Henry Morton Stanley in Africa, many of the first Europeans to visit these societies were, for good reason, enchanted by the people they found there.

As delightful and appealing as the people were, as expansive and exciting as was their culture, one great fact cries out for explanation: many very important aspects of the dark side of human life also made their first appearance in complex societies. Primitive society had no severe class differences, no tyrannical monarchy or aristocracy to rob people of their chances for life. Poor people, aristocratic tyranny, severe political oppression—all this we have inherited from advanced complex society. Strikingly, human sacrifice was the characteristic form of ritual aggression in almost every one of these societies. In primitive society it did not exist; archaic civilization seldom practiced such a ritual. But in complex societies like Buganda, hundreds and thousands were slaughtered each year. This book makes a very serious attempt to answer the question of why all these dehumanizing human forms find their beginnings only after primitive society has been overthrown.

This history of complex society will be told primarily by using data from three representative cultures: ancient Buganda at the northwest corner of Lake Victoria in East Africa; ancient Polynesian Tahiti, one of the Society Islands in the Pacific; and ancient Hawaii, also a Polynesian culture in the Pacific. I do not intend to restrict the argument to these data alone, because this is a rumination about complex society as a whole, and information from other complex societies will be used freely. I am concerned with these societies in their traditional form, before they were transformed by contact with European and American culture. For Tahiti and Hawaii that contact began in the latter part of the eighteenth century; in Buganda, the traditional society was still in full flower as late as 1875.

This book is both a history and a sociological study. It is a history in that one of its primary aims is to describe how it felt to be alive in such a society; what it meant to be a prime minister, or a prime minister's wife, the king of Buganda, a page at the court of the Hawaiian monarch, an itinerant actor, a renowned warrior, or a poor back-country peasant. It is also a sociological study attempting to answer questions about the nature of society and cultural development on the deepest theoretical level. Why was human sacrifice the characteristic form of aggression in complex society? What is the relationship between the destruction of the primitive kinship system and the beginnings of tyranny and the state? After human beings had lived on this earth for two million years or so, why did people decide to create kings and nobles and tax collectors? Why, in essence, did our ancestors destroy the primitive world and create complex society, which ultimately made archaic civilization possible?

In my view, these and other important questions cannot be answered unless we understand the relationship between the development of the individual human psyche and the development of society and culture. It would not be surprising to discover that the stages in the progress of the psyche are intimately and intricately connected with the stages of social development. The ultimate aim of this book is to illuminate these connections.

I

ANCIENT BUGANDA
AND ITS
TRANSFORMATION

1

The Pearl of Africa

The British explorer John Hanning Speke was the first representative of Christian culture to enter the ancient kingdom of Buganda. It was 1862; Speke was looking for the source of the Nile. Even though Speke was no newcomer to African exploration, having tried it twice before, it took him sixteen months to walk the eight hundred miles from Zanzibar on the African east coast to Mutesa's capital. This isolation allowed for the preservation of the ancient society until about 1880, when, first, Christian missionary and Islamic influence, and, subsequently, British imperial interests put an end to the traditional culture.

Previous to Speke's arrival, there had been some slight contact between Buganda and Arab traders operating out of Zanzibar. We even have evidence from oral history that trading goods, such as cups and plates, could be found at the king's palace as early as the 1780s. There is almost certain evidence that Arab traders entered Buganda in the 1850s and strong circumstantial evidence of contacts in the 1830s and 1840s. Regardless of these intrusions, what Speke found in 1862 was a highly developed complex society that had developed over a period of four to five hundred years without substantial contact with more advanced or literate societies.

For twelve years after Speke's departure, no member of European society appeared in Buganda. Islamic influence, however, began to change the culture, and in the 1860s Mutesa carried on a serious flirtation with Islam. When Henry Morton Stanley arrived in 1875, the ancient society was still functioning as such, but change was in the air and Mutesa was no longer the unsophisticated parochial king with whom Speke had dealt.

Stanley sent his famous telegram to England reporting that Mutesa had requested Christian missionaries to come to Buganda. The response was instantaneous. By 1877 the first Protestant missionaries were on the scene. In 1879 a Catholic mission arrived. The speed with which the Baganda were converted was incredible. By 1886 the threat of Christianity to the traditional society was so strong that the unsympathetic king, Mwanga, son and successor to Mutesa, burned two or three hundred martyrs. Conversions to Islam also continued apace. In 1888, about ten years after the first Christian missionaries arrived, the combined forces of the newly converted Muslims, Protestants, and Catholics drove the king out of the country.

True to their European and Arab teachers, the Baganda then proceeded to wage their own wars of religion. First Islam triumphed, and the Christians of both the English (Protestant) and French (Catholic) factions were forced into exile. Then they returned and defeated the Muslims, with the help of arms provided by British traders. Not content with that victory, the English and French Christians fought one another. By this time, British soldiers were in the country, and the French Catholic faction had no chance of success. It was 1892.

Two years later, the British established the Uganda Protectorate. In 1900, the English commissioner imposed a land settlement on the country whereby all the land was given over to private ownership. The principal beneficiaries of this settlement were the nearly three thousand members of the aristocracy, primarily Christian, who had replaced the king as the most important political power in the country. Mwanga had been deposed and his four-year-old son declared king. The regents who ruled in his place were not related to the young king but were the leaders of the newly landed aristocracy. The ancient society of Buganda had ceased to exist.

"Uganda" was the Zanzibari name for Buganda. The Uganda Protectorate created by the British, which eventually became the tragic modern state of Uganda, consisted of several ancient kingdoms, one of which was Buganda. Within this British invention were also to be found various peoples who did not live in kingdoms—peoples living in primitive tribal societies or in early complex societies "ruled" by chiefs. In the twentieth century, one of the most important political questions for the Uganda Protectorate, and subsequently for the independent state of Uganda, was the relationship between Buganda and the other peoples in this political entity.

The country is "Buganda"; the people are the "Baganda"; one per-

son is a "Muganda"; the language is "Luganda." Luganda is one of the
great Bantu family of languages. The Bantu peoples—those who speak
a Bantu language—have, like the Indo-Europeans and the Semites, been
one of the great civilizing peoples in world history. Starting probably
from one small area, they proceeded to conquer and settle most of Africa south of the Sahara. By the middle of the nineteenth century, the
Bantu peoples could be found in every stage of cultural development,
from primitive tribal societies to great kingdoms. By 1850, no Bantu people existed without agriculture or the domestication of animals, and no
Bantu had yet created an archaic state like Egypt or Sumeria. The conquest of the continent by Christian and Islamic cultures, of course,
meant that no Bantu people was to be given the chance to create such
a state.

The almost total isolation of the kingdom of Buganda until 1860,
and the relative isolation from 1860 to 1880, are a tremendous boon to
the scholar who would understand the nature of highly developed complex societies. In the last half of the nineteenth century, almost every
European who went to Africa wrote a book, first explorers, and then
missionaries. As a result of the literary efforts of Speke, Stanley, and
the earliest missionaries, Mutesa, the *kabaka* (king) of Buganda, was a
familiar person to the literate Englishman of 1885.

Buganda historiography was greatly fortunate in that one of the missionaries who entered the country in the latter part of the nineteenth
century, the Reverend John Roscoe, was enthralled by the new study
of anthropology. Roscoe was a friend of J. G. Frazer, the great British
anthropologist, and Frazer advised him how to proceed in his investigation of Buganda society. With the help of Apolo Kagwa, prime minister
and regent to the king, Roscoe interviewed many elderly people who
had lived a good part of their lives in the ancient traditional society.
A person of sixty, interviewed by Roscoe in 1895, would have been born
in 1835, twenty-one years before Mutesa became king. Roscoe's *The
Baganda,* published in 1911, remains one of the most important reports
of a complex society we have.

The Baganda response to Christian and Islamic contact was extraordinarily assertive, and the Baganda did not leave it entirely to anthropologists and imperialists to write the history of their country. Starting
with Apolo Kagwa himself, a group of Buganda historians, most of
whom were born before the great conversions to Christianity and Islam,
began writing histories of their country.

The result of all this activity is that we know much more about the ancient kingdom of Buganda than we know, for instance, about the first dynasties of Egypt, or about Athens in the sixth century B.C. There is the popular notion, still being taught to our children in grammar school, that "history," which really means "our history," begins with Egypt and Mesopotamia, that everything before that is somehow "prehistoric," and therefore of less importance. As this book unfolds, we will see that the history of the great kingdoms of complex societies is as much "our history" as anything else that has ever happened to human beings. To take only one example, the great process of nonkinship politics, by which we live and die today, was the creation of that stage of society. We know practically nothing about the societies that preceded archaic Egypt and archaic Sumeria. From ancient Buganda we can learn what it felt like to be alive in such a "prehistoric" time.

Buganda was a centralized, bureaucratic, hierarchical state, ruled by an autocratic king, the *kabaka*. In theory, there was no law higher than the king's wishes and no man whose advice the king must ask. Such autocracy exists only in dreams. In reality, the king of Buganda had to worry about the political power that existed beyond his reach, and was just as circumscribed by his system of government as Louis XIV, Napoleon, and Josef Stalin were by theirs.

The country was divided into ten provinces, and the ten provincial governors, together with the king's prime minister, provided a political counterweight to the sovereign. A provincial governor ruled only on the sufferance of the king, but no king ever survived the discontent of a large majority of his governors. Each governor was a small version of the king in his own province, and he had subgovernors under him, who in turn had subordinates under them. Political power and authority passed down from the top. Taxes and forced labor and military service passed up the ladder from the bottom.

Such was the state system of politics that was the invention of complex culture. The older, kinship system of clans continued to exist side by side with the newer structures. There were between thirty and forty clans in Buganda, which owned their own burial grounds and shrines, exerted some very loose control over land tenure, and each functioned with a clan head as well as with heads of several subdivisions of the clan. The clan system was also hierarchical, building from small kinship groups into larger and larger ones. The full clan could contain as many as thirty to forty thousand people. There was an important political and psychological tension between the state system and the clan system, which we shall look at later in detail.

Not every complex society was a centralized monarchy. Just as political development could not and did not go from primitive societies like the Nuer or the Zuñi to dynastic Egypt in one jump, in the same manner the social distance from primitive societies to centralized monarchies was too great to be covered in one stage. Centralized monarchies represent the *end* product of the development of complex societies. Between primitive tribal societies and centralized monarchies the stage of chieftainship must be added, and it is possible to talk about the development of complex society from chieftainships to early monarchies to complex monarchies. From nineteenth-century Africa we have evidence of many peoples in every stage of this developmental process.

We do not know when the country of Buganda changed from chieftainship to early monarchy and from that to complex monarchy. We do have a fairly complete oral history of the "kings" of Buganda that seems to go back to around 1300, but we have no way of knowing whether some of the "kings" were merely chiefs. It is a reasonable assumption, based on the oral history, that the centralized state of Buganda as it was known in the nineteenth century was five hundred years in the making, and that there was a steady expansion of the kingdom after the year 1600.[1]

Buganda was not the only centralized kingdom in the area of Lake Victoria. Rwanda was a powerful, centralized state to the south of Buganda, though there was very little contact between the two. Ankole, Karague, and Burundi were states of a lesser degree of power and centralization. In the two or three hundred years that preceded the accession of Mutesa, Bunyoro was the state that provided the strongest competition with Buganda for political control of the region. Buganda won this struggle for dominance primarily because its political system worked better, provided more flexibility, and delivered more military power. By the time of Speke's visit, Bunyoro, though still important, could no longer challenge Buganda for pre-eminence.

We who live in the midst of the cold war—that latest evolution of Western politics—assume that the determination of which state is pre-eminent is an important matter in people's lives. It is of interest to note that members of primitive societies had neither states nor our idea of pre-eminence. An attitude that we regard as inevitable for all people—a result of universal "human nature"—may not have existed for all time, may indeed have been invented or discovered or created by societies in a certain stage of development. That we still care about political dominance in the same way as ancient Bunyoro and Buganda did says only that this attitude is enduring, not that it is coeval with human-kind. The Banyoro and the Baganda killed each other to win the prize of pre-eminence; most of us are ready to do the same. But it was not always so, and this practice may someday cease to plague us.

The fertility of the soil, the climate, and the system of agricultural production were such in Buganda that the men did practically no work in the raising of food. Women provided the agricultural labor, and men were free to build houses, construct roads, clear land, fish, sleep, talk, smoke, hunt, mix in politics, and create a state. Bananas, or plantains, were the staple food crop, and bananas take remarkably little work in the proper climate. Bananas could be raised on the same soil in Buganda for forty years with no loss of yield. Their supply was certain, they required very little labor, and they were harvested all year round. The climate of Buganda was perfect for the growing of bananas: temperature never below 50 degrees Fahrenheit or higher than 105 degrees; an even rainfall; and no particular dry season.[2]

Bunyoro was not blessed with such a banana-beneficent climate and had to depend more on cereal production, which required greater labor to provide the same number of calories. It is not proper to conclude from this, however, that the difference in climate was the main factor contributing to the relative success of Buganda. In neighboring Busoga, just across the Nile, the bananas grew even better than in Buganda, but the Basoga never evolved a centralized state, creating, at their highest stage of development, several strong chieftainships.[3] No materialist explanation will ever be adequate to rule out the spirit of a people as a fundamental fact of human history and development. Everyone of sensitivity who visited Buganda in the nineteenth and early twentieth centuries was immediately struck by the vitality, the eagerness, the intelligence, the life-enhancing quality of the Baganda, by what they had achieved. At first, the British dubbed them "the Chinese of Africa," until the situation in the Far East changed and the Baganda were referred to as "the Japanese of Africa." From the imperial English, these were meant as high compliments. It was the young Winston Churchill who called the country "the Pearl of Africa."

The Baganda did not live in villages but in separate homesteads strung out through the countryside. The only city was the king's capital, with thirty to forty thousand people: the political hierarchy and bureaucracy, the servants of the king, the hangers-on, entertainers, craftsmen, concubines, and wives.

The kingdom that Mutesa ruled lay crescent-shaped along the

northwest corner of Lake Victoria; it contained about ten thousand square miles. What is extraordinary is that Mutesa ruled over a million people. He had the capacity to put thirty thousand warriors into the field at one time, assisted by a naval force of another fifteen thousand troops. The population of England under the rule of Henry VIII was only three million people. As we will observe when we look more carefully at the evolution of political systems, what happens in primitive societies is that as the population grows larger, the kinship system becomes too unwieldy to work as a single entity, and there is a splitting or segmenting. In some primitive societies this happens when the size reaches no more than three hundred people. That a single man could rule a million people was a remarkable achievement, one that required the creation of many new political forms, one that took hundreds of years to develop, one that took a people who desired to have such a state. The creation of such a state was also an accomplishment full of tension, conflict, and anxiety: the goals of complex society were achieved only at great psychological cost. We may admire the courage of the Baganda, who were ready to take whatever risks were necessary to make that political revolution, even as we suspend judgment as to whether or not humankind is better off for having overthrown the primitive world.

2

The Life and Times of Prime Minister Mukasa, Part I

When King Suna died in 1856, the passing of sovereignty to his son Mutesa was accomplished with no great political disruption, even though Mutesa was young and inexperienced. The power of the monarchy held. Political continuity had clearly become a value for Buganda society.

Mukasa, at the time of Mutesa's accession, was a page at the king's court. His father had been one of the ten great provincial governors under Kabaka Suna, ruling the large southern border province of Buddu. This was a great help to Mukasa when he started out in political life—the king was inclined to think well of Mukasa because of his father's position, and anxious to give the young man opportunity to prove himself—but it could not by itself have assured Mukasa the attainment of high office. That he would have to achieve by himself. The situation was similar to circumstances in our own society: a person named Taft running for the Senate from Ohio does not start at the same place as the other candidates, but his electoral success is not certain; the name will not automatically set him at the top.

The Baganda had evolved an elaborate system of sending young men away from home to be raised by people other than their parents, a custom also true of ancient Hawaii. An uncle or some other relative, especially if he held a political office, was the perfect choice for an ambitious family. Many young men were sent to the *kabaka*'s court to become pages and learn the sophisticated life. Mukasa was probably taken from his mother at five or six years of age and sent to be raised properly by a relative living at a distance from his home. At around twelve, he would have started his life as a page at the royal court.[1]

For the young people, the situation at the royal court was not simple. The *kabaka* had a multitude of wives and hundreds of children. Every royal prince was a potential monarch; the mothers of the princes actively promoted the prospects of their sons; rivalry between princes and between mothers of princes was intense. For that reason, it was unlikely that the *kabaka*'s sons would be friendly with one another, and the young pages who attended the court naturally fell into relationships of friendship and companionship with various royal youths. To become the companion of a royal prince who subsequently became the *kabaka* was a most fortunate occurrence for an ambitious young commoner.

Mukasa was an attractive youth, possessing obvious intelligence as well as "a fine set of white teeth, bright eyes, and general good looks."[2] We do not know how close Mukasa was to Mutesa before the latter became the monarch, but soon after his accession, Mutesa appointed Mukasa to a position of great trust: guardian over the imperial lavatory. The Baganda, independent of world history, had invented the privy. No fact of Buganda life drew greater praise from the first English explorers than this. For a page to be assigned to preserve the security of the king's privy was a first-class promotion.

As he was destined to do in every job he would ever attempt, Mukasa performed this first task with distinction, and the reward for so doing was his promotion to the rank of *mutongole,* member of an elite corps answerable only to the king. This corps of *batongole* (plural of *mutongole*) provided the king with a political counterweight to the power of the ten provincial governors, who represented a potential threat to the *kabaka*'s absolute control. A *mutongole,* with no large province to govern, would have less opportunity to create his own local source of political power; he was, therefore, more dependent upon the *kabaka* and could be relied upon to fight for the king should he be challenged by one or several provincial governors.

An appointment such as that of Mukasa to the king's bodyguard was made personally by the *kabaka.* The king might be unable to control everything that went on outside his capital, but within the city no major or minor political act was taken without the *kabaka*'s knowledge and consent. Mukasa was given the special honor of carrying a double-barreled gun. As a sign of even greater distinction, he had control of some gunpowder and a few bullets. Guns were scarce; gunpowder and bullets still more so. Many carried their guns for show only, since they did not possess the means to operate them. Though it was not proper to carry oneself with too much pride, Mukasa began to walk with a different tread after he became a *mutongole.*

The king was constantly sending messages and messengers to all parts of the kingdom, most times transmitting royal commands. Sometimes the messenger had the task of making sure that some particular thing was accomplished. Often this required the messenger to take with him a military force to guarantee that the king's wishes were carried out. For a young page or a humble *mutongole,* frequently the first opportunity for advancement came when he was chosen to perform such a task. Clearly, the king and the others in power were keenly observant of how well the job was performed. It was a politically mobile society: success bred more success; failure usually meant the end of progress.

We do not know what particular errand Mukasa was first sent on, but since he is the hero of this saga, we are not surprised to learn that he performed it so well that the king was pleased to send him out again, this time with an armed force. Now Mukasa could fully demonstrate his capacity for leadership—and this in a society that was drunk on leadership, much as adolescents get drunk when they first taste wine. As he assumed command, Mukasa's back "became rigid and straight as the staff of his spear, and an unusual sternness of face had somehow replaced the bland smiles which hitherto decked it."[3] The truth in the saying "The office makes the man" has come down to us from advanced complex societies. Mukasa knew that on such an errand he became a surrogate king. He barked commands, severely punished any breach of discipline; his soldiers ran to him when summoned, announcing, *"Kabaka,* behold us."

The Baganda had a clear grasp of the principles underlying a stable bureaucratic situation, one of the most important being the existence of enough offices on all levels so that those who performed well could look forward to an early promotion. The efficiency in such a system severely drops if those who are intent on "making it" can see no way of doing so. In Buganda, swift promotions could be depended upon.

Mukasa's diligence was rewarded with higher office and greater responsibility when he attained the position of *kawuta:* overseer of the cooks and provisioners in the *kabaka*'s palace. When two prominent officials were chosen by Mutesa for the awesome task of removing the remains of his father, Kabaka Suna, to a new burial place, Mukasa had the honor of being chosen.[4]

Mukasa's valor and capacity for military leadership were tested periodically, since he was commissioned by the *kabaka* to head various raiding expeditions. The raiding of neighboring peoples for ivory, cattle, children, and women was of such importance for the Buganda economy that some analysts have pronounced it the country's foremost industry. The spoils from such raids helped provide the rewards that the *kabaka* was able to supply his most important subordinates. Booty greased the political machinery.

Those in our society who regard great disparities of wealth among members of the same society as inevitable in human relations may be unsettled to discover that it was not always so. In band societies, the first form of human society we know of, there were practically no differences in wealth between one person and another. In primitive societies the discrepancies were larger, but they were not of great significance. The power and diversity that were developed in complex societies made large accumulations of wealth possible for the first time. The complex political system decreed not that this wealth was to be distributed more or less equally but that some were to be substantially wealthier than the rest. Wealth fell to those who controlled the political system.

In Buganda, riches were measured by the extent of the land and people one controlled, and by the possession of cattle and slaves. The latter were usually taken in raids on neighboring tribal societies or chieftainships, which had no means to retaliate against the mighty kingdom of Buganda. Mukasa soon became an important person in this spoils system and led many such raids; honors, lands, slaves, and cattle were heaped on him by the appreciative *kabaka.* Mukasa had clearly become a big man at court, and his ambition to attain one of the highest stations—that of provincial governor—was soon to be satisfied.

Every office in Buganda had a name, which was assumed by the incumbent when he took that office. When, for instance, Mukasa became governor of Buddu, the province in which his father had held the same post, he was known neither as Mukasa, governor of Buddu, nor as Governor Mukasa, but was now called *"pokino."* In our political system, we have reserved this right for only a few: the president, the vice president, the chief justice; unlike our governors, mayors, senators, they alone need no geographical identification. In Buganda, however, the world was young, and everyone who had made it had the right to his own individual title. *Pokino* himself had a hierarchy of twenty-five important subordinates, each official with his own title attached to the office.

At some point the incumbent *pokino* offended Mutesa; we are not told the nature of the offense, but too great a display of wealth by a provincial governor frequently brought spoliation by the king. The *kabaka* did not care to have anyone rival him in a show of power, and the plundered wealth would make a nice addition to the king's coffers; indeed, Henry VIII felt and acted the same way toward Cardinal Wolsey. The *pokino*'s offense might have been of this order, or it could have been outright rebellion: refusal to give the *kabaka* the customary share of spoils from a raid, or failure to obey an order.* Whatever the case, the incumbent *pokino*'s days were over and Mutesa decided that Mukasa was the perfect replacement.

When the *kabaka* summoned him, Mukasa fell to the ground to hear the king's command. "Take men and eat up *Pokino*'s land and name, for old *Pokino* has forgotten me." After shouting the special "thank you" that the Baganda used when rewarded by the king, Mukasa rubbed his cheeks in the dust but then sprang to his feet, seized his spear, held it in a threatening position, and shouted: "By the *Kabaka*'s orders, I go to eat up *Pokino*. . . . Mukasa shall become *Pokino. Kabaka,* behold me!"⁵ With the help of an armed force, the new *pokino* took the old *pokino*'s name, lands, and authority. The system worked; though the man changed, the office and the pattern of power remained constant.

Mukasa had now attained one of the strongest positions of power in Buganda society. He ruled over a hundred thousand people in a district embracing about fifteen hundred square miles. A hierarchy of twenty-five subordinate officers recognized him as master. His women slaves numbered in the hundreds; he had thousands of young slaves and cattle. He kept court, dispensed justice, granted bounties; hundreds of people were maintained in his personal establishment. To the *kabaka* and only to the *kabaka* did he have to show deference. The king and the king's prime minister were the only people in the whole world more powerful than he.

This kind of political power did not always exist. It is a human invention—as much so as the bow or the wheel or agriculture or the hydrogen bomb. No Zuñi, Kwakiutl, or Nuer ever elevated a man to such power. We know *when* in the history of the development of human society (in advanced complex societies) this conception and reality of power was invented, but we do not know *why*. Unlike technological inventions, which seem to have a certain logic to them, the reasons for

---

*John Rowe suggests that the transfer of power to Mukasa could have resulted from Mutesa's desire to have younger governors who had been appointed by himself.

inventing social forms such as kingship or a great political hierarchy are not so obvious to us. It would be enormously profitable to know what drives human beings to invent new ways of coming together politically. One of the premises of this book is that looking back to the time when these new forms arose may help give the answer.

In terms of cultural time, rather than actual historical time, the political boss of Chicago, making and breaking governors and congressmen, collecting and then sharing out power, is closer to our hero Mukasa than Mukasa was to a kinship headman in a tribal society like the Nuer. This distinction is one measure of the revolution wrought by complex societies.

All inventions rust if they are not used. It was not enough for Mukasa to sit in *pokino*'s capital and feel his power all around him. Nor was it sufficient for Mutesa to sit complacently and take pleasure in what a strong, efficient, courageous underlord he had. Power, to be power, must be exercised. Like sexuality as Freud conceived it, power needs an *object* toward which it can direct itself.

The country of Usongora lay to the west of Buganda. Rich in cattle, and having no king ruling over it, it was a perfect place to send Mukasa to raid, and such was the order. *Pokino*'s own troops were supplemented by warriors from other provinces, though the governors of these provinces did not attend the raiding expedition. Such a large force was needed because the route to Usongora lay quite close to Bunyoro territory. The Banyoro, the Baganda's principal rivals for political hegemony in the lake area, were well acquainted with raiding for bounty. On the Baganda's return from Usongora, there was every chance that the Banyoro would decide to spoil the spoilers.

Pokino Mukasa was in his ripe years and capable of any task. Usongora was despoiled; the journey home did provoke a Banyoro ambush, which was totally annihilated.

Surely no Caesar or Pompey felt greater pride and worth than Pokino Mukasa on the day of the celebration of his triumph. The *kabaka* set the time and received *pokino* and his warriors in state, his harem of three hundred wives behind him, his governors and other subordinates seated to the right and to the left in order of rank; his musketeers on guard, his drummers and musicians filling the air with their conception of victory.

Pokino advanced and prostrated himself before the *kabaka*. With his warriors massed behind him, he told the story of his adventures in Usongora. We may assume that the dangers involved and the skill with which they were overcome are slightly exaggerated in the telling, but glorification, after all, was the reason they were all there.

Large pots of *pombé* (an alcoholic drink made from bananas) rest in front of the king. "Drink, if thou darest," says the *kabaka* after hearing *pokino*'s recital. *Pokino* rises from the ground, advances to the pots, dips a ladle in one of them and fills it, holds the ladle aloft, turns to his warriors, and cries out as loudly as he can: "Am I worthy or not?" "Thou art worthy!" they shout in return. Again he asks; again the response. He drinks the *pombé,* again falls to the ground to thank the sovereign, and withdraws from center stage to let others go through the same procedure. Most are found worthy and are rewarded with their share of the spoils. Some are despised for their lack of courage, do not get the approbation of the troops, are not allowed to drink, and are led off for execution.[6]

Mutesa was so moved by *pokino*'s success that he gave him a royal drum, *serukoma.* Important drums in Buganda, like important people, had individual names. This one had been given Mutesa by his mother. The queen mother was a person of political power in Buganda, and the drum carried with it an estate, headed by a *mutongole* with several subordinates. Drum, estate, *mutongole,* and entourage were all delivered to Mukasa with this one gesture of the *kabaka.*[7]

Mukasa's great success resulted from his capacity to practice all the forms and techniques that were valued in Buganda society. Deception and cruelty were not the least of these. Following the death of the king of Ankole, which bordered on the province of Buddu, a civil war of succession was fought by two contenders for the throne, Mukwenda and Makumbi. Mukwenda, following a practice that has lost many states their freedom, requested the help of neighboring Buganda. Mutesa had no desire to annex Ankole but did prefer to have its king obligated to him, and so ordered *pokino* to do what was necessary to secure the victory of Mukwenda.

Pokino moved his forces to the border and sent word to Makumbi that *pokino*'s real intention was to bring aid to him. *Pokino* informed Makumbi that as proof of this he was ready to take a pledge of blood brotherhood with him—a most solemn act. So convincing was *pokino* that Makumbi and his leading officers came to the Buganda camp to seal the contract. *Pokino* seized them all, executed seventy high officials including twenty members of the royal family,[8] and calmly informed Mutesa and Mukwenda that the mission was accomplished. It is small wonder that a man used to acting out the value system of an Icelandic saga should have presented his wife with her lover's newly severed head.

Adaptability was another important value in Buganda society, and when, in the mid-1860s, Mutesa moved toward conversion to Islam, Mukasa responded quickly, becoming one of the first Muslim "readers." In Buganda, the experience of learning to read and undergoing religious conversion were inexorably linked, because the same person taught both reading and religion. In following Mutesa's moves in the direction of "modernization," Mukasa had the advantage of sharing the king's age and outlook. Many of the older governors resented the *kabaka's* interest in nontraditional ideas. Mukasa was one of those bright young men who, their time having come, will push old men aside not for power alone but also for some vague but nevertheless very real commitment to ideas.[9]

For Pokino Mukasa, favorite of the *kabaka,* there remained only one more step to ascend on the political pyramid: that of the office of *katikiro,* or "prime minister," as the English have translated it. There is not much similarity to the English office, however, since there were no political parties in Buganda. The *katikiro* was literally the king's first minister, more analogous to a sultan's vizier than to an English prime minister.

An inherent danger in the kind of power intrinsic to a large centralized state is that it is enormously attractive. Since it is limited by definition, competition for the power (part of the reason the power exists) could destroy the stability of the state and ultimately destroy the state itself. No king rules a million people without having strong governors or subordinates. What is to stop these leaders from challenging the king's right to rule? No society in history has ever devised a permanent solution to this problem. In advanced complex societies a partial solution was found in the office of the king's first minister, which always had to be someone *not* of royal blood, who could not succeed to the throne. In the history of Buganda, many kings were violently overthrown, but no *katikiro* ever became king. The office of *katikiro* had an enormous stabilizing influence on Buganda political life, especially during the critical time following the death of the *kabaka.* The incumbent *katikiro* played a crucial role in the selection and legitimization of the new *kabaka.*

For the ambitious Mukasa it was the usual two hurdles that had to be passed over: the office had to become vacant, and the *pokino* had to beat out his rivals, since he was not the only cruel, deceptive, adaptable, intelligent young man in the political hierarchy. When Mukasa was promoted from *kawuta* to *pokino,* a clever young man named Ntwatwa was appointed to fill the office Mukasa had just vacated. Ntwatwa was also an excellent Muslim reader, a man of great talent who was held in affection by the *kabaka.*

And then there was Tebukoza, a brilliant reader, one of the best Arabic scholars at court. He had first come to the attention of the capital as a wrestler of great power. To understand the importance of wrestling in advanced complex societies, we must consider the *Odyssey* and the great value wrestling and other games had in the aristocratic life portrayed there, rather than our own society's attitudes toward professional athletes. One of the striking similarities among ancient Buganda, Hawaii, and Tahiti is that in all three cultures wrestling and wrestlers were held in great esteem.

As a reward for reading and wrestling, the *kabaka* gave Tebukoza high office, sent him on what proved to be a very successful raiding expedition, and then used him in delicate diplomatic missions involving the Egyptian military, which was at that time moving south down the Nile, threatening to engulf Buganda.[10]

Mukasa, with it all, is the hero of this story, and to Mukasa belonged the prize. In fact, his patience was not severely tried. Four or five years after Mukasa became *pokino,* the incumbent *katikiro* could not resist the temptation to compete with the *kabaka* and take for himself what was the king's prerogative: from the spoils of a raiding war the prime minister selected some of the most beautiful female slaves before the *kabaka* had made his choice. In the capital there were always people to bring such information to the *kabaka*'s ears; political intrigue and the carrying of damaging tales, true or not, were major occupations. The *katikiro* was removed from office. Mukasa was offered this ultimate power. The year was 1874.[11]

3

The Life and Times of Prime Minister Mukasa, Part II

When he assumed the office of *katikiro*, Mukasa was also showered with honors by the *kabaka*. Hundreds of slaves were sent by the king to Mukasa's enclosure to serve him; four close relatives of Mutesa were given to the *katikiro* as wives, and one of the king's daughters was promised as well. Mukasa was even allowed to retain the governorship of Buddu. They called him *kalyabugatte*, "He who has eaten a combination of offices."[1]

To raise anyone to such high estate was risky for the king, but Mutesa was a sophisticated politician and an expert player of the *kabaka* game of setting one political faction against another, thereby keeping any faction from growing strong enough to challenge the king's rule. It is a tribute to the stability of the Buganda political system and to Mutesa's security in his own power and judgment that he could raise a *katikiro* so high, not fearful that the prime minister's unusual power would be turned against him. Mutesa's judgment was accurate; Mukasa never betrayed him.

Under normal circumstances, a capable *katikiro* could have looked forward to years of pleasurable and leisurely manipulation of power, but the times were far from normal. Buganda society was about to undergo as radical a change as any society has had to tolerate in a short period of time. Outside forces were revolutionizing the Buganda state. Arnold Toynbee explains much of world history through application of the concept of "challenge and response." In the case of Buganda, it *is* helpful to think about the complex and assertive response that this society made to contact with Islam and Christianity. The breakdown of the kinship system, the erection of the state, the creation of new forms in society and culture—all this gave the Baganda a positive view of *change:* What they have, and we do not, may be better than what we have. And it was not merely guns, although guns were sorely wanted. A more satisfying spiritual life, a more exciting intellectual existence, and a greater number of material things were promised by the emissaries from the other, larger world. The Baganda wanted it all.

To remain Mutesa's prime minister at such a time was no easy task. Mutesa had an enormous curiosity and a great appetite for change. His father, King Suna, had kept a zoo near the royal palace, to which any unusual animal that was caught in the kingdom was sent. When reading Speke or Stanley, one cannot help observing that Mutesa was as curious about them as they were about him. Mutesa was unafraid to taste something new.

Mutesa's flirtation with Islam was of almost ten years' duration when Stanley arrived in Buganda in 1875. Mutesa and Stanley took an instant liking to each other; both were energetic, curious, authoritarian, courageous. When Stanley began to attack Islam and praise the virtues of Christianity, Mutesa was moved and suggested that maybe the Baganda should adopt Christianity. Mukasa felt the need to demur: Let the chiefs choose for themselves rather than forsake Islam, he suggested. We don't know the *katikiro's* motivation for speaking thus. Possibly, he was afraid of offending the Arab traders from Zanzibar who were so important for the country, or perhaps he had some real attachment to the spirit of Islam. Or it might be that he was jealous of the attention and response Stanley was getting from Mutesa. Probably all three motives were at work. In any event, the tide was running against him, and when several important leaders announced their willingness to follow Mutesa, abandon Islam, and become Christians, Mukasa, sensing it was time to retreat, announced that he, too, was of that conviction. However, the *kabaka's* enthusiasm for Christianity passed with Stanley's departure, and for the moment the influence of Islam remained predominant at the court.[2]

As always happens in such circumstances, interaction with the larger world did not bring only benefits. Gonorrhea was one result of contact with "advanced" cultures. Mutesa had the disease for years, and in 1876 he suffered a severe attack, which confined him to bed for the last eight years of his life. Such incapacity made him extremely vulnerable to any plot against the throne by rival factions. Prime Minister Mukasa stepped into this vacuum—acting for the king but not replacing him—thus preserving Mutesa's power, Mukasa's office, and the stability of the state. Mutesa expressed his gratitude, and his need, in 1881, when he entered into blood-brotherhood with the *katikiro*.[3]

Though this arrangement preserved the fabric of government until Mutesa's death in 1884, the centralized structure was weakened by the *kabaka*'s illness. The Buganda state existed only as an emanation of the monarchy. If, for instance, the king decreed that no provincial governor was to trade with the Zanzibari Arabs, leaving that solely the king's prerogative, there was no public prosecutor or department of justice to see that such an edict was enforced. Enforcement, like promulgation, was the personal task of the *kabaka*. And fear of the *kabaka*—not just the rational fear resulting from his being entitled to take one's property and life, but, equally important, an irrational fear, the sense that it was psychologically dangerous to do what the *kabaka* prohibited—was an important part of the enforcement of decrees and the maintenance of the centralized state. No matter how strong a *katikiro* might be, no matter how much real power he had to take lives, no one feared him as much as he did the *kabaka*. The provincial governors, knowing that Mutesa was ill, did business with the Zanzibari traders, defying the king's edict. Mukasa *katikiro* did the same.[4]

About a year after the onset of Mutesa's critical illness, at the end of 1877, the first English missionaries arrived in Buganda, a direct result of Stanley's visit. These few, and those who followed, both English Protestants and French Catholics, had an enormous impact on the society. The personal behavior of individual missionaries began to have important implications for the Buganda political system. Prime Minister Mukasa had now to deal not only with the conflicting forces of traditional politics but with this new phenomenon as well. Among the first English missionaries, the one who was most intelligent, most imaginative, most courageous, most irascible, and most difficult was Alexander Mackay. He won Mutesa's affection, not least because he had great mechanical skill and spent much of his time repairing guns that had become dysfunctional. But Mackay's mind was as busy as his hands. His fantasy was that Mutesa should be converted to Christianity and then become a "Christian Bismarck" who would unite the whole lake area into one powerful, godly state. As a first step, Mackay convinced the *kabaka* that he should conquer Ukererere, a kingdom on the southern side of Lake Victoria. Mackay volunteered to accompany the expedition in order to reinforce its chances of success.

Katikiro Mukasa, wanting no competition as secretary of state, resentful of Mackay's insinuation into the councils of power, and determined to keep an eye on this religious rival, himself offered to command the expedition. Mackay decided not to play army chaplain, and Mukasa, no longer having any reason to go, gave the command back to the original general.[5] No one knew better than the *katikiro* how to play the Buganda version of realpolitik. Eventually the prime minister would go down to defeat before the revolutionary forces in the society, but that would happen only when the capacity to win this traditional kind of political contest was no longer the issue.

By 1879, Buganda society had come to a critical juncture: it was no longer possible to preserve things as they had been; radical change was inevitable. We get the feeling that Mutesa understood this, even though he was too old, too sick, or too confused to make a clear decision himself. Four basic alternatives presented themselves to Mutesa: to pursue Islam; to become Christian; to preserve the traditional religion with its gods, priests, and rites; or to let everyone choose for himself. Mutesa changed direction several times and died without ever having made a permanent choice. As always in such situations, the reasons that any particular person of power takes a particular position are complex. These reasons can usually be anything from high principle to cynical self-interest. Mukasa was the kind of person who never had to worry about abandoning his immediate interests in favor of high principle. He was determined not to get too far from the opinion of Mutesa, no matter how many changes of direction that might entail. His one, basic, narrow ambition was to stay on as Mutesa's *katikiro,* and he was prepared to do whatever was necessary to accomplish that.

The conservative forces—those who would preserve the traditional religion—centered around the queen mother. This group included some of sincere belief, who felt that the new religions were bad for society and themselves, as well as political opportunists who were at present "out" and sought any means to get "in." For all of these, Katikiro Mukasa was the main object of attack, because he had supported Mutesa in religious experimentation and because his elimination would open up many political opportunities for those currently out of office. In 1879, this conservative faction convinced Mutesa that he should call a leading god, Mukasa of the lake, to come and cure him of his acute illness. The priests of the god, who spoke for the deity, were instructed by the conservatives to deliver the message that Mutesa would be cured only if Katikiro Mukasa and others were removed from office.

The proclamation was never made. Whether the prime minister reached the priests before they could speak, or whether the priests independently agreed that there was no point in taking on the enmity of the *katikiro,* we do not know. The god commanded a few restitutions of traditional political arrangements that Mutesa had transgressed; Mutesa complied—but was not cured. At this point the brief surge of the conservative tide passed, and Mutesa, Mukasa, and the society as a whole returned to their prior condition of continuing indecision.[6]

In Mutesa's last year, Katikiro Mukasa exchanged his governorship of the province of Buddu, which was distant from the capital, for command over the nearby province of Kyaggwe, because he wished to keep close to the obviously dying *kabaka.* In October 1884, the *katikiro* was on a tour of inspection of his new province when secret messengers informed him of the king's death. He returned through the autumn rains to the capital, not knowing how people might react to the passing; when he rushed into the royal enclosure, not stopping to change his muddied clothes, he found everything calm, with people in a state of shock rather than hysteria.

Two days later the *katikiro* and his party had chosen Mutesa's eighteen-year-old son, Mwanga, to be the new *kabaka.* The succession was not seriously contested; no anarchy resulted. Mukasa, of course, stayed on as the *katikiro.*[7] The Buganda political system had proved its strength after the death of one of its greatest and longest-ruling monarchs. At the time, there were very few who could have predicted that within four years Kabaka Mwanga would be driven from the country by the Buganda followers of Christ and Allah.

From 1884 to 1888, from the accession of Mwanga to his first exile, the pace of events in Buganda accelerated incredibly. Whereas traditional Buganda politics had had four basic sources of power—the king, the provincial governors, the prime minister, and the clans—the new situation created five additional power bases: the Buganda converts to Islam, the Buganda converts to Christianity, the Zanzibari Arab traders, and the English Protestant and French Catholic missionaries. The sources we have do not reveal what Mukasa's relation was to these traditional and modern power structures. We cannot perceive his motives and know nothing of what kind of Buganda he would have wanted, if he could have ordered it any way he wished. Outside of the obvious—that he wished to maintain his power and would use any means to do so—we know only Mukasa's actions, nothing of the ambiguity of purpose that drives all political people.

Kabaka Mwanga was an unattractive person: self-willed, lacking in leadership qualities, changeable of mind, narcissistic. He was definitely

not the man to lead a nation in a critical period. Within three months
of his accession, he had quarreled with the *katikiro* so disastrously that
Mukasa joined with other high-placed leaders in a plot to assassinate
him and replace him with his brother Kalema. The attempt was sched-
uled for the end of February 1885, when Mwanga would be attending
ceremonies in connection with the newly constructed tomb of his father, Mutesa.

The plot was discovered by Joseph Mukasa, a leading Catholic convert, who passed the information on to the queen mother. Mwanga ab-
sented himself from the ceremonies and, three days later, confronted
the prime minister. The *katikiro* protested his loyalty, wept like a child,
and convinced the impressionable Mwanga that he had had nothing to
do with the conspiracy. Mwanga left it to Mukasa to prosecute the plot-
ters. The prime minister dealt with his former associates leniently: no
one was executed, though seventeen people were removed from office.

Mwanga rewarded those whose loyalty had saved him by appoint-
ing several Catholics and Protestants to positions of trust. He also
intimated that Joseph Mukasa and Andrew Kaggwa, two Catholic
converts, would someday assume the offices of *katikiro* and commander-
in-chief of the army.[8] Mwanga should have known that Katikiro
Mukasa was no one to threaten with what might happen someday. Neither Joseph Mukasa nor Andrew Kaggwa was to survive the great persecution of the Christians that took place in 1886, in large part because
Prime Minister Mukasa had a keen interest in their future.

Faced with the possibility of conversion to a modern religion, neither Mutesa nor Mwanga did what other kings have done in similar
circumstances: adopt the religion, force conversion on their subjects,
and use the new religion as a means of strengthening the monarchy
and the sense of nationalism. Clovis, king of the Franks in the late fifth
century A.D.; several Anglo-Saxon kings in England during the seventh
and eighth centuries; and Pomare II, first sovereign of a united Tahiti,
all responded in this fashion. Mutesa and Mwanga probably remained
indecisive in part because there were three religions to choose from:
Islam, Catholicism, Protestantism. Undoubtedly, there were other considerations, but we may only speculate on these because neither *kabaka*
gave firm reasons for his actions. All three religions demanded certain
sacrifices which the sovereigns were reluctant to make: Islam required
circumcision; Christianity decreed only one wife. Mutesa did once suggest to Mackay that he would renounce all his wives if Queen Victoria

would send him one of her daughters to wed. Particularly important in the case of Mwanga was the fact that Christianity took a strong stance against homosexual practice.

Despite the inaction of the sovereigns, conversions to all three religions, particularly by young men at court, proceeded at a rapid pace during the early 1880s. The *kabakas* could not ignore what was happening, although they refused to control it by choosing one of the religions. The result was an acute confusion, especially on Mwanga's part, toward the converted and their faiths. In 1885, the same year that Mwanga praised the Catholics Joseph Mukasa and Andrew Kaggwa, the first Protestant martyrs were executed by order of the *kabaka* on the advice of Katikiro Mukasa.

These executions were the final result of actions that had begun when the English missionary Mackay, for whom the *katikiro* had no love, decided to go in his boat to visit the mission station just south of Lake Victoria. No one could enter or leave Buganda without the *kabaka*'s consent, and Mackay formally asked permission. Mwanga, only a few months on the throne, gave it and, as an act of protection for Mackay, offered to have one of his legates accompany the missionary. Hot-headed Mackay, mistaking the *kabaka*'s intention to mean he was under surveillance, refused. Mwanga did not withdraw the permission to go, but informed his prime minister of Mackay's refusal. Playing on Mwanga's offended vanity, Mukasa induced him to issue a decree for the arrest of all Baganda in the service of foreigners as a way of responding to Mackay's arrogance.

Oblivious of the new edict, Mackay, another missionary, Robert Ashe, and five Baganda boys set out for the shore of the lake. The party was intercepted by soldiers and brought back to the capital, where, after a stormy session with the *katikiro*, the missionaries were allowed to return to their station but the five boys were arrested on the charge of attempting to leave the country. Another mission boy was seized that night, as was a woman named Sarah Nalwanga, who was charged with teaching Christianity to some of the royal princesses—an action that had never previously been declared a crime.

The next day, the missionaries sent Mwanga a present of cloth, thus obtaining the release of the mission boy who had been seized at night. All the others were taken to the execution site Mpima-erebera. Here the two youngest boys were set free and Sarah Nalwanga was returned to prison, but the three remaining were killed after the usual tortures.

Despite the swiftness with which these events proceeded, they did not portend the beginning of a general persecution. More than a year would pass before another Baganda would die for his beliefs.

As much as Mukasa might have wished to eliminate all Christian influence in Buganda society—and many of his actions indicate that this was his inclination—he recognized that Christianity was a growing power, and he was not one who was incapable of hedging his bets. After the execution of the Protestant martyrs, the French Catholic missionaries, who had left the country a few years before, returned to Buganda. Père Lourdel wrote to his superior general:

> Some chiefs are hostile to us, especially the Chancellor [katikiro]. Before our return he had demanded the death of the white men, or at least of those who followed their instructions. Three men who frequented the English mission were seized by his orders and burnt alive. Our return has angered him. It was only after I had presented myself three times at his enclosure that he consented to receive me. He has not even thanked me for the present which I sent. Seeing, however, that we are highly in favor with Mwanga, he has resigned himself to appearing less sulky. Yesterday he sent us a bullock in order to show that, at least for the present, he did not want to declare himself an enemy.[9]

Even in the beginning of 1886, when Mwanga's hatred of the Christians was becoming an uncontrollable force, Mukasa had no wish to make a permanent enemy of anyone who might someday hold power. Mwanga had ordered his chief executioner, Mukajanga, to kill Mackay the next time he brought his mission boat to its accustomed port near the capital. Mackay was warned by the *katikiro* to stay away, and for many weeks he kept discreetly within the mission precinct, until the danger had cooled.[10]

With all his deviousness, discretion, double-dealing, and manipulation, however, even Katikiro Mukasa was unable to control the explosion that rocked Buganda society in 1886, a time of crisis that signaled the demise of the traditional state.

4

The Blood of the Martyrs
Part I: Mutesa

If it had not been for these thing
I might have live out my life
talking at street corners to scorning men.
I might have die, unmarked, unknown, a failure.
Now we are not a failure.
This is our career and our triumph. Never
in our full life would we hope to do such work
for tolerance, for justice, for man's understanding
of man, as now we do by accident.

Our words, our lives, our pains—nothing!
The taking of our lives—lives of a good
*   shoemaker and a poor fishpeddler—*
all! That last moment belongs to us—
that agony is our triumph.[1]

Bartolomeo Vanzetti, having been condemned by his society to enact the role of sacrificial victim, transformed himself with the aid of these words into a glorious martyr.

We may imagine a fairy tale whose heroes are a set of unidentical twins; they share the same hair coloring, complexion, height, and build, but one twin is ugly and the other beautiful. Human sacrifice is the ugly twin, and martyrdom the one of radiant beauty. They were both born of the same mother; the ugly one came first. The beautiful one is supposed to be the cure and antidote to the one whose visage is offensive, but he has brought us only temporary relief. Vanzetti's martyrdom did not end society's need for human sacrifice.

Human sacrifice and martyrdom, like these twins, share many attributes:

In each case, someone dies.

In each case, the "Powers" who demand such killing are evil, but their evil appetites must be satisfied. With human sacrifice, the "Power" is some vague, unnamed hostile Cosmos. Martyrdom deals with real-world powers, which have the same appetite for death.

In each case, people die or are killed in order that something greater than themselves may live. Human sacrifice preserves the life of the king or the stability of society. Martyrdom enhances the causes of truth, justice, human love.

In each case, a heightened sense of the dramatic is crucial to the form. Human sacrifice usually proceeds under circumstances which can easily be described as high drama; the same is true of martyrdom. Christ's death, both a sacrifice and a martyrdom, has immense dramatic force. Martyrs tend toward self-dramatization; they say things of great power; biblical and Shakespearean rhetoric may ornament their speech.

Yet, these twins are not identical. Whatever else human sacrifice is about, it does not concern itself with the advancement of human morality, whereas martyrdom for the martyr is always consciously and deliberately about a greater truth, a greater justice, a greater love. Not only is it about morality, but it is concerned with the *extension* of morality, recognizing that existent morality is not adequate for human needs. With human sacrifice, the victim does not choose to die. Martyrdom contains the notion of choice; the martyr consents in some fashion to his death. Even Vanzetti, who certainly did not choose to die, is accepting his death when he succeeds in transforming it into a martyrdom: "Our lives . . . nothing!" And herein lies the great contradiction in martyrdom. On the one hand, it is the grandest kind of action a human being can take: to give one's life in the cause of morality. And yet, it is a deliberate choosing of death; it is unavoidably related to suicide and its psychological mechanisms.

The real suicide, by fulfilling their supposed hostile intent, identifies with those who he thinks wish to harm him. But he also punishes his persecutors by going far beyond any harm they might actually have wished for him and kills himself imagining how "sorry" they will be. The martyr, similarly, identifies with the aggressors when he accepts the death they are planning for him. However, he also punishes them and triumphs over them with the accusation, implicit in his dying, that their immorality has caused this catastrophe, that his death will bring immortality, whereas his persecutors shall die and be forgotten: "But Sacco's name," Vanzetti said, "will live in the hearts of the people and in their gratitude when Katzmann's bones and yours will be dispersed by time. . . ."

Despite the morality, despite the triumph, martyrdom can never free itself entirely from suicide. It is unable to transform the aggressive need for sacrifice—can never liberate itself from its twin.

It is perhaps not so great a distance from modern Boston to ancient Buganda as it seems. Sacco, Vanzetti, the Buganda Christian martyrs— all were destined to be sacrificial victims whose deaths would cleanse society. All transformed themselves into glorious martyrs for truth, love, justice. In the case of Buganda, it seems a reasonable hypothesis that the notion of martyrdom came so easily to those Christian converts not only because Christian history taught its great value but also because they lived in a society suffused with the forms of human sacrifice.

Support for this proposition is rendered by the fact that when Mutesa persecuted and later executed some of his pages for following the Muslim religion, they behaved in exactly the same manner as the Christian martyrs would ten years later. Islam itself has no tradition of peaceful martyrdom like that of the Christian Church, so these early Muslim martyrs must have found the impulse toward martyrdom within their own society. Much of what happened to Christianity in Buganda was prefigured by the experience of Islam there. That history begins in the reign of Mutesa's father, Kabaka Suna II (c. 1824–56).

The first Arab traders entered Buganda probably in the 1830s, and by the 1840s many Zanzibari merchants had arrived in the country. Along with goods to trade, they brought their belief in Islam. For most, Islam was the usual combination of ritual observance and magic that religion has been for the vast majority of people throughout history. For a very few, the high ethical quality of this great world religion was a major concern. One such trader was Ahmed bin Ibrahim. After he had gained the trust of the *kabaka,* Ahmed felt confident enough to rebuke the king for the seemingly wanton slaughter of people that went on at the court. "On one occasion he rose to his feet and told Suna that both he and his victims had been created alike by Allah, that to Allah alone he owed his kingdom, and that it was a grievous sin before Allah to destroy those whom he had created." Suna, a true father of Mutesa, took the rebuke, which had aroused his respect and his curiosity. Several conversations between Suna and Ahmed ensued, but when the trader left to return to the coast, Suna's interest in the new religion melted away.[2]

By a process that is hidden from us, Mutesa gradually became converted to his own variety of Muslim practice during the first ten years of his reign. He introduced an official calendar along Islamic lines, announced that it was a criminal offense for any of his subjects to greet him except in the Arabic fashion and with Arabic words,[3] had a large mosque erected at his court and several smaller ones in the countryside, took to expounding the Koran to his court,[4] and celebrated Ramadan (ritual fasting) for ten years.[5] Nothing even close to this happened in any other East African kingdom.

For a while, it looked as if Mutesa were serious about converting the country to the new religion—"serious" in Buganda, of course, meaning that those who did not comply would be executed. A dozen of his subjects were put to death for failure to salute him in the new manner.[6] During one Ramadan fast, in about 1875, the *kabaka* gave orders for a mass arrest of "nonbelievers." As many as two hundred were slaughtered "for refusing to embrace the religion ordered by the king." This action had an immediate effect. Tens of thousands professed the new belief, and many mosques were erected in villages outside the capital.[7]

Before resorting to this holocaust, Mutesa had tried milder measures. During Ramadan he sent inspectors into the countryside to make sure that people were observing the fast, which obliges a believer not to eat anything from sunrise to sunset. One infamous inspector, Kakoloboto by name, was himself unable to make the sacrifice: he was caught sucking on a small calabash and eating food that he had hidden on his person. He was severely punished by the *kabaka,* and the phrase "You are Kakoloboto!" was used thereafter to castigate any hypocrite.

If Mutesa had stayed on this path of belief, observance, and forced conversion, the whole history of Buganda would have been different, but sometime around 1877 Mutesa became violently opposed to Islam and converted many Muslim believers into sacrifices and martyrs. We don't know why this happened. It might have been partly the result of Stanley's visit; or perhaps Mutesa had begun to have his own doubts. The one thing we do know is that Mutesa's right to define Islam in the way he wished was seriously challenged. At the beginning, he had felt that he was in total control, that the conversion would go as quickly or as slowly as he wished, that he would decide which observances were to be respected and which ignored, and that he would tell everyone what Islam meant. He discovered he was wrong.

A crucial factor in the change was the arrival in Buganda of a different kind of Muslim from the Zanzibari Arabs, who tended to be very flexible in their beliefs. As the English General Gordon, representing the sultan of Egypt and commanding Egyptian troops, moved south down the Nile and dreamed of annexing Buganda to the Egyptian crown, Islamic people from the north made their way into Mutesa's country. To the Baganda, all of them were known as "Turks." Many of these Turks were determined to change Mutesa's brand of Islam. They found the mosques in Buganda built to face westward instead of eastward. They convinced Mutesa to call a meeting at which they instructed the Muslims never to eat meat slaughtered by an uncircumcised person and never to allow such a one to lead the community in prayer. Since traditionally any bodily mutilation was anathema to the Baganda, Mutesa had refused to be circumcised. Ham Mukasa, the Buganda historian, tells of the consequences brought by these new Turks:

Everybody knows that the Kabaka led prayers in Lubiri [council meeting]. The Turks said this matter was crucial. The Qur'an forbade the uncircumcised to lead in prayer; and this law should be followed in Lubiri also. "Why," they asked, "does not the Kabaka follow the text of the Book?" The pages answered that the Kabaka admitted no authority but his own and that all Baganda were subject to him. He had supreme authority in his palace and his mosque and none could prevent him if he chose to lead the prayers. The Turks insisted the Muslims must obey their ruling. "The Kabaka's supreme authority exists in matters of State; but, when it comes to religion, that is another matter." From this time on, Muslims started to absent themselves from prayers in Lubiri, to pray outside under proper leadership, and to refuse meat killed by non-Muslims.[8]

What this confrontation led to was identical to what would happen with the Christian converts less than ten years later; it was the young pages at the court who defied the power of the *kabaka* and insisted on religious purity. Despite the Buganda proverb that "The ears that do not obey their master mulch the soil,"[9] the Islamic youths became arrogant and provocative in both manner and actions. Consciously or not, they were headed for a martyr's life and a martyr's death:

"Mudduawulira, do you no longer eat meat which is slaughtered in this palace?" demanded Kabaka Mutesa, king of Buganda. "Yes, sir" was the bold reply. "If I kill it myself will you eat it as I have done the slaughter?" "No, my lord, I won't eat it, even if you yourself kill it, I cannot eat it." "Why?" "Because of the religion which commands, and which I follow, as we are taught in the Koran, moreover, as you 'Salongo' know. . . ."[10]

No one had ever talked to the *kabaka* in that way before, and it was so startling that Mutesa did not immediately respond with anger, though he began to sour on Islam: "He no longer read with pleasure, seeing that his servants when he taught despised him in the customs of religion."[11]

The pages continued to press their critical attack, and there were several more incidents like the one involving Mudduawulira. The provincial governors and other high officials who feared the new religion began to provoke Mutesa into retaliation. Finally, he struck. About seventy young Moslems were executed in the capital; another two to three hundred escaped to the coast with the Zanzibaris. Ham Mukasa says that in the country at large, as many as a thousand were slaughtered or exiled because of their beliefs.[12] This Christian historian pays high tribute to the victims: "The Muslims who were dying for their religion at that time were very brave, just like the Christians at Namugongo."[13]

Despite all these troubles, Mutesa's inquiring mind did not turn back to the traditional religion. A short time after the death of the Muslim martyrs, some of Gordon's troops who had been in Buganda left the country and took with them the Islamic teachers who had stirred up the religious controversy. Mutesa wrote to Gordon requesting that he be allowed to keep one of them, Shaykh by name, who, although a proponent of Muslim orthodoxy, was the one man with whom Mutesa enjoyed discussing the large questions of the Islamic faith.[14] Thus Mutesa continued to satisfy his appetite for the modern world, even when he was incapable of dominating the ferment it brought to his country.

5

The Blood of the Martyrs
Part II: Mwanga

The same day Kagwa (Apolo) was called into the king's presence with another youth; a stormy scene ensued. The king, acting on an impulse of uncontrollable fury, attacked the other lad with a spear, gashing him frightfully, and he was hurried away and murdered by the executioners. Then the king turned to Apolo: "Are you a reader [Christian]?" he cried, trembling with passion. "Nsoma, Mukamawange (I read, my Lord)," was the brave reply. "Then I'll teach you to read!" shouted the angry king, and gashed him too with the spear, and then took the wooden handle and broke it over his back. At last, breathless with exertion, his anger having apparently spent itself, he told him to begone. And Kagwa's life was saved, and no more was done to him.[1]

Alexandro Namfumbambi, who often gave us trouble by his inconsistencies, on hearing of the seizure of his fellow-Christians, went boldly up to the court, and when the executioners asked if any readers were concealed in his enclosure, replied, "I myself am a Christian"; and was at once apprehended and made prisoner.[2]

"We served the king," they said, "if we take flight, he will say that we have revolted against him. Let us remain firm. If our master wants to kill us, let him do so; at any rate, we shall die for the religion of God."[3]

PAGAN PIETY

Christianity has given us the parable of the seed that falls on either barren or fertile soil. The great flowering of Christianity in advanced complex societies occurred because that soil was enormously rich. The Hebrew-Christian concepts of piety and the love for and from God met a positive response in Hawaii, Tahiti, and Buganda that even the most optimistic missionaries could not have anticipated.*

John Papa Ii, a major historian of traditional Hawaii who died a pious Christian, tells of his childhood in pagan times. He was religious by nature and expressed keen interest in matters of ritual even as a small child, the result of which was that his father often took him to the altar on the "mornings of Kane" (the twenty-sixth of the Hawaiian month) to observe the god, his priests, and his rites. Ii tells the story of how he was sent by his mother to do some net fishing with a group of smaller boys under his direction. Before they returned to their homes, Ii divided the catch: first he separated out fish suitable as offerings for the male and female gods, then gave each of the boys his share and took his own. When he returned home, his mother counted the fish and requested that some be set aside for offerings. "They are already separated," announced the boy. "My companions have had their share, and this is ours."⁴ We can imagine that such a beamish boy was not rebuked by his mother.

As he grew older, he frequently accompanied the priests of Kane in tasks concerning the altar and the making of offerings.⁵ It seems a reasonable presumption that, had the traditional society continued, Ii would have joined the ranks of the priests. Instead, he became a Christian deeply involved in the Church, got actively involved in national political affairs, and wrote a history of his people. He was one of those sane, caring people who prosper when times are good.

In Buganda, the convert Kalemba told the Catholic missionary Père Livinhac the history of his personal quest:

"My father," he said, "had always believed that the Baganda had not the truth, and he sought it in his heart. He had often mentioned this to me, and before his death he told me that men would one day come to teach us the right way. These words made a profound impression on me, and whenever the arrival of some stranger was announced, I watched him and tried to get in touch with him, saying to myself that here, perhaps, was the man announced by my father.

*Although this section of this book is about Buganda, I feel that comparative material from Hawaii and Tahiti at this point would lend even greater weight to the ideas presented, especially since many of the present concerns relate to complex societies as a whole, not just Buganda.

Thus I associated with the Arabs who came for the first time under the reign of Suna. Their creed seemed to me superior to our superstitions. I received instructions and, together with a number of Baganda, I embraced their religion. Mutesa himself, anxious to please the Sultan of Zanzibar, of whose power and riches he had been given an exaggerated account, declared that he also wanted to become a Moslem. Orders were given to build Mosques in all the counties. For a short while, it looked as if the whole country was going to embrace the religion of the false prophet, but Mutesa had an extreme repugnance to circumcision. Consequently, changing his mind all of a sudden, he gave orders to exterminate all who had become Moslems. . . . I succeeded with a few others, in hiding my conversion, and continued to pass for a friend of our gods; but, in secret, I always remained faithful to the practices of Islam.

"That was how things stood when the Protestants arrived. Mutesa received them very well; he had their books read in public audience, and seemed to incline to their religion, which he declared to be much superior to that of the Arabs. I asked myself whether I had not made a mistake, and whether, perhaps, the newcomers were not the true messengers of God. I often went to visit them and attended their instructions. It seemed to me that their teaching was an improvement on that of my first masters. I therefore abandoned Islam, without, however, asking for baptism.

"Several months had elapsed, when Mapère [Livinhac] arrived. My master, Mackay, took care to tell me that the white men, who had just arrived, did not know the truth. He called their religion the 'worship of the women'; they adored, he said, the Virgin Mary. He also advised me to avoid them with the greatest care. I therefore kept away from you, and probably, I would never have set foot in your place, if my chief had not ordered me to supervise the building of one of your houses. But God has loved me. The first time when I saw you nearby, I was very much impressed. Nevertheless, I continued to watch you closely at your prayers and in your dealings with the people. Then, seeing your goodness, I said to myself: how can people who appear so good, be the messengers of the devil?

"I talked with those who had placed themselves under instruction, and questioned them on your doctrine. What they told me was just the contrary of what Mackay had assured me. Then I felt strongly urged to go and assist personally at your catechistical instructions. God gave me the grace to understand that you taught the truth, and that you were really the men of God of whom my father had spoken. Since then, I have never had the slightest doubt about the truth of your religion, and I feel truly happy."[6]

Although all missionary accounts of such experiences are undoubtedly exaggerated, they seem to be exaggeration elaborated upon a truth. John Papa Ii tells of his own experience, and it is not likely that Kalemba's report of his father's messianic expectations was manufactured by

Livinhac. What seems true is that certain people in these societies, as in all societies, were deeply committed to a religious view of reality and that, for them, the great moral message in the Christian religion resonated with desires within themselves. There was, for example, the old woman in the Congo who, after hearing a missionary preach, rose up and cried out: "There now! I was certain in my heart that there is a God like that!"[7] We don't know how large or small such a group was in complex societies; it was clearly large enough to be significant and to affect the response these particular cultures made to Christianity.

One of the most moving stories concerns Tahiti. Brother Nott was reading the Gospel of Saint John to a large number of Tahitians, and when he finished the sixteenth verse of the third chapter, one listener interrupted him: "What words were those you read? what sounds were those I heard? let me hear those words again." Brother Nott read out the verse a second time: "For God so loved the world, that he gave his only begotten Son, that whosoever believeth in him should not perish, but have everlasting life." The Tahitian rose from his seat: "Is that true? can that be true? God love the world, when the world not love him! God *so* loved the world as to give his Son to die, that man might not die! Can that be true?" Brother Nott read the verse a third time, and announced that whoever believed in God would not perish but would be happy after death. The amazed Tahitian burst into tears, trembled, and left the meeting in order that he might be alone with his feelings.[8]

For people of sensibility, the transition to new beliefs was not always easy. One of the virtues associated with piety is loyalty, and some were deeply troubled by their wish to change religions because it involved a disloyalty to what they had formerly believed. Some, like Chief Sebuta in Buganda, could never decide. For years the Catholic mission struggled to win his soul, without success. Sebuta recognized the value of the new teaching but could not bring himself to baptism and final renunciation of the old gods. When Sebuta became terminally ill, the priest undertook one final effort to "save" him. On his seventeenth visit, the Catholic father found him still alive, even though he had been delirious the previous evening. It was clear, however, that Sebuta was dying. The priest drove everyone out of the room and gave the dying man a sniff of smelling salts, causing him to regain consciousness for about a minute. The priest spoke to him of Jesus and Mary. But even in the jaws of death Sebuta could not resolve his conflict: "Jesus, I don't love him. I am going to Hell!"[9]

An even more complicated situation of attachment-ambivalence-conversion concerns an old man on the island of Huahiné, one of the Society Islands. This man had been the last pagan priest of the war god Oro and had received many human sacrifices for the greater glory of the god. After the conversion to Christianity had proceeded to the point where the political authorities on Huahiné decreed that no one should work on the Sabbath, this priest adopted an attitude of defiance and went to till his garden whenever he pleased. One Sunday morning, "in contempt of the day," he did his usual gardening, returned home, and went blind. In panic he cried out, "I am a dead man!—a dead man." His neighbors ran to his aid, found him alive but sightless. He immediately came to the conclusion shared by everyone: that his blindness had resulted from his violation of the Sabbath. "He humbled himself in the dust, mourned over his sins, confessed them, abjured idolatry, and embraced that religion which had already triumphed over almost every other heart in the island except his own. . . ."[10] Eventually, his sight returned.

Several years after this remarkable conversion, the island of Huahiné was visited by a delegation of the London Missionary Society. They met the formerly pagan priest, heard his story, and, to satisfy their curiosity, asked him if he would perform for them the rites he had enacted for the god Oro in the past. The old man, not knowing which to fear most, the ancient or the modern masters of the island, reluctantly agreed to comply with the request. He hesitatingly walked to the old sacred place and was about to repeat one of the ancient prayers to Oro, when he found he could not do it: "Fear came upon him, and trembling, that made all his bones to shake. . . ." He leaped down from his station and cried out: "I dare not do it—I dare not do it." Apparently fearing death, he fled the scene.[11]

These last two stories help demonstrate the important truth that attachments to custom, to religion, to gods, to place, to family, to one's past have enormous force behind them. In many cases, such attachments can be broken only with great psychological violence. To change a man's religion may be as difficult as separating his arm from his body. We will talk later about the breaking apart of the kinship system. It is helpful to note here what a violation of the psyche such a fundamental change entails.

I heard, too, the story of Walukaga's capture. When they came to seize him, his wife Hannah, a most intelligent woman and clever reader escaped with the rest of the household; but he stood firm, and was taken.

He waited for a definite reason, and it was this: The Christians were
suspected of disloyalty and sedition. Now the most prominent of them
would not run away nor go into hiding, lest they should give colour to
this suspicion. They appealed to the laws of their country, and were
prepared "Kuwoza musango," to plead for judgement, before the proper
tribunal. It was this spirit and this confidence in the righteousness of
their cause which so puzzled the rulers, and which made the Christians
such a power in the country.[12]

While Mackay was vaccinating the children, Kiwube came to him and
said ... "My friend, I wish to be baptized." This was a most extraordi-
nary request at such a time. His teacher, Munyaga, had just been mur-
dered in the most shockingly frightful manner.[13]

TABU AND HOOMANAKII

Polynesians, as we shall have occasion to look at in more detail later,
were of a philosophical bent of mind. They took great pleasure in words
that had a multitude of symbolic overtones. They have given to our
language the words "tabu" and "mana," unquestionably better than any
words in English to describe a certain kind of prohibition or a certain
way of thinking about power. It was natural for the Polynesians, as the
new religion gradually established itself, to make certain philosophical
connections between its symbols and the traditional ones.

The concept of tabu permeated all Polynesian societies. Certain persons, certain acts, certain foods were prohibited. In Hawaii a fundamental tabu even prevented men and women from eating together. But in
1819, before any Christian missionary had set foot on the islands, the
Hawaiians had officially abolished all tabus—an extraordinary act. By
the time the Christians arrived, a critical look at the concept of tabu
was already part of the Hawaiian world view. The connection between
the Sabbath and old methods of prohibition was immediately made by
the Hawaiians, and Sunday became simply *la tabu,* the forbidden day.[14]
When Catholic priests arrived in the islands, intent on conversions, and
told their followers to refrain from eating meat on certain days, the
Protestant opposition threw up the charge: "This is another form of
tabu."[15]

The first Catholic Mass was celebrated on Hawaii in 1827, seven years after the arrival of the Protestants. By that time, most of the high aristocracy had been converted. The Protestant missionaries were militantly opposed to their new rivals, and the Catholics didn't have a chance. One of the main weapons the Protestants used against the Romans was the accusation that Catholicism was a regression to more primitive times. *Hoomanakii* was the Hawaiian word for idolatry, compounded of *hoomana* (to attribute supernatural power or efficacy) and *kii* (image, device, picture, or representation). When the priests conducted their first worship, bowing before pictures and crucifixes, the Hawaiians exclaimed, "It is *hoomanakii.*"[16] Some high officials, prompted either by their consciences or their Protestant teachers or both, went further in their criticism and announced that "this new religion was all about worshiping images and dead men's bones and taboo on meat!"[17]

> *Seeing that the persecution was taking on a more cruel aspect and that it had begun being carried on on a large scale, Mbwa advised us, the youngest of the company, to flee in order that we might live to carry on the work of the Gospel after our fellows had gone. But, fearing lest by running away we might deny Christ, we declined to act upon our friend's suggestion and preferred to stay where we were and to die together with our fellows.*
>
> *As we had definitely refused to quit our place of refuge, Mbwa decided that we should be left alone but that extracts from the Acts of the Apostles should be read out to us between the periods for prayer so that the persecution and imprisonment of the early Christians might inspire us with patience and consolation under our difficulties.*[18]
>
> *"Then Mukajanga gave each of us a small gourdful of plantain wine, it being the custom of the Baganda to give plantain wine to everyone who is about to be put to death. James Buzabaliawo (probably in memory of his Master's refusal on Calvary) refused to drink."*[19]

THE BUGANDA HOLOCAUST OF 1886

Kabaka Mwanga was bisexual, and he preferred young boys to women. He was lucky that what he lusted for was lavishly supplied at the court: beautiful, shiny-faced, cheerful, post-pubescent boys. The existence of a great number of young pages at the royal capital meant that Mwanga did not have to travel far to satisfy his desires, and he took many of the pages to his bed. The missionaries told the young men it was a sin, causing some of them to refuse the king's invitation. Mwanga killed them for holding to their faith.

The corps of pages at the *kabaka*'s court was a crucial cadre in Buganda society. It was the way the most intelligent and promising young men were drawn into the vortex of Buganda politics, since nobody would send a dull-witted boy to be a page. The future leaders of society were chosen from their ranks. For the individual page, being at court was the perfect opportunity to learn the system and to make the alliances that could benefit him for a lifetime.

The pages had been wrenched from their families at the critical stage of adolescence and sent into a world far different from the tight web of kinship in which they had grown up. It is not surprising, then, that they developed fierce loyalties to one another and that they were receptive to a religion that preached idealism and stressed a sense of communion and community among its members—a religion whose founder had said, "He that loveth father or mother more than me, is not worthy of me."[20] Forsaken already by their parents, these best and brightest young men had nothing to give up in order to obtain the great psychological benefits of Christianity—nothing, that is, except the *kabaka*'s approval. Others, who were not pages, also flocked to the Christian standard, but it is safe to say that, had it not been for the conversions of these young men, Christianity never would have become a great power in nineteenth-century Buganda.

Although the motives behind Mwanga's holocaust had a sexual overtone, the real causes differed little from those for Mutesa's persecution of the Muslims ten years before. Mwanga, like his father, refused to be converted to one of the three modern religions and thus lead his country in a cultural revolution. Neither *kabaka,* however, could keep a multitude of others from conversion, and conversions to Islam, Catholicism, and Protestantism were eroding the traditional primary loyalty of the Buganda for the *kabaka* at a tremendous rate. This was the real issue, not eating meat or circumcision, as it seemed to be in the case of Mutesa, or sexual compliance, as in Mwanga's. The *kabaka*'s word had ceased to carry its absolute psychological imperative.

Faced with a radical diminution of his powers, egged on by a ruthless prime minister who had no sympathy for new ideas, Mwanga did what might have been predicted: he had a furious tantrum, lashed out at those whom he could no longer control, and killed two hundred converts, Protestants and Catholics alike.

Even this action could not restore his power. The execution of the martyrs and the bravery with which they met death only increased the attractiveness of Christianity for the Baganda. Equally important, the passion of the young people was finding a response among the older, more established members of society. For example, the queen mother refused to yield her attendants to her son's executioners, and they were saved from the burning.[21] Kabaka Mwanga and Katikiro Mukasa had obviously lost control of their country.

> *Seeing that many of his fellows had already been taken away and killed for their faith and fearing lest he might miss the chance, Buza of his own accord went up to the king's executioners and reported himself as one of the wanted converts. The news of his self-surrender having been conveyed to the king, he gave orders that the prisoner be brought into his presence.*
>
> *"Are you, James Buza, the teacher of the Christian converts?" the king asked. To which the prisoner replied by saying that he would be most grateful to his master if he thus appointed him to such a high position. Incensed by this answer, king Mwanga told his audience that as the prisoner had at one time dared to give him religious instruction and to give him orders, king of Buganda that he was, and as he had answered back with such insolence, there was no other punishment fit for him besides death. At this, Buza thanked his master all the more for the great honor that he had conferred upon him first by giving him the title of leader of Christian converts and secondly by deeming him worthy to die for his religion.* The prisoner was then led away and put to death.[22]*

TRIAL OF THE PAGAN GODS

In the great confrontation between Christianity and paganism, an oft-repeated scene has been that in which a man or woman of the new God violates the tabu of the old gods, and thereby proves their power-

---

*In the traditional society, prisoners always thanked the *kabaka* for sentencing them, even when the sentence was death[23]—a striking confirmation of the idea that the psychology of martyrdom was incipient in the value system of the society.

lessness when no punishment rebounds to the iconoclast. The Anglo-Saxon missionary Willibrord, at the end of the seventh century, cut down with his own hands the great sacred oak of the heathen Frisians. The superb dramatic effect of this act was to accelerate tremendously the rate of conversion to the new God.

In Buganda, Hawaii, and Tahiti, there were many such courageous trials of the pagan gods by people raised in traditional society, with the traditional fears of these deities. Kapiolani, a highborn princess of Hawaii, decided in December 1824 that she would break the spell of belief in the goddess Pele, who was, among other things, the deity of the volcano. Rejecting the advice of her husband and her friends, she made a journey, mostly on foot, of 150 miles, visiting on the way the crater of Kilauea. As she approached the great crater, she was met by the priestess of Pele, who admonished her not to proceed farther. " 'Who are you?' demanded Kapiolani. 'One in whom the goddess dwells' " was the reply.

Then ensued a verbal battle identical to the great contests of riddles or aphorisms that we find in the folklore and mythology of Polynesia and many other cultures. The priestess quoted from a sacred letter she had received from the goddess; Kapiolani cited passage after passage from scripture, "setting forth the character and power of the true God." The priestess was overcome and gave the signal of defeat in such contests: she fell silent. Subsequently, she admitted the goddess had left her.

The trial with the priestess being over, Kapiolani's way was clear to move forward to the crater. Advancing, she was surprised to find Mr. Goodrich, an American missionary who had traveled there in order to accompany her to the crater. He conveyed to her the regrets of another missionary, Mr. Ruggles, who was also anxious to come, but unfortunately had been without shoes for six months.

A hut was built for Kapiolani on the eastern ridge of the crater, where she spent the night. The next morning she led her company of eighty people five hundred feet down to the "Black Ledge," from where there was a clear view of the fiery action of the inner volcano. Kapiolani ate the berries consecrated to Pele and threw stones directly into the crater's mouth: "Jehovah is my God. He kindled these fires. I fear not Pele. If I perish by her anger, then you may fear Pele; but if I trust in Jehovah and he preserves me when breaking her tabus, then you must fear and serve him alone. . . ." When the goddess showed her helplessness by not responding, the worshipers knelt in adoration to the creator and raised their voices singing praises to Him.[24]

Mukajanga, in his count and inspection of the living faggots, which his assistants had thrown onto the funeral pyre, recognized amongst them his son, Mbaga Tuzinde, who, like his companions in glory, was calmly reciting his prayers, a serene and tranquil expression on his face. At the thought of the torment in store, his father's heart revolted. He had the boy untied, and took him aside. Mbaga, his hands still tied behind his back, knelt before his father, who pleaded with him once again. "Give up this folly! Leave this European nonsense in the furnace and come with me to the Kabaka. He will pardon you at my pleading." "Pardon me, Father," replied the boy, "but praying is no crime. I have no desire to give up the service of Jesus, and I am happy to have the chance of dying for Him, my King."

"But I," protested Mukajanga, "do not want you to die. Let me hide you. And, to please me, give up this religion."

"Father, the Kabaka has ordered me to be burnt. He is your master, and you cannot shield me."

"What kind of madness is this," exclaimed Mukajanga, "that drives you to break my heart?"

In spite of himself, the old man could not but admire the determination of all these Christian pages and soldiers. He was heart-broken and distraught at having to commit to the flames his obstinate but lovable son. Out of pity, to spare him suffering, he ordered his assistants to club the boy on the nape of the neck, and throw his lifeless body into the flames. They took him some little distance apart and did so, killing him instantly. I saw all these things with my own eyes.[25]

CHRISTIAN ENTHUSIASM

There are wonderful and rare moments in history when a large number of people have called upon the best that is in themselves to rise with great enthusiasm and spirit above the usual petty, narrow level of human existence. In the past, such periods have usually occurred in conjunction with political or religious revolution, sometimes with both together. The Italian Renaissance of the fifteenth and sixteenth centuries was unusual in that its thrust was *not* primarily moral; it did not address itself to a fundamental change in religion or politics. The period of revolutionary change in Buganda—1888 to 1900—followed the usual pattern of great political and religious transformation and released vast sources of energy in many people.

No social theorist has succeeded in explaining why these periods are so short. Max Weber's thesis that charismatic authority is transformed into bureaucratic authority is true—and sad. Even Weber, however, could not explain why this should be so, and why it happens so quickly. In this regard, Buganda was no exception: the leaders of the revolution became, in the twentieth century, great bureaucrats.

At first, the Baganda were religion-intoxicated. By 1893, "The missionaries were constantly being stopped as they walked about the streets by people racing out of their houses with books in their hands to ask the meaning of obscure passages. What was a winepress? How far was it from Jerusalem to Jericho? In what did the wealth of Capernaum consist? The embarrassed clergymen had to write home to headquarters for reference books and commentaries."[26] The same kind of thing happened in Hawaii, where the new converts were constantly accosting their pastors after church, or waking them at strange hours of the night to discuss their feelings, their thoughts, and "troubling points of doctrine."[27]

The Baganda very quickly became missionaries themselves, dedicated to the task of converting their own people. Only fifteen years after the first European missionaries arrived, the Buganda Christian community sent out 260 evangelists to eighty-five mission stations, twenty of which were beyond the Buganda border. For some of these recent converts, such action represented a substantial sacrifice, a relinquishment of considerable secular power and authority. Apolo Kiuebulaya, a man of remarkable personal piety and dedication, became "apostle to the pygmies," an inspired example for many succeeding generations.[28]

In some political leaders, the combination of weighty ambition and a firm belief that they have been encouraged by God reminds us of the Emperor Constantine or Oliver Cromwell. Apolo Kagwa, great Christian general, foremost Buganda historian, and the first Christian *katikiro* (a post he held for over twenty-five years), says of his part in the wars of religion among the Muslims, Protestants, and Catholics that began after Mwanga was deprived of his throne in 1888: "But the writer of this book and Stanislaus Mugwanya fought from horseback, for we despised those against whom we fought. They were renegade Christians who were fighting for the evil customs of the past. When we saw that they had fled from God, we were unable to fear them. God lifted up our thoughts, for our enemies were firing all around us and we were clearly visible up there on our horses, but they failed to hit us. Then we knew that God was fighting with us."[29]

Christian enthusiasm even succeeded temporarily in changing the rules by which warfare was conducted. The customary procedure in all of East Africa was to despoil those defeated in battle. To win the battle and not take away the booty was an unheard-of thing. When the Christian forces fought their way back from exile after their defeat by the Muslims in 1888, they first succeeded in conquering all of the border province of Buddu. Contrary to everyone's expectations, they took no one's property, not "a needle or even . . . a hen's egg." The Buganda historian Zimbe goes on: "We gave freedom to all the peasants of Buddu by abstaining ourselves from dispossessing them of any of their property, and they then understood that we followed the true religion of Christ . . . in contrast to Muslims who used to plunder peoples and all their property. . . ."[30]

Exactly the same kind of thing happened in Tahiti shortly after King Pomare II became a Christian. Following a crucial battle in the war that would finally unify the island, Pomare's victorious troops were prepared for the usual plundering and killing of their opponents. "Pomare approached and exclaimed, *Atira!* It is enough!"[31] Thereupon the sack ceased.

In 1893, forty Christian Buganda chiefs gave up their slaves voluntarily.[32]

Traditional Buganda society allowed a man as many wives as he was able to obtain. They did all the agricultural work. After the fields were initially cleared, no man worked in the gardens. Christian converts had to give up all wives but one, and some, like the high official Matthias Mulumba, even began to help in growing food: "bent on imitating Christ's example [and] not ashamed of manual labor."[33] When the English succeeded in introducing the growing of cotton—a very productive cash crop—in the twentieth century, it was the men who, after hundreds of years of disdaining such work, became the cultivators.

Not all acts of Christian charity were well received. On the island of Borabora, near Tahiti, the unregenerate criminals who committed most of the thefts and assaults had been designated with the popular opprobrious nickname *tuta auri,* or "rusty iron." The appellation made the ne'er-do-wells extremely angry, and as an act of Christian concern for those less fortunate, the people of Borabora held a large public meeting in which it was decided that henceforth such individuals would not be called "rusty iron," but *feia aroha,* "people to be pitied." While the meeting was in progress, some of the rusty-irons-who-are-to-be-pitied broke into the oven of one of the principal speakers at the conclave, stole the hog and breadfruit that were baking therein, and left the speaker and his family dependent upon the charity of others for their supper.[34]

It is sad to see how quickly Christian piety and Christian enthusiasm give way to Christian hypocrisy. In Hawaii, a short while after the conversion, most Christian energy went into attempts to close the grog shops near the harbor and end the traffic in prostitution on the ships. A gaudy Victorianism spread over middle- and upper-class Hawaiian life, smothering whatever charismatic energy still remained.

> *"As they passed the enclosure of his brother, Bosa, after a two hours' walk from Munyonyo [Bruno] cried out: 'Bosa, Bosa, Bosa! Bring me some plantain wine!' Bosa poured some into a bowl, and brought it to the place where Bruno was waiting, guarded by an executioner. When the brothers met, Bruno said: 'You see, Bosa, that they are taking us off to execution; but we are going (to Heaven) to keep places for you. A well which has many sources, never runs dry. When we are gone, others will come after us.' Bosa replied: 'Here is the plantain wine which you have asked for.' Then Bruno looked his brother in the face, fixed his eyes on him for a moment and refused the wine. Turning to the executioner, he said: 'Let us go on.'"*[35]

OF MARTYRDOM, IDEALISM, AND SUICIDE

It is illuminating to look closely at the last two stories of martyrdom, the one of Mukajanga and his son Mbaga, and the other of the brothers Bruno and Bosa. In both, the usual pathos of martyrdom is heightened by the fact that the terrible split of loyalty occurs within a *family*. Just as Aristotle observed, the most pitiful tragedies are those that set father against son, brother against brother: tragedies about families.[36]

Tragedy and martyrdom are intimately related. Martyrdom is the Christian form of tragedy, tragedy the secular form of martyrdom. In both forms, sorrow and death come because those who hold legitimate power are unjust. In both, the moral cause belongs to the victims.[37] Both tragedy and martyrdom are intimately related to the more primitive religious form of human sacrifice.

So deeply are these things joined that one can justifiably call Christ a tragic figure, a martyr, a sacrifice. And although Prometheus is not representative of all Greek tragic heroes, he, too, is a martyr and a sacrifice as well as a tragic hero, since his suffering came because he would help humankind.[38]

All martyrs give the sense of having been betrayed. They act as if they were somehow promised justice but received instead a violation of their rights, as if somewhere they were promised love and received death. They are intent on converting those who hold power not only into something evil but into betrayers: those who promise benevolence and deliver tyranny. Even Christ, on the cross, cries out that his father has betrayed him. This is remarkable because nothing in the story relates that God had previously promised Christ that he would not have to suffer. Nothing in the story suggests that Christ didn't know beforehand all that was to happen. Why, then, does Christ cry out about having been forsaken, if not because the sense of betrayal is essential to martyrdom?

This atmosphere of betrayal is related to another aspect of family martyrdom stories: the intensity of love and hatred that exists within the victims. The child Mbaga loves God so intensely that he is willing to die for that love, but equally strong is the hatred he feels for his father, a hatred repressed and disguised by the overwhelming commitment to God. Mbaga is intent upon dying because dying will simultaneously satisfy both these passions. Nothing he could do could hurt his father more and, at the same time, prove to himself how much he loves God.

And it is the same with Bruno. He will not let his brother Bosa off the hook. Bosa is not the cause of Bruno's death, but Bruno insists on setting up a situation in which Bosa is forced to deny him. Had Bruno merely asked for wine and a little pity, Bosa could have responded, but Bruno insisted on asking for much more: he wanted Bosa to say, "Yes, you are right," or "I will join you in death." And when Bosa would not say any such thing, Bruno figuratively spat in his face by refusing to drink his wine. The undrunk wine was meant to be transformed into a great burden of guilt and remorse that was to be carried by Bosa.

This same strange combination of intense, seeming idealism and love, on the one hand, and enormous rage, on the other, occurs in our own world in a phenomenon related to martyrdom: left-wing terrorism. Terrorists are not ordinary criminals, although they do most of the things criminals do, because they claim to act in the interest of an ideal. And the rhetoric of their idealism speaks often of great love for others. If the stated goal of terrorist activity is the independence of a homeland or the establishment of an egalitarian society, the sense of brotherhood and sisterhood with large numbers of people is a proclaimed ideal, the same as, but also different from, that of the Buganda martyrs, whose love of Christ and their fellow martyrs brought them death. And yet the terrorist cannot live without killing others, or, at least, thinking about killing others. The rage is enormous. And for many terrorists, the terrorist life becomes a means to suicide: through prison or execution or mishaps with their own bombs or casualties caused by armed attack. Very few live to be old.

This syndrome of idealism, love, rage, and suicide relates intimately to the period of late adolescence—more accurately, the period between adolescence and young adulthood. Student riots and uprisings, intense political idealism, reckless personal behavior, anorexia (that half-suicide), and suicide itself, are all characteristic modes of this time of life. And the rage that exists in so many of these modes is fueled by a cruel sense of betrayal.

The Buganda pages were the perfect candidates for conversion and martyrdom. They were the right age. A sense of betrayal was easily available to them because they had been sent away from their homes. The society in which they lived was in the process of downgrading the kinship system and erecting new forms of political cohesion—a time of social transition and upheaval that is never easy—and they were the cutting edge of this transformation. The *kabaka,* who was meant to be their new father, who was meant to replace their parents, really did betray them when he refused to countenance the idealism of their conversions. Betrayed, they felt, by their parents, betrayed in reality by the *kabaka;* they were left with the idealized love of Christ and Jehovah. Like the suicide, but different from the suicide, consumed by rage and love, they went magically to their death.

6

The Life and Times of Prime Minister Mukasa, Part III

The Anglican Bishop Hannington, in 1885, was making his way to Buganda through the land that eventually would become the country of Kenya. Hannington, intent on visiting the Anglican missions in Buganda, assumed he would be welcomed. He planned to enter the country from Busoga, the northeast neighbor of Buganda. That was a mistake. The traditional lore of the Baganda told how a strange, destructive enemy was to come from that quarter. This tradition played on Mwanga's hysterical nature and, combined with his growing hostility toward Christianity, brought him to the point where he sent out word that the bishop was to be killed in Busoga.

After the murder, Mwanga feared retribution from some vague supernatural source and from real-life English soldiers. Losing control of the situation within his country and of himself, the *kabaka* lashed out at the Christian converts. The first martyr in the great holocaust of 1886 was the same Joseph Mukasa whose information had forestalled the assassination of Mwanga barely a year before. Mwanga had predicted that Joseph Mukasa would someday become *katikiro*, but loyalty to individuals or to ideals was not one of the king's virtues.

Joseph was arrested and brought to the *kabaka*'s house. The *katikiro* was also present. Mwanga lashed out at the convert: he had betrayed state secrets to the white men; he had caused obstruction; he had insulted the *kabaka* by saying it was wrong to kill the bishop and that Mutesa never would have done such a thing; he had tried to poison the king when he asked Père Lourdel to prescribe medicine for the *kabaka*; he had been forbidden to pursue this white-man's religion but did so anyway, even going so far as to teach religion to the *kabaka*'s servants at court, inciting them against him: "They no longer do a thing I tell them."[1]

Katikiro Mukasa joined in, playing on Mwanga's paranoia. "From his attempt to poison you it is apparent that we have a sorcerer before us. Well then, since he wanted to kill you, let him precede you to the abode of death. Give him to me and I will rid you of him." The prime minister called in the executioners who were always in attendance outside the *kabaka*'s doorway, and they immediately bound the prisoner. "You have saved me!" cried the *kabaka*. "Now there will no longer be two *kabakas* at this court. . . . This is the fellow who always wanted to teach me, and told me to put away my charms!"[2]

At the king's orders they took Joseph Mukasa out to burn him: "Do not let him live the night" was the last instruction from Katikiro Mukasa.[3] The chief executioner, Mukajanga, however, was an old hand at *kabaka* fickleness. Many times in the past he had been quite leisurely in carrying out similar commands and was rewarded with the sovereign's thanks after the king changed his mind and retrieved the condemned man. This was most likely to happen in cases like the present one, where the victim was a former close ally of the *kabaka*'s.

Mukajanga, therefore, made no haste in the preparation of the pyre, and indeed, even as his men were working, a messenger was seen coming down the hill. Expecting the usual reprieve, Mukajanga was startled to learn it was an angel of death, not of mercy. It was the prime minister's messenger demanding that the fellow be burned at once.[4] Mukajanga could not resist such an order from the *katikiro,* and Joseph Mukasa became the first Catholic martyr in Buganda. As the flames from the execution fire were dying down, a second messenger did arrive from the *kabaka* ordering that Joseph not be killed but be kept in prison. Once again, the wily, sadistic *katikiro* had outmaneuvered his immature, hysterical master.

The prime minister's cruelty and sadism intensified as events moved forward. He was getting on, and old age, for some people, is a time of indulgence in all forms of aggression. With society changing everywhere around him, he may have felt the necessity of preserving old values, and his kind of cruelty was definitely a value in traditional Buganda society. Or this intensified brutality may have resulted from the fact that he, too, like Mutesa and Mwanga, knew that he was no longer in control of things, that established methods of power would no longer hold. Feeling his power slipping away from him, he must have received some temporary alleviation of his sense of impending impotence in the gouged-out eyes and severed arms of his victims.

Katikiro Mukasa felt no reluctance even to judge members of the royal family. The Princess Muggale, a sister of Mwanga's, had, with everyone's knowledge, been conducting an affair with the youth Bwami. Mwanga himself was aware of the intrigue and would jest about it. As long as the couple were never actually caught together, no official action had to be taken. One day, however, they were discovered, and the event reported to the court. Muggale was forgiven, but, according to Mackay, only after Mwanga had given her a severe beating. Bwami presented a more serious case, since execution was the traditional penalty for such behavior. Mwanga was prepared to pardon him, but Katikiro Mukasa insisted on severe punishment, won his point, and had the youth's eyes plucked out.[5]

When the storm of Mwanga's anger broke on the Christian converts, the prime minister was at the center of the action—urging the king on, making sure the *kabaka* did not change his mind, performing executions on his own, and in general making sure that death, not prison or beating, was the punishment meted out. Appropriately enough, it was the *katikiro*'s son Mwafu who provided the immediate occasion for the persecutions.

"When Mwafu, the son of Chancellor Mukasa, came to Court, he was a pretty boy. Soon, the *kabaka* took a fancy to him and committed sodomy with him," reported a Baganda chief.[6] Mwafu, however, began to study religion and became markedly less receptive to the *kabaka*'s needs. One day, Mwanga noted that Mwafu was not even in attendance at the court, where he was required to be. Furious at his absence, Mwanga sent out an arrest patrol, which found the boy and brought him into the *kabaka*'s presence:

"Where have you come from? Tell me exactly where you have been, and no lying!"

"I have been with Ssebuggwawo," replied the youth.

"What have you been doing?"

"He has been teaching me religion."

"So!" shouted the *kabaka*, striking the boy with his hand. "It is Ssebuggwawo who sets you against me, and takes you constantly to Kisule's to study religion! Did your father send you here to serve me or to learn the religion of the white men?"

Mwanga then turned to Ssebuggwawo.

"Has Mwafu been with you?"

"Yes," replied Ssebuggwawo.

"What business had you with him?"

"I have been teaching him religion."

Turning back to Mwafu, the *kabaka* said angrily:

"So it's true! You're learning religion too now, are you?"

"Yes, I am studying religion."

Beside himself with fury, Mwanga again shouted at Ssebuggwawo:

"And you constantly take the son of my vassal along to Kisule's place to instruct him in religion! Haven't you heard me forbid the teaching of religion here?"

"Yes, I have been instructing him in the Christian religion," replied Ssebuggwawo.

"So, it is you that are responsible for trying to convert him?"

"Yes, I am the one that instructs him. . . ."[7]

By that point, Mwanga was in a raging tantrum. He beat Ssebuggwawo senseless while calling out that the executioners should come and take him away. Ssebuggwawo was killed the next morning. Mwafu, under his father's protection, was saved from sacrifice.[8]

As the number of victims multiplied, Mwanga could not handle all the condemnations himself, and the *katikiro* rendered his own private judgment on certain converts. Matthias Mulumba was not a page but a man of mature years. He was brought into the prime minister's presence: "Why do you pray?" asked the *katikiro*. "What has moved you, a man of standing, to embrace the white man's religion, at your age?" Mulumba replied, "I practice that religion because I want to." But Mukasa did not give up hope of provoking him to anger: "You have sent away all your wives I am told. So you cook your own food, I suppose?" Mulumba let the *katikiro* know that he might take his life but his soul belonged to himself: "Is it because I am thin, or because I practice religion that I have been brought before you?"[9]

A few days after Mulumba's execution, Mukasa learned that the victim had been adopted and brought up by his, Mukasa's, uncle Magatto and was therefore a relation of his. As well as such a man can, he expressed regret over what had happened: "If I had known that, I would not have put him to death, but I would have installed him in my household, and given him charge over all my goods, for I know that those who practice religion do not steal!" This was not just words: the *katikiro* ordered his brother to set up Mulumba's widow on their family estate.[10]

This response to Mulumba's death is one of only a few occasions when we glimpse a Mukasa who is more humane than the vengeful political maneuverer he usually appears to be. Another such occasion occurred directly after the terror had started. Many pages were held prisoner at the court; the question was whether they were to be executed or not. Père Lourdel, having gone to the palace to plead for their lives, was on his way home when he fell in with the *katikiro*. Mukasa treated Lourdel with an exaggerated courtesy as they walked down the hill. Lourdel, not knowing where mercy might come from, pleaded with the prime minister. Banish the missionaries, he said, but do not execute the young Christians. The *katikiro* of Buganda offered him rebuke: "It is our own children that we are killing, not yours. As for your people, you are our guests; we will not drive you away. Teach us as much as you like, but as many as you teach, we shall kill."[11]

Not content with this rebuff, the prime minister could not hold back a final taunt: "You men of God know many things, but you did not know what was going to happen today."[12] Mukasa was also, unconsciously, speaking to himself. It was he who had not known what would happen to his country and could not know what even the near future might bring. For the moment his power held, but only perhaps for the day.

When he had a score to settle, there was literally nothing Mukasa would not do. We recall that more than a year before the 1886 holocaust, Mwanga had praised, and predicted a bright future for, Joseph Mukasa and Andrew Kaggwa, two Catholic converts. Joseph Mukasa had already been disposed of by the prime minister. When the terror began to collect more victims, Andrew Kaggwa fell into the *katikiro*'s hands. The prime minister ordered the executioners to put him to death, and, fearing once again that the *kabaka* might change his mind, added: "Be quick about it, and bring me his arm to prove that you have done your work." Unconsciously recognizing the cannibalistic nature of the proof he required, the *katikiro* added: "I will not touch food until I have seen it."[13]

The executioners were not sure how to respond. They recalled that in the case of Joseph Mukasa, Mwanga's pardon had come too late. If they held off, and Andrew Kaggwa was reprieved by the *kabaka*, their reward would be great. There was a limit, however, to how far one could test the *katikiro*'s anger. The victim, intent on becoming a martyr, helped them decide: "Why don't you carry out our orders? I'm afraid delay will get you into serious trouble. If your master had asked you to serve him a kid, would you keep him waiting? You would go and kill it at once. Well, he wants my arm, and he cannot eat until he gets it. Take it to him without delay!"[14]

What an extraordinary combination, contradiction, resolution of human motives come together in this one speech; even more, in the one phrase "our orders." Human sacrifice, victimization, cannibalism, willingness to die, loyalty, identification with the aggressor, idealism, hatred, suicide, love. How complex is the irrationality of human existence!

The *katikiro* was concerned for his dinner. He had not long to wait, "for in a few minutes the Chancellor's gatekeeper re-appeared, carrying suspended from a length of fibre, Kaggwa's bleeding arm, severed at the shoulder."[15]

With all his excesses, Mukasa still held on to his political wisdom, in contrast to Mwanga, who was completely ruled by his moods. After the great holocaust subsided, and several months had gone by without any such executions, Mwanga grew restless. When one of his Christian pages displeased him, he ordered the page and a number of others arrested. By this time, however, the *katikiro* had had enough. Knowing that the country was becoming profoundly discontented with Mwanga and his hysterical outbursts, Mukasa advised the *kabaka* that the neighboring countries would come to know that the Baganda were killing all their young men and leaving themselves defenseless and open to attack. Mwanga listened and took the advice.[16]

Mukasa was not powerful enough, however, to compensate for Mwanga's pervasive incompetence. As discontent grew, Mwanga tried to overcome it by putting himself in fierce opposition to the Muslims and the Christians, not realizing that such a course would leave him with practically no supporters. In September 1888, Mwanga hatched a plot to rid the country of the foremost Christian converts, an action that was certain of failure. Katikiro Mukasa finally abandoned his young *kabaka,* warned the Christians of the intrigue,[17] agreed with the Muslim party that Mwanga must go, went to the palace, pronounced to Mwanga a Buganda proverb which says, "The dog that you feed will bite your hand," and then asked the *kabaka* to look out onto Lubaya hill across the way. The hill was covered with rebel forces. The *katikiro* withdrew, and, hedging his bets as always, left a son to fight for the king.[18] When one of Mwanga's pages was killed, the king gave up the fight and fled to the lake. That was the extent of the battle. The Muslim, Protestant, and Catholic forces ruled the country.

The first job of the new administrators was to divide up the important chieftainships and governorships among themselves. Before that,
however, they had to settle the matter of Katikiro Mukasa. Here there
was no disagreement. The unanimous decision was that he was to go.
His request for a few days to straighten out his affairs was denied. They
sent him into retirement at Kasubi, the place of his old master Mutesa's
tomb.[19]

The Buganda aristocracy was not yet able to rule the country without a *kabaka*—it did not occur to anyone that the kingship should be
abolished—and Kiwewa, a brother of Mwanga's, was chosen to be the
new king. Very quickly, the differences between the factions of the victorious rebels made themselves felt. The Zanzibari Arabs, who were
in natural alliance with the Buganda Muslims, were not happy with the
new *kabaka,* or with the new *katikiro,* who was a Christian.[20] Kiwewa,
with no experience in political affairs, fell back on the advice of the incumbent *katikiro* and even consulted frequently with the emeritus
Mukasa. Mukasa's advice to the young *kabaka* was not to be too compromising with the Muslim faction. This tactic backfired, however; the
Muslims rose again in revolt and chose another brother, Kalema, as
kabaka. Forced to flee the capital, Kiwewa went directly to find sanctuary with Mukasa at Mutesa's tomb. The wily old retired *katikiro* had
no compunction about abandoning one whose star had fallen. Mukasa
and his followers drove Kiwewa and his cadre away from the tomb,
killing five people in the process.[21]

Kalema, who had converted to Islam, agreed to be circumcised and
became the instrument of the Muslim faction. Mukasa, from his retirement, could not cease from any intrigue that might put him back in
power, and even made overtures to Mwanga, who was now in exile
south of Lake Victoria. Kalema learned of these negotiations, and sent
assassins to visit the former *katikiro:* "When the messengers came, he
behaved with much dignity, and met his death with the greatest courage. He saw that his murder was intended, and made no resistance.
He was shot, and his body cast into one of the houses, which was then
set on fire, so that all that was mortal of him thus perished in the
flames."[22]

The force of Mukasa's character had made a very deep impression
on many Europeans. Emin Pasha called him the one gentleman in
Buganda. The English missionary Robert Ashe, who might have
been Mukasa's natural enemy, found him remarkably courteous and

polite. "He possessed," writes Ashe, "an astonishing insight into
character. . . . When not carried away by the cruel passion of revenge,
he could take a statesmanlike view of affairs."

"This man," says Ashe, "was one of the most remarkable Africans
that I ever met."[23]

II

ANCIENT POLYNESIA: TONGA, TAHITI, HAWAII

7

The Beauties of Tonga

Finow I, a fierce military and political leader, forged in the latter part of the eighteenth century the various chieftainships of Vavau (one of the islands of Tonga in the Polynesian Pacific) into a centralized monarchy, enjoyed several years of military and political power on Vavau and other islands of the Tonga group, and died.

His son, Finow II, succeeded to the throne. This Finow was one of the most remarkable rulers of an advanced complex society that we know about. A "civilizing monarch," he had inherited his father's energy and courage, and chose to use both in the areas of art, craft, and the peaceful pursuit of orderly politics. In order to accomplish this, and particularly to avoid the possibilities of warfare, Finow II decided to cut off contact between Vavau and other islands of the Tonga group. He was especially desirous that intercourse with the people of the islands of Haapai should cease, since contact between the two islands had been particularly close.

Haapai sent a yearly tribute to Finow's island of Vavau, so that year, when the canoe arrived bearing the goods, the new King Finow informed the nobleman in charge that this was to be the last such visit, that no one from Haapai was ever to visit Vavau again.

One final piece of diplomacy had to be settled by means of this canoe. Finow I had been married to Máfi Hábe, who was the daughter of Tooi Bolotoo, one of the main rulers of the island of Haapai. On the death of her husband, Máfi Hábe expressed the wish to return to her father's house, and Finow II had promised Tooi Bolotoo that she could do so. Máfi Hábe was instructed to get herself and her attendants ready to depart with this last tribute canoe.

The problem was that Máfi Hábe, having been the principal wife of the king, had a great number of female attendants, "many of whom were some of the handsomest women"[1] on Vavau. As happens, many of the young men who surrounded Finow had made connections with these attendants, and others hoped to do so in the future. Since the permission granted to Máfi Hábe to leave included, by custom, license to take all of her attendants with her, and since they were deeply devoted to her, if things proceeded in the normal course the sexual and marriageable resources of the island would be seriously depleted. Finow even feared that under such circumstances some of his discontented young men would be tempted to follow the women.

Direct approach seemed the best tactic. Finow sent for Máfi Hábe, informed her of his problem, and instructed her that, "with her leave," he would contrive some stratagem to keep the young women from departing. Máfi Hábe had no objection; she was not planning to live on a grand scale and rather looked forward to living a quiet life with her father; all she needed was two attendants. The rest could stay on Vavau.

Though he had received Máfi Hábe's consent, Finow knew that her female attendants would not agree to being left behind, abandoned by their mistress; force would be necessary to detain them. Because Finow did not want the forcible restraint of the young women to be seen as an authoritarian act on his part, he asked the aid of William Mariner, who was the historian of this event. Mariner, an Englishman, had survived a shipwreck and massacre of the crew during the time of Finow I, and lived to become a trusted adviser to both kings Finow. Not only did Mariner have a gun, but he also knew how to use it—an invaluable political resource. Finow II instructed Mariner how he wished him to behave in this delicate situation.

When the canoe was ready to leave, the widow Máfi Hábe was carried to it; immediately her two designated attendants followed. The remainder of the young women then advanced toward the canoe, but they found their way barred by Mr. Mariner, who seized the foremost woman, threw her into the water, and warned the rest that they would be shot by his ready musket if they tried to follow. Mariner shouted to Finow's male attendants, who by design were seated on the beach, to come to his aid. He was amazed, he exhorted them, that they would let the women leave, when they had so often risked their lives in battle to protect these same women.

The young bravos rushed to Mariner's aid and forcibly held back the women, who raised a fierce lament. At that moment Finow appeared and innocently inquired the cause of their distress. Togi (as the islanders called Mariner) had violently prevented them from joining their beloved mistress, they reported, and Finow's followers had cruelly assisted him.

At this point, clearly by prearrangement, one of the more loquacious of Finow's guards addressed the king: "We have all agreed to lose our lives rather than suffer these women, for whom we have so often fought, to take leave of us for ever. It is possible that we shall soon be invaded by the people of Haapai; and are we to suffer some of the finest of our women to go over to the men who will shortly become our enemies? These women, the sight and recollection of whom have so often cheered our hearts in the time of danger, and enabled us to meet the bravest and fiercest enemies, and to put them to rout? If our women are to be sent away, in the name of the gods, send away also the guns, the powder, and all our spears, our clubs, our bows and arrows, and every weapon of defense: with the departure of the women our wish to live departs also, for then we shall leave nothing worth protecting, and having no motive to defend ourselves, it matters little how we die."

Finow could only bow to this eloquent sentiment, and explained to the Haapaian nobleman in charge of the canoe that he would be obliged to leave without the widowed queen's attendants. Further, Finow instructed him that no canoe from Haapai should ever approach Vavau again, for such action would be considered hostile and appropriate measures taken against it.

Before the canoe departed, the women on the beach earnestly petitioned Finow that they be allowed to take an appropriate farewell of their mistress. Finow agreed. Máfi Háhe returned to the beach and for a full two hours the cries of wailing and consolation filled the air along the shore as the men of Vavau waited impatiently until the canoe should finally make its departure.

8

The Enchanted Isles

The Polynesian peoples, coming most probably from eastern Asia in the years after 1000 A.D., settled most of the inhabitable islands of the central Pacific. The area of Polynesian settlement is approximately encompassed by a huge triangle that has the Hawaiian Islands in the northwest as its apex, with Easter Island to the southeast, and New Zealand to the southwest, as the other two points.

The distances between islands are enormous, but the land masses, with the exception of New Zealand, are quite small. The sides of the Polynesian triangle measure four to five thousand miles. The island of Tahiti has an extent of only four hundred square miles; Hawaii, the largest Polynesian island except for New Zealand, is only four thousand square miles. We may remember that the kingdom of Buganda encompassed ten thousand square miles.

The word "Polynesian," like the words "Semitic" and "Bantu," refers to a family of languages and the peoples who spoke these languages. There was a tendency for Polynesian speakers to share certain physical characteristics, but to go beyond that statement and talk about "racial features" is to wander from the truth. There were many shared cultural attitudes and forms among all Polynesian peoples, but anthropologists have spent years disagreeing about the universality of any specific attitude or form. Enough cohesion existed, however, so that it makes intellectual sense to write about ancient Polynesian society or ancient Polynesian religion. All attempts to make such generalizations about Bantu society in Africa, on the contrary, have produced paltry returns. It may be that the relative isolation of the Polynesian islands helped preserve the similarities among various Polynesian cultures until their first contact with Christian society in the late eighteenth century.

In regard to political development—the creation of a centralized monarchy and state—great variation existed among the approximately twenty ancient Polynesian societies about which we have information. It is possible to arrange these societies on an ascending scale of political development, and several people have done so. Irving Goldman has placed them into three categories: traditional, open, stratified.[1] In the first category we find the Maori of New Zealand, and the Tikopians, among others. It is important to note, however, that even these least developed Polynesian societies cannot be called "primitive," that all Polynesian societies were complex. Though there were no monarchies among the Maori and Tikopians, chieftainship was an important political form.

When we come to look at Goldman's stratified societies (Hawaii, Tahiti, Tonga), we discover monarchical institutions and centralized states—what we have been calling advanced complex societies. No Polynesian society at the time of contact with American and European culture, however, represented the same degree of centralized kingship as existed in ancient Buganda. Such centralized states were created in the Hawaiian Islands and Tahiti during the period of contact. Whether ancient Polynesian society would have taken this step without the stimulus of foreign contact we shall never know, but we do have evidence indicating that, especially in the Hawaiian Islands, there was an unmistakable drive in that direction.

We are concerned in this book primarily with the Hawaiian Islands and Tahiti. The island of Hawaii gave its name to an entire group of four large—Hawaii (4,000 square miles), Maui (700 square miles), Oahu (600 square miles), and Kauai (550 square miles)—and several small islands that formed a single cultural area. All the islands interacted politically with one another in ancient times.

Tahiti was one of several important islands of the group called the Society Islands. Like Hawaii, they represented a single cultural area, but the information we have about Tahiti is so much greater than that from the others, it makes sense to talk of Tahiti alone.

The Tonga Islands also possessed monarchical institutions and were representative of advanced complex societies. Though we will not focus on Tonga, we will make use of a remarkable book, William Mariner's *An Account of the Natives of the Tonga Islands*. This is the same Mariner

whose account of the women of Vavau we have just read. The only
survivor of shipwreck and massacre by the Tongans, he became an important subordinate of the king, lived through the significant reigns of
Finow I and Finow II, returned to England, and wrote an extraordinarily fine history of his sojourn in Tonga, when the ancient society was
still uncontaminated by contact with the West.

People in the same circumstance as Mariner also lived in Hawaii
and Tahiti, including, on Tahiti, the mutineers from Captain Bligh's
Bounty, but since none of these wrote about their experiences, Mariner
is as close as we can get to ancient Polynesian society.

TAHITI

Tahiti was "discovered" by Christian peoples in 1767 when Wallis's ship
anchored there.[2] This landing was quickly followed by Bougainville
in 1768 and Cook, on his first voyage, in 1769. In the thirty years between
Wallis's discovery and the arrival of the first English missionaries in
1797, there was a continual, though intermittent, series of visits by European and American ships. This lovely island quickly gained a reputation
in Europe of being a Garden of Eden as well as a sexual paradise. The
French Romantic writers fell in love with the reports of these noble,
beautiful, sexually unrepressed copper-skinned people. As with all myths,
only part of this one was true.

As in Buganda, the land was enormously fertile and easily provided
the kind of economic surplus that made leisure available to a great many
people, leisure that could be expended on politics and art. Political development lagged behind Buganda or Hawaii; no king had ever succeeded in establishing his hegemony over the whole island of Tahiti,
which act might have been preliminary to someone's ruling all the Society Islands.

Tahiti is shaped like a lopsided figure eight, with a greater and a
lesser peninsula joined by an isthmus. By the time of Wallis's visit in
1767, the political situation in the lesser peninsula had become stabilized
under a single monarch. The larger peninsula, however, still contained
seven or eight major political divisions, some more and some less centralized. The level of political centralization ranged from strong chieftainships to monarchies with a moderate degree of control. The various
states were constantly at war with one another, but the aim of the warfare did not seem to be creation of one ruling monarchy.

We in the great age of nationalism who study, with a sense of manifest destiny, the history of the unification of France or Italy tend to assume that a situation in which several disunited states speak the same language and share the same culture is somehow untidy, unstable, even immoral, frustrating a universal human drive toward nation-states. There is a kind of truth in this, and it is one of the tasks of this book to examine how much and what kind of truth. Nor is there any question that the people of ancient Buganda and Tahiti shared this view.

In Africa and Polynesia, however, as instanced by the country of Busoga, which bordered Buganda, fifty or sixty chieftainships and kingships in which the same language was spoken could exist in one cultural area, apparently without there being any powerful drive to unify the country under a single political head.

In Tahiti this unification did not occur until 1815, under the kingship of Pomare II, who had become a Christian three years before. Pomare's home state had not been one of the most powerful at the time of Wallis's visit, but it was situated very close to the best harbor on the island, which precipitated Pomare I into intimate contact with the visiting ships. Sea captains, although they wrote extensively of their experiences, did not stay very long on any one island; none of them ever succeeded in giving, for Hawaii or Tahiti, the kind of picture of an ancient society that we get from Speke or Stanley. Much of their information was incorrect. Many of the English described Pomare I as king of the whole island, a blatant misstatement of the political reality.

English guns, however, eventually made a truth of English misperceptions. And English gunners—at one time some of the mutineers from the *Bounty* assisted the Pomares in their island warfare. The second Pomare's conversion to Christianity fifteen years after the missionaries arrived also helped his political aspirations. Independent of the great political changes, and despite very slow progress and great difficulties at the beginning, Christianity did take hold among the people, becoming, therefore, a unifying principle. We do not know how much Pomare's conversion resulted from sincere belief or how much he perceived the political advantages to be derived from it. If the latter, he had clearly seen that Tahiti was worth a communion.

The political unification of Tahiti was not the result of external forces alone; something within Tahitian society made it choose this particular response to the challenge offered by contact with the Western world. Clearly, the stage of political development it had already reached was a most important element in that choice.

THE HAWAIIAN ISLANDS

The Hawaiian Islands were found by Europeans eleven years after Tahiti, when Cook, on his third and last voyage, anchored there in 1778.[3]
The process of state formation there was significantly further advanced
than in Tahiti. On Cook's arrival, three of the four large islands were
controlled by single monarchs, and the fourth, Kauai, was in a state of
only temporary instability, to return to single-monarch rule within a
few years.

Further than that, the political system was obviously pushing toward the possible unification of the whole island group under one monarch. The ruler of Hawaii, for instance, had already conquered a part
of Maui. He had made repeated, albeit unsuccessful, attempts to conquer the whole of the island, and the king of Maui had been unable to
drive him out of the subjugated district.

After Cook's visit, there was rapid political change. When the king
of Oahu died, the succession proved unstable, and the king of Maui took
advantage of the situation to subdue the whole island. His brother had
succeeded in bringing back centralized rule in Kauai and put himself
into alliance with Maui. The king of Maui now dominated all the islands
of the group except Hawaii.

By 1786 it looked as if the unified kingship would grow out of the
house of Maui. On Hawaii, the one independent island, the king had
died, and the centralized state dissolved into three smaller ones, each
headed by its own king. There seemed to be no one to challenge the
ruling house of Maui. But at this point, a man of unique capability and
a genius for political rule emerged. Kamehameha I, with the subtle combination of wise statesmanship and ruthless cruelty that has marked all
the great conqueror-rulers of history, first became sovereign of one of
the districts of Hawaii, then ruler of the whole island, then military conqueror of Maui and Oahu, and finally the receiver of obeisance from
Kauai. By the time he died in 1819, he had not only unified the Hawaiian
Islands but also created a dynasty that was to provide stable rule for
many years. The unity of the Hawaiian state was never severely threatened after its creation by Kamehameha.

During the years of Kamehameha's reign, an enormous number of
English, American, French, and Russian ships put into Hawaii for supplies. Kamehameha himself outfitted a ship to traffic in sandalwood with

the Chinese. It was a very sophisticated monarchy that Kamehameha
left to his son. The degree of cultural ferment in those years was stag-
gering: when the first missionaries arrived in 1819 they found that the
new king, Liholiho, had, independent of any message from "the true
god," abolished the tabus that had encumbered ancient society. The
missionaries' task was made much simpler, because they found themselves in a country that had "no religion."

We will never know as much about ancient Hawaii and Tahiti as we
know about Buganda. By around 1825, these traditional Polynesian societies had ceased to exist as such—eighty years before the same thing
happened in Buganda. It was precisely in these eighty years that the
science of anthropology was created and came to its first great flowering. In 1850, there were no great anthropologists, no keen sense of what
questions to ask or what to look for, no army of graduate students waiting to make their mark by exploring "virgin" societies, no scientific
journals eagerly awaiting new word from the world of primitives. And
the missionaries, unlike those in Buganda, did not on the whole feel
impelled to record as much as possible about the ancient society. Even
had the desire been present, the theoretical structure was lacking; no
one could have done for Hawaii and Tahiti what Roscoe did for Buganda. Therefore the work of Reverend Ellis and Reverend Orsmond
has great importance for us, in part because it is all we have.

In the 1830s, 1840s, and 1850s, some residents of both cultures, either
native or naturalized, began to collect and set down memories of traditional society, and these writings are a primary historical source.

Lost, probably forever, is any real understanding of the kinship system or the relationship of that system to the state system of centralized
monarchy. We also know very little of how the various monarchies
worked—how large or effective was the hierarchy, how succession to
the throne was determined, how struggles between royal princes or between the king and his subordinate governors were resolved.

Nevertheless, in one very important area our knowledge of Polynesian society is greater than what we have of Buganda. This is in
the arts—in poetry, dance, theatre, fairy tales, epic stories, riddles,
and proverbs. Buganda and the centralized Polynesian societies were
all advanced complex societies, but each also had its own cultural
individuality.

Buganda had the great virtues of Rome: political and military organization, the hierarchical capacity for expansion, a complex legal

system, the ability to educate competent subordinates to all levels of political power, a religious reverence for the state. Hawaii and Tahiti had the virtues of ancient Hellas: a subtle, imaginative, complex religious life; a central, not peripheral, place in their lives for poetry, theatre, and the dance; a literature unexcelled by any nonliterate peoples anywhere; a sense of grace in personal behavior that astonished the first European visitors.

The concept that society develops in stages, that all societies in the same stage share certain views of the world, should not exclude the idea of the individuality of every culture. Clyde Kluckhohn has said that there is a way in which every society is like *all* other societies; there is a way in which every society is like *some* other societies; and there is a way in which every society is like *no other*. All capitalist societies share certain crucial common attributes, but all have their own individuality. Similarly, all advanced complex societies shared certain essential characteristics, but the life lived in ancient Buganda was far from identical to the lives lived in ancient Hawaii and Tahiti. Human variety is not precluded by any law of human development.

9

The Arioi Society

To dress, to dance, to sing, our sure delight,
To feast or bath by day, and love by night.

Thus reads Alexander Pope's tribute to the Phaeacians, who would finally bring Odysseus home. It was quoted by Georg Forster, traveling with Cook in the Society Islands, in an attempt to find some precedent in history or art that would allow him to understand the Ariois, the most important association of traveling performers in the islands.

They came, in one recorded instance, seven hundred of them travelling in sixty or seventy canoes from Huahiné to Raiatéa (two of the Society Islands), with the principal chief of the association on board the largest canoe, streamers floating in the wind, drums and flutes announcing their arrival, bodies painted with fantastic colors, hair oiled, both body and hair adorned with flowers. Sometimes on such visits, the Ariois would perform a dance or mime or musical exercise in the canoe as it approached the shore, with the surf rolling and breaking on the surrounding reef, the crowd on the beach bedazzled by the spectacle.[1]

Mark Twain and others have written about the explosive impact on the imagination the circus parade had in a small American town. In a culture without newspapers, magazines, books, photographs, phonographs, radios, televisions, or movies, that excitement must have been multiplied tenfold by a visit of the Ariois.

The large house in which they were to perform—either the local king's or else one belonging to the Arioi society of that island—was ready for them. They would stay in one district as long as six or seven days and nights. (Sunlight was not required for the performances—the house was lit by fires and tapers made from candlenuts.) If the house was large enough, three stages were erected, one on each end and one in the center. At times various entertainments went on simultaneously on all three stages. Atop a high platform at one side of the house, stools were placed for the chief Arioi of each sex, who presided over the rites. The royal family of the district had places of honor reserved for them, while the spectators spread all over, on the grass, in the house, in the trees. Such pleasure was bestowed that "even the crickets, it was said, cried with joy on these occasions."[2]

Even for a sexually unrepressed society, it was a time of heightened activity. Excitement is contagious. Among the Ariois, the men outnumbered the women four or five to one; since frequent sexual connection was considered essential to Arioi life, young women from the local district were co-opted for temporary membership in the society. If the Ariois made a tour of a particular island, some of the young women would stay with the group for the entire tour. We may assume that some were tempted never to return home.

Sadly, we do not have nearly as much information about the content of the actual performances as we would like. There was music: drums and pipes were the instruments; singing could be either solo or choral, or a combination of the two. All Polynesian peoples were mad for dancing; at a performance one might dance alone, or in twos, or fours; but intricate ensemble dancing, with or without a leader, made the greatest impression on the English officers who witnessed these performances.

The dramatic performances proceeded either with dialogue directly from the actors, or by narration while the actors mimed the parts. Legendary and epic material, as well as fairy tale, were the principal subjects of these dramas. We don't know whether new stories were created for the performances or not, but political satire and portrayal of local news was kept up to date. Neither the king nor the most sacred priest was exempt from the possibility of seeing himself and his foibles portrayed on the stage. It was a license, much like that granted to political cartoonists in our society. Humor, and sometimes not very subtle humor, was a fundamental ingredient of the show.

And then there were what the English missionaries were fond of calling "unutterable abominations."[3] For the Frenchman Moerenhout, however, the abominations became utterable, and we learn that the dramatic subjects were not limited to history and myth. Love and the details of lovemaking were also exhibited, with "young men and young

women actually offering their sacrifice to the goddess of love in public."
Such scenes were preceded by chanting and dancing, the chants "re-
volving around the delights of sensual pleasures, which were depicted
with utmost candor and ardor," while the dancing was "everything in
the way of lasciviousness that their voluptuary geniuses could invent."[4]
It is a remarkable commentary on the beginnings of class status in a
society that we are told that only the lower-class members of the Arioi
would enact such scenes. The concept that the lower classes are sexually
less inhibited and more capable was clearly not invented in recent times.

For the Ariois, the display of sex in a social context went further
than these performances. The "beautiful handmaidens," those "daughters of the local adult population" who accompanied the Ariois on tour,
would sleep with the players at night, but in the day they would offer
themselves indiscriminately: "Fornication, our wares are copulation,"
they would call out.[5] The writer of this text (a Christian) uses the word
"prostitution," though he gives no details of payment or the distribution
of revenue. It is not clear that prostitution, as opposed to general license
and exuberance, was the case. Like Georg Forster quoting Pope, the
Reverend Orsmond, the writer of the text, when faced with something
he could not comprehend, tried to relate it to something he had seen
or thought about before. Prostitution was as close as he could come to
that kind of indiscriminate sexuality.

One thing is clear: the purpose of the behavior was to de-privatize
sex. The players would travel from place to place, at times making a
complete circuit of Tahiti, while the handmaidens of the Ariois,
adorned with "ti fronds and scented oil and crimson dye," called
out as they came to a new village: "Fornicating! Fornicating!
Fornicating!"[6]

In an attempt to understand what was happening in such circumstances, analogies of Berlin in the 1920s or the "combat zones" of our
large cities do not seem appropriate. From these and other descriptions
we have of sexual theatre in Tahiti emerges a sense of good humor and
exhilaration that is absent from the concept of pornography. When an
end to much sexual repression in our own society occurred in the 1960s,
the musical show *Hair* opened on Broadway, presenting completely
nude people of both sexes for the first time on the "legitimate" stage.
The treatment of sexuality in this performance was exuberant with a
sense of breaking out of confined experience. At one point in the play,
the actors strolled through the audience chanting: "Fellatio! Cunnilin-
gus! Masturbation!" Perhaps, similarly, the Ariois crying "Fornicat-

ing!" were the heralds of the lifting of sexual repression. Perhaps, as in our day, experimentation, variety, flexibility were the new order. And, possibly, the sexual performances were the only kind of illustrated sex manual that could exist in a society without printing—or possibly they preferred to take such instruction in a social context and not in private.

It may very well be that the hankering after public sex was closely related to the breakdown of the kinship system, that the breaking of intense family ties allowed for, or made necessary, the search for a social—and socially approved—sexual experience. The Arioi society was a voluntary association, and in the history of human society voluntary associations have played an enormously important role in those circumstances where large numbers of people are leaving familiar and familial environments and going to live in places where their parents have never lived. In eleventh- and twelfth-century Europe, there was a revival of cities and city life, after the five or six hundred years of "Dark Ages." The new inhabitants of these cities came from the countryside, where their ancestors had lived for centuries. Nobody makes such a move without great psychological cost; one way to lessen that cost is to create quasi-family associations that replace the kinship networks left behind. The guilds of the reviving cities of Europe served such a function, as did and do all the ethnic associations in the United States of people who came from elsewhere. The Masons in the eighteenth century provided a similar solace for those who had separated from the family-encompassing Church. Without such associations, we may wonder how much separation from inherited circumstance would be possible.

These associations began in primitive societies, where they were of either a voluntary or an involuntary nature. Many primitive societies had associations of dancers, or witchcraft practitioners, or cannibals, or medicine workers, wherein membership was voluntary; one joined, usually through a process of individual initiation and as a result of individual initiative. It might make a difference if one's father or brother was, or had been, a member of such an association, but what is most significant is that membership *was not* based on kinship. Practically all the political and social activity in primitive society *was* based on kinship: people prayed together, worked together, celebrated together, and fought together as kin. Voluntary associations marked the beginnings of political and social action on a nonkin basis.

In some primitive societies, and in many early complex societies, especially in Africa, we find the phenomenon of age sets. All the boys of a tribe, let us say, from twelve to sixteen will be put in the same set and all initiated at the same time; they will remain in that set for life. When they come of fighting age, they will fight in the ranks of others of their set, not with others of their village or clan. They may all be allowed to marry in the same years, and certain political responsibilities such as counseling or ruling may be reserved, in progressive years, for members of a set as they reach a certain age.

Here, again, the crucial thing for the development of society is that these age-set groupings are *like* kinship, but they are *not* kinship; they are a transformation from the kinship system that allows people to over-come the kinship system. Without nonkinship forms of social cohesion, the state as we know it would be impossible.

The Arioi was a voluntary association, but it existed in a society emerging from the kinship system and committed to the preservation of social classes and the importance of social status. Lower-class members of society were allowed to be Ariois,[7] but there was a limit as to how high up in the association they could climb, and it has already been noted that it was from their ranks that the sexual performers were taken.[8] Upper-class members presided over the formal and ritual aspects of the performances. And, clearly, if a person of very high rank wished to join, he had merely to give the word to some of his fellow aristocrats, rather than going through the usual steps of application and initiation, just as in our society many "exclusive" clubs waive certain procedures if a high-ranking member of the plutocracy applies.

The ordinary candidate had to demonstrate that he was possessed of the god Oro, who was the most important god in the Society Islands at the time of contact and was also the patron of the Arioi society. During a performance of a local lodge of the association, the applicant painted his face scarlet, fastened yellow leaves around his waist and over his eyes, oiled and flowered his hair, and ran out onto the dancing ground, acting deranged, raving, and howling to establish his possession by the god. In between howls he was supposed to join in the dance or the mime, thereby demonstrating his capability in these arts. If all went well, the highest-grade Arioi present called him by name, tapped him on the shoulder, and said to him: "You are one of us, come hither."[9]

One of the great functions of voluntary associations (guilds or Ma-sons, for example) is to arrange for the burial of its members. When an Arioi died, his kin were not left with the entire responsibility for his burial; the Arioi society played a significant role in the funeral rites.

They resorted to the house of the deceased, lamenting loudly, bringing presents for the family, and preparing a feast, then holding a wake at night during which they called out to the dead spirit to return to the body. After two or three days, the corpse was taken to the temple of Oro, where the high priest of the god invoked prayers for the dead man. Finally, the body was buried within the temple precincts.

We all have a tendency to feel that most of the ideas, forms, and values by which we live our lives are coequal with humankind, have always existed, and are the result of an unchanging "human nature." We easily accept the concept that there is a public sphere and a private sphere to our lives; we live easily with the notion that people who have achieved fame or power are buried in a public ceremony and people who have lived essentially private lives are buried by their families and friends. What we find difficult to comprehend is that the public sphere did not always exist, that it is a human invention. In primitive society, funeral rites were the business of kin alone. The public funerals that we can observe in complex societies result from the invention and elaboration of the idea "public." It is of great importance to ask, and try to answer, the questions why people invented a public sphere, why they were not content to stay only with kin, and what were the pleasures and costs of this movement away from kinship.

Certain activities surrounding the visits of the Ariois call attention to what seems to be a peculiar feature of advanced complex societies: legitimate (that is, legally permitted) plundering of one part of society by another. "When a party of Areois arrived in a district, in order to provide a daily sumptuous entertainment for them, the chief would send his servants to the best plantations in the neighbourhood; and these grounds, without any ceremony, they plundered of whatever was fit for use. Such lawless acts of robbery were repeated every day, so long as the Areois continued in the district; and when they departed, the gardens often exhibited a scene of desolation and ruin, that, but for the influence of the chiefs, would have brought fearful vengeance upon those who occasioned it."[10]

This seems peculiar. Why didn't the king merely levy a special tax and send his men out to bring it in? Why did they become plunderers instead of collectors? Although no ready answers to these questions present themselves, what seems to have been expressed in these circumstances was uninhibited aggression. Methods of undisguised dominance, and the aggressive satisfaction these afforded, were preferred to legal process.

Lest we imagine that this was somehow peculiar to Tahiti, it is of interest to note that in Buganda, anyone traveling as messenger for the king was expected to feed his troops by plundering the countryside through which he passed. When Speke arrived and settled in the capital city, he complained to Mutesa that his men didn't have enough to eat. Mutesa couldn't understand the complaint, for he assumed that Speke's men, as guests of the king, were supplying themselves free of charge from the surrounding farms.

With the Ariois, the plunder privilege went even further. The gallant Captain Bligh writes in his log: "The Erree-oys also began to play their part which was to rob every Woman of her Cloathes if it was worth taking. These people it seems have the Power and privilege whenever they are in want of Cloth to take it from any Woman they see, and now it came within my sight the depredations they committed on many of the Sex. As I was passing a party of them, they were dragging a Young Woman along the ground who held fast her cloth and opposed them taking it, for that is allowable. It was of the best quality and she had it so disposed about her as drew my attention to the Violence they were committing to take it away, and observing me take notice of them, she held out her hand asking my assistance, which I had no sooner given than they desisted, and being freed from them she thanked me and I saw her no more."[11]

One explanation of this behavior, since Bligh's description reads as if the act were a mock rape, is that in a previous, more violent time the privilege the Ariois enjoyed was that of sexually assaulting any woman they might find walking alone. In some primitive societies, a woman walking by herself outside the village could "legitimately" be raped. Since the taking off of her cloth would have been a preliminary to the sexual assault, it would make ritual sense to continue to permit the disrobing even after the actual ravishment had been prohibited. The forcible removal of the cloth is clearly a sexual violation of the victim and could easily be the shadow of a former, more brutal act.

And they killed almost every child who was born to them. Most Ariois refused to become parents. It was, in its way, a religious act. They were enjoined to kill their children, a kind of celibacy after the fact. Maybe all celibacy is related to infanticide—a most irrational insight, but one that may very well be true. Since celibacy itself is irrational, it would not be surprising if its explanation were equally so.

Compulsory infanticide—and its relationship with celibacy—is certified in the myth of the origin of the society. The two brothers who founded the Arioi society were made gods and kings and lived in celibacy. They naturally had no descendants and were determined that their followers should have no progeny, either, but they obviously felt that it was too much to ask of the followers that they abstain from sexual activity. Thus, profligacy and child murder became the Ariois' wont.[12] When a novice was initiated, he had to promise to obey absolutely the commands of the Arioi chief, and not to allow any of his offspring to live.[13]

In all fairness to the Ariois, it must be remarked that infanticide was a widespread practice in Tahiti, a fact we will look at more closely later. There is also a disagreement among the sources as to whether *upper-class* Ariois were also required to do away with their children. Teuira Henry says that "children born to the highest ranks were regarded as descendants of gods, and were spared to inherit their parents' titles." Moerenhout claims that a high noble person would save the firstborn son, and a chief of an Arioi lodge would keep alive all male offspring except the firstborn.[14] The data are not very complete: we do not know whether it was necessary for both the mother and the father to be noble; nor is it clear how, in a situation of indiscriminate sexuality, one could be sure who the father was, unless the upper classes were more inclined toward permanent sexual pairings than lower-class Ariois.

If Arioi infanticide was related to celibacy, it would follow that there may be a connection between all insistence on adult celibacy and the desire to kill offspring. What is of interest is that two observers, one in the eighteenth and one in the twentieth century, have made the same connection. Georg Forster, on Cook's voyage, wrote of the Ariois that "we have great room to suppose that the original institution required their living in perpetual celibacy. As this law was too repugnant to the impulses of nature, which must be uncommonly strong in their climate, they transgressed it; but preserved the intention of the prescribed abstinence, by suffocating their unfortunate offspring immediately after birth."[15] And J. C. Beaglehole, the editor of Cook's journals, commented in 1955: "Their practice of infanticide being perhaps the equivalent, for the dedicated life, of celibacy in more sexually inhibited culture-systems."[16]

One version of the story of King Oedipus of Thebes tells us that Oedipus' parents, Laius and Jocasta, lived together for years without producing a child. Laius consults the Delphic oracle for remedy and is told that, if he does produce a son, the son will kill him. Laius' response to this prophecy is to become *celibate* and refrain from connection with his wife. One night, however, overcome by intoxication, he procreates a son. As a defense against the fulfillment of the prophecy, the child is exposed to the elements immediately after his birth, to kill him.[17] We know the rest of the story. What is important here is that the myth confirms that *infanticide* is made necessary by the failure of *celibacy*.

One may find this linkage strange, but how much more strange—when looked at from a distance—is the notion of the great Saint Paul that a person becomes nobler and holier, a moral leader of the community, when he or she denies himself or herself two of the greatest human pleasures. What kind of god would enthrone celibacy as one of the highest human virtues and thereby deny human beings the happiness of sex and children? Certainly not a rational god. There is a deep logic within all great religious notions, but it is the logic of the repressed, not the expressed—the logic of the irrational, not the rational.

Even among the Ariois, there were some who could not stay within this adolescent paradise forever: the drive to grow up pushed even them. When they decided to spare the lives of their children, they were disenfranchised. They could no longer keep the company of the most orthodox Ariois, but might associate only with those who likewise had decided to become parents. "They went no more into the space-of-the-head-players-in-which-the-cloth-and-were-divided.* He had been in the high rank but was now deformed. His red loin-girdle was taken away, the sacred pig. He went no more on the high scaffold from which was pronounced the names of those to whom . . . belonged the sacred hog and loin girdle. On being told go up no more. He wept, the excrements streamed from his nose, he fell behind, ashamed, washed off his scented oil and red dye and went to dwell with players of old who had also been put out for having families." [18]

Like the aging Prospero, he abjures his magic in the interest of becoming a real parent to a real child. Nothing, it seems, moves forward without cost.

---

*This sentence is admittedly not clear, but it is the sentence in the text. Since it provides some sense, albeit not accurate sense, I have included it here.

10

Finow, Father and Son

In the Tonga Islands, the three largest—Tongatapu, Haapai, and Vavau—developed into centers of political power. Traditionally, political and religious pre-eminence belonged to Tongatapu. The Tuitonga, the most important religious personage in the islands, more of a sacred king than a high priest, resided there. The secular king of Tongatapu customarily wielded the strongest political power in the group. At the end of the eighteenth century, all this changed. The centralized state of Tongatapu collapsed; the Tuitonga was removed to Vavau, and that island assumed political leadership of the cultural area. None of this resulted from contact with American or European societies; it all proceeded from the internal development of the traditional polity.

Before this political upheaval, Toogoo Ahoo was the king of Tongatapu, receiving tribute from Haapai and Vavau, and practicing cruelty even beyond the limits of that indulgent society. It was he who ordered the amputation of the left arms of twelve of his cooks, "for the vanity of rendering himself singular by this extraordinary exercise of his authority."[1]

Toobo Nuha, a great chief, brother to Finow, who was the lord of Haapai, could no longer abide the tyranny of Toogoo Ahoo and resolved to assassinate the king or die in the attempt. He enlisted Finow's aid. One evening, the two chiefs and their followers paid attendance on Toogoo Ahoo, giving the customary respect and presents of cava root (used to make the Tongan intoxicating drink), a pig, and several baskets of yams. The food and drinks having been dispatched, all retired for the night, but Toobo Nuha, Finow, and their cadres returned about midnight. Finow and his troops stood guard outside the king's hut, which Toobo Nuha entered "armed with his axe, and burning with desire of revenge. As he passed along, on either hand lay the wives and favorite mistresses of the king, the matchless beauties of Tonga, perfumed with the aroma of sandalwood, and their necks strung with wreaths of the freshest flowers. . . ."

Such a sight did not weaken the intent of Toobo Nuha, who found the king buried in a profound sleep. Not wishing the monarch to die in ignorance, Toobo Nuha struck him on the face with his hand. The king awoke, startled. "Tis I, Toobo Nuha, that strike," announced the tyrannicide, and delivered him a tremendous blow with the axe. Toobo Nuha then caught up the king's three-year-old son, whom he needed for political maneuvering, and fled the hut. Finow and his guards poured in and permanently silenced those who were crying out in alarm.[2]

Like the assassination of Caesar, the killing of Toogoo Ahoo did not resolve political matters, the settlement of which required a civil war between the conspirators and the loyal followers of the dead monarch. The issue was finally decided in one of the greatest battles in Tongan history. Tooi Hala Fatai led the loyalists, while the regicide Toobo Nuha, ably assisted by his brother Finow, commanded the rebels.

Tongan warfare was not a matter of high strategy conceived by commanders immune from fighting. It was a general melee, with all on one side against all on the other. Individual warriors of exceptional skill stood out and were crucial to the determination of victory. At the end of the day, a man knew how many he had killed. Achilles would have been at home on such a field.

The evening before the great engagement, Tooi Hala Fatai, the loyalist chief, felt himself acutely ill and growing worse by the hour. Fearful that he might die of the sickness, he insisted that the battle commence as early in the morning as possible, so that his death would occur gloriously on the field of battle. He had his wish; the armies engaged: "The plains of Tonga had perhaps never before witnessed so tremendous a battle."[3] The rebel chief Toobo Nuha was invincible; his "resistless arm performed prodigies of valor; when he stood, he stood like a rock—when he rushed, it was with the impetuosity of a hurricane; he raised his ponderous club only to give death to his victim; and as he moved forward he strode over the bodies of fallen chiefs."[4]

On another part of the field, the ailing warrior Tooi Hala Fatai was making sure that many would go with him when he left the earth. At last, unable to continue, he rushed with one final burst of energy "into the thickest of the battle, and fell, pierced with spears, beneath the clubs of his adversaries."[5]

Our chronicler, official historian of the house of Finow, does his best to include the latter in the superlative heroics of the day, but his prose reveals that Finow was not yet at the ripeness of his power. The day belonged to the dying Tooi Hala Fatai and the conqueror Toobo Nuha. The rebel chief, it is reported, slew forty warriors with his own hand. His ferocity and the death of their chief threw the loyalists into a state of panic. They fled in all directions. The kingdom of Tongatapu belonged to Toobo Nuha.[6]

He died not very long after conquering the island, leaving neither son nor brother who could succeed him. Finow was in no position to assume the kingship because he needed to attend to political commitments on his own island. Several distant relatives put in claims for the sovereignty, but since no one was able to establish authority, civil strife ensued. The island became divided into twelve or thirteen petty states, each with a garrisoned fort, each insistent on its own independence.[7] We see how fragile, how dependent on individual leadership the centralized state in complex societies was. Dissolution was an ever-present possibility. Although the centralized state was an invention of advanced complex societies, a stable state, one in which the possibility of dissolution was remote, was another, equally difficult achievement, one beyond the power of most complex societies.

With the demise of the state of Tongatapu, the center of political action moved to Finow and the islands of Haapai and Vavau. Starting as chief of Haapai, Finow conquered Vavau, set his capital there, and established another as chief of Haapai, tributary to himself. Eventually, Finow took advantage of the political chaos on Tongatapu and moved the sacred king Tuitonga to Vavau as well. Finow became the most powerful person in all the Tonga Islands, in a position to mold them into a unified, centralized state. If two or three powerful kings had followed Finow, and if there had been no serious interference with traditional Tongan society by outside forces, it is a reasonable assumption that the Tongan state would have attained the kind of unity and stability achieved by many African kingdoms. Finow's son and successor, however, did not want an empire, and the larger world did not let Tongan society be.

For all this achievement, it is not Finow's military and political skills that draw us to him—we find these qualities in many individuals in ad-

vanced complex societies—but, rather, his humanism. He was a hero—
and a humanist. Odysseus could claim no more.

Mariner relates that, after he had learned the Tongan language,
many young warriors, particularly those who had been active in the
conquest of Mariner's ship, would crowd around him, ask about the
use of certain articles they had taken from the ship, and boast of how
difficult it had been to obtain them. They would continue to expound
on who had killed whom, how a certain man had been convulsed before
he died, how deeply some of the Englishmen had groaned before they
met death. "Finow passing that way, and overhearing the discourse,
would command them not to talk upon a matter which must be so disagreeable to Mr. Mariner's feelings; that the fate of his companions was
too serious a subject to be thus slightly spoken of: to which some of
the chiefs replied, 'but he does not make that a subject of consideration,
for none of them were his relations.'—'Though none perhaps were his
relations,' rejoined Finow, 'they were nevertheless his countrymen.' "[8]

We who live still in the great age of nationalism and have transferred
our feelings for kin onto our countrymen have no problem in understanding what Mariner must have felt and what Finow spoke of. That
Finow, raised in a kinship society where the notion of country hardly
existed, should see so easily this connection is indicative of the kind of
imaginative insight available to him.

We are talking of an expansiveness of ideas and of feelings. The feeling of pathos, for instance, is crucial to all great epic poetry. In Homer's
Iliad this feeling ripens because we care for both sides in the war.
Homer, in fact, takes no sides. Although one faction is called "Danaäns"
or "Achaeans," and the other "Trojans," both parties speak the same
language, worship the same gods, have identical feelings toward family,
have the same culture. Though the combatants come from different
countries, these warriors kill people exactly like themselves. In human
terms, it is a civil war.

When Finow conquered the island of Vavau, the country was
politically divided. He championed one side, became victorious, and
eventually ruled the whole island. In one of the battles of that civil war,
Finow's forces approached a garrisoned fort. A shower of arrows descended upon them, but Finow did not immediately engage. He sent
a high subordinate ahead to request an armistice, "that each party might
take leave of what friends and relatives they might have among their
opponents." The request was granted. Many from the garrison came

out to take farewell of their kin: "Here ensued a moving scene; many
tears were shed on both sides, and many a last embrace exchanged."[9]
When old Priam in the *Iliad* requests a truce from Achilles in which
to bury his great son Hektor, Achilles asks Priam how long he will require. The father explains in detail the schedule of the funeral: "On the
eleventh day we would make a grave-barrow for him, and on the
twelfth day fight again; if so we must do."[10] With all their humanity,
that same "must" drove the king of Troy and the king of Vavau.

The memory of Greek epic and legend produces many a "shock
of recognition" when one reads the chronicles of King Finow I. *The
Trojan Women* springs to mind with the following tale: Finow's rise
to political pre-eminence did not proceed without the usual demurrals
from those whom he cast down in the process. When a conspiracy
against him was discovered, all the conspirators were captured and executed. The widows of those would-be assassins petitioned Finow to be
allowed to perform the usual rites of burial for their deceased husbands,
"which the king readily acceded to." Nowfaho, one of the leaders of
the conspirators, had sent messages of deep affection to his wife before
he was killed. On hearing these words, "she appeared greatly moved,
for, though she scarcely wept, her countenance betrayed marks of violent inward agitation. . . ." She retreated to her house, armed herself
with a spear and a club, and went out to enlist the aid of the other widows in her plan to avenge herself on Finow by killing as many of his
wives and principal chiefs as possible. None of the others would join
with this Polynesian Hecuba, however, and she was forced to abandon
the plan. Finow, naturally, learned of the forsaken project, but had no
need of further revenge: "On hearing her intention . . . he praised it
much, and approved of it, as being not only a meritorious act of bravery,
but a convincing proof that her affection for her deceased husband was
great and genuine."[11]

What the usual epic hero loves almost as much as killing is talking.
In the *Iliad,* for instance, it seems that equal time is given to these two
occupations. Finow, we are not surprised to learn, was an eloquent
speaker:

During the time Finow was addressing the Vavaoo people, the matabooles
[people of the higher class] and warriors that surrounded his canoe (among
whom was Mr. Mariner) appeared much moved, and several shed tears, for his
powers of persuasion were such, that, in defending his own cause, he seemed
to be the most worthy, the most innocent, and the most unjustly used: on this

account the greater chiefs and old matabooles of Vavaoo remained in the fortress, fearing to listen to his arguments lest, being drawn aside by the power of his eloquence, they might mistake that for true which was not, and even lead the young and ardent warriors into an error, by persuading them that what he said was reasonable and just.[12]

Finow used the Polynesian institution of *fono*—whereby the most prominent people met in public council to discuss the problems of the day—to harangue his subjects about how they should behave. Like Fidel Castro in Cuba with his four- and five-hour speeches, he must have felt that he could transform society by the power of his voice. Young *matabooles* in Tonga, for instance, would frequently molest women they met on the road. When the women complained to their husbands, the husbands would bring the matter to the attention of the older *matabooles*. The king would call a *fono* that all the young bravos had to attend, preach to them on the impropriety of their behavior, and order them to desist from such actions in the future. We get the feeling, though we are not directly told, that such a performance was as effective as most sermons usually are.

Finow I, king of Vavau, tributary lord of Haapai, restless in his power, periodically cast envious eyes toward the independent island of Tongatapu. There, a certain stability had set in; the days of large warfare were over, and only an intermittent—if unending—raiding between the various petty states kept the spears from total neglect. Several small kingdoms began to gain a certain pre-eminence over the others. Hihifo was one such provincial kingdom, and its sovereign had earned a wide reputation for the training of hunting birds. One particular bird, which the monarch had long had in his possession, was so extraordinary in its capacity that people who had been to Hihifo could talk of nothing else. It was "the envy of every chief that had seen it."[13]

Finow, an aficionado of hawking himself, had never seen the bird, but its reputation began to gnaw at his vitals. He started to think of nothing else: he must have that bird. He sent one of his chief ministers to Hihifo with a few presents and the request that the lord of Hihifo satisfy the craving of the king of Vavau. The chief declared that the bird was necessary for his existence, but he would be glad to send the great king of Vavau two other birds that he was sure would please the monarch. "Finow received the present, but was by no means well pleased with the refusal of the bird, on which he so much set his heart."[14]

The following morning, however, he decided to try out the two birds he had been given. The results were extraordinary, but instead of satisfying Finow, this only made him more determined to obtain the great bird. Again he sent one of his chamberlains, this time with more lavish presents: "sea-horses' teeth, beads, axes, a looking-glass, several iron bolts . . . a grinding-stone, all of which he had procured from European ships," as well as many fine mats and a great quantity of cava.[15]

We are not told whether the threat was delivered at the same time as the presents, or whether the niceties of Tongan diplomacy were such that nothing of the sort was actually spoken. Whatever the case, this second request the ruler of Hihifo did not refuse. He, "after some consultation, answered, that as he could not make any use of the bird himself, his time being so much taken up in constant warfare with his neighbors, and as *it would not be consistent with the character of a chief* to retain from another that which he could not use himself, he would, at once, resign the bird to Finow, notwithstanding the high value he placed on it, and the immense care and trouble it had caused him." Finow was delighted, but the bird proved less spectacular than he had hoped. He grew tired of the sport, and his infatuation melted away.[16]

Any intensity of human feeling, whether of satisfaction or denial, was of interest to Finow. A famous hermit, Tootawi by name, lived on the island of Vavau. Tootawi found himself in the same ironic circumstance as that of the famous Egyptian Christian hermits of the third and fourth centuries: in their complete withdrawal from the world their reputation was made, and the world insisted on flocking to them in their isolation. Finow, having conquered the island, "had a most lively desire to see"[17] this famous anchorite.

Tootawi, although unacquainted with the life of Saint Anthony, knew how a hermit was to behave and received the new temporal lord of Vavau as he would anyone else, with a certain understated contempt. Finow, far from being dismayed, acted as if he knew that no famous hermit's life was complete without a subtle tempter, a role he decided to play. The monarch "spoke kindly to [Tootawi]; inquired if there was anything that could render his situation more comfortable, and offered whatever could be thought of to induce him to return to the habitation of men. . . ." Tootawi, of course, would have none of it: "Canoes, houses, and plantations were to him matters of no value whatsoever; conversation had no charms for him, and the luxuries of life were insipid things."[18]

Finow then played what he hoped was his trump card: would Tootawi not select a wife from among Finow's female attendants? That, replied the recluse, was the one thing he wanted least. The king persisted and entreated Tootawi to take something, anything, from the king's great possessions, and we know how seductive Finow's eloquence could be. By compromising a little bit, the hermit won the day—he would take one small wearing mat, and that was all.

Finow departed, giving voice to his admiration and confirming the previous edict that the hermit's privacy should be respected by all.[19]

When he wasn't thinking about assassination, conquest, political dominance, people's feelings, hermits, or birds, Finow, like many of us, was thinking of God—more accurately, of the gods and those who claimed to speak for them. He was representative of a phenomenon that is observed in many complex societies—a political personage of strong will who is free of belief in the gods or fear of the priests. "His want of religion was, indeed, almost proverbial, and on this account, the people often wondered that he was so successful in war." Before the invasion of Vavau, the priests sought to dissuade Finow with the information that the gods advised an offer of reconciliation with the Vavau people. But Finow took the priest's advice only when it "tallied with his own opinion." [20] Despite their opposition, he proceeded with the invasion.

Finow's atheism did not prevent him from feeling at times that he was possessed by the spirit of a former king of Tongatapu. He often stated to Mariner that he doubted the gods existed and thought people fools to believe what the priests told them. When Mariner wondered aloud how Finow reconciled these beliefs with his conviction that the dead king's spirit would possess him, the sovereign hedged: "True . . . there may be gods; but what the priests tell us about their power over mankind, I believe to be all false."

In regard to possession by a famous personage of the past—very commonly believed in complex societies—Mariner tells a remarkable story about Finow's son and heir—who was to assume the throne as Finow II—a story that makes us think of our own literary and mythic past. Many people have observed that two of the most powerful stories of Western literature—Orestes and Hamlet—have remarkable similarities: In both, a king has been murdered by a close relative, the son of that king has the obligation to avenge the murder on someone who is, naturally, a relative of his. In each case the ghost or the spirit of the dead father plays a crucial role. In *Hamlet* it actually appears in the action; for Orestes, the evocation of his father's spirit is a pivotal act before he kills his mother.

As for Finow II, his father was a king but he had been the assassin, along with Toobo Nuha, of a greater king, and not the victim of assassination. When he had grown to be a young chief, Finow II became intermittently possessed by the spirit of Toogoo Ahoo, the late king of Tongatapu who had been murdered by his father and his uncle.

No tragic consequences resulted from this possession, for if the spirit of Toogoo Ahoo urged Finow II to avenge Toogoo Ahoo's assassination, the king's son said nothing of it. Mariner, who was a great friend of the young man, asked the prince how he felt when the spirit of the dead king entered him. He replied that "he felt himself all over in a glow of heat and quite restless and uncomfortable, and did not feel his own personal identity, as it were, but seemed to have a mind different from his own natural mind, his thoughts wandering upon strange and unusual subjects, although perfectly sensible of surrounding objects."[21] Hamlet, after the meeting with his father's ghost, decides to act mad in order to disguise the fact that he is intent upon avenging his father by murdering his uncle: "As I perchance hereafter shall think meet to put an antic disposition on."[22]

When Mariner inquired of his friend how he knew it was the spirit of Toogoo Ahoo, the prince replied: "There's a fool! How can I tell you *how* I know it; I felt and knew it was so by a kind of consciousness; my *mind* told me it was Toogoo Ahoo."[23]

Despite whatever turmoil there might have been in his mind about his accession to his father's office, the young Prince Finow behaved in a rational manner. Unlike some royal princes in complex societies who grew impatient with their aged fathers and resorted to revolt in order to obtain the throne, Finow II stayed on excellent terms with his father until the latter's death elevated Finow II to the kingdom in what proved to be an easy and successful transition. The relationship of young hotbloods to kingly authority is the subject of another play by Shakespeare, and we are reminded of Prince Hal when we read of young Finow and his friend Hala Api Api. The latter, though a brave warrior and not a coward, forcefully recalls Sir John Falstaff and his ambiguous place between old king and young prince:

No man performed more mischievous tricks than he, at the expense of the lower orders, and yet they all liked him. If any other chief oppressed them, they flew to Hala Api Api for redress and he always defended their cause as if it was his own, often at the risk of his life, and this he did seemingly from pure motives of pity. He would weep at the distress of which they complained, and the next moment his eyes would flash with indignation, at the injustice of the oppressor, and seizing his club, he would sally forth to redress their wrongs. If he committed any depredations himself he would sometimes be equally sorry, and make ample reparation. On other occasions, however, his mind would remain for a considerable length of time in the same wild and ungovernable disposition; and the report of his depredation would reach the king's ears [Finow I] . . . who would say, "What shall I do with this Hala Api Api? I believe I must kill him." But Hala Api Api neither feared death, nor the king, nor any other power. There was nobody but what liked him, and yet everybody feared him. . . . Talk to him about battles, and he looked as if he were inspired. Relate to him a pathetic story, and the tears would run down his cheeks faster than you could count them. Tell him a good joke, and there was nobody would laugh more heartily than he. . . . No sooner did the younger Finow come to be king, than his friend, Hala Api Api, (to the astonishment of everybody), left off his mischievous tricks, and ceased to commit any acts of depredation. On being asked by Mr. Mariner, his reason for this, he replied—"The present king is a young man, without much experience, and I think I ought not to throw obstacles in the way of his peaceable government by making him uneasy, or creating disturbances. The old king had great experience, and knew how to quell disturbances: besides he was fond of fighting, and so I gratified my humour, without caring about the consequences, but such conduct now might be very bad for the country."[24]

The accession of the young Finow to the throne caused a radical change not only in the life style of Hala Api Api but in the entire political situation on Vavau. Finow II was determined to institute a cultural revolution no less thorough than that attempted by Ikhnaton when he radically altered the religion, the arts, and the value system of ancient Egypt. Finow II wanted to eliminate war as an activity of Vavau life and devote energy to the arts of peace—building, cultivation of the land, poetry, and music. Toward that end, he was determined to isolate Vavau from the other Tonga Islands.

The island of Haapai, whose lord was now Toobo Toa, paid tribute to Vavau. Shortly after Finow II's accession, Toobo Toa, Finow, and Finow's uncle Finow Fiji had a short meeting of state, in which Toobo Toa expressed his desire to remain tributary to Vavau because he felt it helped preserve the stability of his tenure in office. Finow refused the offer, explaining to Toobo Toa his intentions for Vavau. The lord of Haapai was not pleased with the plan and felt humbled that he had to accede to the wishes of so young a king. He mused out loud that his own restless warriors would find mischief if they were kept idle, might even plan war on Vavau or the overthrow of himself, and therefore he planned to direct his resources toward Tongatapu. The king of Hihifo (on Tongatapu) was an ally of his, and that state had recently become so militarily weak that there was a possibility it would be destroyed by its enemies. Toobo Toa declared that he would lead an expedition to Tongatapu to support his ally as soon as he returned to Haapai.[25]

One connection between Vavau and Haapai could not be severed. The Tuitonga still resided on Vavau, and all islands were required to send him annual tribute for the *inachi* ceremony: "It could not be dispensed with, because it was a religious act, and was necessary to be performed to ensure the favour of the gods, and to prevent calamities which might otherwise be inflicted on them."[26]

An opportunity to solve this problem arose not long after the reign of Finow II began. The Tuitonga died. Finow decided to have no more Tuitongas and to put an end to the *inachi* ceremonies. It was a revolutionary act, no less so than Luther's treatises on the church door. Having found the courage to do such a thing, the reasons to support it were easily discovered: "it must be noticed," argued Finow, "that the island of Tonga had, for many years, been deprived of the power, presence, and influence of the Tooitonga," and notwithstanding that, remained "not less favoured with the bounties of heaven and of nature than the other islands, excepting the mischief and destruction which arose from human passion and disturbances: and if Tonga could exist without this divine chief, why not Vavaoo, or any other island?"[27]

The chiefs and *matabooles* agreed with the king. The common people raised no objection and were pleased that the *inachi* tax was eliminated. The deed was done, an extraordinarily rational act that demonstrates how far this complex society had come from the primitive world, how far the human spirit had succeeded in freeing itself from supernatural dread.

The son of a powerful, murderous father could abandon the father's warlike value system, either out of a fear of competing or the courage to surpass. One of Hamlet's problems is that he himself does not know whether he prefers philosophy and civilized interests to the warrior's value system because they are intrinsically better or because he hasn't got the courage to be a great fighter. The existence of Hamlet's contemporary young Fortinbras highlights that confusion in Hamlet's mind. Mariner's description of Finow II—and allowance must be made for the close friendship between the two—would indicate that the young king could easily have excelled in the traditional military values of kingship had he so desired. "His general deportment was engaging: his step firm, manly and graceful: he excelled in all athletic sports, racing, wrestling, boxing, and club-fighting: he was cool and courageous, but a lover of peace."[28]

He was also a lover of justice and spent much time judging cases between people. His subjects were eager to refer their grievances to him, because if a case required that a day or two be taken to collect information, he had no reluctance to put off the decision until all the facts had been assembled.

He was fond of mirth and good humour: he was a most graceful dancer: he was passionately delighted with romantic scenery, poetry, and vocal concerts: these last had been set aside in a great measure, during his father's warlike reign; but when the son came into power, he revived them, and had bands of profess[ional] singers at his house almost every night. He used to say that the song amused men's mind, and made them accord with each other—caused them to love their country, and to hate conspiracies.[29]

When Finow I was not at his house, one generally looked for him at some public place or another chief's house; Finow II could be found at the houses of carpenters or canoe builders, or possibly upcountry supervising the cultivation of some new ground.[30]

We don't know how the Great Experiment ended. Not many years after young Finow's accession, Mariner managed to return to England and write his book. If he had stayed, we possibly would have learned the whole history of Finow II. But, then again, maybe the book would never have been written and published, and we would be that much poorer in our attempt to understand how full of possibility and variety human life has been.

11

"The Taboos Are at an End. . . . The Gods Are a Lie"

The first missionaries to Hawaii came from the United States and arrived in the islands in March 1820. The year before, the great King Kamehameha I had died. The missionaries both hoped and assumed that they were coming to a land rife with savage superstition and dark religious rites, a place where they could struggle with Satan for the souls of people. As their ship *Thaddeus* approached the islands, a boat was sent ashore under the command of Mr. Hunnewell, the ship's first officer. He returned from the visit and announced to the startled shipboard company: "Liholiho is King; the taboos are abolished; the idols are burned; the temples are destroyed. There has been war, but now there is peace."[2] The Hawaiians had clearly taken care of Satan by themselves and "presented to the world," in the words of James Jarves, "the strange spectacle of a nation without a religion."[3]

The crucial tabus had to do with women and eating. Men and women were not allowed to eat together. The burden of maintaining this separation fell on both sexes: "The man first started an oven of food for his wife, and, when that was done, he went to the house *mua* and started an oven of food for himself."[4] In addition to this restriction, certain foods, including pork, bananas, and coconuts, were prohibited for women.[5] When the English Captain Vancouver brought certain European domesticated animals to the islands for the purpose of introducing herds, he cautioned the Hawaiians that they should not eat the animals for ten years, that they be given a chance to thrive, and that women as well as men be allowed to partake of them once the time for slaughtering had arrived, "as the intention of their being brought to the island was for the general use and benefit of every inhabitant of both sexes."[6]

Understanding this particular Hawaiian configuration of tabu imperatives requires many more historical data about the development of Hawaiian society than we possess. We know almost no history for Hawaii before the meeting with the West; what remains, primarily, is a picture of the society at the precise moment of contact. Therefore, we cannot tell why the Hawaiians developed this specific system of tabu. Every culture, including ours, imposes certain restrictions in the areas of eating, sexuality, and aggression. Liberated as we may think we are, we still do not eat every animal available for food (dogs and cats, for instance), though no law forbids it. The fact that Hawaiian women were aggressively discriminated against by being deprived of some choice foods was not unique to that culture; many primitive societies denied certain favored foods to all except adult males. The tabu against men and women's eating together has also been found in many societies. What specific unconscious conflicts between men and women in Hawaiian culture were being expressed, and repressed, by the system of tabu is difficult to say.

During the early years of the nineteenth century, the absolute power behind these prohibitions was consistently being undermined by the interaction between Hawaiians and American and European seafarers. Throughout the whole of Kamehameha's reign, nonetheless, severe penalties were meted out to violators. In the first decade of the century, three men were caught eating coconuts with some aristocratic women; the men were imprisoned and sentenced to death.[7] Around the same time, two aristocratic young girls were seen eating a banana. They were obviously of too high a rank to be punished easily; their tutor, being judged responsible, was put to death by drowning.

As late as 1816, the Russian explorer Otto Kotzebue found a woman's body floating in the harbor. She also was a commoner and had been executed for breaking the food tabus.[8] And just before the prohibitions were ended, a little girl had one of her eyes put out for eating a banana.[9]

Kaahumanu was the principal consort of the King Kamehameha at his death in 1819. A woman of extraordinary power, not only did she announce that Kamehameha had designated her as a coregent to rule with the new king, Liholiho, but she also led the struggle that resulted in the permanent destruction of the tabus: "But as for me and my people . . . we intend to be free from the taboos. We intend that the husband's food and the wife's food shall be cooked in the same oven, and that they shall be permitted to eat out of the same calabash. We intend to eat pork and bananas and coconuts . . . and to live as the white people do. . . ."[10]

She then orchestrated a dramatic performance to take place, with the new king as principal performer. Liholiho acquiesced in her arrangements and set sail for Kailua. For whatever reasons of ambivalence, he spent two days on the water, completely inebriated. Finally, Kaahumanu dispatched a large double canoe to bring him to the appointed place. A great feast had been prepared with, as was the custom, separate tables for men and women. At the king's table, a number of important foreigners were being entertained. Before sitting down, Liholiho smoked and drank with some noblewomen. When everyone was seated, the monarch arose and deliberately walked to the women's table, sat down, proceeded to eat what had been prepared, and then asked his female companions to do the same.[11] The feast was observed by a large group of common people who anxiously awaited the consequences of so terrible an act. When nothing untoward happened, they began, either at the prompting of their own progressive hearts or by prearrangement of Kaahumanu, the joyful shout: "The taboos are at an end. . . . The gods are a lie."[12]

The effect of it was like that of displacing the keystone of an arch. The whole structure of both idol-worship and of the taboos fell at once into ruins. The high-priest himself set the example of setting fire to the idols and their sanctuaries, and messengers were sent even as far as Kauai to proclaim the abolition of the taboos, which was termed the *ai hoa* or free eating, in opposition to the *ai kapu.*[13]

The supporters of the traditional religion, however, were not insignificant and were determined to fight for the religion of their ancestors. They raised an armed revolt and included in their ranks several highly placed aristocrats with military capacities. But the new establishment was too powerful for them, and one battle put an end to civil contention. The revolution was complete.

The American missionaries, unlike the English and French ones who would go into Buganda sixty years later, were a distinctly mediocre lot. They succeeded powerfully well, in their terms, because the way had been prepared for them by the profound response of the Hawaiians to contact with the outside world. No set of missionaries ever landed in a more fertile climate. The brand of Christianity that they planted there was a paltry thing morally, concentrating its energies on

the control of alcohol and prostitution. A people so capable of transforming their own lives deserved better.

The revolution of 1819 against the old religion had been forty years
in the making. Cook had landed in Hawaii in 1778, and from that time
on, more and more ships visited the islands, mostly to replenish their
supplies. Correspondingly, more and more Europeans and Americans
settled there, either temporarily or permanently. Western culture was
becoming a familiar thing, especially among members of the Hawaiian
aristocracy.

The restrictions on eating were already being treated in a flexible
manner by women of noble rank. Kotzebue, who noted in 1816 the execution of a common woman for breaking the tabu, also remarked that
male and female aristocrats came on board his ship and took meals together.[14] The explorer Archibald Campbell wrote:

Notwithstanding the rigour with which these ceremonies are generally observed, the women very seldom scruple to break them, when it can be done
in secret; they often swim to ships at night during the taboo; and I have known
them to eat of the forbidden delicacies of pork and shark's flesh. What would
be the consequence of a discovery I know not; but once I saw the queen trans-
gressing in this respect, and was strictly enjoined to secrecy, as she said it was
as much as her life was worth.[15]

The same kind of easing of restrictions occurred in Tahiti as well. Pomare I was already eating with women by 1789, and the practice spread
to one or two other chiefs soon thereafter, though it did not by any
means become a general practice immediately.[16]

There was a precedent for violating the tabus that had nothing to
do with contact with the Western world. Following the death of the
king, or any high aristocrat, the Hawaiians indulged in a period of interregnum anarchy. Until the accession of the new monarch, aggressive
feelings were allowed free reign, and almost all sexual prohibitions were
disregarded. In addition, women's eating tabus were suspended—they
ate bananas, coconuts, and pork—and they were also permitted to
climb on the sacred places, which was ordinarily forbidden. From one
point of view, what Liholiho did was to continue the period of free
eating.[17]

It was not only that the Hawaiians felt impelled to imitate all Western ways; in the matter of the food tabus, there was deliberate encouragement from the Westerners:

When Kamehameha was residing on Oahu many of the chiefs learned to talk a little in English, and Liholiho, the King's son, desiring to learn English, a trader (Mr. Marshall, I mistake not), undertook to teach him to read. When Mr. Marshall had gained his confidence and made some progress in teaching him, he took the opportunity to give him in substance the following advice: "When you have learned to read, it will be the first step of true knowledge to renounce tabu." [18]

One last factor that undoubtedly contributed to the Hawaiian action was the news that Pomare II had converted the whole of Tahiti to Christianity and had abolished the tabus.[19] This took place four years before the death of Kamehameha.

What appeared as a near miracle to the first missionaries was, in reality, a reasonably predictable sociological process. Forty years of contact with Western culture, combined with the heightened vitality of a society that believed in change and experimentation, produced the Hawaiian "revolution" of 1819. It was a classic demonstration of Toynbee's concept of challenge and response, and unlike many other results of cultural contact, it redounded to the credit of both cultures.

III

O BRAVE NEW WORLD

12

O Brave New World . . .

A Love Poem

Alas! I am seized by the shark, great shark!
Lola-Kea with the tripled-banked teeth.
The stratum of Lono is gone,
Torn up by the monster shark,
Niuhi with fiery eyes,
That flamed in the deep blue sea.
Alas! and alas!
When flowers the wili-wili tree,
That is the time when the shark-god bites.
Alas! I am seized by the huge shark!
O blue sea, O dark sea,
Foam-mottled sea of Kane!
What pleasure I took in my dancing!
Alas! now consumed by the monster shark! [1]

And a fragment worthy of the great Sappho:

Love carries me off with a rush, and I cry, I cry,
Alas, I'm devoured by the shark, great shark! [2]

To be a bird, to be a fish, to escape the limitations of human existence—only in this century have people learned to fly, giving technological reality to that longing. But to be a fish—the Greek vase painters knew that nothing in the whole world was as happy as a dolphin. Ships

came close, but not close enough. Exesias in his great painting of Diony-
sus alone in his boat knows that the god, no matter how liberated, is
still earthbound—only the dolphins encircling the boat are truly free.
The ancient Hawaiians came as close to being dolphins as anyone has
ever come.

"Twenty or thirty of the natives, taking each a long narrow board,
rounded at the ends, set out together from the shore. The first wave
they meet, they plunge under, and suffering it to roll over them, rise
again beyond it, and make the best of their way, by swimming, out into
the sea. The second wave is encountered in the same manner with the
first; the great difficulty consisting in seizing the proper moment of div-
ing under it, which, if missed, the person is caught by the surf, and
driven back again with great violence; and all his dexterity is then required to prevent himself from being dashed against the rocks. As soon
as they have gained by these repeated efforts, the smooth water beyond
the surf, they lay themselves at length on their board, and prepare for
their return. As the surf consists of a number of waves, of which every
third is remarked to be always much larger than the others, and to flow
higher on the shore, the rest breaking in the intermediate space, their
first object is to place themselves on the summit of the largest surge,
by which they are driven along with amazing rapidity toward the shore.
If by mistake they should place themselves on one of the smaller waves,
which break before they reach the land, or should not be able to keep
their plank in a proper direction on the top of the swell, they are left
exposed to the fury of the next, and, to avoid it, are obliged to dive and
regain the place, from which they set out. Those who succeed in their
object of reaching the shore, have still the greatest danger to encounter.
The coast being guarded by a chain of rocks, with, here and there, a
small opening between them, they are obliged to steer their board
through one of these, or, in case of failure, to quit it, before they reach
the rocks, and plunging under the wave, make the best of their way
back again. This is reckoned very disgraceful, and is also attended with
the loss of the board, which I have often seen, with great terror, dashed
to pieces, at the very moment the islander quitted it. The boldness and
address, with which we saw them perform these difficult and dangerous
maneuvers, was altogether astonishing, and is scarcely to be credited."[3]

It is enchanting to discover that the same conflict between surfing and
the spirit of capitalism existed in ancient Hawaii as exists in our own
culture. When the surf was up, the work ethic was forgotten. One

month in the Hawaiian calendar was called Ikuwa, which means "deaf-
ening," because it was the month of coastal storms, rain, wind, and
thunder. It was also the month of high surf

that lures men to the sea-coast. For expert surfers going upland to farm, if part
way up perhaps they look back and see the rollers combing the beach, will leave
their work, pluck ripe banana leaves, ti leaves and ginger, strip them, fasten
them about their necks and stand facing the sea and holding sugar-cane in their
hand, then, hurrying away home, they will pick up the board and go. All
thought of work is at an end. . . . The wife may go hungry, the children, the
whole family, but the head of the house does not care. He is all for sport, that
is his food. All day there is nothing but surfing.[4]

Alas, it was even worse than neglect. Nature abhorring a vacuum, licentiousness rushed in when hard labor was abandoned. Women joined
the surfing: "There is fine sport; from innocent pleasure they turn to
evil pleasures; so it goes!"[5] We have also learned the incompatibility
of surfing and our Puritan heritage.

When one is reading and thinking about advanced complex society, the
enormous explosion of imaginative energy that was central to that culture is striking. As one looks for an analogy, the Renaissance and the
admiration one feels for those who created it immediately come to
mind. In ancient Buganda, Hawaii, and Tahiti, however, it was not a
rebirth, but the birth, of certain imaginative forms. There were no prece-
dents to resurrect; people used only the energy of their own minds.
A more appropriate comparison would be the birth of lyric poetry in
seventh-century B.C. Greece and the beginnings of tragedy in fifth-
century B.C. Athens. We owe as much to the creators of advanced complex culture as to any people who have gone before us. The Buganda
and Polynesians are not of course our direct ancestors, but similar advanced complex societies must have preceded the archaic civilizations
of Egypt, Mesopotamia, Crete, and China. We are accustomed to ac-
knowledging our debt to archaic civilizations, but not to the advanced
complex societies they grew out of. Real people lived over that theoretical wall we have erected to separate "history" from "prehistory," and
it is both fascinating and instructive to get to know them.

   The great explosion of imaginative forms was not antagonistic to
orderliness; these two virtues seemed to reinforce each other. Those Europeans who first visited Buganda and Polynesia were themselves

deeply committed to cleanliness, order, and efficiency. If they had not
been, they might never have made their discoveries and returned to tell
of them. In the English navy, the second half of the eighteenth century
was an important time, marking the conquest of disease aboard ships
on long journeys. Cook himself was an innovator in matters of diet and
cleanliness. And in "darkest Africa" no European lived to write about
his journey unless he had taken great care in the preparation of guns,
food, medicine, scientific instruments, items to trade, paper to write on,
books to read, chairs to sit upon. Stanley, for example, transported, in
five sections, a forty-foot boat weighing two tons, and launched it on
Lake Victoria, almost a thousand miles from the coast.

These intrepid, organized Englishmen had nothing but praise for
the orderliness of the ancient kingdoms they encountered. Stanley, as
he loved to be, was rapturous:

There is a singular fascination about this country. The land would be loved
for its glorious diversified prospects even though it were a howling wilderness;
but it owes a great deal of the power which it exercises over the imagination
to the consciousness that in it dwells a people peculiarly fascinating also. "How
comes it," one asks, "that this barbarous, uneducated, and superstitious monarch builds upon this height?" Not for protection, surely, for he has smoothed
the uneven ground and formed broad avenues to approach it, and a single torch
would suffice to level all his fences? Does he, then, care for the charms of the
prospect? Has he also an eye to the beauties of nature? . . .
    This man builds upon a hill that he may look abroad, and take a large impe-
rial view of his land. He leaves ample room; his house is an African palace,
spacious and lofty; large clean courtyards surround it; it has spacious quarters
for his harem, and courtyards round those; he has spacious quarters for his
guards, and extensive courtyards round those; a cane enclosure again is a wide
avenue running round the palace fences. His people, great and small, imitate
him as much as lies in their power.[6]

And Speke pays the palace of Mutesa the greatest of compliments: it
makes him think of home. "The whole brow and sides of the hill on
which we stood were covered with gigantic grass huts, thatched as
neatly as so many heads dressed by a London barber, and fenced all
round with tall yellow reeds."[7] And "The whole land was a picture
of quiescent beauty. . . ."[8]

In Buganda it was the roads that were most impressive. Every district governor had the obligation to maintain the road, twelve feet wide,
from the royal capital to the provincial capital. In the case of Buddu,

almost a hundred miles was traversed. Each provincial governor had several subgovernors under him, who had the responsibility of maintaining a roadway, although not as wide, from their seat of government to the provincial capital. What most impressed Speke was that, unlike all other public ways in Africa, the roads in Buganda ran *straight.*[9]

In Hawaii the residence of any reasonably well-to-do man contained six separate buildings: a chapel where the statues of the family ancestors were kept, which was used for private worship; the eating house of the men, which was tabu to women; the house where the wife lived; the eating house of the women; a structure where the women beat the *kapo* bark in bad weather; a house where the wife lived during her menstruation.[10]

Even more than Buganda, Tahiti and Hawaii were lands where "every prospect pleaseth." Of the Hawaiian island of Maui, Menzies wrote: "Even the shelving cliffs of rocks were planted with esculent roots, banked in and watered by aqueducts from the rivulet with as much art as if their level had been taken by the most ingenious engineer. We could not indeed but admire the laudable ingenuity of these people in cultivating their soil with so much economy. The indefatigable labor in making these little fields in so rugged a situation, the care and industry with which they were transplanted, watered and kept in order, surpassed anything of the kind we had ever seen before."[11]

Concomitant with the orderliness of the landscape was the personal cleanliness of the people. The Polynesians were as obsessed with bathing as we are; so, too, the Baganda, especially the men, who often bathed twice a day. The Baganda even brushed their teeth, using a fibrous stick.[12]

The people of Buganda provided a remarkable contrast to their neighbors. They were clothed from head to foot and did not smear their bodies with oil or fat. They had an abhorrence of any manipulation or mutilation of their bodies: they did not tattoo themselves, or extend their ear lobes, or cut lip plugs; they practiced no circumcision, or filing of teeth, or ritual extraction of teeth. As we have seen, this rejection of any bodily mutilation worked seriously against the attempts of the Zanzibari Arabs to convert the Baganda to Islam, since the Arabs insisted on circumcision as a prerequisite of conversion.

This pride in landscape and in one's body seems related somehow to the self-esteem—or vanity—connected with the erection of large buildings. Our society is obsessed with building, and we respond to ancient societies that shared this obsession. For years our historical imagination has been stirred much more deeply by ancient Egypt and its pyramids than by ancient Mesopotamia, even though the contribution of Mesopotamia to the development of our civilization was much greater. In our culture, usually the first imaginative contact with archaic civilizations is reading the Bible, in which much more is made of the sojourn of the Hebrews in Egypt than of the fact that Mesopotamia created the literary, philosophical, and moral background out of which Old Testament religion developed.

The Tahitians and Hawaiians were great builders. In Hawaii three types of stone construction were used to increase food production: terraces were built for growing taro plants submerged in water; irrigation ditches and aqueducts brought water to the terraces and fields; fresh- and saltwater fishponds allowed for a steady supply of fish.[13] On the island of Kauai, for example, in Waimea Canyon, there was an aqueduct that carried water four hundred feet around the face of a cliff that jutted out above a rapidly flowing stream.

On Tahiti and the other Society Islands, the most impressive stoneworks were temples, or *marae*. The typical stone *marae* consisted of an enclosed rectangular court with a step pyramid forming one of the shorter sides. The largest *marae* in Tahiti was constructed between 1766 and 1768 for Teriirere, who was heir to the kingdom of Papara. Since his parents built this temple as part of an attempt to establish his political hegemony over neighboring kingdoms and eventually over the whole island, the size of the *marae* was meant to overawe those who might be inclined to oppose these political ambitions. The inner court measured approximately 260 by 360 feet.[14] The step pyramid had ten or eleven steps and reached a height of 50 feet. At its base the pyramid measured 260 by 90 feet, and the top level measured 180 by 6 feet.[15] This attempt to make Prince Teriirere into a great monarch resulted in a miserable failure, for the unification of Tahiti had to await Christian ideas and Christian guns. Nevertheless, consider the fact that Papara was just one of several Tahitian kingdoms at the time. How a small political entity could muster the enormous amount of labor required to build such a structure—and do it in three years—is still beyond anyone's comprehension, although there is no question that such was the case.

The Hawaiian island of Maui had achieved something that even the great road builders of Buganda could not boast of—a paved road, 138 miles in length, that ran around the entire perimeter of the island. Oral tradition attributed the road to the great King Kihapi'ilani, who unified the whole island into one kingdom and lived (according to modern estimates) in the sixteenth century. The road was in neglect when the Eu-

*Mutesa, king of Uganda, walking with the
characteristic step of the* kabakas

The arrival of Speke's expedition at Mutesa's palace in Uganda

Mutesa reviewing his troops

A queen being dragged to execution

Human sacrifice at Mutesa's court

Kimenya the Dwarf: entertainer of
Speke's expedition. Right: Kamrasi,
the king of Bunyoro, takes his
first lesson in the Bible.

Musicians in an East African kingdom

A noble of the Hawaiian Islands.
Right: A woman of Oahu.

A dancer from Hawaii

Tereoboo, king of Hawaii,
bringing presents to Captain Cook.
Right: *A ritual offering made before*
Cook in the Hawaiian Islands.

A view of Huahine, the great
harbor of Tahiti. Left: A dance
performance on Tahiti

The reception of Cook on Haapai in the Tongan Islands. Right: *A night dance by men on Tonga.*

A temple on Tongatapu.
Left: *A ceremony for the king's son on Tongatapu*

A boxing match in the Tongan Islands

ropeans arrived, which might indicate that centralized monarchy was stronger in times previous to the 1770s. A developmental view of the growth of centralized monarchies does not preclude an ebb and flow of centralization, a buildup and then a breakdown of powerful kingship. We know that in ancient Egypt, for example, there were two major periods of breakdown of the centralized state that lasted for hundreds of years, the causes of which are unknown. The monarchies of advanced complex societies may have been subject to similar periods of collapse and decentralization.

As impressive as the Polynesian building in stone was the construction of the large double canoes that were used for transportation during the period of migration, and afterward for long sea journeys. A voyage of twenty-five hundred miles could be done in less than a month. With a sailing canoe making eight or nine knots, such an expedition could easily cover a hundred miles a day, since the crew paddled during periods of no wind.

Some of these canoes were over a hundred feet long and four to five feet wide. During the migration, whole groups of families set out in these vessels, along with pigs, chickens, dogs; coconuts, taro, breadfruit, banana to plant; and provisions for four to six weeks. Water was carried in joints of bamboo or coconut bottles. Small fires were kindled on board on top of a mixture of sand, earth, and stones. Fish and birds were caught along the way.[16]

Oral tradition tells us that journeys of several thousand miles were made in such canoes. The settlement of Easter Island, Hawaii, and New Zealand would have been impossible without the existence of these conveyances.

Face-to-face competition between two great poets was a traditional form of some early poetry. The Greeks invented a fictitious confrontation between the two champions Homer and Hesiod. On the island of Tonga, the poet Falepapalangi dared his opponent Mamaeaputo to compose a chant:

> To be bitter as if it were Kava,
> To swim as if it were in the ocean,
> To fade as if it were a rainbow,
> To go about crying as if a Katafa bird,
> . . . to cause a gardenia to flower, and to cause
> me to eat with my back turned, ashamed.[17]

A complexity of cultural forms seems to develop hand in hand with complexity in politics; it is impossible to say which causes the other. When culture reaches a certain level of complexity, formal teaching becomes necessary for its preservation from generation to generation. Schools, which barely existed in primitive culture, are characteristic of all advanced complex societies.

In ancient Tahiti, most teaching was done by chanting. "The main subjects in the teacher's schools were: history, heraldry, geography, navigation, astronomy, astrology, mythology, time, numbers, seasons, genealogies (by which they counted the generations, which marked their chronology), and studying enigmas and similes . . . a favorite pastime."[18] As happens in all aristocratic societies, those at the highest level were not required to learn in the same atmosphere as ordinary people. The kings of Tahiti kept "dancing masters" to instruct the court in music, dance, and dramatic performance. They also kept certain priests as teachers who were known as *"tahu'a parau tumu fenua,* 'experts in basic knowledge of the world.' "[19]

Schools meant teachers, and teachers meant a group of people who spent all their time dealing with things of the mind; it was the birth of intellectualism and intellectuals. Intellectuals meant esoteric learning, since intellectuals, like any producers of a product for the market, want their wares to be scarce—it keeps the price high. And from esoteric learning came philosophy. The Polynesian Maori of New Zealand, although politically less developed than other Polynesian societies, had an elaborate system of schooling in traditional lore. For the Maori, Rangi and Papa were the Sky and the Earth, the first gods, who began the world. But some pre-Socratic Maori philosopher invented the genealogy of Rangi and Papa. First there was Development (as in the womb); from Development sprang Growth; from Growth, Energy; from Energy grew Thought; from Thought, Mind; from Mind developed Desire; until, eventually, we come to Rangi and Papa.[20]

Greek philosophers before Heraclitus and Socrates produced the same kind of abstract cosmogonic myths. And the study of complex societies indicates that such a manner of thought was not unique to the Greeks—that it was a product of many complex societies.

Along with schools, teachers, and intellectuals developed a conscious concern with language. Self-consciousness about language is one sign of advancing civilization. In ancient Buganda, the purest Luganda was spoken in the county of Busiro. A great number of princesses lived there, and their speech was considered cultured and refined; many people began to model their own speech after that of the Busiro princesses. The people of Bulemezi County had a reputation for being adept at all sorts of humorous phrases. Governors and subgovernors, who held small courts, would encourage people from Bulemezi to visit, making feasts for them and giving them gifts as a reward for the amusement they offered.[21]

The people of Rwanda, a kingdom neighboring on Buganda, could state that their primary ambition was for children and cows, but if asked why, they revealed that these goods were merely means to more abstract ends. What they really cared about, they said, was *amaboko* (power) and *ugukomera* (reputation).[22]

These leaps of the imagination, this great revolution in the creation of symbols, also had an effect on religious ritual. In advanced complex societies we can observe a profundity in prayer and ritualistic action that did not exist in primitive society. The world had become fuller, deeper, rounder, more ambiguous, more invested with meaning. One aspect of the Hawaiian harvest celebration was a system of divination to determine the prospects of future harvests. A great net was filled with food and shaken so that part of the contents fell through the mesh; the greater the fall, the greater the future harvest. This net had first appeared in a mythical time of intense famine, when it was let down from heaven, scattering food all over the earth:

KAHUNA [*The Priest*]
    Oh deep-blue sea, oh god Uli!
    Oh blue of the wild, tossing sea!
    Net of heaven, oh Uli!
    Green are the leaves of god's harvest fields.
    The net fills the heavens—shake it

PEOPLE *Shake down the god's food!*
    Scatter it oh heaven!
    A season of plenty this.
    Earth yield thy plenty!
    This is a season of food.
    Life to the land!
    Life from Kane,
    Kane the god of life.
    Life from Kanaloa!
    The wonder-working God.
    Life to the people!

Hail Kane of the water of life! Hail!
Life to the king of the Makahiki [the harvest festival]
Amana.* It is free

KAHUNA *Free through whom?*

PEOPLE *Free through Kane.*[23]

When the priest came to the words "shake it," exactly that was done to the net, forcing the food to fall through. After the full prayer, the priests rose and held their hands aloft, while the people raised only their left hands, shouting, "It is free! It is free! It is free!" At each exclamation, they clapped their right hands under their left armpits.[24] We may trust that the priests were good enough shakers so that the prediction was for a bountiful harvest next year. It was a ritual of abundance and optimism of a complexity unknown in primitive society.

From a Hawaiian Legend

When the people saw Kaeweaoho they at once recognized their lost king, and with tears of joy they rushed to the sea, and, seizing the canoe, carried it into the palace yard on their shoulders, with the king and all the sailors in it. Before the palace they lowered the canoe. The king gave his great aloha to all.[25]

A Piece of Missionary History

When the Christianization of the Society Islands began to accelerate after several years of little progress, the separate islands of the group were impatient to obtain their own missionary, who would bring the message to them. When the missionary Orsmond arrived at the island of Raiatea, the inhabitants were so anxious for his presence that: ". . . on my arrival, the king, the chiefs, and great numbers of the people, ran into the water, laid hold of my little boat, and carried it, including myself and all my cargo, upon their shoulders, about a furlong inland, into the royal yard, with masts, sails, and rigging all displayed; the bearers and the accompanying multitude shouting as they went, 'God bless our teacher, Otomoni!' "[26]

---

*This word is impossible to translate; it is equivalent, in part, to our word "Amen." Some of its meanings are: "It is ended," "It is over," "It is free," "It is settled," "The tabu is lifted," "So be it."

One mechanism that human beings have invented to facilitate cultural and social development is that of first creating a legend or a myth in which something new happens or some attribute is given to a god or a hero, and subsequently imitating it. First people create the myth of a just god, and then they try to act justly. Or people invent a myth that says that human sacrifice is unnecessary, and subsequently give it up. In Polynesia, the heroic legends of those who reigned over a whole island, or the entire group of islands, existed before such centralized power was realized. Not knowing the legend, the Reverend Orsmond may have supposed they made up this triumphal entry for him alone.

It is a reasonable assumption that legends of autocratic, powerful kings whose very word or gesture was an imperative for their subjects preceded the actual establishment of such a kingship, although data are lacking to assert this definitely. There has been much discussion about whether the *kabaka* of Buganda was "divine" or not. What is beyond dispute is that the king was a *very special person* and that such special persons had not existed in societies that preceded advanced complex cultures. The king was special not only in the power he wielded, the fear in which he was held, or the unlimited pleasures of the world to which he was entitled—these kings, Polynesian and African, had a sense of themselves as individuals. Their power and position made them not just cruel but inventive of ways in which human beings could act. Some of them had imaginative as well as political capabilities. They were what we like to call the "great men of history," and had what all great men have had: a sense of personality and self-advertisement that could match their achievements.

When Captain James Cook visited one of the Tonga Islands, he was cordially received by the reigning monarch, King Finow I. Cook and Finow recognized in each other the same qualities of command, curiosity, and competitiveness. At their formal meeting, each tried to outdo the other in the complexity of the welcoming entertainment. First Finow's people put on an exhibition of music, singing, and dancing that, Cook reluctantly admitted, was remarkably impressive. The English captain—straight out of Gilbert and Sullivan—refused to be bested by the accomplishments of his hosts and, "In order to give them a more favorable opinion of English amusements, and to leave their minds fully impressed with the deepest sense of our superior attainments, I directed some fireworks to be got ready; and, after it was dark, played them off in the presence of Feenou [Finow], the other chiefs, and a vast concourse of their people. . . . Our war and sky-rockets, in particular, pleased and astonished them beyond all conception; and the scale was now turned in our favour."[27]

But Finow was as tough a competitor as Cook, and the fireworks "seemed only to furnish them with an additional motive to proceed to fresh exertions of their very singular dexterity; and our fireworks were no sooner ended, than a succession of dances, which Feenou had got ready for our entertainment, began."[28]

We do not have Finow's version of what happened, but even Cook's description makes it clear that the contest ended in a draw. Human history, one sometimes thinks, could be described as the alternate choosing, by people for their entertainment, of Finow's dancing and Cook's war rockets.

Finow I, with his high spirits, political acumen, imaginative response to events, and capacity for cruelty, reminds one of Henry VIII, who would dash off a tune or kill a queen with equal felicity. For a time, the shipwrecked William Mariner was the only European at Finow's court, but circumstance brought another, and one day Mariner and Finow engaged in a discussion of writing and what it could do. To test Mariner, Finow whispered things for him to write down; once written, the words were delivered to the other man to be read aloud. Amazed at the accuracy of this magic, Finow kept Mariner busy for three or four hours writing down the names of persons, places, things. This entertainment took place in front of the whole court, which included both men and women, and Finow used the occasion playfully and domineeringly to whisper some "love anecdotes," which were written down and subsequently read aloud, "not a little to the confusion of one or other of the ladies present . . . which was all taken in good humour."[29] We wonder what alternatives to good humor were available to the women who had just had their sexual secrets made public by the playful king.

The kings of Buganda, likewise, exhibited a powerful sense of themselves and held an expansive view of what life could bring. This included a sense of the dramatic and of their own place in the drama. Kabaka Suna, the father of Mutesa, had a great interest in anything in nature that was unusual or novel. All freaks, including unusually colored animals, or human dwarfs or albinos, were shipped to Suna's palace. He also kept a zoo stocked with dangerous animals.[30]

Mutesa grew from the tentative, immature king of Speke's visit to the imperial monarch portrayed by Stanley. A year before Stanley arrived, Mutesa had sent an embassy to Zanzibar, on the coast. While returning from the mission, some of the men had disappeared in a part of the countryside that was dominated by a notorious military chief named Mirambo. Mirambo was becoming a hindrance to trade, and word got out that Mutesa intended sending fifty thousand spears to put an end to his predatory activities. Mirambo sent three men to Mutesa's court to declare that there was no cause for fighting between the two and to bring gifts of placation: "So many cloths, so much wire, some half-dozen dinner plates of European make, an ample brass coffee tray, an Arab dagger silver-hilted, and a scarlet coat."[31]

The gifts were impressive, but Mutesa was no small-time chief to be bought off with goods: "Tell Mirambo from me that I do not want his gifts, but I must have the head of his man who slew my chief Singiri a year ago . . . or I will hunt him up with more Waganda [Baganda] than there are trees in his country. Go!"[32]

Two Hawaiian Prayers for the Cutting of the Thatch for a New House

I *Cut the umbilical cord of the house*
A house that resists rain and strong elements.
A house for a man to dwell in.
O Lono, behold the house,
A house in the presence of the giver of life.
Grant life to those who dwell therein,
Grant life to the visitors that come,
Grant life to the landlord.[33]

II *Severed is the navel-string of the house, the thatch that sheds the*
*   rain,*
that wards off the evil influences of the heavens,
The water-spout of Haukula-manu [Deluge personified].
Cut now!
Cut the navel-string of your house, O Mauli-ola [demigod of
*   health].*
That the house-dweller may prosper,
That the guest who enters may have health,
That the chiefs may have long life.
Grant these blessings to your house, O Mauli-ola.
To live till one crawls hunched up, till one becomes blear-eyed,
Till one lies on the mat, till one has to be carried about in a net.
Amana. It is free.[34]

No steps in the development of society and culture are taken without the creation of new symbols and new symbolic forms. In one way, these steps consist precisely of the invention of symbols and symbolic forms. (I use "symbolic form" as Cassirer does, to indicate a complex system of symbols, one that carries a broad and deep meaning.[35] The crucifixion is a symbol, but Christianity is a symbolic form. Culture and society are themselves symbolic forms.) Through symbols and symbolic forms, we know the world and ourselves, and through them we act in a public and a private manner. Another way of describing complex society as more developed than primitive society is by saying that its symbols and symbolic forms are more complex.

Some larger forms of complex society, such as kingship, the state, hierarchy, and the division of labor, deserve chapters of their own. Here we look at a few particular symbols, the creation of which demonstrated the workings of new imaginative energies. The *niau,* the leaf of the coconut tree, was a symbol of authority in the Society Islands. A king who sent out a request for labor or goods, or who called an assembly of other kings or lesser governors, or who announced preparations for war, would send along with the request a leaf of the coconut.[36] In former times, an actual gift of food was probably sent, and the coconut leaf remained as the memory of the need to make and receive a gift. The leaf softened the command because the commander, by sending it, admitted that he could not just issue orders; it was a complicated way of saying "please." On the other hand, the leaf strengthened the order because it lent a tradition and a history of respect to what was being asked. The office was asking, as well as the individual king.

After Captain Cook landed on the Hawaiian Islands in 1778, he departed for further explorations in the north, and returned almost a year later. Between the first and second visits, several children had been born to Hawaiian women, the result of liaisons with Cook's men. When it became apparent that Cook's ships were again going to depart, never to return this time, and that the fathers had no intention of settling on Hawaii, the mothers took the dried and preserved umbilical cords of the children and placed them in the cracks of the deck and other parts of the ship, thus to maintain some connection between the fathers and their children.[37]

The symbolism of the eternal fire that burns, for example, beneath L'Arc de Triomphe or on the grave of John Kennedy has probably come down to us from complex societies. In Buganda, such a fire burned day and night in the capital when the king was in residence there, and was carried from place to place when he traveled. The original fire was said to have been kindled at the time of Kintu, the first *kabaka* of Buganda.[38] When each *kabaka* died, the fire was extinguished.

In Polynesia, fire was put to a more playful use than the certification of the solemn eternity of the state. On the Hawaiian island of Kauai, a multitude of firebrands of various light woods were burned at night on top of the northern cliffs; the whole giant conflagration was then pushed over the cliff to descend slowly into the sea. The lightness of the wood and the upward currents of the wind contributed to a leisurely descent, heightening the sense of magic and delight.[39]

So many primitive peoples entertained an intense fear of the dark that one is struck by the desire of people in complex societies to extend the daylight by artificial means. Polynesians not only held dramatic performances and political councils at night with the aid of various torch mechanisms, they also fished by torchlight. From everything we know of them, it is reasonable to conclude that they took pleasure not just in the fish, but in the setting itself, as did Reverend Ellis: "Few scenes present a more striking and singular effect than a band of natives walking along the shallow parts of the rocky sides of a river, elevating a torch with one hand, and a spear in the other; while the glow of their torches is thrown upon the overhanging boughs, and reflected from the agitated surface of the stream. Their own bronze-coloured and lightly clothed forms, partially illuminated, standing like figures in relief; while the whole scene appears in bright contrast with the dark and almost midnight gloom that envelops every other object."[40]

> *Thou, silent form! dost tease us out of thought*
> *As doth eternity. . . .*
>
>   —JOHN KEATS,
>   *"Ode on a Grecian Urn"*

13

'Ban 'Ban, Ca-Caliban

"Every day there is a wanton slaughter going on of innocent victims. For a time, after we came here we were ignorant of this. It may have been done more quietly on our account, or our ignorance of the language and people prevented our detecting it sooner. Now at any rate, before our eyes the terrible crime lies bare. No more is it the king himself who says, 'Go slaughter such a one and such a one.' Now each executioner—we do not know how many executioners there are, but on every road diverging from the court there is at least one—has orders to capture and kill mercilessly all or any who pass on the highway. Unsuspecting peasants coming in from the country with plantains on their head are seized upon in a moment, and dragged into the executioner's court, secured in forked sticks till morning, and slaughtered at dawn. . . . It is especially men who have no friends or powerful chiefs as their protectors who are the victims. No crime have they committed, nor been guilty of the most trivial offense. It is the king's pleasure that so many be butchered every day by each executioner . . . and the owner of the slaughter office must find his victims where he can.

"It is dark, about 10 p.m. All is quiet, the last drum heard being the executioner's across the small valley, announcing that he had secured his victims for the day, and will spill their blood in the morning. Suddenly a sharp cry in the road outside of our fence, then mingled voices; an agonizing yell again, followed by the horrid laugh of several men, and all is still as before. 'Do you hear?' says one of our lads; 'they have cut the fellow's throat—hee, hee, hee!' And he laughs too—the terrible Buganda grin of pleasure in cruelty. So it is."[1]

In Buganda there were several official places for the execution of human sacrifices. One was Kitinda, a sacred spot on the island of Damba dedicated to crocodiles. It was inhabited by a medium who became possessed; moving his head from side to side, opening his mouth wide, and snapping it shut. His official function was to feel out people who were planning rebellion against the *kabaka*. Accurate or not, such motives were ascribed to all his victims. Those who were to be killed were taken to Damba, given some doctored beer to drink, and marched to the beach. Their arms and legs were broken. They were laid on the beach in a row. The lake crocodiles did the rest.[2]

"Someone of the name of *Mayanja* (whether a sorcerer or not we do not know yet) has advised the king that to hasten his recovery it is necessary to slaughter people on several hills round the capital. For days the dozen or more executioners, each with his gang of twenty or thirty men, have been laying in wait for people on the roads. *Bakopi*, or common people, only are caught; while sons or petty officers of chiefs, if caught by mistake, can generally purchase their release by a goat or by a cow. The other night five were suddenly apprehended at our own gate; two days ago the executioner (*Sabata*) opposite went to catch men on another road, as it had been noised abroad that he was catching everyone that passed this way. People who had gone the other way to avoid this one, thus fell into the trap, and by evening we heard that Sabata had captured forty men and thirty women. Last night we heard that he had made a similar 'take.' . . . Some will have their throats cut, while others will be tortured to death—their eyes put out, nose and ears cut off, the sinews of their arms and thighs cut out piecemeal and roasted before their eyes, and finally the unhappy wretches burnt alive."[3]

What is so remarkable, and what cries out for explanation, is that this kind of cruelty could exist in conjunction with—even in intimate relationship with and almost indiscriminate from—the most imaginative, most joyful, life-enhancing human experiences. And this intermingling existed not only within the same culture, or within the same person, but actually within the same ritual. At the birth of King Pomare II (who would become the first king of a stable, united Tahiti), his father, as was the custom, sent two messengers in opposite directions to circle the island. Their function was to announce and celebrate the birth of the king's son and to assert the political hegemony of the king. By letting the messengers pass through, the people of a district acknowledged the political superiority of the sovereign. Should the assertion of this hegemony be presumptuous on the king's part, the people of a district would refuse the messenger, and war might result. The rite gave promise that the child, grown to manhood, would rule those districts. The heralds went gaily decorated and carried beautiful ensigns made of mats with fringed edges and decorated with the most colorful feathers available. Bunches of black feathers borne in hand completed the ensemble. A great crowd gathered to watch the dispatch of the heralds from the national temple at Papaoa, the birthplace of the prince. Before they left, a man was ritually slaughtered and dedicated to the god Oro.

Circling in opposite directions around the larger peninsula of Tahiti, the heralds met at the isthmus between the two peninsulas and then proceeded to the smaller one, where, at a temple in Tautira with an island-wide reputation, they slaughtered another man to Oro. In this particular instance, no one challenged the messengers and, with their unharmed banners held aloft and the pride of accomplishment illuminating their faces, they returned in triumph to their king's temple.[4]

In Hawaii, the temples of the gods were more elaborately decorated than those in either Tahiti or Buganda. Large statues representing the deities were carved in the mountains, where the largest trees grew, and taken to the temples. The day on which a completed statue was conducted from its carving place and installed was one of celebration. The people gathered large quantities of ferns, which they carried on their backs, and filled their hands with the fruit and flowers of the mountain apple. The journey from the mountain to the ocean, where the temple lay, was accompanied by tumultuous noise and shouting. "I go to victory," they cried out. Arriving at the temple, the people placed the image on the pavement, covered it with leaves, and left. Anyone they met on the way who was not part of the celebration was butchered on the spot.[5]

From this speech given to potential Christian converts on the Polynesian island of Mangaia we have evidence of what it felt like to be a potential victim of these holocausts:

Young people, look on me. Do you know that I was one of those appointed for sacrifice to Rongo? These ears and this nose of mine were to have been cut off and divided out to each chief in token of office. This head was . . . "a feast provider." It would not actually be eaten; but until I or some other suitable victim had been offered to the god of war, no culture of the soil was lawful and no feasting permitted, bloodshedding alone being the order of the day.

Our family was one devoted to sacrifice, our god being Utakea. . . . Most of my ancestors in past generations have been slain and then placed on the altar of Rongo. Without a human sacrifice the drum of peace would not be beaten nor a new paramount chief be appointed.

The first narrow escape I can recollect was a day or two after the battle of Rangivra, when Makitaka became supreme lord of Mangaia. I was then a mere youth, and passing along over the hills fell in with two armed men, Putiki and Tavare, who were in search of suitable sacrifice. Patiki seized me by the arm and said to his companion, "This will do." But to my great joy Tavare released me, declaring that I should not die, for I was his near relative. They passed on, and I fled home as fast as my legs would carry me. It then dawned upon my mind for the first time that at some future period I too should be offered in sacrifice.

But the presidency [sic!] of Makitaka was unfortunate. There was nothing to eat but candle-nuts and wild . . . roots. It was evident that the gods were displeased: a new "lord of Mangaia" must be chosen. The chief fixed upon was Pangemiro. New sacrifices to the god Rongo were required to ratify the change. I was carefully hidden by relatives of the dominant tribe not eligible for sacrifice until we heard that Teata had been slain and offered on the altar of the god of war.

At that period my uncle Kariuna . . . lived under the protection of Meduatipoki, not far distant from my home in Veitatei. Little did he dream of danger one morning when he watched the chief Kino, accompanied by a few friends, crossing the hills . . . and making for his guardian's dwelling. Kino asked Meduatipoki to let him have . . . "the insignificant minnow," yonder. Consent was at once given, and in a few minutes my poor uncle was clubbed and borne all warm to Rongo's bloody altar. As Kino advanced to kill him he made no attempt to escape, for to whom could he go?

During the reign of Pangemiro I lived secure, took a wife, and became a parent. But . . . Teao contested with Pangemiro the temporal lordship at the battle of Aracva, the last heathen fight. A second time the chieftainship fell to the victorious Pangemiro. A human sacrifice was again required, and I trembled lest I should be fixed upon.

With the rest of the conquered party I lived after the battle at Butoa. On one occasion a party of us went to our old quarters at Veitatei. . . . I paid a visit to an aged relative residing in a very secluded spot. As soon as Teare saw me he said, "Fly for your life. Yonder are Erui and others waiting to kill you and offer you in sacrifice." I was not slow in taking the old man's advice; and when I had gained the other side of the taro plantations I saw the killing party walking discontentedly away.

Ten days afterward we heard that Erui had slain the beautiful Mukimaki, the young wife of one of their number. I felt angry with Erui, himself one of the vanquished, for thus meanly striving to ingratiate himself with the victorious party. . . .[6]

Vaitamana's story of betrayal and narrow escape sounds remarkably like the stories told by those with the tattooed numbers on their arms. The word "holocaust" means *"sacrificial offering."* How strange, and full of insight, that it should now be applied to a seemingly "meaningless" slaughter. Maybe the Mangaians and the Nazis shared the same nightmare. I have no wish to equate those who created complex societies with those who produced the German catastrophe, but I do wish to bring together one sacrificial offering—one "cleansing of the world"—with another, and ask why either of them was "necessary."

Vaitamana concludes his speech and reminds us of another form of sacrifice: "But for the gospel you would not see my face this day. Now we all live in peace, as our ancestors never would. They longed to see a period of peace and of plenty, but passed away without ever enjoying such privileges. Let us value our mercies. They all flow to us through the Son of God, who offered himself on Calvary to save us from eternal death. For more than thirty years I have served Christ."[7]

Reverend Ellis tells a somewhat similar story about Tahiti. In the early days of the missionaries a young man was converted to Christianity and therefore banished from his father's house. Not content with this punishment, his persecutors decided that he should be the sacrificial victim at an approaching ceremony. A delegation with insidious intent sought him out in his place of retreat, urging him to come down into the valley because the priest or some of his friends wished to speak with him. Having perceived their purpose, the youth answered: "I know a ceremony approaches, that a human victim is then to be offered—something within me tells me *I am to be that victim,* and your appearance and your message confirms my conviction. Jesus Christ is my keeper, without his permission you cannot harm me; you may be permitted to kill my body, but *I am not afraid to die!* My soul cannot hurt; that is safe in the hands of Jesus Christ, by whom it will be kept beyond your power."[8]

Unable to deceive him into going down voluntarily, they clubbed him to death, put his corpse in the appropriate long basket made of leaves of the coconut tree, bore it to the temple, and dedicated it to the god.

And then, in telling the story, the Reverend Ellis says a remarkable thing: those who heard the dying man's words and witnessed his firm resolve would probably become more receptive to the religion that he professed. The Church would grow as a result of his death because "The blood of the martyrs has ever been the seed of the church. . . ." [9] Ellis was not appalled that the young man was transformed into a sacrificial offering, as long as it was an offering to the right god.

Of course, in Ellis's religion the god himself was a human sacrifice. In all the great theological debates of the fourth and fifth centuries, the orthodox position, that which triumphed at the Council of Nicaea, insisted that Christ was human as well as divine, that he had died on the cross as a human, had suffered pain there as a human, that his body rose to heaven in its human form. Christ was a divine *and* a human sacrifice. Perhaps we all share the same nightmare with the Tahitians and the Nazis, although many of us, individuals and cultures, seem to have learned to deal with that nightmare and no longer act it out in the real world. If this is so, Christ's sacrifice is intimately connected with the capacity to deal with this unnamed terror. An anonymous Tahitian gave voice to a powerful insight as he questioned one of the first missionaries. He wanted to know whether Jesus Christ was the Father or the Son, and "which was killed for a sacrifice." After he was answered, he further inquired "whether if Jesus Christ's being made a sacrifice is the reason that we do not kill men for sacrifices?"[10]

Assuming that Christ's suffering and human death were necessary so that we might be forgiven our sins and attain eternal life, it is an extraordinary thing that Christ would choose to succor us in that manner. But by whose decree was that sacrifice necessary? It has to be explained why forgiveness of sin and eternal life were not free gifts, freely given. It may be asked who invented the system whereby such God-given rights could only be purchased at the most excruciating cost. There is no question but that the Tahitian is correct: we no longer sacrifice men to the gods, in part because we invented a religion in which the central god dies a symbolic death as a sacrifice for all men. But what law of human nature is it that decrees that *some* dying is necessary? There must be some terrible fear deep in every human psyche that causes human moral and developmental progress to be measured against the awful question: Who dies?

If Christ died so that we could give up ritually killing men, it may also be that human sacrifice in complex societies served the function of making worse killings unnecessary. Many people find it difficult to acknowledge that our society—full as it is of unlimited narcissism, rac-

ism, poverty, warfare, and the threat of world destruction—is morally
and developmentally advanced. Most of us maintain a pessimism about
the future that makes difficult an accurate view of the past. How much
harder it is, then, for us to see that human sacrifice—with all its cruelty
and irrationality—may have been, for the cultures it served, a remarkable invention that freed people from the prisons of kinship and cannibalism and allowed them the energy required for great developmental
advances.

If all this is true, it seems a wildly irrational system, immensely
wasteful of human life. We wonder if all that suffering was inevitable.
To which we can again respond, Was Christ's suffering *necessary?* It
is this necessity of unnecessary suffering that we long to understand.

To do this, we must first go back and deal with ritual homicide
to see what it looked like, when it was done, who were the victims,
what functions it served. We will return later to the great question of
necessity.

Human sacrifice had no significance in primitive society. A few
scarce examples may exist—although I know of none—but in no primitive culture was it important. The use of ritual homicide as a sacred
act begins in complex societies, rises to a frenzied climax in advanced
complex societies, and then ceases to exist as archaic civilization
develops.

Archaeology reveals the existence of human sacrifices in first-
dynasty Egypt, very early China, and predynastic Sumeria,* all points
where the societies were in transition between complex and archaic civilization; afterward, *ritual homicide ceases to exist* in these areas. There
is no hard evidence that it survived in ancient Greece, though myths
of human sacrifice abound and rumors of its existence were retailed.
The only undisputed evidence of such sacrifices in a society beyond
the complex stage comes from ancient Phoenicia (where children were
frequently the offerings) and from the wife-killing rites at the husband's
funeral in India and other Asian countries, a practice that was not dis-
continued until the nineteenth century.

I cannot comment as to why the practice continued to exist in India
and Phoenicia, but it was exceptional, and in neither case did it involve
the holocaust of large numbers of people—such as five hundred at a

*Leonard Woolley's discovery in Ur ("of the Chaldees") of royal tombs containing over
a hundred human sacrifices was the most spectacular find in Sumeria.

time in Buganda, Dahomey, and Benin, for example, and thousands on single occasions among the Aztecs. Ritual homicide was the characteristic form of sacred aggression in complex societies, and, allowing for the two exceptions, *it was unique to that stage of cultural development.*

Furthermore, its dominion over the spiritual lives of people increased as complex societies developed into advanced complex societies. If one takes the twenty or so Polynesian societies about which we have adequate information and ranks them in a progressive order reflecting the degree of centralized statehood—as Irving Goldman[11] and Marshall Sahlins[12] have done—one finds that, in general, as one moves from bottom to top of that order, human sacrifice becomes increasingly important. At the very top of this scale, Sahlins and Goldman are agreed to put Tahiti, Hawaii, and Tonga, and it is precisely in these societies that ritual homicide played the greatest role. In ancient Africa, there is no question that there was a significant correspondence between the degree of political centralization and the importance of human sacrifice. As for Aztec society, the power of its polity and the orgiastic qualities of its ritual killing are well known. I am aware of no advanced complex society that did not practice ritual homicide.

With pitifully few exceptions, in all societies some human beings have killed others, but the way in which that killing is done changes as society develops from one stage to another. On the one hand, one may argue that it is all killing and must be done for the same reason; but on the other hand, it seems that different modes of killing must serve different psychological purposes.

It can be argued that these differences have no moral significance, that it is immaterial whether people are killed and their bodies eaten, or killed and their heads hung up to decorate some hut, or killed and dedicated to the god Oro, or die from lack of adequate medical care in "the most powerful nation in the world"—in all cases, the people are dead. It may indeed make no difference, but one has no right to argue that point unless one can explain why people kill one another in different ways at different stages of development, and what that means. It could be of enormous importance to understand why people in complex society invented human sacrifice, became intoxicated by it as they moved into advanced complex society, and abandoned it as they took the revolutionary step into archaic civilization. Only when we understand this can we know whether it makes a difference or not.

But let us take a look at the rite itself and some of its possible origins.

ANXIETY

All situations requiring the ritual slaughter of human beings are infused with unusual anxiety. The king is ill (will our protector disappear?); the king dies (can we and the state survive?); a new king is inaugurated (will he be able to hold things together?); there is famine in the land (will we all die?); war is declared (will we win? will we be killed?); the king's palace is dedicated (will the gods permit such an assertion by human beings?); the king's ancestors are unhappy (will they curse the land?); the gods are angry (will they eat us? can we turn their anger to someone else?); the king's son is circumcised (will the hope of the country survive this dangerous passage?). The fact that human sacrifice may be accompanied by an open display of sadistic pleasure does not signify that that is the only reason for its performance. No ritual killing is *mere* sadism, although sadism has a role in it. The reduction of anxiety, or, more properly, the containment of the fear of annihilation by reducing it to mere anxiety, is an essential purpose of the rite.

William Wilson, who captained the ship that brought the first missionaries to the South Seas, tells a story of Tonga. Moomooe lay critically ill. One of his sons, Colelallo, who lived some distance off, was sent for on the pretext that he must perform the ceremony of cutting off his little fingers, an act that would appease the anger of the god Odooa and cause the father's recovery. What those who were tending the father really wanted, however, was Colelallo's life, not his fingers. Colelallo arrived, was greeted cordially by his older brother, went in to see his father, and was seized by the father's attendants, who intended to strangle the son. Though Colelallo struggled for his life, he was finally subdued when three men from Fiji who were used to doing such dirty work were called in, along with Colelallo's sister. They slaughtered him, that the father might live.[13]

As irrational as it sounds to us, people really believed that one life could be ransomed by another, that someone or something (the gods, fate, the universe, unknown powers) would take a life hostage but would be ready to release it provided another life was given. Within limits, one could negotiate with the Power. What was not negotiable was that something terrible had to happen to someone; who that someone would be was subject to bargaining: "I will give you Colelallo, if you agree to spare his father." The Power also knew the value of the life it held and could raise the ransom if the life was valuable enough: "A life for a life, is fair enough, but to spare the *kabaka* of Buganda, I will need a hundred or two." They were given.[14]

The system was irrational but its logic was relentless. If killing two hundred peasants when the *kabaka* was ill would cure him, then a periodic prophylactic slaughter could assure his continued good health. Several years after a new *kabaka* had assumed office, he went on a ritual journey to visit the *nankere* for the purpose of prolonging his life. The *nankere*, head of the lungfish clan, was never permitted to see the king except on this occasion. When the time for the ceremony had been agreed upon, the *nankere* selected one of his sons, who was fed, clothed, and treated like a prince, and housed in a special enclosure where the ceremony was to take place.

The *kabaka* left the capital and stopped on his way at the temple of the god Mukasa to change his clothing. Most particularly, he took off whatever anklets he was wearing and made certain he did not put on any others. At their meeting, the *nankere* and the *kabaka* exchanged gourds of beer. The king's mother attended the ceremony and saw her son for the last time. The *nankere* intoned a solemn speech: the mother was urged to build a new house, for she was no longer to behold her son now that he had reached his maturity. To the *kabaka* he said, "You are now of age; go and live longer than your forefathers."

To assure the prophecy, the *nankere*'s son was brought in and presented to the sovereign, who turned him over to the bodyguard. They removed him and killed him by beating him with their fists. The muscles of the back of the victim were taken out and made into anklets for the king. A piece of skin was taken from the victim's body and turned into a whip, which the *kabaka* kept in his enclosure to be used on special occasions.[15]

The presence of the king's mother for the last time suggests that this was a ceremony of separation from the mother, and that such separations are always accompanied by anxiety and ambivalence. The killing of the *nankere*'s son seals the act, makes it irreversible. Deep in the unconscious, where such ceremonies are born, is the slaughter of the *nankere*'s son a reminder to the *kabaka* of what may happen to him if he refuses to grow up and leave his mother? Is it a warning to the mother of what will happen to her if she refuses (psychologically) to let him go? When we describe a society as being in the process of destroying the kinship system as the primary basis of political life, that is an abstract theoretical way of saying that many people are in this pro-

cess of leaving the mothers who raised them. It is a reasonable hypothesis that ritual homicide was intimately connected with, and probably
a means of trying to cope with, the anxiety and ambivalence of such
leavetakings.

Death is the most irreversible separation of all, and the death of the
king was inevitably accompanied, in advanced complex societies with
strong centralized kingships, by a holocaust of victims. Wives of the
king were chosen particularly, and in Buganda[16] and Dahomey,[17] for
example, a long list of persons who filled specific offices around the king
during his lifetime were killed as well. In Buganda, the death of the
kabaka's mother was responded to with ritual homicide.[18] The king of
that country visited the grave of his father once during his reign;[19] a
ritual function equally important with the visit was the inauguration
of a new hut over the grave of the kabaka's father.[20] This last act required only ninety-five human victims; the grave visit by the king resulted in the death of hundreds.

In our own society, we have many ceremonial occasions, both public and private. The private include baptism, christening, circumcision,
first communion, marriage, funerals, and so on. The public ceremonials
deal with the inauguration of a president or governor, the dedications
of buildings, dams, and bridges, and public holidays. When concerned
with a very public person, the usually private ceremonial tends to become public—the funeral of a president, the marriage of a royal child,
the birth of a royal child. This same transformation occurred in advanced complex societies. In Tahiti, for example, the washing of the
royal firstborn, the first presentation of a royal child to the public, and
the circumcision of the firstborn prince were all public ceremonies.[21]

In advanced complex societies there was a tendency for every public
ceremonial to be accompanied by an act of ritual homicide. We may
find this easier to comprehend if we can see that all public ceremonials
in all societies, even those that on the surface seem to be purely joyous,
arise in good measure out of anxiety. The purpose of the rite is not only
to express public joy but equally to handle the anxiety that the situation
provokes.

Take the cutting of the ribbon to open a great bridge. It is certainly
a time for celebration of the accomplishments of those who built such
a bridge and the politicians who had the foresight to back them, and
that is the subject of the speeches. But underneath there is a current
of anxiety: Will the bridge hold? Should human beings really dare to
do such things? Will we be punished for striving too high? In the deep,

irrational part of our mind we preserve the view that the powers of the universe are hostile to our proud ambitions and that we shall be punished for pursuing them. In complex societies people were slaughtered and placed in the foundations of buildings. With bridges, mention is still always made in speeches and the press of those who lost their lives in the construction. Concerning the Verrazano Bridge in New York, the story became established—totally unsupported by actual events— that a man had fallen from a scaffold into the still-liquid concrete foundation, that his body was never recovered, and that it remains in the heart of the bridge. Myth may provide the human sacrifice even when society has outwardly given up the practice.

Henry gives a long list of the occasions for human sacrifice in Tahiti. The mixture of celebration and anxiety is apparent:

> Laying the foundation stone of a national temple.
> Washing of the royal firstborn.
> Tearing of the royal flag.
> First introduction of the royal child to the public.
> Circumcision of the firstborn prince.
> Coming of age of the firstborn prince or princes.
> Inauguration of the sovereign.
> Perforating tapa cloth to make a royal feather girdle.
> First piercing the needle into the cloth.
> Completing the [girdle].
> Canoe-roller for the sovereign or heir apparent in visiting a new land.
> Awakening the tutelar god to preside over battle.
> In opening hostilities at wartime.
> In equipping a canoe to go with an offering of peace to 'Oro.
> To support a king after defeat in battle.
> Fish [the man sacrificed] for pledging international friendship.
> In erecting a house of sacred treasures of the [temple].[22]

DREAMS

Even sleep, one of the sweetest things that interlace our lives, has high potential for anxiety. The Orthodox Jew arises each morning with gratitude for Jehovah, who has let him live out the night. The most popular nighttime prayer we teach our children rivals "Rockabye Baby" in its anxiety for and aggression toward the young: "And if I die before I wake" is the dramatic focus of the prayer.

The king of Dahomey, a centralized, sophisticated monarchy on the west coast of Africa, arose each day grateful for a good night's rest. He killed two slaves every morning to demonstrate that gratitude. The reason given for this action was that the slaves' souls "transported his message of thanks to his ancestors for having vouchsafed him a good night's rest and allowed him to awaken to yet another day of life."²³ One must be wary of such explanations, which are similar to those that insist that the attendants and wives of a king were killed at his death in order to serve him in the next world. If the *only* purpose of the rite was that the king of Dahomey should thank his ancestors, then any adequate symbol would have succeeded: lighting a fire, or beating a drum, or ringing a bell, or even intoning a prayer. The king may have wanted to show gratitude to his ancestors, but he also wanted to kill someone, and the anxiety of the night may have had more to do with it than anything else.

The very first missionaries to Tahiti gave this report: "Manemane arrived from Opare, and privately informed the brethren Pomere [Pomare I] had killed a man for a sacrifice. . . . Pomere dreamed in the night his god came to him, and told him he must sacrifice a man to him, or he should be angry. In obedience to this he arose, and laid hands on the first man he caught suitable for his purpose, whom he murdered without hesitation."²⁴

The *kabaka* of Buganda periodically had dreams that produced human sacrifice. Mutesa believed that if he dreamed of a specific person, it was because the person was planning treason. No doubt there were nights when this happened; it was also a convenient way to pay out a political score. Dreaming of his dead father was particularly terrible for the king. In one recorded case, Mutesa slaughtered five hundred people after such a night vision.²⁵

WHO DIES?

The young students of the Buganda missionaries, on hearing the story of the crucifixion, inquired of their teachers how it was that Christ was sacrificed—was he such a poor person, and had he no family of any influence? There were no severe class distinctions in primitive society. The tyranny of social class and status was an invention of complex society, and tyranny saw to it that when the gods were angry and had to be appeased with human flesh, the flesh of the poor provided most of the feast. It has been that way ever since. When a person of rank or wealth was caught in the Baganda executioner's dragnet, a gift of a good-looking woman or a large number of cattle either to the executioners or to the *kabaka* would generally purchase his release.[26] The ordinary peasant had no means of escape.

Buganda had a class system based upon differences in wealth and political power, but there was no pariah class set aside for unusual contempt, nor was there a certain group of people from whom human sacrifices were chosen, as was the case in Mangaia. On Tahiti the victims were war captives kept alive for that purpose, or people of political importance who had become anathema to the ruling powers, or anyone from the lowest class, called *manahune*. Once a Tahitian victim had been taken from a particular family, the members of that family were marked to end their lives in the same manner. When ritual homicide was called for, such people fled and hid themselves until the drum announced that a suitable man had been taken. The king would send a warrior bearing a club who would inquire of a provincial governor: "Have you got a broken calabash here? Have you not seen a stray dog here?" The governor nodded in the direction of the doomed man, the king's warrior dispatched him with his club and carried him off. "Captain Henry was once present at a meeting of natives in a large house where he saw an instance of a treacherous murder of this kind. At a signal given by the chief, which was merely a downward glance of the eye, a poor man was suddenly despatched from the midst of the unsuspecting assembly and borne away. . . . " [27]

Some advanced complex societies—Rwanda in East Africa, for example—established a particularly despised group of low-status persons similar to untouchables. In Rwanda the Twa were racially different from the majority of the population and the separation was easily made, but it would be wrong to conclude that racial differences were the cause of this degradation. On the island of Hawaii, the Kauwa people, racially indistinguishable from the Hawaiians, were set aside in certain areas and so despised that not even Hawaiian commoners were allowed to associate with or marry them.

Any non-Kauwa who walked in Kauwa territory was considered defiled and was put to death. A Kauwa was permitted to travel to the house of his lord and nowhere else; to make the journey he had to cover his head with a large handkerchief and keep his eyes cast downward.

When a sacrifice was called for at the temple and no criminal or war captive was available, the local bailiff went to the boundary of Kauwa land and selected a victim, "as one might select a fowl in a barnyard." The Kauwa could not refuse the summons.[28]

In all these societies, people of high rank were also ritually slaughtered on occasion. Already mentioned is the circumstance where the king would use the excuse of sacrifice to eliminate a politically undesirable person. In addition, in Hawaii, faithful adherents of the sovereign and people of high esteem were killed on the death of the king.[29] In the kingdom of Bunyoro, neighbor of Buganda, it is related that

the king stood erect in the hut of the *Mpango,* on the threshold of the large door of ingress, dressed in the traditional habit; a great mantle of stuff made from the bark of trees, surmounted by a leopard-skin hanging at his back and round his neck; his head crowned with talismans, his wrists, neck, and ankles ornamented with large glass beads, and holding his lance in his right hand. The members of the *conde* and all the nobles were arranged in a semicircle in the great court, sitting on their little benches; the guardian of the *Mpango* stood at the right hand of the king, holding high the fatal axe. . . . A large cup was on the ground. . . . Terror and silence rested upon the assembly.

The king made a sign with his head; the great men rose, and, bowing in a sign of reverence, approached him; he touched one of them with the point of his spear on the shoulder; the chief advanced and extended his neck; the horrid axe descended; the blood was caught in the cup; the king with his finger sprinkled some of it on his own forehead and cheeks, then on those of the great men; grasping the vase he poured the remaining blood on the drum and on the little seat. . . . At a sign from the king the sorrowing parents took away the body of the unhappy Kisa, late chief of the district of Muenghe.[30]

Our knowledge of the politics in such societies indicates that the king would not feel free to dispatch the most powerful nobles on such an occasion. Kisa was probably a young man who had just started to rise on the bureaucratic political ladder. He could be dispensed with, and his death would cause no serious threat of revolt or revenge. The power to kill, however, can become a maddening thing, and the oral histories of Buganda and Hawaii are full of stories of kings who could not stop killing at a sensible point, who insisted on the deaths of people of high station, and who were eventually overthrown and replaced. In the case of this particular *Mpango* ritual, it certainly magnified the power of the Bunyoro king that he could slaughter a person of high rank. Anyone could kill a few peasants.

WHO EATS?

Toward the great religious symbols of the past—for instance, belief in the devil—three fundamental stances are possible. First, one may believe in the symbol: that there is a devil whose function is to tempt people into unrighteousness. Second, one may reject it and express disbelief either in a sympathetic or a hostile manner: "I know there is no devil; the evil that people do comes from something in themselves, but I can understand how people once held this belief." Or "That's all nonsense; how could any rational person profess such a view?" There is a third stance, in between belief and disbelief, where one does not really believe but finds the symbolism boldly and directly moving. Thomas Mann wrote a novel late in his life about the Faust legend not out of belief in the devil but because the symbolism of the devil, the psychological things that the Faust legend concerns itself with, were of immediate importance for him. The Faust legend spoke to him in a way that the crucifixion, for example, did not, although he believed in neither the devil nor in the sacrifice of Christ.

What do we make, then, of the religious symbolism that says the gods are angry and will not cease their anger until a man is killed and dedicated to them? One may register disbelief by emphasizing the absurdity in the notion: There are no gods; if there were gods, why should they be angry? Can't they have everything they want? Why would the killing of an innocent human being make them feel better or relinquish their anger?

But emphasis on the rational absurdity of this symbolism is not helpful in understanding why people once believed passionately in such a proposition. It is of enormous importance to try to become sympathetic to the symbolism, to let it speak to us, because, in my view, such absurd associations are still active in our lives, in our political lives especially. Politically, we think that we are acting out of a fundamental rational commitment, when actually we are moved to assume certain positions by deep, irresistible, irrational symbolism. The fact is that our secular twentieth-century democracy maintains the need to sacrifice someone to the angry gods, whether it is the slaughter of the president in the public-opinion polls, or the periodic ritual homicide of our young men in wars to save the world for something or from something, or the persistent, unrelenting degradation of one class of people whose means for

"pursuing happiness" are consistently being taken away. Thinking we
are free, we may be more in the hands of an angry god than ever, and,
finding ourselves in that place, we may be doing exactly what the *kabaka*
of Buganda did—attempting to satisfy the god by acting out "Take
them and not me!" We behave as if our own lives would be endangered
should society's victims cease to exist, that we are somehow safer as long
as some other people are oppressed.

The Cosmos is a hostile place. To assert that is not the same as saying
the world is a hostile place. The evils of the world—disease, famine,
earthquake, wild animals, other human beings who kill us for their
profit or pleasure—are realities, not symbols. The Cosmos, in the religious sense, is a symbol, the product of people's imagination, as are the
gods and demons who exist there. The Cosmos could have been made
up any way people wanted, but they chose to make it hostile:

In the days of Umi, that king was sacrificing at Waipo, when the voice of
Kuahiro, his god, was heard from the clouds calling for more men. The king
kept sacrificing, and the voice continued to call for more, till he had slain all
his men except one, when, as he was a great favorite, he refused at first to give
up. But the god being urgent, he sacrificed him also, and the priest and himself
were the only two that remained of all his company. Upwards of eighty victims,
they said, were offered at that time in obedience to the audible demands of the
insatiate demon.[31]

On Tahiti, the priest at the temple would roll himself into a bundle of
cloth and imitate the god by speaking in a shrill, squeaking voice: "I am
angry; fetch me boys, kill a man, and my anger will be appeased. . . ."[32]

And what did the gods do with all these human victims who were
slaughtered on request? They ate them, of course. One Hawaiian myth
says that after the bodies had been placed on the altar, the disembodied
tongue of the god descended from heaven. It "quivered downward to
the altar, accompanied by thunder and lightning, and took away all the
sacrifices."[33] On Raiatéa in the Society Islands, fish and human bodies
were hung in the trees around the temple, and the god Oro invoked:
"Now eat of the long legged fish (man). . . . Eat of thy fish of the sea."[34]
In the Polynesian Marquesas Islands the gods were impatient; instead
of waiting for people's compliance with their requests, they would let
down a hook from the heavens and catch a victim to satisfy their appetite.[35]

The giants and witches of our fairy tales are the remnants of these man-eating gods. But though with us the only creatures who still eat people are unreal beings in made-up stories—our gods no longer ingest human beings—in advanced complex societies, there existed beings who used to feed on men, although they had ceased to do so; these were the people themselves. Some Polynesians—the Maori, the Marquesas—practiced cannibalism on a regular basis, but this was not true of Hawaii, Tahiti, and Tonga, the most advanced Polynesian societies. Though on occasion a warrior on Tahiti would ingest two or three mouthfuls of a slain enemy, it was not a regular practice.[36] East African kingdoms—Buganda, Bunyoro, Ankole, Rwanda—did not practice anthropophagy. In general, no advanced complex society with a strong, centralized kingship regularly practiced cannibalism. Significantly, whatever cannibalism did exist in such societies usually occurred in connection with human sacrifice.[37]

The Aztecs are the one outstanding exception to the absence of regularized anthropophagy in advanced societies. I cannot offer any insights into Aztec society, but even here cannibalism took place in intimate connection with ritual homicide. People were not eaten until they had first been dedicated to the gods.

"It were much to be wished, that this deluded people may learn to entertain the same horror of murdering their fellow-creatures, in order to furnish such an invisible banquet to their god, as they now have of feeding corporeally on human flesh themselves," wrote Captain Cook, an anthropologist before his time, about Tahiti. "And, yet, we have great reason to believe, that there was a time when they were cannibals. We were told (and indeed partly saw it), that it is a necessary ceremony, when a poor wretch is sacrificed, for the priest to take out the left eye. This he presents to the king, holding it to his mouth, which he desires him to open; but, instead of putting it in, immediately withdraws it. This they call 'eating the man,' or 'food for the Chief', and, perhaps, we may observe here some traces of former times, when the dead body was really feasted upon."[38]

Why the eye? Ellis gives some examples of the way people curse one another out in Tahiti. The language of aggression can tell us much of what people are really feeling and can be, as Freud said of dreams, a royal road to the unconscious. For example, people had been calling one another "mother-fuckers" for centuries before Freud discovered the Oedipus complex. In Tahiti, mothers were no less the objects and subjects of verbal aggression: "Mayest thou be baked as food for thy mother," and, most significantly, "Take out your eyeball, and give it to your mother to eat."[39]

When King Oedipus finally discovers the whole truth of his tragic life, including the fact that his mother had given him out to be killed when he was an infant—had been willing to sacrifice him—he rushes into the palace to put an end to her life. Finding her dead by her own doing, he takes *her* brooch and puts out his eyes. He sacrifices his own eyes. To her? That she may eat?

Orthodox psychoanalytic criticism pronounces Oedipus' self-blinding a symbolic castration, but if one wanted such a symbol, a finger or a nose would be more accurate. It is difficult to see how the eyes stand for the penis, unless Oedipus, like all of us, first ravished his mother with his eyes.

In Tahiti, then, there was a symbolic eating of the sacrificed victim: by the gods, by the king, by mothers. On certain great occasions, this symbolic eating was extended to the general populace. Although no actual eating of the corpse took place in recorded time, what did occur was a general distribution of pieces of the sacrificed body to different areas of the country. There seems no question that in the past these pieces were distributed to be eaten. Of the Aztecs, we are told that they divided the sacrificed bodies and distributed the parts for consumption. On Tahiti: "The king has lately sent over to this district a piece of a human body, said to be one of the men who was lately killed in Eimeo. He sent it, we understand, as a confirmation of friendship between him and the district. The Rateras [people of high rank] . . . seemed much pleased with it, and have had various meetings on the occasion."[40]

It is a sad irony to discover that Cook, who wrote so well about the possibilities of giving up ritual homicide, should himself have been transformed into a sacrificial victim. Cook was killed by Hawaiians in a scuffle on the island of Hawaii. Several days after the fracas, peace was made between Cook's people and the local government. The new English commander demanded that Cook's body be returned for proper burial. Certain parts were brought back, but others could not be. Some had been burned. The head had gone to the great governor, Kahoo-opeon; the hair to Maia-maia; and the legs, thighs, and arms to Terreeoboo.[41] These parts were to serve as trophies and were not to be eaten. Headhunters had long ago discovered that one makes a trophy of what one has forbidden oneself to eat.[42]

We who only very recently have given up executions in public should realize how close we still live to the psychological mandate that produces human sacrifice. The great public debate surrounding the question of capital punishment is nothing less than a discussion of whether or not we are to give up this remnant of ritual homicide.

Our culture, our values, and our law come most directly from England, which in its time also "has been one of the dark places of the earth."[43] In the early fourteenth century, King Edward II took as his lover Sir Hugh Despenser. Sir Hugh not only ruled the king but also tyrannized over a large part of the nobility. Having had enough of the king and his favorite, the nobles rose up and dethroned the sovereign. Despenser was marked for execution:

After the feast this same Sir Hugh, who was not loved in these parts, was brought before the Queen and the assembled nobles. All his deeds had been written down and were now read out to him, but he said nothing in reply. He was condemned by the unanimous verdict of the barons and brought to suffer the following punishment. First, he was dragged on a hurdle through all the streets of Hereford, to the sound of horns and trumpets, until he reached the main square of the town, where all the people were assembled. Then he was tied to a long ladder, so that everyone could see him. A big fire had been lit in the square. When he had been tied up, his member and his testicles were first cut off, because he was a heretic and a sodomite, even, it was said, with the king. . . . When his private parts had been cut off they were thrown into the fire to burn, and afterwards his heart was torn from his body and thrown into the fire, because he was a false-hearted traitor, who by his treasonable advice and promptings had led the King to bring shame and misfortune upon his kingdom and to behead the greatest lords of England. . . .

After Sir Hugh Despenser had been cut up in the way described, his head was struck off and sent to the city of London. His body was divided into four quarters, which were sent to the four principal cities of England after London.[44]

Froissart does not tell us what was done to these quarters. We may assume that, in fourteenth-century England, they were not eaten. The purpose of the distribution was to share out the pleasure in the revenge on Sir Hugh, so that all parts of the country could taste (if only symbolically) of vengeance.

This story of the end of Hugh Despenser is not told in order to demonstrate that there was no difference morally or developmentally between ancient Polynesia and medieval England. A whole society cannot be judged by one outrageous act of public violence, just as one should not conclude—although many have done so—that the Nazi experience proved that all of Western culture was potentially mad. Fourteenth-century English society must be seen in its totality before one can say what this particular act meant. These incidents are presented, first, because the treatment of the dead body has a remarkable similarity to Polynesian experience, and was clearly undertaken for the same underlying psychological motives. Second, it is remarkable that a "civilized" country preserved so intact the psychological need and the ritual forms of human sacrifice. This should make us ask whether in our own society, in a more disguised but no less important way, we do not continue this same attitude toward the hostile Cosmos.

Returning to complex societies, it is important to underline how intimately ritual homicide was connected with kingship. Almost all human sacrifices were either concerned with the king—his coronation, his health, his death—or performed by him or with his sanction. In Dahomey, for example, it was specifically stated that anyone who sacrificed a person without the authorization of the monarch would himself become a victim of the rite.[45]

In their control over human sacrifice and, in the case of Tahiti, in their symbolic eating of the corpse, the kings in advanced complex societies became godlike. This godlike power was itself one of the foundations of kingship. "In fact, so powerful a function was human sacrifice, so apparently *necessary* was it to chiefly [kingly] authority, that some chiefs [kings], upon being urged by Europeans to give up the practice, exclaimed, 'If we do there will be no chiefs.' "[46]

Powerful anthropomorphic gods and omnipotent kings are both inventions of the human spirit and joint products of the complex age. When we read of an omnipotent king, we tend to describe him as "godlike." In advanced complex societies, it is equally accurate to describe powerful gods as "kinglike." People did not invent the gods first and then the monarchs in imitation of them. The creation both of powerful kings and of powerful deities was the result of a more fundamental invention—that kind of power itself. In primitive society, no person or supernatural being had the type of power possessed by the god Mukasa or the Kabaka Mutesa. Political and religious omnipotence did not become an ideal until the stage of advanced complex society, and in primitive society it was unimaginable. In our society, a desperate struggle seems to be under way to give up that ideal of omnipotence and replace it with a view that embraces power but not omnipotence.[47]

In advanced complex societies, the capacity to kill ritually another human being seems, unfortunately, a necessary attribute and undeniable certification of the highest power. We do not fully understand why this was so. It seems to have been intimately connected with the destruction and breakdown of the kinship system, and it will be profitable, after dealing with that revolution, to return to the question of the necessity of ritual homicide. It also seems reasonably certain that the rite of human sacrifice was the final step of a long process that began in primitive society and did not reach completion until the advent of archaic civilization: the permanent repudiation of anthropophagy.

THE RENUNCIATION OF CANNIBALISM

It seems clear that the symbolic meanings in the ritual of human sacrifice had to do with eating. Ritual homicide was renounced in archaic civilizations, and animal sacrifice put in its place. The central religious ritual of the ancient Greeks, Romans, Israelites, and Babylonians included the killing and, in almost all cases, the eating of an animal. In the *Agamemnon* of Aeschylus, the Chorus cries out against Agamemnon's having sacrificed his daughter instead of the usual animal, emphasizing the horror in such an act by describing the victim as "unholy, untasted."[48] *All* sacrifice has to do with eating. Even Christ's sacrifice we do not let pass without symbolically tasting of his flesh.

Many of the sacrificial victims in advanced complex societies were either war captives saved for that purpose, or dead enemy warriors whose corpses were brought to the temple for dedication to the war god. People who practiced cannibalism, in contrast, *ate* the bodies of dead enemies. When a Tahitian war commander brings the corpse of an enemy to the temple for dedication to the war god Oro, we say he is practicing human sacrifice, but what is it that he is giving up? The corpse has no value for him except as food to eat, and it is precisely the pleasure of eating human flesh that he is renouncing.

The god eats instead of men. The god eats in order that men may repudiate eating. When the great Hebrew moralists urged men to forswear vengeance, they did not seek to eliminate revenge from the world. Instead, they sought to have men renounce it in favor of the god. "Vengeance is mine," proclaimed Jehovah. Freud writes: "In the development of the ancient religions one seems to find that many things which mankind had renounced as wicked were surrendered in favor of the god, and were still permitted in his name; so that yielding up of evil and asocial impulses to the divinity was the means by which man freed himself from them."[49] Human sacrifice was one means by which humankind freed itself of cannibalism.

The sequence cannibalism–human sacrifice–animal sacrifice can also teach us something about when in the course of cultural development each particular ritual is abandoned. Human sacrifice, the means for re- nouncing cannibalism, is itself repudiated when there is no longer any real possibility of anthropophagy. People adopt animal sacrifice when they are sure that they can never regress into cannibalism, and people renounce animal sacrifice when it is clear that they have permanently given up human sacrifice.

It is difficult to see how the optimistic, moral-development view that humankind progressively abandons more primitive forms of satisfying aggression can be reconciled with the other insight that our democratic polity preserves the absolute necessity of human victims. In the presi- dential election of 1980, during the primary campaign, a leading candi- date for that powerful office began to boast publicly about the way to "win" an atomic war with the Soviet Union. If you asked such a man if he would buy a slave and slaughter him in order to assure electoral success, he would look at you as if you were insane, and yet he seemed willing to sacrifice more than half the people in the world for "victory," and only a few cried out that *he* was mad. We are both more and less than we seem. We are both more wonderful and more terrible than our conscious, rational minds are willing to admit. Having renounced human sacrifice, we continue to practice it in more subtle, more deeply hidden ways. Our humanity is circumscribed within this great contra- diction.

14

... *That Has Such People In't!*

Thickly falls the small rain on the face of the sea,
They are not drops of rain, but they are tears of Oro.[1]

People in complex societies took great delight in imposing a symbolic order upon the world through the use of number and the establishment of categories of existence. As with us, they had a need to ask, and a pleasure in answering, the questions "How big?" "How many?" In Hawaii and Tonga, people measured Cook's ship, some stretching their arms and determining how many lengths long and broad the ship was, others actually using a line to make the calculations.[2] The Baganda took pleasure in counting and, in the early days of their contact with Western culture, whenever they got a book into their hands the first thing they did was to count the pages. Their game of *mweso* depended upon a considerable capacity to calculate numbers.[3] Both Buganda and Polynesia had simple-to-use number systems that extended beyond the hundred thousands.

As we have seen, the Baganda loved giving names to hierarchical positions. The office of the first assistant to a provincial governor had a name, as did the second, the third, and the fourth. Even the wives of a polygamous husband had names that indicated their position: the first was *kaddulu-bale,* the second *kabeṇa,* and the third *nassaza.*[4] In this regard, as in so many other things, the Polynesian imaginative capacities tended more toward abstraction and less toward politics and hierarchy. The Hawaiians had divided space and named its divisions. That which we see directly over our head "when standing erect" was called *luna-ae; luna-aku* was the space above that; *luna-loa-aku* came next; then *luna-lilo-aku, luna-lilo-loa,* and the firmament where the clouds floated, which was called *luna-o-ke-oa;* above that were the three divisions of solid heaven, *ke-ao-ulu, ka-lani-ul,* and *ka-lani-paa.*[5]

In both cultures there was a highly sophisticated system for the determination of day, month, year. The moon determined the month; each month of the year was named, and each day of the month had its designation, usually related to the phases of the moon.[6] In Polynesia, it was recognized that the lunar year did not correspond with the actual year, which was determined by the annual reappearance of certain constellations. The Polynesians began each year with the rising of the Pleiades at sunset, about November 20. In Hawaii, this marked the beginning of the first month, Makalii.

Twelve lunar months are always less than a year. This discrepancy between the lunar and the actual year was dealt with by many ancient peoples by adding a thirteenth month every three years or so. Exactly how this was done in Hawaii and Tahiti is not known to us, but the Polynesian people of Manihiki in the Cook Islands had a cycle of nineteen years, in which a thirteenth lunar month was added in years three, five, eight, eleven, thirteen, sixteen, and nineteen.[7]

It begins to appear that some of the scientific information that was available to archaic civilizations such as Egypt and Babylonia was not necessarily discovered by these societies and could have been an inheritance from the advanced complex stage. Our historiography has assumed that early-dynasty Egyptians or Sumerians invented the calendar, because it is in those societies that we first observe it. However, since ancient Polynesians and Baganda invented a reasonably accurate calendar, it is a fair assumption that the cultures that preceded dynastic Egypt and the great city-state of Babylonia could have done the same.

Those of us who still hold in awe the capacity of human beings to create a written language tend to be incredulous that complex societies could have accomplished what they did without that particular advantage. Why the beginnings of writing have been equated with the beginnings of "civilization," why the invention of writing has become the great divide whereas the invention of science, law, the state, medicine, and epic poetry are not, is an important area of study, but it is not the question here. There must be something in the relationship of human beings to writing and reading that has caused us, when thinking about historical development, to attribute godlike qualities to these skills.

The overemphasis on the importance of writing does not take into account the capacities of oral communication or, for example, the ingenuity of tax collectors the world over. A tremendous amount of information can be passed from one generation to another through oral traditions. Nonliterate societies, as we have seen, have schools, teachers, students, curricula, graduation exercises, and specialists in various areas of learning.

Tax collecting requires the storing of great quantities of information, difficult without writing. It is clear from the first deciphered Linear B tablets from Greece and the earliest Sumerian records that receiving taxes and giving receipts for same was the first great spur toward writing. On the island of Kauai in Hawaii, tax information was kept principally by one man on a line of cordage about twenty-five hundred feet long. Each district had its place on the cord, and each individual taxpayer was indicated. "Knots, loops, and tufts, of different shapes, sizes, and colours" were used to discriminate between districts and individuals, as well as to indicate the manner in which the tax was paid, whether in hogs, dogs, sandalwood, taro, or whatever.[8]

In Buganda people used a system of tied knots on plantain fiber to enable them to remember the days of the month.[9] The collection of taxes in that country was preceded by a census of each subdistrict, in which one cowry shell was brought to the tax collector for each house. After the households had been counted, and the total tax to be collected calculated, the tax officials went back to make the actual collection.[10] Although the Baganda still traded and paid taxes by means of goods, they had succeeded in adapting from others an adequate, stable form of money. Cowry shells were the medium of exchange, and the Baganda were capable of calculating the price of a cow or a slave or a hoe in terms of the number of cowry shells, which circulated as money.[11]

Observation of the heavens led to the development of astronomy. We know, for instance, that the Hawaiians were readily capable of distinguishing between the planets and the fixed stars.[12] They used this knowledge in, among other things, the practice of astrology, that lesser twin of astronomy. The art of divination, through a multitude of means, was as pervasive in advanced complex societies as it was in archaic civilizations. For the Hawaiians the relationship of the planets to the fixed stars gave indication of the success of a new enterprise or the fate of a battle, and could even presage the death of a high official.[13]

Polynesian navigators knew that the fixed stars rose from a certain point on the eastern horizon, followed a set pattern through the sky, set at a definite point in the western horizon, and would do exactly the same thing the next night. The course of the stars through the sky, bounded by the rising and setting places, was called the star's *rua,* or pit. Navigators knew what stars belonged to each specific pit, knew the courses of many stars, and could name at least 150 stars individually.[14] Polynesians knew that the moon affected the tides and predicted the state of the tide by observing the moon.[15]

One of the first books published in the Hawaiian language in the early nineteenth century contained a few pages on the basics of astronomy, including the notion that the earth was spherical. Some seriously objected, but the astrologer Hoapili remarked: "Stop; do not be so quick with your objections to the foreign theory. Let us look at it. This is what I have always seen. When I have been far out to sea on fishing excursions, I first lost sight of the beach, then of the houses and trees, then of the hills, and last of the high mountains. So when I returned, the first objects which I saw were the high mountains, then the hills, then the trees and houses, and last of all the beach. I think therefore that these foreigners are right, and that the earth is round."[16]

Observation of the order that prevails in the universe is not only of astronomical, scientific, practical value; the regularity, the certainty, of the ebb and flow of the year is the basis of one of the world's great metaphors. Those people who have lived their lives most closely with metaphor—priests and poets—have been enormously responsive to the time for sowing and the time for reaping, to predictable order. Order is a defense against chaos and panic; no people will take any developmental step forward unless they have learned new ways to defend themselves against disorder and anxiety. On the first night of the first month of the new year, which was always the first night of the new moon, the king in the Hawaiian Islands placed a signal in front of the temple to indicate that the old year had passed. In the evening, outside the temple, the celebration of the new year took place. The people were arranged in two rows; a priest stood up with a branch of *ieie* fern in his hands: " 'My brothers, it is well; we are safe.' " Then all stood up, "from front to rear, with loud rejoicings."[17]

A Tahitian Creation Myth

All was darkness, it was continuous, thick darkness. Rumia (upset) was the name of that shell of Ta'aroa.

Ta'aroa was quite alone in his shell. He had no father, no mother, no elder brother, no sister. There were no people, no beasts, no birds, no dogs. But there was Ta'aroa, and he alone.

There was sky space, there was land space, there was ocean space, there was fresh-water space.

But at last Ta'aroa gave his shell a fillip which caused a crack resembling an opening of ants. Then he slipped out and stood upon his shell, and he looked upon his shell, and he looked and found that he was alone. There was no sound, all was darkness outside.

And he shouted, "Who is above there, oh?" No voice. "Who is below there, oh?" No voice! "Who is in front there, oh?" No voice. "Who is in back there, oh?" No voice! There was the echo of his own voice, and that was all.

And Ta'aroa exclaimed, "Oh, space for skies, oh, space for hosts, oh space for land, extending high above and far below!" Then he swam in the space without land. He swam up, far up, and down, far down; and then he returned to Tumu-iti (Little-foundation) in Fa'a-iti (Little-valley) within his shell, and he dwelt there in close confinement and thick darkness.

At length, Ta'aroa got wearied of that shell, and so he slipped out of a new one, and stood outside upon the old shell [which was named] *Rumia.*

And he took his new shell for the great foundation of the world, for stratum rock and for soil for the world. And the shell, Rumia, that he opened first, became his house, the dome of the gods' sky, which was a confined sky, enclosing the world then forming.

Then Ta'aroa dwelt in the confined sky in total darkness, and did not know of light outside, and thus he became a lad. But these were the persons within himself, memory, thought, steadfast-gaze, and observation; these persons knew the land. Who gave this boy his name, Ta-aroa? He named himself, Ta'aroa.

He grew and became matured; but how great was Ta'aroa! What gods were all the others? They were only minor, dependent gods!

By Ta'aroa all things existed. The storm, the rain, the sea, were in the hollow of his hand.

Ta'aroa made the great foundation of the earth to be the husband, and the stratum rock to be the wife; Haruru-papa (Rock-resounder) was the name of that foundation, and he put his spirit into it, which was the essence of himself, and named it Ta'aroa-nui-tumu-tahi (Great-unique-foundation). Ta'aroa hailed Tumu-nui (Great-foundation) as king, but Tumu-iti hailed him as king without land.

And Ta'aroa said: "Oh, Tumu-nui, crawl hither as a husband, to espouse this wife Papa-raharaha (Stratum-rock). Tumu-nui had an audi-

*ble voice as he answered, "I will not crawl thither, I am the foundation
of the world."*

*Then Ta'aroa said: "O, Papa-ra-ha-raha, crawl hither to espouse this
husband, Tumu-nui." The rock had a real voice as it answered, "I will
not crawl thither. I am the stratum rock for the earth." The one did not
go nor did the other go.*

*Ta'aroa dwelt on for ages within the close sky [named] Rumia; he
conjured forth gods, and they were born to him in darkness. For this
reason the sky was called the sky of gods.*

*When Ta'aroa stood within and turned his face to call to darkness,
it was to create gods. It was much later that man was made. Tû was
with Ta'aroa when he made man.*[18]

Although the practice of medicine in complex societies cannot be described as "science," such practice went far beyond magic and mere
practical remedy. What did exist was a medical mode of thought, a confidence that doctoring could be of value, and a desire to base it on evidence rather than magical wish fulfillment. Medicine was thus on the
way to becoming science.

On the practical side, people in both Buganda and Polynesia were
capable of resetting bones that had been broken, even including compound fractures. Ellis reports (we have no way of checking the accuracy
of the statement) that in the Society Islands successful trepanning operations were conducted on people whose skulls were damaged in battle,
using a coconut shell to replace fractured bones in the skull. "It is reported that there are persons living on the island of Borabora on whom
it has been performed. . . ."[19] Such an operation would not have been
impossible, for we have reports from both cultures of the capacity to
stitch wounds together to enable them to heal.

In Hawaii, the field of symptomatology and the classification of
diseases were highly developed. Legendary material tells of two great
doctors, father and son, who began the practice of cutting open the
body of a person after death to determine what disease he had died from.
The father, Puheke, had instructed his son, Palaha, to do exactly that
after Puheke's death. Palaha became a famous person in the priestly-
doctoring order of the *kahuna kapa'au.*[20]

The treatment of disease was taught in Hawaii by means of the
"table of pebbles." Hundreds of pebbles were arranged on the ground
in the shape of a man. The pupils sat around this figure while the

teacher, beginning at the feet and working slowly up to the head, taught them the name—and the treatment—of almost a thousand diseases that could afflict the body. Some of these "diseases" were merely descriptions of symptoms: "a ridge . . . a lump . . . an immovable ridge . . . severe cramps . . . cloudy secretions. . . ." We should not forget, however, that until the seventeenth century, most of what passed as medicine in Europe consisted of the description and haphazard treatment of recognizable symptoms. Hawaiian medical instruction went beyond the use of the pebble table: "Then the teacher would bring in a man who had many disorders and would call the people one by one to go and 'feel,' *haha,* for the diseases. If the diagnosis *(ike haha)* was the same as that of the teacher, then the teacher knew that the pupil had knowledge of the *haha.*"[21]

It is comforting to learn that the sharp ambivalence about doctors that people feel in our culture already existed in complex society. Doctors, it seems, have *always* made too much money. Some felt that medical practitioners were in need of defense: "Some of them, perhaps, did seek wealth by deceiving and lying, but there were others who did not—they really did have medical knowledge and they did heal many people."[22]

The great psychological benefit that people derive from science is a sense of control, even if the control is not actual. Doctors are valuable, not only because they contain disease and preserve life, but also because they give people the feeling that someone can do something about a threatening situation. Faced with helplessness or panic, the healthy reaction is action. People confronting a truly hopeless medical situation will resort to false medicines or practitioners and feel better because they are actively meeting the threat, although their rational minds may know that nothing will help. That our science and technology give us a sense of control can easily be observed in the panic that results when technology fails. A temporary power breakdown, for instance, always produces an immediate irrational sense of tremendous danger, totally out of proportion to the real consequences. Science does not develop automatically; people, or a society, must desire control before science can arise.

What struck the first visitors to Buganda and Polynesia, and what strikes one today when reading their reports, is the pleasure that the Baganda and the Polynesians took in areas where they had created a sense of control, whether politics, technology, games, or art. Art is as much about order as is science, and the peoples of complex societies used art for pleasure and for the pleasure of control. We do the same; a joke or a humorous cartoon about some frightening aspect of the world political situation temporarily makes us feel better. Nothing will have changed to lessen the threat of war or economic depression or political chaos, but the joke will provide at least a temporary sense of dominating the situation.

Lacking newspapers and magazines, complex cultures used the mechanism of the topical song to comment upon the latest news, or the latest threat. Syphilis came to Buganda in the reign of Kabaka Mawanda. In wars waged against neighboring tribes, some women who had the disease were captured and quickly gave it to their captors. When the king observed that the hands of his warriors were turning white, he inquired as to the cause and was told that the new disease was the agent. He then ordered his musicians to play this song:

> *Why is it that syphilis whitens hands?*
> *Syphilis whitens hands because of its cruelty.*
> *Syphilis whitens hands because of its fierceness.*[23]

Under the rule of Kabaka Kamanya, the neighboring country of Busoga was invaded, bringing about a disastrous famine in which many died and people ate foods they would ordinarily avoid. The king's trumpeters composed a song on their return to Buganda:

> *When trees were eaten, here we come*
> *You may disregard anything but hunger.*[24]

When Mutesa built the new city of Banda, he seized and killed many of his subjects as a sacrifice. Afterward, people would comment about a man who had been killed: "I warned so-and-so not to go out on the street but he would pay no heed." The king, on hearing the comments, enjoying the fear he had inspired, ordered his musicians to sing this new song:

> *I warned you but you paid no heed*
> *Now the lion [Mutesa] has devoured you.*[25]

In Hawaii and Tahiti, topical songs were no less in evidence. In the 1820s on Tahiti, two people were disputing whether Captain Bligh had lost the buoy of his anchor when he had harbored in the bay of Papara

almost forty years before. The argument went on for some time with
no resolution until the disputant who had stated the affirmative remembered the ballad that confirmed his position:

> *Such an one a thief, and Tareu a thief,*
> *Thieved . . . the buoy of Bligh.*[26]

The seemingly limitless imaginative energy penetrated deeply into the
area of sport. In Polynesia, almost all the great religious festivals that
were island-wide or district-wide, like the Makahiki harvest celebration
on the island of Hawaii, included boxing or wrestling matches as an
integral part of the festival.[27] One sport popular at the Makahiki was
the *holua,* or sledding downhill. A long course was laid out on a steep
incline; first rocks, then earth was laid and beaten hard, and finally a
layer of slippery grass to enable the sled to slide with ease.[28] Such was
the speed and the danger that the thrill was like surfing on land. Since
the nature of the trails limited the number of participants, the sport was
primarily engaged in by aristocrats, but the crowds of spectators and
the gambling on the winners were all very democratic.

In the great wrestling matches on the Society Islands, five thousand
people would gather at a space covered with grassy turf or on a wide
expanse of beach. Everyone dressed in the brightest costume he or she
could muster. The air was laden with color and excitement. After a fall,
for instance: "One party were drumming, dancing, and singing, in the
pride of victory, and the manner of defiance; while, to increase the din
and confusion, the other party were equally vociferous in reciting the
achievements of the vanquished, or predicting the shortness of his rival's
triumph."[29]

The wrestlers of one district would challenge those of another, and
the whole population of a kingdom would gather to see the result. Even
grander matches took place between wrestlers of different islands. This
entailed an elaborate visit by sea of the king, his court, his wrestlers,
and as much of the population as could get transportation.

The proceedings took place under the aegis of the gods, and we are
reminded of the Olympic and other games in ancient Greece when we
read the description of how the athletes repaired to the temple before
the match, presented an offering, and asked for victory.

When, as often happened, famous wrestlers represented both sides,
challenges would be made beforehand and individual matches arranged.
Otherwise, six to ten wrestlers from each side would enter a ring about

thirty feet in diameter, each wearing nothing but a loin covering, some with their arms and legs oiled. The challenge was given by violently striking the left hand, which was cupped over the side of the body, with the right hand. As the left hand hit the body, a loud hollow sound resounded in the air. The challenge accepted, the parties engaged. Sometimes only two wrestled while the others watched; at other times, several pairs struggled simultaneously.

While the match was on, the spectators were deathly still. As soon as a victory was scored, there was a shout of exaltation, the drums began to speak, and the women on the victor's side rose and danced in triumph over the fallen wrestler. His side, in turn, let forth the loudest noise it could muster in order to dampen the triumph of its rival. Victory consisted simply in throwing one's opponent, and any means was legitimate. Ellis was acquainted with Mape, a famous wrestler who was strong but not very large and found himself once in the ring with an unusually tall man. They grappled and separated. Mape clearly understood that the usual tactics could not prevail and therefore walked casually up to his opponent, who extended his arms in order to engage again, lowering his head in the process because Mape was significantly shorter than he. Mape ran at the surprised wrestler, using the crown of his own head to ram the unsuspecting forehead of his opponent, and "laid him flat on the earth."

People of the highest rank engaged in the wrestling matches. Women also wrestled, many times against men: "The sister of the queen has been seen wearing nearly the same clothing as the wrestlers wore, covered all over with sand, and wrestling with a young chief, in the midst of a ring, around which thousands of the people were assembled."

When the great matches were over, the wrestlers returned to the temples and made offerings of young plantain trees. Ritual provided the order that bounded the excitement of the day and allowed aggression to be expressed within limits. With the help of the gods, people returned to ordinary life.

Ordinary life was for ordinary people. For some, the most important thing was to live a life that was in no way common. The whole notion of aristocracy is distasteful to most Americans today, so that it is difficult to consider that, at some point in the development of society, the concept of living an aristocratic life may have been a progressive force. The aristocratic life has a double thrust: it is exalted, allowing human beings to realize new ideals of behavior, but it is exclusive—only a few can live it. Balzac says, "The noble of every age has done his best to invent a life which he, and he only, can live."[30] To exclude most people from the best life is an act of tyranny, but to invent such a life is an act of imagination.

In primitive society, there was no aristocracy. The invention of a noble life—and the exclusion of most people from it—belongs to complex societies. As this book proceeds, I shall try to answer the question of *why* people would invent an aristocracy and the aristocratic life, but we will not get even close to the answer unless we first see that there was something liberating in such symbolic behavior. It is necessary to remember that the effete nobles at the court of Louis XIV or the snobs of the British aristocracy inherited the institution when it was already old, and to recall what living by aristocratic ideals—courtesy, respect for strangers, the perfection of the body in sport, valid notions of honor, a real concern for music and poetry, the sense that every noble participated in a heroic life—meant to someone like Odysseus when the world was new.

One of the best descriptions we have of the aristocratic life in advanced complex society comes from Rwanda, whose ruling class, Tutsi, were physically taller and lighter-skinned than the commoners they ruled. That they represented a conquering people who had moved into the country at some time in the past is probable but not yet proved. The Tutsi ruled with a tyrannical hand.

All young Tutsi were instructed in the traditional sports and those dances that were considered becoming to a nobleman. There was a very complicated training in the composition of poetry and intense competition among nobles for the approval of their poetic efforts. All were expected to be able to carry on witty and eloquent conversation. The techniques of warfare and military courage were an essential part of the curriculum.

Tutsi youth were constantly being reminded of the aristocratic ideal toward which they must strive. That ideal had three main components. *Ubutware* was military courage, the willingness to risk one's life in the defense of aristocracy and its privileges. *Ubugabo* referred to the qualities of manliness: trustworthiness, generosity toward friends, charity toward the poor, fidelity in all personal relationships, and the willingness to accept all one's responsibilities. *Itonde* meant self-mastery: "The demeanor of a Tutsi was always to be dignified, polite, amiable, and a little supercilious."[31] Any intense expression of emotion, especially of anger, was strictly forbidden. Cato the Elder or Scipio Africanus would have been perfectly at home in Tutsi society; indeed, one can see how little the ideals of aristocracy have changed through the ages, probably because the goals of the aristocratic life have scarcely varied from one society to another.

Tutsi were organized into companies for military purposes, in which the training in self-control was intense. People were jeered at and provoked in a hundred ways in the attempt to make them display anger, until they learned to remain quiet and polite no matter what the occasion.[32]

Status that is determined by class is always based on genealogy: one's ancestors define one's position. Genealogy is only one element in that much broader symbolic ordering of the world that is a sense of history. The development of a sense of history in advanced complex societies was remarkable.

Every society that we know about has a symbolic relationship to the past. There is no society that does not retain a memory of ancestors, forebears, or those who went before and invented certain customs or artifacts, whether mythical or not. There seems to be a universal human need to answer the question: Where do we come from? A sense of history differs from this general sense of the past because it takes as its goal the elimination of all mythical and legendary material. People have been in no hurry to do this, and it has developed very gradually; Herodotus, "the father of history," still has many unbelievable stories to tell us.

In ancient Buganda, a sense of history began to dominate the sense of the past before any contact with more developed cultures. Oral tradition preserved the memory of the usual legendary material, but it also told in what king's reign certain provinces had been annexed to Buganda, when particular governorships had been wrested from clan control by the *kabaka* and put under his appointive aegis, when particular offices had been created and why certain of them belonged to certain clans, when particular customs had been established by edict of the sovereign.[33] The past lived in people's lives. The head of any clan, and of each division and subdivision of the clan, took the title the first holder of that office had owned. "The holder of the office spoke of past events as though he had been present and had taken part in them, and to such an extent identified himself with the original holder of the office that he would speak of himself as the leader of an expedition which had taken place a hundred years previously, or as the father of persons who had been long dead."[34]

Mutesa, oral tradition said, was the thirtieth *kabaka* of Buganda.

This would indicate the establishment of the country three to five hundred years previous to his accession. The tomb of every king from the founder, Kintu, to Mutesa was preserved until the middle of this century, and they may still be in place. When Roland Oliver paid a visit to the tombs in June 1958, he was startled to discover how completely the memory of the *kabakas* was preserved in people's minds. Between Kakiri and Kiziba, he stopped to ask directions to the turn-off for Dambwe and was asked if he was going to see the place of Kigala[35]—Kigala being the fifth *kabaka,* who had lived sometime around 1500. The tombs were watched by one or two guardians; the people of the surrounding countryside made the necessary repairs to keep them in order. One must admire the staying power of such a society.

It is a corollary of Santayana's dictum that "those who cannot remember the past are condemned to repeat it" that he who *can* remember the past has more control over his present and his future. Neither Hawaii nor Buganda suffered the usual postcontact fate of "primitive" peoples. This had nothing to do with better policies on the part of the conquering imperialist nations but resulted from the power and flexibility already present in these societies. Kamehameha, united Hawaii's first king, created a dynasty of rulers that lasted over fifty years, and the unity of the country was never dissolved. A hundred years after Cook, the islands were still independent; the eventual submission to United States authority subjected the individual Hawaiian to capitalist much more than to imperialist exploitation. In the twentieth century, Hawaiians lived in a twentieth-century world.

The Baganda were not so fortunate. Shortly after they were "discovered," the European powers, especially England, Belgium, and Germany, entered into their most intense period of imperialist competition. Africa was one of the main areas of contention. At first there were some German attempts to counter British influence in Buganda, but a subsequent European agreement left Buganda to the British, and they promptly ate the country and all the surrounding countries. Buganda's chance for independent development was lost when the English created the Uganda Protectorate, which included many surrounding kingdoms, chieftainships, and tribal societies as well as Buganda. For years, the Baganda enjoyed a predominance in the protectorate as a result of their advanced culture, but when tragedy and cultural dissolution struck the enlarged country in 1971, the Baganda were completely tied to its fate and no longer had any way of pursuing an independent course.

   The response of countries in earlier stages of development to the modern capitalist-democratic-technological, rapidly changing society of the West is one of the great themes of twentieth-century history. Japan, China, and Russia are as much a part of that story as Ghana, Indonesia, Brazil, and Iran. The initial response of Buganda and Polynesia to the modern world was remarkably assertive; the presence of centralized kingships was crucial. When Kamehameha learned of the great profits to be made from the sale of sandalwood, plentiful on Hawaii, to merchants in China, he was not content merely to lumber it and sell it to foreign captains. He fitted out a ship under a Hawaiian flag and sent a cargo of wood to Canton for his own profit.[36] Nor was Mutesa passively willing to let others come to him. He undertook several trading expeditions to Zanzibar, and the Baganda became great traders. "Whenever prospects of trade open up, the Buganda [*sic*] will go," a missionary wrote home in 1906.[37]

   Mutesa's son and successor, Mwanga, was defeated for the last time in 1897 and deposed from office; his one-year-old son was proclaimed king. In effect, there was no longer a *kabaka,* but the political stability held. A whole new generation of politically effective people, trained by Christians and Muslims, and tempered in the wars of religion, had come to a ripeness that was rare in any "underdeveloped" country. For sixty years this oligarchy ruled the country—under British control. "Administrative officers of experience in this Protectorate are agreed," wrote a senior official in 1907, "that the best method of developing the country is through the native governments, and that these governments should be upheld and established in every possible way...."[38] And to a large extent it was done; the Buganda politicians proved adequate to the task.

   Three years after Mwanga was deposed, the British proclaimed a new land settlement. "At one stroke all the tenures based either upon the claims of heads of clans to control clan lands, or of the Kabaka to distribute land to whomsoever he wished ... were ... swept away. In their place there now appeared the so-called *mailo* tenure; and it did not take the oligarchies very long to seize the opportunity which the Agreement presented to them of parcelling out all the land which was at their disposal ... to their own immediate followers.... Since, moreover, land could henceforth be freely bought, sold and bequeathed in Buganda it soon began to pass into the hands of an increasing number of independent farmers."[39] Buganda became a country of small and large farmsteads owned by *Africans,* unlike neighboring Kenya, where

British settlers dominated the land and paid in violence when the situation became intolerable. The Baganda remained more in control of their own lives than practically any other native people in Africa.

Christianity, political sophistication, capitalist enterprise—in fifty years the Baganda had come as far into the modern world as any previously nonliterate society had ever come in so short a time. Despite their great capacity for assertiveness, the modern world was to cheat them of their expectations; in this regard, however, the Baganda were not alone.

15

Of Drums, of Cruelty, and Pissing on the King

Nobody really understands the relationship between the control of excretory functions and the advance of civilization. Some psychoanalytic writers, such as Karl Abraham[1] and Otto Fenichel,[2] give us tantalizing hints, most of which consist of asserting, either implicitly or explicitly, that there *is* such a connection. Deeper than that, no one seems to go. The privy, just like the state or voluntary associations or the theatre, did not always exist—it is obviously a human invention. But what kind of invention? Some would argue that it is the beginning of repression and has brought us nothing but evil. Others may see in it the very foundation on which humankind has erected double-entry bookkeeping, the banking system, rational bureaucracy, a legal system, the ethos of capitalism, and the demise of slavery.

It makes no sense to deny the connection between excretory functions and cruelty. Tiled bathrooms or no, we still "treat people like shit," describe certain war activities as "mopping-up" or "cleaning-up" operations (killing the survivors is the true function), humiliate people (symbolically) by making them eat shit, and describe lower-class people in terms of filth: riffraff, rubbish, garbage.

The tenth of February passed. The sun hastened towards the west—a blow was struck on the grand drum, deep and solemn.

In a moment songs ceased, all sounds were hushed, the market was empty; every one went to his own habitation; the roads were deserted and for three long days silence and stillness reigned around. Only the slow dismal ring of blows struck at interval on the great drum told they

> *were fulfilling the mysterious rites of the* mpango, *which caused the miserable inhabitants to shudder with fear.*
>
> *It is a popular belief that the* nuggare [the great drum] *sounds without being beaten whenever the angry spirit of Kamrasi wishes to be appeased by human victims.*
>
> *The period of the mysterious rites was passed; the sun approached the end of his journey; the great* nuggare *gave forth its deepest sounds; cries of terror mixed with reverence echoed everywhere, and spread from village to village, following one another like the waves of the sea; the miserable passers-by, the peaceful husbandmen, were seized, bound with cords, and their throats cut, as a holocaust to the Great Father.*
>
> *In Juaya ten unhappy creatures paid tribute with their blood to this superstition.*[3]

Cruelty is the great excretory vice, control the great excretory virtue. The relationship between cruelty, control, and society is the fundamental question raised here. No answers will be found in this discussion; it is to be hoped that there will be a helpful sharpening of the questions. In ancient times, when the world was younger than it is today, people were less inhibited about giving expression to certain connections that we have ceased to recognize. A society in which certain people urinated and defecated on the king as part of the coronation ceremonies is certainly worth looking at in the attempt to understand the intricate connection between culture and the bowels.

In many literatures of "the heroic age" we are presented with a great archetypal scene of confrontation between a king or ruler and a prophet. As developed to its highest point in the Old Testament and in Greek tragedy, it symbolizes a cosmic conflict between raw, real-world, political power and transcendant notions of justice and morality. The great confrontation between Oedipus and Tiresias in *Oedipus the King* is one ultimate development of a theme that began, it seems, in the literature of advanced complex societies. From Buganda we have such a story, but the subject of the confrontation may startle us.

In the reign of King Suna, the father of Mutesa, we are told, the *kabaka* appointed Lumwemo Nakirindisa to levy taxes in one province. When the task was completed, Lumwemo's men informed him there was a very famous prophet named Kigemuzi in the district. Lumwemo sent a subordinate to seek from the prophet an oracle concerning the outcome of the tax collecting. The sage unreluctantly gave a thorough response: "Your master Lumwemo will make an excellent report of his tax-collecting campaign. But do tell him that, on his return to the capital, he should [say to the] King 'Why did you prevent your people from excreting in the capital and why did you execute others for allegedly violating the so-called sanitary laws? Where do you yourself excrete?' "[4] Kigemuzi the prophet, the champion of freedom, further added that unless the king permitted the people to excrete freely in the capital, disaster would overcome him.

Immediately on receiving report of the prophet's threats, Lumwemo resorted to the *muwemba,* a highly placed subordinate of the king, who called the seer into his presence and inquired, "Was it you who uttered these words?" "It was I," responded the prophet, as such prophets have responded in thousands of stories. The *muwemba* arrested Kigemuzi and handed him over to Lumwemo for deportation to the capital.

After proceeding directly to the *katikiro,* the prime minister, Lumwemo made report of his successful tax campaign and then acquainted the *katikiro* with the problem presented by Kigemuzi the seer. Wanting to hear for himself, the prime minister questioned the prophet, who, in the tradition of prophets, loved to reiterate his pronouncements: "Why does the king execute people for excreting in the capital? Where does he excrete himself?"

Fuming with rage, the *katikiro* took the prisoner to the king. "Give the same oracle as the one you gave to Lumwemo," demanded the *kabaka.* This time Kigemuzi refused, stating that he would continue silent as long as he remained a prisoner. The *kabaka* was furious. He ordered one of his soldiers to stitch up the lips of the prophet. Kigemuzi replied that as his lips were stitched, so "yours will also be stitched."

At this point Kigemuzi was struck by one of the outraged courtiers (the man who did it was the grandfather of Apolo Kagwa, who is the teller of the story and was the first Christian *katikiro* of Buganda). "You will also be struck," threatened the prophet.

The soldier stitched the prophet's lips, branded his whole body with a red-hot iron, and took him off to prison to await execution in the morning.

But King Suna was to suffer as King Pentheus suffered when he tried to keep the god Bacchus in jail. A torrential rain filled the night with more thunder and lightning than anyone could remember. The *kabaka* himself was seared by lightning on his leg, shoulder, and cheek. When the storm abated, the *katikiro* released Kigemuzi from the stocks, took the stitches from his mouth, and brought him into the presence of the king.

"Did I not warn you that you would also be burnt? But to strike a child is not to kill it, you will recover soon."

The story as we have it ends with an anticlimax. Kigemuzi advises the *kabaka* to leave his capital and establish a new one at another place. Kigemuzi goes home and, four days later, King Suna does as the prophet has suggested. The tale ends without telling us what the shitting arrangements were in the new capital city.

A strange story, and yet . . . The last and most complete of the Dead Sea Scrolls banned toilets anywhere in the capital city of Jerusalem and forbade anyone, anywhere, to defecate on the Sabbath. Control of instinctual behavior was an important virtue for our Hebrew ancestors. The same scroll announces that anyone who lived in the "shadow of the temple in a permanent state of holiness must be leading a single life." All sexual relations were forbidden in Jerusalem.[5] If control is the great excretory virtue, for the Hebrews that particular virtue had become a vice.

The story of Kabaka Suna and Kigemuzi seems to be a garbled version of something important that was really going on during Suna's reign. Oral tradition does tell us that during that *kabaka*'s term of office people were forbidden to walk naked in a public place and severe penalties were inflicted on anyone caught promenading without a barkcloth covering on the body. Some Baganda continued to discard their clothes when inside their own houses, but public modesty was enforced.

We also know that the Baganda had privies at the time of Speke's arrival, in Mutesa's reign, although we don't know when the custom originated. Such an invention was unique to the Baganda; their neighbors, even those as politically advanced as the Banyoro, did not avail themselves of like sanitary arrangements. The privy may have been invented during Suna's reign; or possibly it had existed before but its use had been confined to the royal enclosures or the capital city, and it was Suna who insisted on the extension of its use throughout the whole country. It is a reasonable presumption that the prohibition on nudity, for instance, was first applied in the king's presence, then spread to the capital city, and ultimately was extended to the whole country.

If Kabaka Suna issued a decree that everyone should build a privy, the tax collectors who roamed the country would be the natural enforcers of the order. We can assume resistance from those in the provinces to the change of ancient practice. Knowing the manner in which the society worked, Suna would probably claim some religious sanction for his decree; he might insist that a god or his father's ghost came to him in a dream commanding that it be done, as indeed may have happened.

The story as we have it may be a garbled version of what was a real conflict between old religious notions of freedom to defecate anywhere, as represented in the person of Kigemuzi, and the new purity and control demanded by that ancient Calvin, Kabaka Suna.

The war drum played an important role in the old wars, and was given the rank of a high personage, and the whole expedition was known ever after by the name of the great war-drum used on the occasion.[6]

The myths and legends of Polynesia—more so than those of Buganda—are full of stories that relate the importance of excretory functions. The great Hawaiian warrior Lupeakawaiowainiha not only had a war club that required 120 men to carry it, but he also flooded the land every time he urinated.[7] A legend in regard to King Kanaloa-Kuaana tells us that he was a weak and poor king, and that since his old priests and aged counselors were without *awa* (the Hawaiian intoxicating beverage) to drink or rich foods to feast upon, and had to make do with water, their urine was clear. Distressed by their humiliating position and angered with the king who was responsible, they went into his presence and urinated as proof of their poverty. "What must I do?" asked Kanaloa-Kuaana, who could not deny the truth of the situation. "Make war on Umi-o-ka-lani and take the whole kingdom to yourself." And so he did, conquering the districts of Kona and Kohala on Hawaii, proving his manliness, putting color in the urine of his priests and counselors, and in the process making the same connection between strong urine and courage as we do in, say, describing a person of excessive energy as full of piss and vinegar.[8]

"So long as Bagyendanwa [the great, sacred drum] *remains in Ankole,"* the people say, *"so long will the country and the people prosper."* The *Banyankole do not think of* Bagyendanwa *as a symbol of abstract unity, but as a concrete power capable of helping men in need.* "Bagyendanwa is like Mugabe [the king], only greater. Ankole is the land of Bagyendanwa *and we are the people of* Bagyendanwa. The Mugabe is his servant," *is the way in which a Munyankole describes the power of the drum over the king and the people.*[9]

We are familiar with the fairy-tale theme in which the hero befriends some person in distress who then, out of gratitude, supplies the hero with the magic words or required answers that secure the quest or defeat the forces of evil. A Hawaiian version concerns the island of Kauai, the hero Kepakailiula, and a wicked king who was used to engaging traveling heroes in riddle contests and executing them when they failed to solve his riddles. This king had a servant called Kukaea, whose only food and drink were the feces and urine of the king. While traveling on an errand for the monarch, Kukaea was purified and fed real food by Kepakailiula.

"What should I give you as payment for your kindness? Here I have lived from my birth to this day with my king and have just completed the circuit of Kauai, but no one has ever given me food to eat. . . . I will give you the answer to the king's riddle, for I am the only person that knows the answer. The riddle is this. . . .

> Plaited all around
> Plaited to the bottom
> Leaving an opening.
>
> The men that stand
> The men that lie down
> The men that are folded.

"The answer to the first part is 'house.' The house is plaited all around and from top to bottom and an opening is left, the door. The answer to the second half is also 'house.' The sticks are made to stand, battens are laid down, and the grass and cords are folded."[10]

The end of the story is easily guessed at: Kepakailiula answers the king's riddles, executes the sovereign, and reigns in his stead.

It is not mere coincidence that a shit eater knows the answers to riddles. For ancient Tahitians and Hawaiians, the process that we describe as thinking took place not in the head but in the bowels. Cook was the first outsider to make note of this, and he very correctly made reference to biblical language in order to comprehend it: "They have one expression, that corresponds exactly with the phraseology of the Scriptures, where we read of the 'yearnings of the bowels.' They use it on all occasions, when the passions give them uneasiness; as they constantly refer pain from grief, anxious desire, and other affections, to the bowels, as its seat; where they likewise suppose all operations of the mind are performed."[11]

In our culture, we make a split between thinking and feeling. We not only *know* that thinking takes place in the head but can also *feel* it going on there. As for emotions—fear, love, excitement, hatred—we *know* that we experience these also in the head, but we *feel* them as much in our bodies. In everyday speech, we continue to use metaphors to describe emotions as taking place in the body—in the heart, the gut, and, in matters of great intensity, even in the bones.

Ours is an age that represses memory of the stage in psychic development when excretory functions dominated psychic life, what psychoanalysis calls the anal stage. When Piaget, the great explicator of the steps by which children in our culture learn to understand the world, asked the youngest children where they thought thinking was done, a vast majority answered "with the mouth." This is exactly what one could have predicted on the basis of the psychoanalytic theory of the stages of libidinal development.*

Piaget, however, found no stage at which children ascribed thinking to the bowels or the stomach. "The second stage is marked by adult influences. The child has learnt that we think with the head. . . ."[13] Yet we know, from the evidence of advanced complex societies, that bowel thinking was a definite period in the development of culture. Our commitment to reason has made us forget what our intestines knew; only recently has our language described the sense of really knowing something as a "gut feeling."

Reverend Ellis observed that, for the Tahitians, "thoughts were in the body, and not in the brain; stating, in proof of the accuracy of their opinion, that the bowels or stomach were affected or agitated by desire, fear, joy, sorrow, surprise, and all strong affections or exercises of the mind."[14]

Vancouver failed in his efforts to argue the Tahitians out of these notions concerning body thinking: "I have frequently held conversations on this subject, with a view to convince them, that all intellectual operations were carried on in the head; at which they would generally smile, and intimate, that they had frequently seen men recover whose skulls had been fractured, and whose heads had otherwise been much

---

*When we were discussing this chapter in my seminar on the origins of the state, one student, an anthropologist who was an outspoken critic of my "psychoanalytic-developmental" approach, reluctantly, but with good humor, informed me that the Tannese people on the island of Tanna, Melanesian agriculturists living in what I would call a primitive society, felt that all wishes, desires, demands, and orders were in the mouth. The Tannese say, "One's will is one's mouth."[12]

injured; but that, in all cases in which the intestines had been wounded, the persons on a certainty died."[15] Like many philosophers who would come later, they were already capable of using sovereign reason to put away reason.

Does the control exercised by reason depend on the repression of the bowels? Control is good, repression bad. How much control is possible without repression? In the raising of a child, one is constantly inquiring whether one is teaching control or establishing a regime of repression. To masturbate or not to masturbate, to defecate on the floor or not to, to let a child hit a younger sibling with a blunt instrument or keep him from doing so—these are portentous questions not only for children and parents. Our society as we know it may depend more on how we answer these questions than we allow ourselves to think about.

In ancient Buganda, the commitment in regard to excretory functions was clearly to control *and* repression. Mary D. Salter Ainsworth went to Buganda (by then part of modern Uganda) in the 1960s to study child-rearing practices and discovered that the teaching of bowel control began when the infant was two and a half to three months old. This bowel training was not the result of Western influence but was the traditional mode. The mother would watch the baby very carefully even when it slept; at the first signs of awakening, the mother would take the infant and hold it down in a squatting position so that the bed would remain unsoiled. After feeding, the child would be taken outside the house, around a corner, and similarly held down.[16]

The children observed were not scolded or punished for accidents, and they learned the system with such facility that, "In the cases of babies whom we visited before control was acquired, the range of ages at which bed-soiling ceased was from five to eleven months."[17] Does all this relate, somehow, to the Baganda's becoming "the Japanese of Africa"? Is there a real connection between these precocious infants and the complex system of politics, taxation, administration, and warfare that the ancient Baganda used to dominate the area in which they lived? These are questions worth paying attention to.

The most important drums were the royal ones . . . they numbered ninety-three in all. Two were very large, forty were large, gradually diminishing in size, and fifty-one were small. . . . Each drum had its name, and each man his special work in beating them.[18]

> *The drums for the temples were next in importance after the royal drums;*
> *they had their own rhythm, and all contained fetiches; they were sounded*
> *at the time of the new moon or some special feast.*[19]

> *A particular drum was attached to each chieftainship and conferred with*
> *the office on each chief; it was known and recognized by the whole*
> *country.*[20]

> *When the King conferred a chieftainship on a man, the latter took a*
> *representative from the King to beat his drum, as he proceeded to take*
> *over the chieftainship. . . .*
>   *Each chief, in addition to the drum of office of his chieftainship,*
> *had also his own private drum belonging to his clan, which was beaten*
> *from time to time to ensure the permanency of his office. On this latter*
> *he would beat the rhythm of his own clan.*[21]

Even though there are no data to support the proposition, it seems a reasonable assumption that any control of excretory functions, even on the simplest level, requires a measure of repression, and that elaborate control requires elaborate repression. Human beings never wholly consent to having a drive or a need repressed, and would therefore resent any such tyranny over themselves and have an unconscious desire to throw it off—in other words, to defecate anywhere they damn well please. If such is the case, there would be a permanent, unresolvable ambivalence about the control of bowel and urinary functions: every human being would both want that control and, at the same time, desire to see it ended.

Ambivalence about control seems to be demonstrable in a hundred ways. Humor is one great form that human beings have developed to deal with situations of temporary or permanent ambivalence. Aggression and sex, about which all people are ambivalent, are prime subjects of much humor, and so are bathroom topics, especially among children and in societies other than our own. One may venture to say that if jokes about aggression, sex, and excretory control were eliminated from the whole corpus of the world's humor, only 10 to 20 percent would survive.

One symptomatic way of *not* being able to deal with the ambivalence toward control is to overidentify with the controller and, at the same time, to express one's anger toward her or him by becoming retentive of one's feces. That this was a problem in ancient Polynesia we know from the fact that the priests of medicine in Hawaii had added to their store of equipment another of humanity's great inventions—the enema. There is a lovely myth that ascribes the invention to a priest named Palaha who reasoned that water in a stagnant stream is filthy and that a fresh flow cleans it of trash. Meditating on this fact, he first tried the enema on a dog (shades of twentieth-century medical research), who responded with renewed vigor. This encouraged Palaha to use the treatment on his ill and declining father, Puheke (he who performed the first autopsy, according to legend), where it naturally produced the same beneficent effect.[22]

We are aware that people under circumstances of extreme fear or stress will lose control of their bowels. For the Hawaiians, this throwing off of control in certain situations was considered a sign of good fortune. "If one had been brought to account for transgression, and he felt that he would be condemned before the king or court, and if, while on the way he labored with excrement then he knew he would not be found guilty."[23]

A great ambivalence produces great contradictions, and great contradictions may be expressed in symbols that simultaneously give satisfaction to *both* sides of the contradiction. A symbol that both exalts and degrades something at the same time is an expression of a pervasive ambivalence. Men have expressed their age-old ambivalence about women by creating symbols that both exalt and degrade: the whore with the heart of gold; the vagina with teeth in it; the ambitious, capable woman who is "too manly"; the "dumb blonde"; the woman of intellectual power who is ugly and sexually repressed; and Mom! We do the same thing about excretory control when a person in the bathroom is described as being "on the throne." We refer to money, the thing we most want in this world, as filthy, and describe a person of whose wealth we are enormously jealous as "filthy rich." In days gone by, the high aristocracy of Europe had chamber pots made of gold.

The ancient kings of Hawaii had no metals at all, so gold chamber pots were unavailable as a symbol for them, but they exalted their bodily wastes by having a special family whose job it was to take charge of the king's excrement and carry it secretly to the sea, in order that no one could obtain it and use it to render harm to the king by sorcery. Failure in this duty meant execution. "This family held the position by perpetual inheritance, it never passed away from them. It was a thing of shame."[24]

Some people in Hawaii worshiped Nuu, a god of excrement. They had to be careful to see that fire never touched their feces.[25] The creation of such a deity may strike our repressed intellects as pushing the idea of polytheism a little too far.

> *These drums were beaten to announce the coronation of the new King, to announce war, at the death of one of the King's children, at the time when the King entered a new house, and at new moon.*
>
> *When the special drum, Kaula, had a new skin put upon it, not only was a cow killed for the skin, and its blood run into the drum, but a man was also killed by decapitation, and his blood run into it, so that, when the drum was beaten, it was supposed to add fresh life and vigour to the King, from the life of the slain man.*[26]

> *In the succession rights, as we shall see, it is the drum which makes the successor a Mugabe, which gives the final stamp and seal. The accession war is for the possession of the royal drum, and many Banyankole claim that if a foreign king were able to capture the royal drum he would automatically become King of Ankole. . . . Perhaps the most conclusive evidence to the statement that* Bagyendanwa *is greater than the Mugabe is the power of the drum to provide sanctuary. If, after being condemned to death by the Mugabe, a Manyankole were able to dash to the shrine of* Bagyendanwa *and to touch the drum he would not be killed. The Mugabe would forgive him; he would be freed and given his former rights.*[27]

> Bagyendanwa *is the tribal drum or fetish of the Banyankole. In the past, it is said, that at the accession ceremonies human sacrifices were made to it.*[28]

Similar to our notion of the toilet as throne, the Polynesian Maori of New Zealand had an exalted view of the latrine, which often was near the spot where religious ceremonies were performed. In one particular rite, which ended a tabu that had been imposed on sacred scholars, the acts of cleansing included biting the horizontal beam of the latrine while the priest intoned certain chants.[29] This act of biting something having to do with feces brings us to what may be the fundamental ambivalence about excrement, one we can see small children struggling with: whether to eat them or not. The captain of the boat that conveyed the first missionaries to Tahiti learned of a practice "of a kind so abominably filthy as scarce to be credited . . . that there had been a society at Otaheite and Eimeo, who, in their meetings, always ate human excrement, but that it had been suppressed by the other natives at Otaheite."[30] There is the possibility, of course, that this story was not true, but in that event it would be legitimate to ask why someone made it up and why so many people (Tahitians and Europeans) believed it.

> *When the King came to the throne, he was said to have "eaten Uganda," or "to have eaten the drums"; the latter expression was used of a chief when he came into office.*[31]

> *In Nkore anyone who is appointed to a position of authority is said to have "eaten the drum," no matter how low or high that position may be.*[32]

A way people have resolved their intense ambivalence about the exalted and degraded aspects of human waste, a way that has brought humankind great misery, is to identify with what is exalted and put others in the category of the degraded. This does not really resolve the contradiction, but, unfortunately, it works; that is, it makes those who have seized power feel better. On the Polynesian island of Mangaia, the warrior status was the most exalted, and those killed in battle went to the highest heaven. The legends are full of tales of old warriors, hardly able to walk, being led to battle in order to die there. In this soldiers' paradise one of the greatest pleasures was defecating on those below, who had attained only a secondary afterlife status.[33]

And in Tahiti the ambivalence about excretory functions, the union of exaltation and degradation—one might even say exaltation *through* degradation—expressed itself in the strangest rite of all. As part of the king's coronation ceremonies, when his exalted status was at its highest point, "The chief or king, while reclining on a mat near the god's image, received what was termed the populace's *ultimate* mark of respect. This consisted of dances and gestures of shocking filthiness, of the grossest kind of obscenity, wherein stark naked men and women surrounded the king and attempted to touch him with various parts of their bodies—even including their urine and excrement."[34]

> *The drum is one of the great human symbols, and like all great symbols, it stands for more than one human attitude. It is capable of expressing simultaneously the human needs for opposing satisfactions. The drum can serve the need for order or indulgence in disorder. It is frightening and reassuring. Its steady beat—its pulse—echoes bodily rhythms, which reassures our sense of ourselves; and yet, especially at night, it portends*

horror. Our own drums give us courage; the enemy's drums turn us into cowards. In ancient East African kingdoms drums were extensively used, on the one hand, to call people together for action in time of crisis, to reinforce the political order, kingship, hierarchy, authority, control, justice, and mercy; on the other hand, or with the other beat, the drum was a call for human blood, either of the sacrificed person or of the warrior.

The English psychoanalyst Melanie Klein, who has done much to illuminate the origins of the drive toward cruelty, has hypothesized that such desires are present in the infant in the first few months of life. It is impossible to know for sure what a two-month-old child may be thinking, feeling, or fantasizing, but anyone who has cared for an infant of that age knows that it is already responsive to music, to certain rhythmic patterns, and to vibrations that resonate in the body. It is a reasonable assumption that the rhythmic patterns of heart and lungs (of both the mother and the child itself) and the vibrations in the vocal cords, the ears, and the upper and lower cavities of the torso provide one mechanism by which the child assimilates the good and the bad nurturing it receives from the world outside itself. Recent colloquial usage, in which "good vibes" has become synonymous with a nurturing ambience, helps to confirm this view. The concept that the lower cavity of the body, which contains the bowels, resonates with the sound of the drums may explain why drums have become archetypal symbols of both cruelty and control—those great transmutations of anality.

A direct connection between excretory functions and cruelty is made in the legends and histories. A legend from Hawaii tells us that Kila wished to avenge himself on Mua. Kila tricked him into lying face downward in a canoe, whereupon Kila's men held Mua down and urinated on him until urine covered his body. For two days they held him under until he drowned.[35] Hawaiian history relates that Ka-lani-opuu, who ruled the island of Hawaii when Cook arrived, was defeated in battle and took his rage out on the common people of a district he had captured, killing some of them, but punishing others by urinating in their eyes.[36]

In Buganda, the puritan King Suna was traveling as Buganda kings always traveled, on the shoulders of a bearer, when, in the camp of a people called Abakeerere, the bearer slipped on some cow dung and nearly dropped the *kabaka*. Since such an accident was the bearer's fault, he lied and said it was human feces that had caused the near accident.

Such waste had no right to be on the path. Suna believed the bearer and executed three hundred Bakeerere.[37]

The kind of cruelty exercised by Kabaka Suna was not unusual in advanced complex societies. In addition to the high incidence of human sacrifice, there was an enormous amount of deliberate, gratuitous cruelty, especially on the part of those who held political power. When reading incident upon incident of such self-indulgent brutality, one feels one has been delivered into the insane world of the Red Queen in Wonderland, only here the cry "Off with her head" runs real blood. Grant, who traveled with Speke, tells of an officer of Mutesa's who was given a single slave by the king in return for some service performed, and had the audacity and the stupidity to ask for more. He was cut to pieces in the court with reed knives. "His limbs were carried away openly, while the trunk was wrapped in cloth."[38] Speke adds that Mutesa himself, having learned how to shoot from Speke, observed a woman being led away to some punishment, fired at her, and killed her outright.[39] And lest we think these two travelers were feverish and in-clined to fanciful horrors, we also have the testimony of the explorer Linant that Mutesa, boasting to him of his aim, "levelled his gun deliber-ately at one of his female attendants, and blew her brains out."[40]

So pervasive was this kind of arbitrary suffering at the court that some chiefs and clans who were supposed to send their children to the royal palace as pages sent their servants instead, in order to preserve the lives of their offspring.[41] This despite the fact that, if the *kabaka* ap-proved of a page, political advancement was the reward. One of the praise names for the *kabaka* was "He who does not pity the parents of the man he kills."[42] When a page was executed at the court for some minor offense, his parents were expected to come and thank the king for dispatching their disobedient son—and they had to bring another child to replace the executed one.[43]

So grotesque are some of these stories that there is an inclination to defend against them by believing that they are not true and must have been invented. However, from Hawaii we have the testimony of John Papa Ii, who was himself a page to the son of Kamehameha, Li-holiho, who became the second king of the united Hawaiian state. Ii, who talks of himself in the third person, says he "was carrying the young chief's spittoon in front of him, had a brush with death when somehow the cover slipped off, struck his knee, and bounced up again. He was able to catch it and so was saved from death, for had it dropped to his feet, his fate would have been [execution]. As it was, he was criticized for forgetting the rite that the spittoon should be held at the back of his neck or shoulder, in which case the cover would not be stepped over if dropped. The boy became very nervous with chiefs watching him and talking about his narrow escape. When they reached home, the chiefs told some of the people how he had passed the hill of death."[44]

Indeed, lest one think that the sunny, happy isles of the Pacific could not compete with darkest Africa in the perpetration of cruelty, the record shows that some of the chief governors under Kamehameha in Hawaii killed people to use their flesh for shark bait,[45] and that Finow I, in the presence of William Mariner, requested, and the request was met, that one of the king's followers be shot down out of the topgallant mast of a ship, merely because "he was only a low, vulgar fellow (a cook); and that neither his life nor death was of any consequence to society."[46]

In regard to cruelty in Buganda, we can observe how close to myth people lived their lives. As happened so often in advanced complex societies, myth and legend seemed to legitimize certain types of behavior. We tell stories of giants who eat people, but we know that people don't do that any more. There is a feeling that those living in complex societies, however, had not clearly distinguished between mythic and actual ways of behavior. The legend of the Katinvuma clan, as Roscoe tells it, sounds no more improbable than Mutesa's casual cruelties.

Katinvuma are small seeds that were worn as beads before glass ones were available. Some children were playing together, and one of them snatched from another the katinvuma beads she was wearing and put them in her mouth. Unwilling to give the beads back, the culprit swallowed them. The mothers of the two children appeared on the scene. Though the mother of the guilty child offered to replace the beads, this offer was rejected by the victim's mother. She would accept only the *identical* seeds. Following the custom of retribution, the girl who had swallowed the beads was handed over to the parents of the girl who had been deprived of them. "They killed her, opened the body, and took the seeds from the stomach. From that time onwards, the relatives of the murdered child refused to wear beads, and they became the totem of the clan."[47]

Before we can understand the nature of cruelty, we must begin to see that it does serve a psychological function for those who resort to it; it is a mechanism of defense used by the ego to ward off the threat of annihilation. The ego, when threatened with destruction, for reasons that are almost impossible to explain, can reaffirm its existence by making others suffer. Admittedly, we are not talking of a mature or healthy ego, but the continued presence of so much brutality in the world gives indication of how rare such healthy and mature egos are. Recognizing that cruelty is a form of defense, that it serves a psychic function, allows us to see that it has a close relationship to control. What brings these two modes of human behavior together in the mind and in the bowels is that they are both methods of dealing with panic. Panic is the problem—cruelty and control are "solutions."

First we must understand panic, fear, anxiety, terror. After we have learned more about what people living in advanced complex societies were afraid of, we may understand more about the particular ways in which they expressed cruelty. It seems clear to me that the breakdown of the kinship system produced an enormous increase of anxiety as people in these societies separated from their kin and the securities of a known structure. The king, who was the great symbolic manifestation of the antikinship state, was allowed to indulge in, was even expected to engage in, the grossest forms of cruelty. He was the surrogate, whose job it was to assuage the anxiety of the whole society. We shall return to this after we have looked in sharper detail at both kingship and the kinship system. For now, it may have been profitable merely to bring together cruelty, control, the bowels, and the drums.

16

Sing Muse: Of Bards, Jesters, Riddles, and the Birth of the Theatre

"A messenger now invited us to sup with the governor, and we soon after joined him and his friends around his hospitable board. Our repast was not accompanied by the gladsome sound of 'harp in hall' or 'aged minstrel's flowing lay,' yet it was enlivened by an interesting, youthful bard, twelve or fourteen years of age, who was seated on the ground in the large room in which we were assembled, and who, during the supper, sung, in a monotonous but pleasing strain, the deeds of former chiefs, ancestors of our host. His fingers swept no 'classic lyre,' but beat, in a manner responsive to his song, a rustic little drum, formed of a calabash, beautifully stained, and covered at the head with a piece of shark skin. The governor and his friends were evidently pleased with his lay, and the youth seemed repaid by their approbation."

Through this tranquil shock of recognition, the Reverend Ellis, journeying through Hawaii in the 1820s, found himself transported back to the heroic age of Greece. Had the bard in the governor's hall begun to sing the woeful tale of the sack of Troy, it might even have seemed appropriate to the dreamlike quality of the experience.

Official court singers of tales were found in almost all complex societies. No matter how much Hawaiian, Tahitian, and Buganda cultures may have differed in regard to kingship, kinship, religion, or world view, they were agreed on the necessity of poets to sing of their ancient past and their present glories and sorrows. In Hawaii, individual bards became attached to the households of the kings or important governors. There were also groups of itinerant musicians who traveled through the islands, being welcomed at the homes of great lords and reciting their lays at public festivals. The songs might recall the past glories of a local noble house, but the ones that provoked the most response re-counted events of national significance. The position of bard was hered-itary, passing from father to son; some poems were sung only by particular poetic families. The king's personal singer inherited and com-posed songs recounting the history of the sovereign's family. "What-ever defects attach to their performances, considered as works of art, they were not wanting in effect; being highly figurative, and delivered in strains of plaintive sadness, or wild enthusiasm, they produced great excitement of feeling."[2]

Like Homer of old, many of the singers were blind. In Hawaii, we are told only that the bard of the late king lacked sight,[3] but of Buganda the record indicates that all poetic singers were blinded. Some Baganda said this made the bards "more proficient in their art."[4] Others advised that, being sightless, the bard would be less tempted by the beautiful women at the court. The stage of societal development, it seems, does not alter the fact that an entertainer of power exerts a strong sexual attraction.

Yet these explanations, though plausible, do not seem adequate. We close our eyes at a concert in order to let the experience sink in deeper; some do the same on the analyst's couch to allow irrational material to rise to the surface. The poet is a shaman of sorts; he goes to places others cannot find. When Oedipus had an insight into the irrational part of the mind—an insight with awesome power—he blinded himself. The bard in Buganda gave up his eyes that his poetic gift might be en-hanced. We are back at the place of sacrifice.

The tradition that great Homer was blind may have been more than an imaginative legend. There was a complex society that preceded the archaic civilization of Greece. In that society, the singers of tales might also have been required to give up their eyes. The story of blind Homer could easily have been the shadow cast by that time.

In a society lacking newspapers, books, radios, phonographs, mov-ies, and television, it is easy to imagine how hungry people were for the presence of a skillful poet or storyteller. On Tahiti, where strong monarchies had not yet blossomed, such artists traveled from place to place and "were not only welcomed but were invited to return again and again everywhere they went."[5]

Hawaiian circumstances resembled those of Anglo-Saxon or Norse times, when a bard would seek out the court of a strong king in order to take up permanent residence. Some of these shaman-poets in Hawaii were so renowned that legends grew around their memory. One, in

the generation immediately preceding that of Kamehameha I, was
named Namaka. He came from the island of Kauai, where he had become expert in "politics, oratory, genealogies, spear-throwing, the con-
formation of the earth's surface, bone-breaking, cliff-leaping, and the
interpretation of omens."⁶ Determined to find a lord to whom he might
devote all his accomplishments, and having chosen Kalaniopuu of Hawaii to be that person, Namaka set out from Kauai and arrived first at
Oahu. Hearing that a certain Pakuanui there was skillful in debate and
bone-breaking, Namaka challenged him to a contest of wits. It was no
real match, but a smashing triumph for Namaka. "The shafts of wit
flew, brilliant as the rainbow arching over the *hau* trees of Kahaukomo
that lends its color to the *ulalena* rain blown by the *kiowao* breeze against
the *pali,* bending the *kawelu* grasses of Lanihula; swift as the gusts that
lift the leaves of the tangled *lehua* of Malailua. There was no limit to
his knowledge. He slipped out of the grasp of Pakuanui like an eel or
wormed his way through his fingers like a slim *opule* fish; a hard question he dodged like a blow aimed at the nose."⁷

Angered at his defeat, Pakuanui, with a skillful movement of his
foot, sent Namaka over the cliff as they were descending a very steep
path. Observers said that Namaka flew like a hawk, sailed like a kite
as the wind changed, and finally settled on the top of a tree. Namaka
moved on to Maui, where he leaped some cliffs to impress the populace,
and then journeyed to Hawaii.

Having reached the end of his travels, Namaka was disappointed
to discover that the King Kalaniopuu was already under the tutelage
of another Kauaian marvel worker. So Namaka found a patron in
Hinai, a chief in Waimea. His hope was that, once he demonstrated
his capabilities to Hinai, the latter would extol him to the king. He
therefore taught Hinai some of his skills, particularly cliff leaping, and
the cliffs they leaped were pointed out to people years after Hinai and
Namaka had died.⁸

Hawaiian and Western oral poetry differed in their method of composition. The West, according to the work of Milman Parry, Alfred
Lord, and others, has laid great emphasis on the singing of *individual*
poets. With this in mind, it is striking to discover that in ancient Hawaii
most long epic poems were composed by a committee of bards. Having
met together, the group would decide on a topic. One poet would offer
the first line; others would criticize and correct it until its final shape
was agreed upon; then another singer would volunteer the second line.
Poems of thousands of lines were composed in this manner. So perva-

sive was the poetic spirit in this culture that almost everyone qualified as a maker of verses. Sometimes to compose an epic poem a high official would call together his important subordinates and his ablest warriors, then choose the subject for the song and appoint each subordinate to prepare a line of verse. Individual verses were criticized by the whole group until the full poem was accepted by all.[9]

Hawaiian poetry was enormously complex and has, so far, proved to be impossible to translate adequately. The Western poet Padraic Colum has commented that "Every Hawaiian poem has at least four meanings: 1) the ostensible meaning of the words; 2) a vulgar double meaning; 3) a mythological-historical-topographical import; and 4) the Kauna or deeply-hidden meaning. I have sat gasping while, in a poem of twelve or twenty lines, meaning under meaning was revealed to me by some scholar . . . who knew something of the esoteric Hawaiian tradition."[10]

Hawaiian poetic tradition was more fertile than that of either Tahiti or Buganda. Like the ancient Greeks, to whom they may be compared, Hawaiians had a great variety of poetic forms, and the need to think about poetry in a systematic way: *mele kaua*, war songs; *mele kuihuna*, genealogies and songs celebrating the achievements of historical and legendary figures; *mele kuo*, songs of praise; *mele oliole*, lyrics and odes; *mele paeaea*, "provocative songs, of a vulgar sort, which we need not take up"; *mele inou*, name songs and panegyrics; *mele ipo*, love songs; *mele kanikau*, dirges and laments; *mele pule*, prayers.[11]

Ancient Buganda resembled ancient Rome in that the state was supreme, and much poetic imagination was sacrificed on the altar of political power. What the blind bards of Buganda sang primarily were songs in praise of the king or other high officials, war songs, dirges for dead officials and warriors, and, above all, the dynastic histories (genealogies) of the *kabaka*.[12] The recitation of these genealogical texts was a dangerous occupation: one mistake could mean death for the bard. In the ancient African kingdom of Ashanti, when these histories of the kings were sung, two executioners stood behind the poets, ready to punish any mistakes.[13]

For Hawaiian lords, ancestral history was equally important:

The work of weaving genealogies into a hymnlike chant commemorating the family antecedents was the work of a *Haku-mele* or "Master-of-song," attached to the court of a chief. . . . He held an honored place in the household. It was his duty to compose name chants glorifying the family exploits and to preserve

those handed down by tradition, but especially to memorize the genealogical
line through all its branches. Since writing was unknown . . . a master of song
usually gathered together two or more of his fellows to edit and memorize the
line or themselves to contribute passages. Especially must genealogies be mem-
orized by more than one reciter.[14]

We have no evidence as to whether or not certain bards were free of
the need to serve the monarchy or the aristocracy, free to sing only their
own songs. All indications are that they did not lead independent existences. It was an age of epic, not lyric, poetry, and epic poetry has always sung of kings and nobles. The evidence from complex societies
suggests that epic poetry did the same at its birth. Heroes and the poetry
that sings their praise are the stuff of individualism; the communal
equality of primitive society was alien to both. Individuation from the
kinship system was a necessary condition for the birth of epic poetry.

In one regard, the bards of complex society did serve the needs of
the whole community; that was in warfare. Of Tahiti, Ellis tells us:

The principal object of these Rautis [bards] was, to animate the troops by recounting the deeds of their forefathers, the fame of their tribe or island, the
martial powers of their favouring gods, and the interests involved in the contest.
In the discharge of their duties they were indefatigable, and by night and day
went through the camp rousing the ardour of the warriors. On the day of battle
they marched with the army to the onset, mingled in the fray, and hurried to
and fro among the combatants, cheering them with the recital of heroic deeds,
or stimulating them to achievements of daring and valour.[15]

The two great themes of epic poetry are aristocratic heroes and warfare:
"I sing arms and the man." It has been so from the beginning.

Aristocracy as a class relates to commoners as a class, as adults to
children, or as parents to children. There is something absurd in the
notion that some are born to the status and power of adults, regardless
of their capacity, similar to the absurdity that gives adult power to parents regardless of their competence to assume that role. One objective
correlative of both these absurdities is the dwarf—a being who becomes
an adult while continuing to look like a child; the face grows older even
as the body refuses to grow. Aristocracy and monarchy, out of a human
need to tell the truth, have entertained the desire to mock the absurdity
of their own position. The dwarf, the jester, and the fool appeared simultaneously with the lord and the monarch and their pretensions to
power. The fool and the jester have been there to underline—sometimes

comically, at other times tragically—the discrepancy between inherited adult status and individual incompetence. King Lear's fool and Captain Ahab's cabin boy, Pip, poignantly insist on the catastrophic implications of situations in which those appointed to power refuse to exercise it in a responsible adult manner.

Such tragic insight was not available to the first wielders of aristocratic power, but they did have need for the dwarf, the jester, and the fool. In Tonga, there were no official jesters, but from time to time certain individuals assumed the role of *fakatakataka* and amused the nobles with their antics. One man of Vavau, named Kahu, took on such a position for the lord of that island. He would mock the foibles of other people and was permitted great license in his speech in his attempts to make the lord laugh. On one occasion, he had himself trussed up like a pig to be roasted and was carried to a feast.[16]

Speke, on his way home from Buganda, passed through Bunyoro, which was ruled by Kamrasi, a sovereign reluctant to have much contact with the white explorers. As a gesture of friendship but also of distance, Kamrasi "directed a dwarf called Kimenya to be sent to us. . . . A little old man, less than a yard high, called on us with a walking-stick higher than himself, made his salaam, and sat down composedly. He then rose and danced, singing without invitation, and following it up with queer antics. Lastly, he performed the tambura, or changing-march, in imitation of the Wakungu [Speke's men], repeating the same words they use, and ending by a demand for simbi, or cowrie-shells, modestly saying, 'I am a beggar, and want simbi, if you have not 500 to spare, you must at any rate give me 400.' "[17] It wasn't very much of a performance, but it was, after all, a long way from Piccadilly.

The ancient kingdom of Rwanda in East Africa was a society with an inflexibly stratified class system. The Tutsi aristocracy tyrannically dominated the Hutu commoners. At the bottom of the social scale were the small group of Pygmie-related peoples called the Twa. They were considered vassals of the king, though many were attached to members of the high nobility, fulfilling a variety of specialized functions: choreographers, musicians, buffoons. Also, in the manner of the Italian Renaissance, they performed a series of sinister labors as assassins, executioners, torturers, and procurers of young girls for their aristocratic masters.[18]

Even as dwarfs and fools mock the pretensions of the aristocracy, they also emphasize the permanent subordinate position of the commoners, who will never achieve equality with the nobility. A commoner has as much chance of becoming a noble as has a Twa to grow to the height of a Tutsi. Like so many of the symbols that relate to social and political life, the dwarf, the fool, and the jester have meanings with a double thrust.

There was a time, in the history of the world, when riddles were more than the playthings of children, a time when, so the stories tell, a riddle contest could be a matter of life and death. In the ancient Grecian land of Boeotia, a malevolent sphinx had put the city of Thebes under its curse and sat at the city gate asking all travelers a not-very-difficult riddle—what creature walked on four legs at dawn, on two legs during the day, and on three legs in the evening. At first, all travelers were unable to give the correct answer and paid with their lives. Oedipus of Corinth, having been marked by the gods to live an unusual life, knew the answer was man. Following the rules of the contest, Oedipus killed the sphinx and liberated the city.

In ancient Hawaii, according to the tales, the same rules applied to legendary riddle contests. One faithful son, journeying for the purpose of avenging the death of his father, meets the killers and engages them in a fierce contest of meanings and riddles. After an exhausting battle, the boy wins out. The men were then executed and cooked in an oven, "and the bones were stripped of all their flesh. Thus did he punish those who had caused the death of his father."[19] It is a reasonable conjecture that in an earlier form of the story the flesh stripped from the bones was eaten, just as there may have been an earlier Theban version in which the sphinx ate those who failed to solve the riddle.

In some Hawaiian legends, the travels of the hero have no particular purpose, and life-or-death riddle contests are engaged in for the same reason that the knights in European romances, traveling through the forest and meeting other knights, fought one another—for the pleasure of fighting.

On the day appointed, Kepakailiula and his friend went to the king's house. As they came in the king saw them and called out: "Let the stranger be seated here." As soon as they sat down, the king said: "Will the stranger join in the fun?" Kepakailiula replied: "Yes." "I have two riddles," said the king. "If the right answers are given to them, I will be cooked in the oven. If they are not answered correctly, you will be baked in the oven. Those are the conditions." The king then gave the first riddle.

> *Step all around, step to the bottom,*
> *Leaving, reserving a certain place.*

"The second one is this:

> *The men that stand*
> *The men that lie down*
> *The men that are folded.*

"These are my riddles, I want the stranger to understand. If you give the right answers you will indeed live but if you fail, I shall kill you. I will bake you in the oven." When Kepakailiula saw that the oven was heated, he gave the answer to the first riddle.

"It is a house. It is thatched all around, reserving the doorway." "Yes, you have given the right answer to my riddle; my second one is yet to be answered. If you fail, I shall kill you." Kepakailiula looked at the oven and when he saw the stones being thrown to the side he answered the second riddle:

> *It is also a house.*
> *The timbers that stand.*
> *The battens that are laid down.*
> *The grass that is folded.*

"What! Who has told you?" While he was expressing his wonder he was thrown in the oven by Kukaea.[20]

We are used to the idea that swords, spears, stones, sticks, guns, and bombs can kill. We only dimly remember that there was a time when words could kill, when answering word puzzles could give a person an uncontestable potency.

Not all riddles were so lethal. The riddles of the Anglo-Saxons, who were very close to being a complex society, are some of the great joys of a fertile literary tradition. Some were very elaborate, consisting of more than twenty-five lines of poetry. Hawaiian riddles were simpler, without the complex development of their Anglo-Saxon counterparts: "My man that cannot be cut." What is it? "A shadow."[21]

Riddle contests were not the only form of word battles in Hawaii, and here again the Polynesians resembled the ancient Greeks in their desire to turn everything into a contest. Some great battles of agonistic vituperation became legendary. The kings of Maui and Hawaii entertained each other at a great feast. After the effects of the intoxicating *awa* had begun to wear off, the king of Maui asked his counterpart from Hawaii: "After you have ruled until you are old, need the help of a cane, and become as bleary-eyed as a rat, who will be your successor?" When the Hawaiian king indicated the man at his side, the heir of the Mauian king commented: "Short of stature, stout and short, a shelf easily reached by a dog." The object of this attack quickly came back: "I may be a small person, but I am the small *maika* stone that can roll over the field and win [reference to a game played with small stones]. I am the small sugar cane stalk of Kuhala [whose fuzz] can irritate the nose."

It was now the Hawaiian's turn to attack. He inquired of the Mauian: "After you have ruled until you need the support of a cane, become as bleary-eyed as a rat, and sprawl helplessly on a mat, who will be your successor?" The king of Maui indicated his younger brother. Now the short, stout Hawaiian heir delivered his critique: "Tall, thin, spindly, and too slender. Falls easily with a gust of wind." Coming to his own defense, the Mauian heir responded: "I am the tall banana tree of the wild mountain patch whose fruit does not ripen in a week. I am the long anchoring-root of the mountains. Though the wind blow, I do not fall."[22] Those who listened could feel confident that the future of both kingdoms lay secure.

Riddles existed in Tahiti and ancient Buganda as well. Riddle battles seem to have been absent in Buganda; at least, there are no recorded instances, and it seems unlikely that such an exciting event would have escaped Roscoe's eye. For Tahiti, such battles could have existed, but because there are no records the knowledge is lost to us.

All the information I have about the birth of the theatre in complex societies, however, comes from Polynesia. In Buganda, although musical performance had reached a sophisticated level, and although certain dance entertainments—similar to those in primitive societies—were performed, there was no theatre as such. Here again, the Polynesians seem similar to the Greeks, the Baganda to the Romans, whose theatre, after all, was not original but resulted from contact with Etruscan and Greek cultures.

Like its counterpart in ancient Greece, the theatre in Polynesia was born under religious auspices. The imaginative aspects of religious ritual were much less developed in Buganda than in Polynesian culture, and this may have contributed directly to the difference of experience in regard to the theatre.

Some aspects of culture—such as bards, epic genealogies, kingship, human sacrifice—were universal in advanced complex societies. Other forms were dependent upon the individual genius of the society. The Baganda invented neither the theatre nor philosophical speculation; Polynesia did not enjoy the kind of complex, sophisticated administrative machinery that delighted the Baganda. We who are the heirs of a multitude of cultural traditions think it "natural" that human beings should do everything, but thousands of years of cultural development were necessary to reach this position.

The theatre began with the dance. Ancient Polynesian dance performances have now entirely vanished, and we have no way of judging their quality, but almost every witness whose testimony we have was moved by the complexity, sophistication, and polish of these entertainments. Cook, whose mind was responsive to any form of human perfectibility, wrote of Tongan dancers:

They formed the triple semi-circle, as the preceding dancers had done; and a person, who advanced at the head on one side of the semi-circle, began by repeating something in a truly musical recitative, which was delivered with an air so graceful, as might put to the blush our most applauded performances. He was answered in the same manner by the person at the head of the opposite party. This being repeated several times, the whole body, on one side, joined in the responses to the whole corresponding body on the opposite side, as the semi-circle to the front; and they finished, by singing and dancing as they had begun.[23]

The religious possibilities of these entertainments are illustrated by the use made of them in the Hawaiian Islands to assure the successful outcome of a pregnancy. When the wife of a high noble was in her sixth month, a dance performance was arranged as a compliment to her, and Vancouver was told that it would be repeated many times until the child was born.[24] Thus art grows by co-opting the functions of magic.

Greek tragedy began as a simple contrapuntal form of opposition between a solo voice and a chorus. All our evidence indicates that the earliest solo part was the chorus leader, gradually developing into the first actor. Subsequently, other acting parts were added, with the chorus relegated to a significant but not a dominant role. The second-oldest Greek tragic drama we have, the *Suppliants* of Aeschylus, is essentially a dramatic dialogue between the chorus and one actor. This simple form is already refined in Aeschylus, reflecting the many years of development that preceded the writing of his play. Nothing is preserved of the primitive dramatic forms that antedate Aeschylus, and we may only speculate on their nature.

It is exciting to discover that, on the Polynesian island of Mangaia, the Reverend William Gill, in the second half of the nineteenth century, found a plenitude of examples of dramatic performances with precisely this solo-chorus form. One cannot call these poetic entertainments "plays," but it is easy to see how this form could have developed into full tragic drama. They provide us with a remarkable view of what sixth- and seventh-century-B.C. Athenian theatre might have been like.

> *A Farewell Chanted at a Reed-Throwing Match for Women.*
> *Composed in memory of Vaiana,*
> *by her Husband Naupata, in 1824*

SOLO *Whither has she gone*

CHORUS *She has sped to Avaiki [Place of the dead],*
She disappeared at the edge of the horizon,
Where the sun drops through.
We weep for thee!

SOLO *Yes, I will for ever weep*
And ever seek for thee!

CHORUS *Bitter tears I shed for thee;*
I weep for the lost wife of my bosom.
Alas! thou wilt not return.

SOLO *Oh, that thou wouldst return!*

CHORUS *Stay; come back to this world!*
Return to my embrace.
Thou art as a bough wrenched off by the blast!

SOLO *Wrenched off, and now in Avaiki—*
That distant land to which thou art fled.[25]

Many of these dramatic poems were laments for the dead, expressing either a private grief, as in the example above, or giving voice to public sorrow over the passing of a politically important personage. It raises the question whether Greek tragedy began with such laments. The tragic nature of death would provide a continuity of emotion with tragedy, but even more than that, the pity and terror that Aristotle identifies as our primary feelings during a tragic performance are exactly the emotions with which we regard the recently dead. If the perception of death is one of the beginnings of wisdom, there would be a natural flow from dramatic lament to the moral world of tragedy.

Not all Mangaian dramatic odes dealt with death. Some, such as the following, had mythic themes. Composed about 1814, it tells of the invention of tattooing by the legendary figure Ina:

> *Song of Ina*
>
> CALL FOR THE MUSIC AND DANCE TO BEGIN
>
> > *Here we are, Ina's little fish,*
> > *On whom the tattoo was first performed.*
> > *As we bore her on her voyage.*
>
> SOLO *Go on!*
>
> CHORUS *On her way to Tinirau*
> *Ina invented tattooing.*
>
> SOLO *Ah, thou shore-loving little fish!*
>
> CHORUS *When did Ina imprint so distinctly*
> *Those lines on thy body?*
>
> SOLO *As I, a little fish, bore her on my back.*
>
> CHORUS *Brave fish that bore her to her husband,*
> *So that she became the happy mother*
> *Of the dance-loving Karo.*[26]

It is noteworthy that the performance consisted of music, dance, and dramatic poetry—exactly as was the case with Greek drama.

The lament that follows, composed around 1770, makes reference to the Mangaian mythological belief that the spirits of the dead are first gathered together by the god Vera on the eastern shore of the island and then led by him over difficult rocks and unyielding thickets to the southern portion of the island, where all turn west until they reach the westernmost point. Here the entire troop takes its final leave before departing to the land of the shades, which resembles the ancient Greek Hades and the ancient Hebrew Shiloh, where dead spirits continue to exist in a joyless, painless state. About half the ode—the middle part—is omitted here.

> SOLO *List, Vera, to the music of the sea.*
> *Beyond yon dwarfed pandamus trees*
> *The billows are dashing o'er the rocks.*
> *'Tis time, friends, to depart*

CHORUS *Our garments are mourning weeds and flowers.*

SOLO *Advance to yonder level rocks;*
There to await the favouring wind
That will bear thee o'er the sea.
(Thy father) Mitimiti looks sorrowfully on

CHORUS *The departing band led by thee.*

SOLO *List, dear Vera,*

CHORUS   *to the music of the sea*
Thou art a wretched wanderer
Almost arrived at Iva—

SOLO   *Yes, at Iva . . .*

SOLO *Ah! Mitimiti is following hard behind,*
Beckoning me to return.
Here let us halt awhile.
'Tis time, friends, to depart;

CHORUS *Our garments are mourning weeds and flowers.*

SOLO *Thy feet, Vera*

CHORUS   *Are entangled with wild vines.*
Art thou bound for Vavau, the home of ghosts?
Over

SOLO   *the foaming billows*

CHORUS   *Wilt thou voyage?*
Thread now thy way through groves of pandamus,
The favourite haunt of disembodied spirits;
Near where the royal Utakea landed,

SOLO *A level beach laved by the sea.*
The cricket-god is chirping to direct thy path,
Through the thickets to the shore
Where the spirits of the dead wander
Bathe thy streaming locks, Vera.
Grant me a new life, O light of morning!
'Tis time, friends, to depart;

CHORUS *Our garments are mourning weeds and flowers*

SOLO *Descendant of the kings*

CHORUS   *of Mauke;*
Favoured one, led by a prosperous wind

> *From the root of the skies to these shores,*
> *Ere taking a long farewell, turn back!*
> *Idol of my dwelling, remain awhile,*

> SOLO   *Decked with the buds of sweet-scented flowers*
> *And fragrant leaves brought from Tutuila.*
> *'Tis time, friends, to depart;*

> CHORUS   *Our garments are mourning weeds and flowers.*[27]

Max Müller, an early, great mythologist, having read this material, was moved to remark: "We know that mythopoeic period among the Aryan and Semitic races, but we know it from a distance only, and where are we to look now for living myths and legends, except among those who still think and speak mythologically, who are, in fact, at the present moment what the Hindus were before the collection of their sacred hymns, and the Greeks long before the days of Homer?"[28]

In most of Polynesia, it was comedy, not tragedy, that dominated the theatre. Satiric representations of public figures, including those with the greatest power, provided comic revenge for common people against the personages who enjoyed the benefits of class. The songs of the *hula ki'i* in Hawaii are characterized as "gossipy, sarcastic, ironical, scandal-mongering, dealing in satire, abuse, hitting right and left at social and personal vices,"[29] like the political cartoons of our own day. James Morrison, an officer on Bligh's *Bounty*, described an elaborate entertainment on Tahiti:

When the Weomen retire to take breath their place is supplyd by the Music and singers which is no way disagreeable when understood being soft and pleasing—at other times a set of Actors supplys their place—the principal part of which the(y) perform is Satyr, which is often directed at their Chiefs, and they never fail to expose such Characters as draw their attention and tho they treat their Chiefs with great freedom they incur no displeasure so long as they keep to the truth—by this Method they rebuke them for their faults in Publick, having first diverted them to draw their attention—this is done in a kind of Pantomime at which they are so good that any person who knows the Man they mean to represent may easily perceive who they are making the subject of their sport.[30]

In Hawaii, very serious acts of tyranny on the part of the aristocracy were mockingly portrayed on the stage. The marionette Ki'i-ki'i was "a strenuous little fellow, an *ilamuku,* a marshall, or constable of the king. It was his duty to carry out with unrelenting rigor the commands of the [rulers], whether they bade him take possession of a taro patch, set fire to a house, or to steal upon a man at dead of night and dash his brains out while he slept."[31]

So free and sharply developed was the capacity to mime satirically the attitudes and actions of people that the early European visitors also became the subject of such presentations. Bligh was much amused by a comic representation of his sailors managing their small boats, the officers finding fault with infractions and inefficiencies, and the sailors demonstrating exaggerated fears of being rebuked.[32] Cook, stuffier than Bligh, claimed not to understand the comic stance of such scenes: "We, our Ship and our Country they have frequently brought on the Stage, but on what account I know not. I make no doubt but it was intended as a Compliment. . . ."[33] Cook could not imagine anyone treating His Majesty's Navy with levity.

Any bit of the latest news could be seized upon by the players for serious or comic comment. When the ships left Tahiti on Cook's second voyage, a young woman, probably attached to one of Cook's sailors, stayed on board a ship as the expedition made its way first to Raiatéa and then to Huahiné of the Society Islands. On Huahiné, some of the ship's company, including the young woman, went to see a dramatic entertainment. Some Society Island satirist had determined to find out whether or not it was true that "guilty creatures sitting at a play, have, by the very cunning of the scene, been struck, so to the soul, that presently they have proclaimed their malefactions."[34] The entertainment depicted a young woman leaving her homeland to adventure with Cook's men. Most poignantly, her not-very-sympathetic reception by friends on her return was portrayed in detail. The woman in question, like Claudius, was intent upon fleeing the theatre, but her European companions prevailed upon her "to see the play out" and "refrain from tears while it was acting."[35]

The same kind of interplay between players and audience—an interaction that is always fraught with the sense of tabu broken—was part of the *hula ki'i*, a marionette performance, in Hawaii. Four attractive young people, two men and two women, are portrayed in one *hula.* In addition to the play itself, as an interlude one of the marionettes will point to someone of the opposite sex in the audience but say nothing. "What do you want?" asks the puppeteer. The marionette remains silent, continuing to point steadfastly. As if slowly comprehending, the

master asks, "Ah, you want So-and-so." The marionette nods assent.
"Do you want him to come to you?" Now the marionette is all action,
its nods and gestures indicating delight. By this time, of course, the audience members are derisively laughing at the object of the marionette's
passion, pleased that their own fantasied sexual involvement with a lifeless object has remained anonymous.[36]

The narrative part of this marionette show is remarkably familiar
to us. Our experience of the *commedia dell'arte* and all its derivatives
has prepared our response to the story, which begins with the braggart
soldier, "a rude and boastful son of Mars, at heart a bully, if not a coward,"[37] always asking for a fight, but dependent more upon his bluster
than his skill to overcome his opponent. A blowhard, but by no means
unattractive. Maka-ku is his name.

His antagonist, Puapuakea, is a modest man, but of "genuine courage." Having heard of the achievements of Maka-ku, Puapuakea challenges him to a test of valor. First javelins, then slingshots, and finally
stone throwing produce only a stand-off. Neither is victorious.

With the contest undecided, it is time for the Hawaiian game of
lua, which was a combination of something like the ancient Greek pen-
tathlon, including boxing and wrestling, along with various actions similar to Japanese *ju-jitsu,* joined with the special Hawaiian privileges of
"choking, bonebreaking, dislocating, eye-gouging, and the infliction of
tortures and grips unmentionable and disreputable,"[38] a sport in which
having your opponent by the balls was no metaphor. For a long while,
the contest remains undecided, but since virtue has the necessity of triumphing, gradually Puapuakea's quiet courage wins out.

Meanwhile, two very attractive sisters have been watching the actions of these heroes and conceive passionate likings for them. Fortu-
nately for all, the sisters' attentions settle on different bravos, and it takes
little time to turn the four into two pairs. "The two men had previously
allowed their fancies to range abroad at pleasure; but from this time they
centered their hearts on these two . . . and settled down to regular married life."[39] True to the archetypal comic form, this performance ended
with marriage.

One form of entertainment found in Tahiti seems alien to our sense
of comedy and of tragedy. A group of adolescent boys are selected and
fattened up to the point where they can hardly walk. "When the period
of fattening is completed they get up and anoint their bodies all over
with coco-nut oil; and fix plaits of palm leaves on their heads which,

when placed above the forehead, keeps their faces shaded from the sun when it shines on them. They furthermore gird themselves about with a long strip of native cloth of various colours, over the breech-clout." They march as a group to the noble's house, where the leader of the group enters and reports to the lord, rendering an account of all those who have been fattened, mentioning each by name and the district from which he comes. The objects of this presentation remove their bark-cloth coverings and hand them to the leader, who in turn hands them to the lord, as meanwhile the gathered crowd rushes in and rips off the multicolored girdles, leaving them with only their breechclouts. After some time to admire the obese bodies, a normal entertainment was performed by a separate group of players, consisting of music, dance, and a pantomime of a man and his jealous wife.[40]

It is difficult to assign a meaning to such actions. Is it the memory of a time when fattened ones were eaten? Is it a defiance of famine and anxiety about starvation? A mode of announcing, "Look how rich and secure we are, that we have no end to eating"? Other complex societies did have fattening rituals, especially in parts of Africa, mostly applied to certain wives of the king. In some societies, people were made so fat they could not walk unaided. This was considered attractive: a grotesque image of abundance.

Another grotesquerie, with comic dimensions, was so popular in Tahiti that we have several versions recorded by the men on Cook's expedition. Georg Forster tells of a farce about a man whose daughter has a lover the father disapproves of. The father, as we would expect, guards his daughter jealously, but in the dead of night the lovers manage to meet, and the unwelcome lover persuades this Polynesian Jessica to run away with him. As time moves on, a fine baby boy is born from this alliance, but here the course of action diverges from all counterparts in the Western theatre—the labor of the mother and the birth of the child are portrayed onstage. A full-grown boy emerges from the coverings that have hidden the mother's labor, and he proceeds to run around the stage, trailing behind him a large representation of the placenta and a very long umbilical cord, while the midwife gives chase to her new charge, who always manages to slip from her grasp. The audience, of course, is rooting for the child to escape capture. All ends happily: "The girl's father upon seeing the cleverness of his grand-son, is at last reconciled to his son-in-law."[41]

A second account appears in a journal kept by Wales, one of Cook's officers:

The Concluding Piece, they called *Mydiddee Arramy*. Which I know not how to translate better than *The Child-Coming*. The part of the Woman in Labour was performed by a large brawny Man with a great black bushy beard, which was ludicrous enough. He sat on the ground with his legs straight out, between the legs of another who sat behind him and held the *labouring man's* back hard against his own breast. A large white cloth was spread over both which was carefully kept close down to the Ground on every side by others who kneeled round them. The farce was carried on for a considerable time with a great many wrigglings and twistings of the body . . . until at length after a more violent than ordinary struggle out crawled a great lubberly fellow from under the Cloth, and ran across the place between the Audience and Actors, and the *he*-Mother straddled after, squeezing his breasts between his fingers and dabing them across the youngsters Chaps, & every now & then to heighten the relish of the entertainment mistooke and strooke them up his backside.[42]

It was a time and a place wherein neither Aristophanes nor Aeschylus would have felt alien.

17

The Heroic Age

The "heroic age" is an ambiguous term—the kind of term people enjoy using under the assumption that everybody knows what it means. But what does it mean? Odysseus and Achilles and bards strumming lyres in courts; small groups of brave warriors surrounding a king, conquering and dying with him; fierce, bearded Scandinavian warriors with tusks in their helmets and icicles on mustache and beard? Was the heroic age a time when people acted as they do in the legends, or does the term refer to a time when people told those legends and believed them to be true? Are we dealing with history or literature or both?

It was the adolescence of the race, says H. Munro Chadwick in *The Heroic Age.* That sounds intriguing. One may agree or disagree as long as the terms of reference are ambiguous, and no hard questions are asked, like: When and where was it? Did people really behave in that manner? What stages of culture preceded and succeeded this heroic age? Then again, maybe it was all invented. Perhaps there was no great Dorian invasion or world-shaking sack of Troy or Abraham from Sumer.

There are those who delight in using legendary material to "prove" theories about real societies. They make the assumption that the society that appears in the legends existed in actuality. When people begin to write about the beginnings of aristocracy, for instance, and use legendary material for their data, they are not writing history, but are keeping alive the art of composing epic poetry. The one place there clearly has been a heroic age is inside our own heads.

And yet, the excitement of the heroic age—with all its lack of clarity—is genuine. All the barbarian peoples of Europe—Anglo-Saxons,

Celts, Norsemen—really did have bards who sang in the lord's hall, and individual warriors of superlative skill, and small groups of loyal followers dying with their lord in the defense of a bridge, and a great literature all of which was oral.

There was a time when people talked and felt and responded and acted like Homer's heroes. People create literature to satisfy, imaginatively, psychological needs. Culture and society are created for the same reason. Epic poetry is partly a true memory of the way things really were and partly an idealized memory. The story of Odysseus at the court of the Phaeacians is no more moving than the account we have of Apolo Kagwa at the court of the king of Ankole, by Bartholome Zimbe, a Buganda historian who witnessed the event, a man who certainly had never read the *Iliad*.

After the Baganda Moslems and Christians had succeeded in driving Kabaka Mwanga from the throne (1888), the victorious religious factions warred with each other. In the first flush, the Moslems succeeded in driving the Christians (Protestants and Catholics) from the country. One of the Christian leaders was friendly with a border governor of the neighboring kingdom of Ankole, and that governor offered refuge and asylum to the troops. Gradually, three to four hundred Christian soldiers found their way to this place of exile. The king of Ankole had no quarrel with his governor's action, but he feared the presence of such a force, inactive, within his boundaries. The king also wished to see what kind of men these godfearing warriors were and invited them to be received at his court.

After all had assembled, with much ceremony and with much keen observation, the king of Ankole introduced his champion wrestler and invited his Baganda guests to provide a challenger who would engage the king's pride. The Ankolean champion was almost seven feet tall and no Muganda was anxious to challenge him. Everyone became uneasy contemplating the shame that would adhere to the Christians if no one answered the call. The king of Ankole might decide he had taken cowards under his protection and might ask them to find refuge elsewhere.

Finally, after a silence that seemed like ages, Apolo Kagwa, a leader of the Protestant faction, a man of enormous personal courage, stepped forward. He was a good eight to ten inches shorter than his opponent. The Baganda inwardly groaned at the thought of what would happen to their beloved general. But God, or fate, or justice, or Apolo's strength, decreed that the impossible should happen. With the fate of his people and his country riding on his actions, Kagwa seized the An-

kolean champion, raised him off the ground, and was about to dash him
to earth.

"When the Ankoleans saw that he was certainly about to drop him
on the ground," writes Zimbe, "the Ankoleans rose up and about 20
of the people held him by the hands and prevented him from being
thrown on the ground saying in their language 'Ayah-yah-yah—he is
killing him.' They accordingly held and took him away from him, then
Kagwa Mityana Apolo in his youthful strength was raging just in the
same way as a man-killing buffalo rages, and Kagwa died with his
strength. Then all of us Baganda rose up and rallied round the wrestling
ground and no Munyankole dared anymore to ask the Baganda for
wrestling; and we were then as Israelites in the case of the giant and
brave Goliath whom however David hit and killed with a slung stone
and all the Israelites shouted joyously with the voice of victory we similarly did in Ankole: we rejoiced. . . ."[1]

As far as warfare and other forms of aggression are concerned, the
available data reveal a striking relationship between the events of epic
poetry and the actualities of life in advanced complex societies. In the
Iliad, when two great warriors face each other, armed to the teeth, death
in their eyes, itching for the kill, they do not immediately go at it. First,
they talk at great length—boasting of their family connections or their
past accomplishments or their intentions toward their opponents. As
literary or "unreal" as this convention may seem, the fact is that, in
ancient-complex Tahiti, warriors fought one another in exactly that
style:

When their modes of attack were deliberate, the celebrated warriors of each
army marched forward beyond the first line of the body to which they belonged, and, on approaching the ranks of the enemy, sat down on the sand
or the grass. Two or three from one of these parties would then rise, and advancing a few yards towards their opponents, boastfully challenge them to the
combat. When the challenge was accepted, which was often with the utmost
promptitude, the combatants advanced with intimidating menaces.

These often addressed each other by recounting their names, the names and
deeds of their ancestors, their own achievements in combat, the prowess of their
arms, and the augmented fame they should acquire by the addition of their present foes to the number of those they had already slain; in conclusion, inviting
them to advance, that they might be devoted to their god, who was hovering
by to receive the sacrifice. With taunting scorn the antagonist would reply
much in the same strain, sometimes mingling affected pity with his denuncia-
tions. When they had finished their harangue, the *omoreaa,* club of insult, or

insulting spear was raised, and the onset commenced. Sometimes it was a single combat, fought in the space between two armies, in the sight of both.[2]

And Henry tells us that, as one champion fell, another would take his place. Subsequently, more men arose to challenge one another, until both armies were completely involved.[3]

In ancient Tonga, warfare also resembled epic, in that the warriors on each side were frequently known to one another. Before combat, warriors of individual reputation would work themselves up by running over to their king, striking their spears violently on the ground, and announcing, "This is a club for so and so."[4] Mariner says that these heroic fighters would take the names of the particular persons they intended to kill; in other words, they ate them before they were dead. At the time of the Tongan King Finow I, after firearms had been introduced, one brave combatant, "instead of assuming the name of one of the enemy, proudly called himself *Fanna Fannooa* (a great gun) declaring that he would run boldly up to a cannon and throw his spear into the mouth of it."[5]

The heroic legends of many peoples tell of warriors of superlative skill and of remarkably named weapons. The military history of the Zulus in South Africa indicates that many legendary fighters and weapons may have been based upon real circumstance. In a crucial battle in their wars of conquest, the Zulus were aided by certain allies in guarding the central ford of the river. Included among these was Njikiza Ngcolosi, a veritable Ajax who carried a club no other man could wield, and who worked it to such prodigious effect that many Zulu enemies never saw another sunrise. In honor of that accomplishment, the club was named Nohlola-Mazibuko, "The Watcher of the Ford," which also became a praise name of its owner.[6] If Her Majesty's troops had not put an end to the heroic age of the Zulu, who knows what great songs some Zulu Homer might have elaborated and sung about Njikiza Ngcolosi?

A warrior hero's glory and troubles were not over even when the war itself was terminated, as the great Greek King Agamemnon discovered. From the Polynesian Maori we have a true story of a chief named Waka Nene who returned from a raiding expedition with a concubine captured in the raid. His wife, a veritable sister to the famous Clytemnestra, took her husband's new delight sea fishing, had her sit in front of the canoe, killed her with a tomahawk, and threw the corpse overboard. When she returned home, she informed her husband of the affair and announced that she would do the same with each new wife he brought home. "It is said that from that time the chief was strictly monogamous."[7]

Within this same Maori culture, it was the custom that when an important chief visited a village, he was not suffered to enter by the usual gate, but, in deference to his high rank and the distinction he was conferring on the village, a part of the defensive wall was taken down and he entered through this special opening. Best comments: "Here the memory wheels backward to Greece and the winner of the Olympian games, who was not allowed to enter by the city gates, but for whose passage a part of the city walls was broken down."[8] We may imagine that in both ancient Greece and ancient New Zealand the myth preceded the rite, and that the myth told of a conquering hero either so powerful a warrior that he could singlehandedly break down the walls of the city, or else so powerful a magician that his magic could cause such destruction. In any event, the ritual gave the illusion that some men, at least, held enormous power and were entitled to great deference.

No great work in this world is done without the courage to abandon and transform old modes of attachment, and if courage is five parts realistic appraisal of one's powers, it is equally five parts magical belief in one's omnipotence. In order to take a great step forward, it is necessary, like Antaeus with the earth, to touch continually the source of strength. The hero, stronger than strong, larger than large, more cunning than cunning, is a person whose task is to make the illusionary real, either in the world or in the mind, since we live in both places. In the heroic age of advanced complex society it was hard to tell, at times, where legend stopped and the real world began. For magic's sake and courage's sake, it was of no importance to make that distinction.

On the Tongan island of Vavau, a king was assassinated by a group of conspirators, who allowed his body to be buried by his mourning chiefs. After forming a circle around his grave, they lowered his corpse into it; then one of the conspirators, Chioolooa, "a great warrior and a powerful man," advanced into the middle of the circle brandishing his club, stood at the side of the grave, and addressed the chiefs: "If there be any among you harbouring secret thoughts of revenge, keep them no longer buried in your bosom, meditating plans of future insurrection, but come now forth and fight me on the spot, for by sacrificing me, you will revenge his death; come on, then, one and all, and wreak your vengeance on my head!" Nobody accepted the challenge. The Vavau chiefs had not forsworn vengeance, but felt it could be accomplished with more success at some future, and secret, time. "The stone was put over the grave, and the company dispersed."[9]

One of the most moving scenes in the *Iliad* takes place on the battlements of Troy between the doomed Hektor and his wife, Andromache, when the fate of Hektor's young son after his father's death is predicted. He will go at the common feasts from table to table, begging for food, because he has no father to buffer him against the world. Just so, the Tongan chief Booboonoo, having conspired against Finow I and lost, said that "he only died unhappy on account of his infant son, who would be left friendless and unprotected; but, calling to a young chief in the larger canoe, of the name of Talo, begged, for the sake of their gods, that he would befriend his child, and never see him want either clothes or food suitable to the son of a chief; upon which Talo made a solemn promise to take the most attentive care of him, and Booboonoo seemed quite satisfied."[10]

So pervasive is the focus of "heroic" material on battle, killing, and revenge that it is restful to come upon a correspondence between complex societies and heroic poetry that does not concern competition or killing. Many of the Homeric heroes were proficient in playing the lyre, partly because it was the mark of an aristocrat to be versed in this art. In Rwanda, the Tutsi aristocracy cultivated the art of dance and of creating verse; among Tongan aristocrats, it was "considered a mark of great ignorance to be unaccomplished in the graceful, manly, and expressive movements of this dance."[11]

In Hawaii, legends collected around the memory of the great King Kamehameha I to the point that it is often no longer possible to separate accurate oral history from elaborated legend. Actual battles became the occasion for exaggerated telling:

Kamehameha and Hema went down till they reached this limited space, when they met Keoua's warriors. Forty of them with their spears and javelins jumped on Kamehameha, but they were as nothing to him. He stretched out his hands, caught the warriors, and broke them in two, one after another, all the time moving onward. Thus Kamehameha slaughtered the soldiers until there remained only ten, when he became exhausted. He then told his servant, "Say, help me out." Hema immediately jumped into the fray, killing the remaining ten; and on that day he became a chief of Kamehameha, being released from his position as attendant.[12]

More important than the question of whether this tale is mostly, partly, or vaguely true is the question whether or not Kamehameha could have sustained the will to conquer the principal islands of Hawaii and become the first emperor of that archipelago without at least some belief that he was just such a legendary hero, capable of disposing of thirty out of forty warriors singlehandedly. Without this dream of heroism, would there have been any advanced complex society or Roman Empire or Catholic Church or Thousand Year Reich or October Revolution or Declaration of Independence? Would anyone write a book or compose a symphony or paint if he or she did not feel it would result in immortality? It is a very thin line that separates the healthy heroic from paranoiac megalomania. The heroic age of the mind nurtures both.

Early in his conquest of the island of Hawaii, Kamehameha found himself in straitened circumstances during one skirmish. His foot got caught in a lava hole, and while he was in this helpless position, a fisherman who lacked a spear splintered his paddle over the future king's head. When he assumed sovereignty over the whole island, Kamehameha called the fisherman before him; the latter admitted his assault. Instead of executing the man, the king gave promise of a beneficent rule by decreeing the "law of the splintered paddle," whose purpose was to protect innocent people from molestation on the public roads. It stated that henceforth old people and small children could sleep on the roadways with no fear that their safety was endangered. Kamehameha undertook a vigorous campaign to effectuate this ideal of civil order.[13]

There are many stories of powerful kings who roamed their capital cities at night, in disguise. We all do, under cover of darkness, what the day forbids. There were the pious sultans of the *Arabian Nights* who sought in the darkness to know the true thoughts of their subjects, and the mad Emperor Nero, who traversed the streets of Rome, beating and even killing unsuspecting victims. Kamehameha, we are told, loved pious people. While he and his chiefs were living at Kawaihae, Kamehameha and Ho'okaukau went out one night to spy. At midnight an old man rose up to pound *awa*. Hearing the pounding, the chief and his companion came up close to the house. After a while, the old man strained the *awa* and poured it into a cup. Then he prayed for the preservation of all the chiefs, and after that he prayed for the preservation of all the chiefesses, then for the life of Kamehameha, saying, "Let Kamehameha, the good king, live to be old, until his eyebrows are wrinkled like a rat's, his skin parched like the dry *hola* leaf, until he lies help-less, so let him live, god, and let me live also." Then the old man drank the *awa*. At the end of his prayer Kamehameha asked, "Is all your *awa* gone?" The old man answered, "The *awa* is gone. I only have scraps left. Last evening I gave most of it to the god, and since I could not sleep I awoke and pounded a little and drank it without any food to eat after it." Kamehameha said, "I have a little *awa;* let my man bring you some." After they had gone away he said to his companion, "Bring him forty *awa* stocks . . . five tuna fish, forty *aku* fish, forty *mamaki* tapas, and twenty heavy loin cloths." When the things were given to the old man he said, "It must have been Kamehameha and his man who came here last night."[14]

Legendary material, like this story of Kamehameha, concerns itself either with real people who take on heroic aspects or with heroes who might or might not have had a real existence. It is difficult with much legendary matter to know whether the tales themselves are true or not. Only when the feat related defies nature can we be sure that the act described is false. There may or may not have been, in the twelfth century B.C., a great warrior named Achilles, but we can be reasonably positive that his horses did not speak. While legends may or may not be true, folklore and mythology do not deal with real situations or people. In the heroic age of the mind, distinctions among legendary material, folklore, mythology, heroes real and fancied, magical acts, and unusual but possible human achievements are blurred and tumbled together so that it is no longer possible to distinguish between real and not-real. So insistent is this quality of the mind that even today sophisticated people look incredulous when informed that there is absolutely no historical proof of the existence of Jesus, and the Viennese founder of "scientific" psychology wrote a book about Moses as if there were no doubt that he had been a real person.

We need it. The goals of our ambitions are too great, and take us too far from home, to be sustained by the rewards that only reality can bring. Those societies that first sought the breakdown of the kinship system have given us the first stories of superhuman heroes who live their lives midway between the gods and humans.

The folklore and mythology of Buganda, Hawaii, and Tahiti rejoice in many of the great themes that are shared by oral literatures the world over. They share the "Delilah" theme, whereby a great hero loses his heart and then his secret to a daughter of the enemy and is betrayed by her;[15] the lost god who returns to earth and then disappears again because of the misdeeds of mortals;[16] the hero who, out of kindness, with no thought of recompense, helps some animals or birds in their distress and is rewarded when they return to extricate him from an impossible crisis.[17]

On the island of Hawaii there was a great king, Imaikalani, "famous for his strength and skill in warfare. . . . If he threw a long spear to the right or to the left hand there was a roaring as of thunder, and flashes as of lightning, and a rumbling sound as of an earthquake. . . ."[18] But he was blind. He had two wild ducks who watched for his opponents and instructed him in which direction he was to aim his weapons. No one could stand against him.

The great Hawaiian King Liloa traveling one day through his lands decided to escape the day's heat by bathing in a cool stream. As chance would have it, he discovered there a woman whose beauty and grace were a match for his imperial power. So satisfying was their embrace that they both knew that a child had been conceived. "When the child is born," he commanded her, "if it be a girl, name her for your side of the family; but if it be a boy, name him for mine. He shall be named Umi. I am Liloa, and these are the tokens for the child when he grows up and seeks me in Waipio: the feather cape, ivory pendant, helmet and *kauila* spear."[19]

The woman was married to a man of common blood, who, not knowing the truth, raised the child as if he were his own, beating him severely when he misbehaved. The mother was enraged that the son of a king should be consistently beaten by an "insignificant, low commoner," and, one day, told her husband the truth, showing him the tokens as confirmation of the story. Fear flooded the stepfather upon learning that he had laid himself open to retribution from the king, and he desisted from mistreating the boy.

Shortly thereafter, Umi, who knew of his parentage, asked his mother if he might travel to see his real father. She gave him her assent and the tokens that certified the story. He traveled to the court, broke the tabu concerning admittance to the king's presence, walked straight up to the monarch, and leaped into his lap. "Whose child are you?" "Yours! I am Umi-a-Liloa." Noticing the tokens, Liloa kissed and wept over his son.

"He ordered the kahunas [priests] to fetch the *pahu* and *kaeke* drums at once and to take the boy to be circumcized and dedicated, as was the custom for children of chiefs. The chiefly drum Halalu, and the smaller *kaeke* drums were sounded. . . . 'It was for this child of mine that I girded my loins with ti leaves and covered my shoulders with banana leaves. . . .' "

This charming story of abandonment and reconciliation leads us to one of the most important mythic themes in all culture, which Otto Rank elaborated in *The Myth of the Birth of the Hero.* It is essentially the same tale told of Sargon, ancient king of Sumer and Akkad; of Cyrus, founder of the Persian Empire; of Romulus, mythical founder of Rome; of Oedipus of Thebes; of Moses and Jesus; and of many others in both the West and East. No other story, it seems, has spoken so deeply to so many people as this elaborated infanticidal fantasy. In some versions the parents of an unborn child are warned that if the child lives great harm will come to them (in most instances, he will kill the father). Putting their own lives before his, but unable to commit the horrid deed themselves, they either give the child to someone else to be done away with, or abandon the child to the elements or wild animals. However, someone (a herdsman) or something (a wolf) saves the child from extinction. Here the stories begin to diverge. The doomed and rescued offspring can then be reconciled with the father (Cyrus) or kill the father (Oedipus) or merely go on to do great deeds (Romulus)

A brilliant effect of the tale is that it arouses our sympathy for and causes us to identify with both parties—the parents and the child. We can fully comprehend the panic of Oedipus' parents when they receive the certain prediction of what will happen should the child be allowed to live. In one part of our mind, we cannot and do not blame them for what they did. And yet, we feel with the child, want it to survive, and even grab the sword with Oedipus when he rushes into the palace to avenge himself on the mother who had intended to rob him of his life. The story allows us no sentimental way out, no simple opposition between cruel, evil parents and good, innocent child. If we would know ourselves, we must comprehend how both the parents and the child feel.

The Hebrew-Christian versions of the story represent a remarkable moral advance. The traditional tale tells of parents with infanticidal needs and the child rescued by others. In the case of Moses and Jesus, the threat to the child comes from *others* (Pharaoh and Herod), and the saving of the child is the task of the *parents*. Moses can be saved only by being given away to be raised by others, but the narrative of Jesus goes even further toward a loving reconciliation between parents and children: the whole family leaves and travels to Egypt so that the child may escape destruction. The child's life is preserved within the structure of his own family. Only the donkey, so prominent especially in the paintings of the flight to Egypt, keeps us in touch with the old tales in which something nonhuman rescued the child.

Many psychologically oriented analyses of literature—the psychoanalytic mode is only one of several possible—make a connection between universal needs in the human psyche and the existence of certain basic themes in literature. Whether one talks of archetypes (Hercules, Odysseus, Eve) or fundamental motifs (Cinderella, the youngest son, helpful animals), the implications of this kind of analysis are that all people share the same needs, that the need for literature is universal, and that the reasons literature is created and listened to are psychological. This way of thought does not have to reduce literature to the psychological or explain artistic creative accomplishments, as Freud did explain them, as merely the outward projection of unresolvable neurotic problems. A humanistic analysis not only makes psychology a part of literature, but also insists that literature is a part of psychology. Human beings are, among other things, a storymaking species.

The universal psychological needs that drive the literary imagination to adopt certain basic archetypal motifs also drive society to create certain basic social and cultural forms. The archetypal Hercules exists in a thousand variations because there is a human need for this particular symbolism. The institution of kingship was invented in a thousand places because there was a human need for that particular symbolism. Human society is a human creation. Whatever symbolic structures exist in the world must have existed first in the human psyche.

In the heroic age of the world, people not only told stories of how the sons of kings were abandoned, recovered, and reconciled—they actually acted out that drama in a regularized, institutionalized series of actions. In that age, this great world-myth was no myth. On the Polynesian island of Mangareva, when the male heir to the king was born, he was immediately removed to a secluded spot in the mountains where he spent his first twelve years. Another six years were spent in isolation at some other location. When the child was eighteen, he returned to Mangareva and took over the ritual aspects of the sovereignty from his father, who continued as regent and as the war commander. Indeed, this institution was not restricted to Mangareva and was found in many islands of western Polynesia.[20]

And Roscoe tells us this true tale of the kingdom of Koki, neighbor of Buganda—a nineteenth-century variation on the flight to Egypt:

It is the custom with the royal clan that the firstborn child of a king shall be a girl; should a male be born, he is killed at birth, and the midwife says that the child was born dead. The present ruler is an exception to this custom, for he was the firstborn child of his father, but escaped death owing to the introduction of Christianity. In the course of developing its work, the Uganda church sent a catechist to Koki, who was successful in reaching numbers of the better class. Among the early converts was the King Kamswaga; after his baptism he was informed of the existence of his son, and he allowed him to be brought to his capital. The child had been taken into the country at the time of his birth and placed with some of the royal herdsmen, and the father had been kept in ignorance of his existence, and told that the child was still-born, according to their old custom. There are instances on record of princes having been thus taken away and cared for, where there was little hope of there being a successor to the king, and of men having come forward at the king's death to prove the prince's legitimate claim to the throne. In this case the introduction of Christianity removed the difficulty, and the father acknowledged his son, and received him back in the capital during his own lifetime.[21]

Was it the same herdsman who saved Oedipus and Cyrus? If our realities begin in dreams, then myth is as real as anything in the world. The society we live in is as much a myth-dream as the tale of King Oedipus. It is good or evil, loving or hateful, as we choose to make it. We have made it up and remake it with each generation. The great revolutionary advances in society come only after the creation of a new myth-dream that cries out to be actualized. We remain, today, bogged down in our own inadequacies and mediocrities, because we lack the belief in a new myth that would transcend our present notions of what it means to live together in human society. It is time we moved beyond our current morally and imaginatively impoverished culture, which insists that the heroic age was *only* a myth.

18

The Slaughter of the Innocents

"In point of number, the disproportion between the infants spared and those destroyed was truly distressing. It is not easy to learn exactly what this disproportion was; but the first missionaries have published it as their opinion that, not less than two-thirds of the children were murdered by their own parents. . . . The first three infants, they observed, were frequently killed; and in the event of twins being born, both were rarely permitted to live. . . . We have been acquainted with a number of parents, who, according to their own confessions, or the united testimony of their friends and neighbors, had inhumanly consigned to an untimely grave, four, or six, or eight, or ten children, and some even a greater number. I feel hence, the painful and humiliating conviction which I have ever been reluctant to admit, forced upon me from the testimony of the natives themselves, the proportion of children found by the first missionaries, and existing in the population at the time of our arrival—that during the generations immediately preceding the subversion of paganism, not less than two-thirds of the children were massacred. A female, who was frequently accustomed to wash the linen for our family, had thus cruelly destroyed five or six. Another, who resided near us, had been the mother of eight, of which only one had been spared."[1]

Thus writes Ellis about Tahiti, and other evidence is more than adequate to confirm his contentions. The documentation from Hawaii is slighter, but there is no doubt that the killing of newborn infants was a regular practice in that society also.[2] For Buganda, I have only one citation, from Roscoe,[3] and therefore, it is not possible to form an opinion concerning the general existence of infanticide.

When we of the Hebrew-Christian world are first confronted with this kind of evidence of human behavior, we immediately seek to deny the full impact of the phenomenon. We prefer, and many insist upon, any other possible explanation of why people acted in this manner except the one that says they did it out of aggressive feelings toward their own children. We have a great reluctance to admit that human beings can maintain an acutely hostile stance toward the whole process of bearing children, and toward the consuming demands, psychological and biological, that the existence of a new human being places on us. We much prefer more rational explanations: it was a method of birth control (after the fact) or population control (especially on a small island). Captain Bligh was convinced that it could not be what it seemed:

The most remarkable instance, related to me, of the barbarity of this institution, was of Teppahoo, the Earee [lord] of the district of Tettaha, and his wife, Tetteehowdeah, who is sister to Otow [Pomare I], and considered as a person of the first consequence. I was told that they have had eight children, every one of which was destroyed as soon as born. That any human beings were ever so devoid of natural affection, as not to wish to preserve alive one of so many children, is not credible. It is more reasonable to conclude, that the death of these infants was not an act of choice in the parents; but that they were sacrificed in compliance with some barbarous superstition, with which we are unacquainted. What strengthens this conjecture is, that they have adopted a nephew as their heir, of whom they are excessively fond.[4]

The profound ambivalence apparent in the actions described by Bligh—killing all one's own children and adopting someone else's child—should alert us to the fact that something profoundly irrational is being expressed. In a similar fashion, parents in Buganda gave their own children out to be raised by others, and raised in their own homes the children of others. There is no more profound ambivalence than that displayed, though not necessarily consciously expressed, by parents toward their own children.

The "Malthusian motive," as Ellis puts it, for infanticide has a certain credulity to it, but we have to reckon with the fact that we are dealing with societies that had an abundance of natural resources and absolutely no shortage of land. These were affluent peoples; the threat of famine and poverty did not hang over them. It is also interesting that people today are willing to ascribe such a rational explanation to the behavior of complex societies (they did it to keep the population down on small islands), while we ourselves are incapable of dealing rationally with our own population pressure even when, at the least, it is ruining the quality of our lives, and, at the worst, it threatens to drive us into an atomic war in order to preserve our sources of energy. That the Tahitians calmly and soberly solved the problems of population explosion, and that our society is incapable thus far of doing so, does not seem plausible.

The killing of newborn infants, no matter what the motive, can never be done coldly and rationally. The state of depression that visits those in our society who have had a child aborted (a year after abortion, or nine months after conception) lends weight to that assertion. Ellis felt that the population explanation was only rationalization: "A Malthusian motive has sometimes been adduced, and they have been heard to say, that if all the children born were allowed to live, there would not be food enough produced in the islands to support them. This, however, has only been resorted to when other methods of defending the practice have failed."[5]

One fact of fundamental importance argues against the claim that infanticide was practiced for rational reasons: in almost every case in which a people have practiced regular, legitimate infanticide, the percentage of girls done away with is much higher than the percentage of boys. No common-sense reasons for killing infants would make that kind of distinction between males and females. Something much more irrational, something much deeper in the psyche, is being spoken to. Tahitian women's "sex was often, at their birth, the cause of their destruction: if the purpose of the unnatural parents had not been fully matured before, the circumstance of its being a female child, was often sufficient to fix their determination on its death. . . . In the adult population of the islands at the time of our arrival, the disproportion between the sexes was very great. There were, probably, four or five men to one woman."[6] It is interesting to note that in the pagan world of ancient Greece and Rome, infanticide was widespread, and, here again, the number of growing boys in the population greatly outnumbered the number of girls.*

Over half the people whom I have confronted with these facts have

---

*John Rowe has suggested in a personal communication that the reason there was no such discrepancy between boys and girls in Buganda is that women were highly valued because they did almost all the productive farm labor. The more women a man "had," the more food he could control.

argued that the killing of a greater percentage of girls was a rational way to population control. Since women are the bearers of children, this argument runs, the most efficient means of birth control in such societies is to kill them before they can perform that function. The most efficient method, no doubt, is to abstain from sexual intercourse, although that "solution" can also be considered irrational since it denies people the pleasure of expressing a biological and psychological drive. What is important to observe, however, is that the disproportionate infanticide of girls results in an abstention from intercourse by a large percentage of the adult population: those males who are unable to obtain marriage partners. Most of the data we have on the results of gender-differential infanticide point toward the "impossible" figures of the remaining population, which then consists of three, four, or five males for each female. Does that mean that the vast majority of men in such societies never got married? Early marriage for females and late marriage for males might possibly compensate a little, but certainly not enough. We have to ask why the males, who controlled such societies, put themselves in such an unfortunate position. It seems doubtful that they did so from rational motives. This question must remain open until we have conclusive evidence, which we now lack, from primitive, complex, and ancient societies that would indicate exactly what were the infanticidal and marriage practices.

In my view, institutionalized infanticide was practiced in order to satisfy intense feelings of aggression, not just toward children and women but, maybe more fundamentally, toward the whole psychological process of child bearing and child rearing, a process that is carried out by women and produces children. That the great pleasure of sex results in the pain of childbirth and the terrible burden of raising a new human is something people have enormous difficulty accepting. Today, some women in childbirth curse the husbands who got them there, even though they love those husbands and are destined to love the children who result from the process. It is not unreasonable to surmise that postpartum depression, which all new mothers suffer to some extent, has to do with a deep, irrational conflict over infanticide. We hate the blow to our narcissism that the reality of birth pain and of a new human being who must have all our attention brings. If we lived in a pre-Hebrew, pre-Christian world, we would feel free to express that anger by killing the infant. More infant girls are killed than boys, not only because boys are more valued than girls—true in all previous societies—but also because women stand for the whole child-making process. As crazy as this may sound, let us recall that the Tahitians, in no way a psychotic people, killed over half the children born to them. If the child was allowed to live, even for a day, Ellis tells us,[7] there was no longer any danger of its being killed. It was not against *the child* that the act was done but against *the idea of the child.* Once the child was allowed to become real, infanticide was impossible.

The mother, or father, or some near relation could deal the actual death. Sometimes a conflict arose as to whether the child should be permitted to live or not. In such cases, it was invariably the mother who argued for the life of the child and the father and his relatives who urged destruction. In a society permeated with class differences, status considerations played their role in this area as well as in others. "The marriage tie was dissolved whenever either of the parties desired it; and though amongst their principal chiefs it was allowed nominally to remain, the husbands took other wives, and the wife other husbands. These were mostly individuals of personal attractions, but of inferior rank in society. The progeny of such a union was almost invariably destroyed, if not by the parents themselves, by the relatives of those superior in rank, lest the dignity of the family, or their standing in society, should be injured by being blended with those of an inferior class."[8]

The story of Abraham and Isaac has such power because it brings together the great themes of human sacrifice and infanticide, or, more accurately, filicide. The notion that the birth of an infant boy somehow represents a threat to the life of the father must arise from the same mad place in the mind that assumes we are made safer by sacrificing others. So many of the myths of abandonment have that as their thrust: if Oedipus lives, his father's life is threatened. In Buganda, it was assumed that the birth of a son to a clan head indicated that the father would die. The answer to this threat consisted in strangling the first male child. After that sacrifice, subsequent males were permitted to live.[9]

So sacred were some temples in Tahiti that, should a stray man appear in the precincts during the prayers to the gods, he would be seized and killed on the spot and his body buried in the temple. Should some unsuspecting Isaac break away from home and go to his father at the temple during the celebration of these rites, the father would announce to the high priest: "Take this child and slay him for the gods! Behold the order of the marae [temple] is disturbed by him, the thread of the prayers to the gods is entangled. He is my son, I begot him, but I must not regret (losing him), because he has erred in coming here to the assembly of the gods."[10] Like Abraham's obedience to Jehovah, it was an act of piety.

We have been misled by our own narcissism as well as by biological concepts of adaptability and survival of the fittest into thinking that whatever the human species has that other species do not have is more functional, more adaptable, increasing the chances of our survival. Our pelvis allows us to walk upright; our large brain enables us to invent weapons; therefore, our prospects of survival are enhanced. All this does not logically contradict the idea that we may have certain inheritances in our animal nature, including what can only be called "psychological impulses," that are dysfunctional, unadaptive, decreasing the chances of survival. One may admire the wonderful biological evolutionary process that has programmed the "ascent of man" without falling into the narcissistic trap of imagining it as a scenario for perfection.

In the course of reading for and writing this book, I have tried to think very hard and unsentimentally about the problem of infanticide. It makes so little sense biologically and psychologically that it seems to have no cause. And yet, it is there. Primitive people did it, as did peoples in complex societies and our Roman and Greek ancestors. I cannot speak for the ancient Egyptians, Sumerians, and Minoans, but it would be no shock to discover the same about them. Human beings seem to have a nonrational biopsychological impulse—as if they carry within themselves some strange, nonadaptive beast—to destroy their own young. In a way, it seems to take a great act of grace to let the child live. To ask what function the impulse to infanticide serves, to look for a logical reason for people's carrying out these destructive impulses, is grossly to misrepresent the perfectibility of the species.

That impulse is clearly only a part of our biopsychological inheritance, and not the greatest part. Were it the latter, we would have left this earth after one or two generations. How many children can be killed and the species survive?

That destructive drive toward the newborn has been a burden that human beings have carried and still carry. In the history of the development of Western society, it was not until the rise of the ancient Hebrew religion, which celebrated a world triumph in Christianity, that the practice of infanticide was declared illegitimate. For most of human history, there has been no moral sanction against destroying newborn children. We contemplate it with horror from a unique, and very recently achieved, vantage point: it was less than two thousand years ago that

the abandonment of Oedipus on Mount Cithaeron gave way to the
flight to Egypt.

And a psychologically primitive involvement with the problem of
infanticide still disrupts our own polity in the form of debate over
whether abortion is only another form of child killing. The question
whether aborting a fetus and killing a child are the same act is a
psychological question, not a legal or an intellectual one. Everyone answers that question for himself or herself on the basis of psychological
considerations. In essence, abortion is murder if you want it to be so.

It is possible that to admit the legitimacy of abortion is to be able
to deal, inwardly and not consciously, with one's own infanticidal impulses. Perhaps those who cry out against abortion are not able to admit
to themselves that they, being human, have a nonrational part of their
psyche that would do away with the newborn. That knowledge is so
frightening that their energies are spent keeping the knowledge of those
terrible impulses repressed, so much so that they will not even allow
others the freedom to do as conscience dictates. They insist on the question of abortion and infanticide because their concern with the latter
has become obsessional.

Even those who are fairly free in this regard are not able to be
entirely rational. The act of abortion cannot be completely severed,
especially for the woman who carries the fetus, from the feeling of term-
inating a life. An abortion will never be as lightly treated as an ap-
pendectomy. To insist that it can be is to deny the complexity and
nonrationality of the psyche.

A case can be made that both society and morality progress in a dialectical manner. It is possible to suggest such a development with infanticide. The Tahitians killed over half of their newborn with hardly any,
if any at all, conscious ambivalence about such actions. It is difficult to
know how much unconscious sense of guilt adhered to the act, since
society completely approved such behavior. When Hebrew-Christian
morality put an end to the pervasive infanticide of the pagan world,
a great moral advance was institutionalized—the value of human life,
especially of children, was enormously enhanced. But that great step
was taken within a moral context that also included the elevation of
chastity to a great virtue, a severe condemnation of premarital sexual
experience (mostly for women), and the prohibition of birth control
and abortion: guarantees that most women would live their lives imprisoned by child bearing and child rearing. The social process that made

infanticide illegitimate also carried with it much that resulted in dehumanization.

Lifting these prohibitions does not mean returning to the Tahitian notion of newborn children as something that can be disposed of as one throws away a broken plate. Our belief in the legitimacy of abortion and family planning grows out of the enormously high valuation we place on those children whom we do rear, and we owe that stance in part to those great early Christians who established orphanages—a form of institution not found in the pagan world.

The lifting of the prohibitions should produce a synthesis, provided it incorporates into the new position the advance that the first prohibition represented. We progress in such a slow and roundabout manner because the nonrational part of what we have to deal with has such enormous power, and we shall never comprehend ourselves until we are willing to admit how vulnerable, frightened, and potentially destructive a place we all harbor within ourselves. The history of infanticide can teach us a great deal about that terrible place.

19

Male Homosexuality
and Male Bisexuality

The evidence of homosexual experience in primitive society is so sparse as almost to be suspect: one wonders whether it was the societies or the reporters of data who were more willing to repress the knowledge of such needs in human beings. Though there undoubtedly was more homosexuality and bisexuality in primitive societies than we know about (there is always more), there does seem to have been remarkably little. Even the anthropologists most willing to look at the sexual aspects of primitive society have reported an exceptionally small amount of data. Malinowski, in a book of over five hundred pages on sexual life, devotes only a few pages to homosexuality, and these are listed in the index under the headings "contempt for and repugnance to" and "unnatural conditions conducive to."[1] Mead, examining sexuality in three societies, says of two out of three, "There was no homosexuality among either the Arapesh or the Mundugumor."[2] There was the well-known institution of *berdache* among the Plains Indians of North America, whereby certain men opted for a woman's way of life, dressed as women, did women's work, and "married" other men. Such patterns of behavior, however, seem to have been rare in primitive society.

As infrequent as are the reports of male homoerotic experience, my statistically untested impression is that female homosexuality and bisexuality were even less frequent. There is also very little evidence of female homosexuality in complex society, though it is possible either that I have missed some or that those who have written the data have. The paucity of data on females is the reason this discussion deals exclusively with male experience.

In regard to male homosexuality, the contrast between primitive and complex societies is startling. We have ample evidence from Buganda, Hawaii, and Tahiti of homosexual and bisexual experience. It is remarkable to discover that Kamehameha I, the founder of the united Hawaiian state; Pomare II, who accomplished the same thing for Tahiti; and Mwanga of Buganda, the son of the great Mutesa, were all bisexuals. And Mutesa was accused by one Catholic missionary of practicing the "vice."[3] This last remains unproved, but of the other political leaders, there is no question. The openness with which bisexuality was practiced, the institutionalized modes established for its gratification, and the degree to which the most powerful in society sought such pleasures—all this is profoundly reminiscent of ancient Greek society.

In Rwanda, the Tutsi overlords sent their adolescent sons to court to be trained for aristocratic life. While there, they were isolated from women, and homosexual experience was considered normal. The Tutsi themselves attributed the homoerotic activity to the lack of heterosexual contacts.[4] The real question is why they invented a system in the first place, wherein the young men would have no alternative to homosexual experimentation. For the Dahomeans of West Africa, homosexual experience was ordinarily looked down upon, except during the period of middle adolescence, when contact between young girls and young boys was prohibited.[5] It was assumed that male youths would use masturbation as a substitute for heterosexual experience. Solitary masturbation was regarded with disdain by the Dahomeans, who felt it would make a man become "like a dog"; mutual masturbation by adolescent males was considered normal.[6]

Tutsi and Dahomean custom was different from that in Buganda and Polynesia. In the former cultures, a certain developmental stage was set aside for homosexual experimentation between youths of the same age. This seems similar to the experience of many individuals in our society, who engage in homoerotic experience during early adolescence but subsequently go on to a heterosexual life. Polynesian men, on the contrary, frequently lived a bisexual existence all their lives, and much of the actual sexual experience was between males of disparate ages. The Buganda data on male bisexuality is much thinner, and there is some sense that the alien presence of Arab traders in the country did much to encourage and legitimize the kind of activity that Mwanga engaged in with the young pages at court.

Whether or not bisexuality was practiced primarily by the aristocracy is an open question. Maquet says that in Rwanda both Tutsi lords and Hutu commoners engaged in homosexuality,[7] but Kamakau says

of Hawaii that the common people there did not gratify such inclinations.[8] The officers on English ships who have left us their diaries associated with, and were primarily interested in, those of the upper class.
When we read, therefore, that "every Aree [nobleman] according to
his rank keeps so many women and so many young men . . . for the
amusement of his leisure hours,"[9] or that "Terreeoboo has five of them
[male sexual companions], who are men of the first Consequence, indeed all of the Chiefs had them,"[10] we cannot know whether the common people differed in their preferences.

It is very possible that homosexual experience was far greater among
aristocrats than among peasants. There seems no question that cultural
repression can lessen actual homosexual practice and that, conversely,
the lifting of repression results in more people's trying this mode. The
rich, full, imaginative life that we observe in complex societies was primarily that of the aristocracy and those commoners in close contact
with high nobles. Country louts did not write epic poetry or dance in
the theatre or become medical healers. It would not be surprising to
discover that heterosexual practice between aristocrats was less repressed, more imaginative, than among people of lower status. The
same relative absence of repression could easily have resulted in a more
widespread homosexuality. People of the lower class still lived their
lives within the confines of the kinship system, auspices that were usually hostile to the expression of homosexual needs.

People of the lower class quickly learned that all appetites were to
be curbed, whereas aristocrats were used to getting what they wanted
and were educated to indulge, not bridle, their cravings. Karana-tua,
brother of a politically powerful noble in Hawaii, came on board Cook's
ship *Resolution* one day and immediately espied a handsome young
sailor who caught his fancy. He offered Cook six large hogs if he could
have use of the fellow for a little while. Cook, naturally, did not indulge
"the strange depravity of these Indians."[11]

The mythic imagination, delighting in tales of origin, which explain
how everything came into existence, provided in Hawaii a legendary
origin for homosexual experience. The King Liloa, who may or may
not have existed in actuality, was skilled in warfare, concerned himself
with religious affairs, and reigned a long while. During his years in office, there was much speculation as to why he retained a certain man
as a favorite. No one could tell what it was about the man that appealed
so much to the king. When Liloa died, the people approached his favor-

ite directly: " 'Why were you such a great favorite with Liloa?' " Sodomy was the simple answer. "When the people heard this, they tried it themselves, and in this way the practice of sodomy became established and prevailed down to the time of Kamehameha I."[12] The need to explain the beginnings of homosexuality in no way indicates that it was regarded as unnatural, since the mythic imagination feels it necessary to account for the existence of many natural things, such as sun, moon, aggression, death.

The most elaborated institutionalized form of homosexual connection in the three cultures existed in Tahiti, and Bligh provides us with a full description:

On my visit this Morning to Tynah [Pomare I] and his Wife, I found with her a person, who altho I was certain was a Man, had great marks of effeminacy about him and created in me certain notions which I wished to find out if there were any foundation for. On asking Iddeeah [Pomare's wife] who he was, she without any hesitation told me he was a friend of hers, and of a class of people common on Otaheite called Mahoo. That the Men had frequent connections with him and that he lived, observed the same ceremonies, and eat as the Women did. The Effeminacy of this persons speech induced me to think he had suffered castration, and that other unnatural and shocking things were done by him, and particularly as I had myself some Idea that it was common in this sea. I was however mistaken in all my conjectures except that things equally disgusting were committed. Determined as I was either to clear these people of such crimes being committed among them, or to prove that they were so, I requested Tynah to inform me, which as soon as I had requested it, a dozen people and even the Person himself answered all my questions without reserve, and gave me this Account of the Mahoos.

These people, says Tynah, are particularly selected when Boys and kept with the Women solely for the caresses of the men, here the Young Man took his Hahow or Mantle off which he had about him to show me the connection. He had the appearance of a Woman, his Yard & Testicles being so drawn in under him, having the Art from custom of keeping them in this position; those who are connected with him have their beastly pleasures gratified between his thighs, but are no farther Sodomites as they positively deny the crime. On examining his privacies I found them both very small and the Testicles remarkably so, being not larger than a boys 5 or 6 Years old, and very soft as if in a State of decay or a total incapacity of being larger, so that in either case he appeared to me effectually a Eunuch as if his stones were away. The Women treat him as one of their Sex, and he observed every restriction that they do and is equally respected and esteemed.[13]

Remarkably, this unusual mode of sexual copulation was also a characteristic form of ancient Greek homoerotic experience.[14] It seems that not only does the stage of cultural development dictate the attitude of society in regard to homosexuality and bisexuality (repressive, neutral, permissive, encouraging), but it may even, in some strange way that we cannot as yet understand, indicate what sexual positions are to be preferred.

The correspondences between ancient Greek and ancient Polynesian attitudes toward homoerotic experience are striking. In both cultures, although there were male individuals who led a totally homosexual life, such as the *mahus* of Tahiti, the men who held power in society, if they inclined toward homoerotic satisfaction, were bisexual, not exclusively homosexual. Sophocles, Socrates, Alexander the Great, Alcibiades were all bisexual, as were Pomare II and Kamehameha I. A certain stage in cultural development seems to call up great military conquerors who are bisexual. Julius Caesar was another example.

The Hebrew-Christian aversion to, and repression of, homosexuality and bisexuality were clearly not true of other societies. The value system in a society, and no society exists without one, makes a judgment on homoerotic experience and, on the basis of that judgment, decides to repress, permit, or encourage such activity. That decision, however, is not made in an arbitrary, random way. No society "just decides" that it is now going to be more permissive of homosexuality. The decision—which is never consciously arrived at, although its results are openly proclaimed—depends upon many other things going on in that society at the same time and upon the society's stage of development.

Two factors, not unrelated to each other, seem to have affected the great change from primitive to complex society in regard to permissiveness of male homoerotic experience: the breakdown of the kinship system, and the lifting of repression in general and in sexual matters particularly. Intense parental disapproval of strong homosexual inclinations makes it difficult, well-nigh impossible, for a person to stay at home and openly or covertly satisfy such inclinations. The response is to move away from the family to a large city. What happens, however, in a society where there are no cities to move to, where a person is obliged to live continually under the eye of kin? In such circumstances, people repress their homoerotic inclinations and live heterosexual lives, more or less, deriving from those lives whatever satisfaction they can get. When Mead tells us that there was *no* homosexuality among the Arapesh and Mundugumor, we must assume that a very efficient repression was at work.

In complex societies, many people did not live their whole lives under the shadow of the kin, and the royal courts provided a place to get away from home. At these courts there was much more sexual license, homosexual and heterosexual, than in most primitive societies. Especially in Polynesia, sexual experimentation seemed to be the order of the day. When sexual repression is lifted, when sexual flexibility and experimentation became valued, many who would not do so in a more repressed situation openly express their homoerotic propensities.

One is, of course, reminded of our own cultural circumstance. Once people escape from the tyranny of parents, either through the dissolution of the kinship system, or as a result of the emergence of a more humanist way of raising children, a definite lifting of sexual repression results. Certain legitimate questions suggest themselves, such as how much of a mixed blessing this lifting of repression was, and is: how much of the present increase in pornography and rape (if, indeed, they have actually increased) and the breakdown of marriage (if, indeed, it was worth preserving as it was) has been caused by the easing of sexual restraint? Complex society saw the development of many new social forms, such as prostitution, that did not enhance the value of human life, in great part as a result of the dissolution of the kinship system and the lessening of sexual repression. What seems clear is that, when sexual repression is lifted, many different things happen, and by no means can all of them be described as good for human beings. Such is the essential concern behind the great "eros and civilization" debate. The fundamental question is not whether sexual freedom is all good or all bad, which it clearly is not, but whether the diminishing of repression is worth the price.

The interaction of a relatively repressed English culture and the uninhibited Polynesian people produced several humorous instances at the turn of the eighteenth century. The English missionary Jefferson, on Tahiti, wrote in his journal that one of the brethren inadvertently witnessed an act between two men "which perhaps had not existence in Sodom and Gomorrha." The brethren were conducting a language exercise, which was attended by Paeeta, the chief of Hapyano. Tired of the teaching, the chief lay down on one of his attendants' cloths. The class being over, the brethren left the chief and his man in the apartment. "Not long after, having the occasion to go back for something

and entering suddenly, [Brother Henry] saw sufficient to assure him
a most singular and horrible species of bestiality was committing; the
chief having in his mouth the other's ———."[15] One wonders what
Brother Jefferson thought went on in Sodom and Gomorrha.

Even the more worldly sailors on the ships, however, were in for
a few surprises:

Now I am upon the subject of these kind of entertainments, I cannot help relat-
ing a very droll occurrence that happened in consequence of one of their noc-
turnal Heivas. Attracted by the sound of drums, and a great quantity of lights,
I went on shore one night with two of our mates to one of these exhibitions.
We seated ourselves among some of our friends, whom we found there; when
one of the gentlemen who accompanied me on shore took it into his head to
be very much smitten with a dancing girl, as he thought her; went up to her,
made her a present of some beads and other trifles, and rather interrupted the
performance by his attentions; but what was his surprise when the performance
ended, and after he had been endeavoring to persuade her to go with him on
board our ship, which she assented to, to find this supposed damsel, when,
stripped of her theatrical paraphernalia, a smart dapper lad. The Otaheiteans
on their part enjoyed this mistake so much that they followed us to the beach
with shouts and repeated peals of laughter; and I dare say this event has served
as a fine subject for one of their comedies.[16]

One thing seems true of all stages of cultural development: people repress only what they are frightened of and learn to laugh at certain
things only when these things have ceased to be so threatening.

20

Gambling, Prostitution, Exhibitionism, and Adultery Games

It is a reasonable proposition, I feel, that primitive society may be characterized as more inhibited and repressed in matters of sexuality than complex society. This does not signify, however, that kinship societies were rigid, unbending, or unconflicted. Adultery abounded; more or less legitimized rape existed in many primitive cultures; sexual matters were freely discussed and joked about in the company of both sexes and all ages; children often had unlimited opportunities to observe their parents' sexual activities; in many primitive societies, premarital sexual experience was freely available to people of both sexes, and in some groups, as instanced by the Trobrianders studied by Malinowski,[1] our period of so-called sexual latency was a time of sexual indulgence; wife swapping and wife lending were not unknown; and some peoples, like those of the Australian desert, had institutionalized a period of great get-together, when sexual license was the order of the day.

With all that, the sexual practices of complex society take on a different tone. It is not so much the difference in specific institutions as the fact that complex society had institutionalized such forms as prostitution and sexually exhibitionistic performances, which were nonexistent in primitive society. I can give no better name to the difference than the old-fashioned notion of vice. There was no vice in primitive society, no sense that performing certain acts has a double pleasure: the pleasure of the thing itself and the additional satisfaction that comes from having broken a tabu, having done what is forbidden. Guilt and shame congregate around the concept of vice, even if in negative disclaimers: It is not a vice, because I feel no shame or guilt about doing it. Decadence is a related notion. Contemplating sexual license at the Australian corroborees, it does not occur to one to use the word "decadence," but if the quoitslike game played by Hawaiian aristocrats to determine how married people would switch partners for the evening was not decadent, one feels there is no decadence.

Our own manner of thinking about so-called deviant behavior has changed so radically in the last twenty-five years that it is difficult to know today whether the concepts of vice and decadence can teach us anything. What used to be vice, and came under the purview of the police vice squad, is now "sexual preference." Twenty years ago, in writing this, one would have referred to Tahitian pornographic sculpture; today it is designated "erotic art." But the consumption of alcoholic beverages, pornography, gambling, prostitution are still regulated by the state, even in the most advanced democratic societies. The concept of vice, along with the obligation of the state to keep it within limits, still pervades our law. And vice, if it exists, began in complex societies.

The most extensive evidence of ordinary and compulsive gambling comes from Hawaii. The Hawaiians would bet on anything: "foot racing, canoe racing, surfing, boxing, hand wrestling, pulling with the fingers, wrestling, dragging a person, sliding. . . ."[2] As with us, spectators of sports could increase their sense of participation by laying a bet. As always happens when gambling is widespread, some people could not keep their involvement within reason. Goods, clothes, farms, wives, and children could all be lost by the compulsive gambler. Many of the famous heroes of Hawaiian legendary history were enormous gamblers. Great chiefs and petty kings even won or lost their sovereignties in some of the more famous betting contests. Both the Tahitians and the Hawaiians had a god of gambling.

One Hawaiian myth tells of a man from the small island of Molokai named Kane-ia-Kama, who joins a gambling contest at the famous gambling place Ka-lua-koi and wins the entire pot. On his way home, he finds he cannot live with his winnings, stops to gamble at another famous gambling center on Maunaloa, and loses everything he has except his own body. He is so exhausted by this cycle of love and rejection that he falls dead asleep; and that night, the god Kane-i-kaulana-ula ("Kane in the red flush of victory") appears to him in a dream, urges him to stake his life in tomorrow's game, promises him victory if he will take Kane-i-kaulana-ula as his god. He promises; he gambles; he wins; he carves a statue of his new god from the *nioi* tree that he saw the deity enter during his vision.[3]

We get no sense, in the Hawaiian culture, of a concept of Dame Fortune who dictates the ups and downs of the political game and the swings between celebration and sadness in life. We get no conceptualization that life itself is a great gamble. We get, simply, gambling, on a day-to-day basis. Though gambling is raised in the legends to heroic proportions, there is no cosmic connection.

The evidence for prostitution in complex societies is rather sparse, but it does seem to indicate that professional sexuality, like so much else in these societies, began at the royal court. Douglas Oliver, our foremost authority on ancient Tahitian culture, has observed:

The presence of Europeans turned many . . . females to prostitution, but prior to that some leading chiefs evidently attached a few young women to their households for purveyance to distinguished visitors. Nothing further is known about these females, save that their mode of employment seems not to have prejudiced to any significant degree their eventual marriage. As for compensation, they probably received a comfortable keep along with some respite from work ordinarily expected of females of their social class.[4]

The great elegance of the comparative method is that by turning to African societies at the same stage of development as Tahiti, we can test and elaborate on Oliver's conjectures, thereby rounding out the Tahitian picture. In traditional Dahomey, there was a group of "public women,"[5] and in Rwanda there were a few women at the courts of the king and high-placed chiefs who lived as courtesans. Surprisingly, these courtesans were not commoner Hutu but ruling-class Tutsi, although they were also, at the lowest end of the upper class, "either the daughters of Tutsi clients of the chief or king, who had been invited by the chiefs or king to come to the court as servants because of their beauty, or divorced women. They received costly presents and were often well-off, having their own herds of cattle."[6] The most complete information comes from Bunyoro, neighbor and rival of Buganda, and from this it seems clear that the old-fashioned notion of courtesan is more appropriate to describe the situation than the more common label of prostitute.

In Kabrega's [the king's] establishment a great number of girls live as servants to his wives. They are usually good dancers, or are distinguished by corporeal advantages, and enjoy unlimited freedom at night. They are called *vranga*. As soon as their day's work is finished, they go out, and if they are addressed by a man they go with him, and remain at his house from four to five days, according to his wishes. It often happens that they follow a man who pleases them of their own accord, and stay with him. He is bound to comply with their wishes, and to provide them with food, etc. Their reward consists of cowries, bark clothes, dressed hides, and even slaves, according to the circumstances of the man they fall in love with. Should the reward fall below their expectations, they always appeal to Kabrega, who, in most cases, decides in their favour, although he derives no benefit whatever from them. All that they earn belongs to them, and should one of them amass a fortune, she sets up a *zeriba* [homestead] of her own, and perhaps marries one of the king's slaves. Should one of them bear a child, it belongs to the king as a slave; if it be a boy, it is placed later on, among the pages (*vagaraggara*), and when grown up is enrolled in the bodyguard, always as a slave, but no reproach clings to him because of his illegitimate birth. If it be a girl, she is brought up to her mother's profession, and also remains, of course, a slave of Kabrega, who comes into no personal contact with these women. The institution seems to be very old, and Kabrega told me that the first of such women were not Wanyoro.[7]

Prostitution thrives on the split between affection and sexuality. It did not exist within primitive society, either because sexual feelings were not yet developed enough and expansive enough to become discrepant with affectionate feelings toward mother, father, spouse, and children, or else because affectionate feelings were still underdeveloped. Perhaps both circumstances were true. The conflict that is reflected in the idea that there are two types of women, the kind one marries and the kind one goes to bed with before marriage—still a shibboleth in my adolescence—requires a certain amount of inequality in the development of sexual and affectionate needs. For the individual psyche, and for culture as a whole, nothing guarantees that these two related but disparate drives must expand at the same rate.

Women have, in most societies, been much more repressed sexually than men, and until recently women were thought to be incapable of the kind of split between sex and feelings that men were accomplished at. Women, it was said, could only have sexual relations with men whom they cared for deeply. With the lifting of repression against women's sexuality, we find that young women are growing as capable as men are of taking a more casual attitude toward sexual experience, insisting that sexual satisfaction is possible even when the heart is not fully engaged. Sexual "vice"—pornography and attendance on prostitutes—still remains, by and large, the monopoly of males, but the male go-go dancer is already with us and the future may call for an enormous increase in male prostitutes. Perhaps this process will not become complete until men assume the role of nurturing their young children. One possible uninvited offshoot of such a change might be that girls will grow up as ambivalent and as split about their nurturing/nonnurturing fathers as men are at present about their nurturing/nonnurturing mothers. Then women may invest as much energy into keeping feelings and sexuality separated as men have in the past.

The lifting of sexual repression is only the first step in a dialectical movement, and initially creates almost as many problems as it solves. It requires another turn of the dialectic, a negation of the negation, before the full humanistic possibilities of the process can be clearly revealed. Only the ultimate synthesis of affection and sexuality will make this whole developmental movement morally valid. From the beginnings of complex society until yesterday, we have been living primarily within the first stage of this process.

The issue of repression and the conflicts it creates, as well as the conflicts the psyche attempts to resolve through the use of repression, both relate directly to the institution of public sexual performances, whether these deal in nakedness only or involve more elaborated sexual acts. The Nuer walked the earth with breasts, buttocks, and genitals completely exposed. Other primitive peoples did the same, but many, if not most, did not, even in climates that easily allowed for such undress. One cannot equate general nakedness and the primitive, but no advanced complex society allowed regular public exposure of the genitals. There is, at least with us, a symbolic equation of clothes to hide sexuality and the notion of "civilized." There is the nineteenth-century idea of the naked savage, and the story in Genesis in which Adam and Eve's fall from innocence is revealed to Jehovah when he sees their attempts to hide their genitals from public view: "Who told thee that thou wast naked?"[8]

People have a desire to look at other people's nakedness; when the desire is repressed by the wearing of clothes, the matter does not end there. The repressed has a way of taking its revenge. "Civilized" people insist on the wearing of clothes in public and then invent various forms of entertainment in which the forbidden nakedness is revealed. Even before the latest sexual revolution, there were plenty of respectable places, night clubs or music halls, where people went to observe, if not nakedness, certainly more flesh than could be seen on the street. And today there is no need to prove how powerful is the drive, especially in men, to reduce sexuality to its visual aspect.

In some complex societies, the striptease and more elaborate sexual performances were established forms. In addition to the previously discussed formal performances of the Arioi society on Tahiti, there also seem to have been, at least on Tonga and Tahiti, more casual open displays of sexual intercourse. William Anderson, on Cook's last voyage, says that the Tongans "have been seen to cool the ardour of their mutual inclinations before the eyes of many spectators."[9] Cook gives much more detail when reporting an incident on Tahiti:

This day closed with an odd scene at the Gate of the Fort where a young fellow above 6 feet high lay with a little Girl about 10 or 12 years of age publickly before several of our people and a number of the Natives. What makes me mention this, is because, it appear'd to be done more from Custom than Lewdness, for there were several Women present particularly Obarea [the wife of Pomare I] and several others of the better sort and these were so far from shewing the least disapprobation that they instructed the girl how she should act her part, who young as she was, did not seem to want it.[10]

Whether the girl was a virgin and this some kind of initiation, or whether she was the daughter of a courtesan beginning to learn her trade, or whether it was merely some spur-of-the-moment exercise to drive away boredom, we do not know.

When Cook first landed on Tahiti, he established a temporary fort on land, where the Tahitians could come to trade or bring gifts. On one occasion, a delegation appeared at the gate of the fort, for what purpose Cook's men did not know. The Tahitians brought gifts of plantain trees, smaller plants, and rolls of barkcloth. The trees were given directly to Mr. Banks, Cook's representative at the fort; the barkcloths were spread on the ground, whereupon a young woman stepped on them and, "with as much Innocency as one could possibly conceive," proceeded to expose her nakedness from the waist down, and turned herself around once or twice. More cloth was spread; the same ceremony of exposure was repeated; the cloths were rolled up and given to Banks; the two women who had brought the presents, including the one who had stepped on the cloths, gave Banks an affectionate embrace, and the ceremony was over.[11] We have no indication that this was a sexual overture, that the young women were offering themselves to Banks, and it is not impossible that the English misread the situation, since they had no command of the language at that time.

The Tahitians had a certain game played by girls using a breadfruit as a football. The prize for the girl who won the match was "the Liberty of exposing her nakedness to the croud about them & this right they are always sure of asserting."[12] Anderson, who clearly had an eye for such things, gives us an account of an exhibitionist performance on Tahiti:

In the evening a great many of them [women] having collected together stood upon the side of a small river near the middle of the Bay and exhibited a sort of dance that rather bespoke of excess joy and licentiousness, though perhaps it might be their usual custom. Most of these were young women, who put themselves in several lascivious postures, clapp'd their hands and repeated a kind of Stanzas which every now and then began afresh. At certain parts they put their garments aside and expos'd with seemingly very little sense of shame those parts which most nations have thought it modest to conceal, but in particular a woman more advanc'd in years who stood in front & might properly be called the tutoress or prompter of the rest, held her cloathes continually up with one hand and danced with uncommon vigour and effrontery, as if to raise in the spectators the most libidinous desires and incite her pupils to emulation in such a wanton exercise. The men flocked eagerly round them in great numbers to see their performance and express'd the most anxious curiosity to see that part just mentioned, at which they seem'd to feel a sort of rapture that could only be express'd by the extreme joy that appear'd in their countenances.[13]

We may wonder whether the rapture and the joy were experienced only by the Tahitians.

On Tahiti, men also exhibited their nakedness as part of a performance, but such exhibitions seemed to have had a grotesque-comic, rather than a sensual-erotic purpose. Bligh witnessed a spectacle in which three men physically distorted their penises, testicles, and scrota to an extent almost difficult to believe. One tied some twine around his penis so that it swelled up, then pulled it out into an erection. The second pulled his testicles up to the head of his penis, tied them all together with a bandage, and then stretched the whole package out to a foot in length up toward the stomach. The last man "was more horrible than the other two, for with both hands seizing the extremity of the scrotum he pulled it out with such force, that the penis went in totally out of sight and the Scrotum became Shockingly distended."[14] By this point, Bligh had had enough and asked the players to desist. The Tahitians who were watching had great fun with the exhibition.

The desire to possess a superhuman penis was also expressed in art.

The erotic sculpture of both Hawaii and Tahiti laid emphasis on the Priapian aspects of human anatomy,[15] another similarity between Polynesia and the Greek-Roman pagan world. Graphic depictions of sexual congress filled the art of many advanced complex cultures. Primitive societies were not devoid of such productions, but erotic art appears to be much more characteristic of complex societies. The great majority of the art that fills our current books under the heading of "primitive" erotic art comes from complex cultures.

Since bourgeois narcissism is the current fixation of many American intellectuals, and since my own narcissistic interest is in chalking up as many "firsts" for complex society as possible, it is pleasing to note that baby contests were the rage in some parts of ancient Hawaii. Certain children of unusual charm or good looks were fastened upon by their grandparents and *paii punahele,* "made favorites." They received the best food, mats, and clothing, and every few years a carnival was held so that these favorites could be displayed by their sponsoring elders. Before a large crowd, each *punahele* was exhibited while name songs emphasizing particular points of praise were chanted by the relatives. The winners were determined by the loudness of the shouts from the spectators. Once the show was concluded, a great feast was engaged in by everyone and various nonsexual dances were performed. It was an event conducive to laughter and high spirits.[16]

The strain on the psyche that is produced by the ideal of marital fidelity did *not* first become evident in complex society. A large percentage of primitive societies were polygamous; in many of the monogamous ones, divorce was common and led to the same kind of serial monogamy we witness today. Adultery was widespread, though mostly illegitimate. Some societies permitted certain modes of adultery: either periodic public festivals allowing sexual license, or a system whereby a man had legitimate sexual rights to three or four married women other than his wife. In some cultures, a group of brothers would retain rights to one another's wives.

The conflict over marital fidelity is related to the strain of maintaining a consistent heterosexual stance. Loyal monogamy requires the abandonment of a general sexual excitation, and straightforward heterosexuality requires the repression of homosexual impulses. Certain kinds of sexual activity have the advantage of breaking both these repressions in one act. Two men who knowingly go to bed with the same woman, even if it is at different times, are exchanging sexual experience with each other. Brothers who share their wives are also sharing sex with each other. All group sex, wife and husband swapping, and adultery games have a homosexual affect.

We have some evidence that brothers had sexual access to one another's wives on Tahiti, but what is striking here, and is different from primitive society, is that while a man engaged in such sexual congress, his own wife might be looking on. Bligh also says that it was "a common thing for the wife to assist the Husband in these Amours."[17] He does not say that the wife of the man participated in the sex, but that would have been the next logical step. We would not be shocked to hear that threesomes and foursomes were known to the sexually experimental Tahitians.

In Hawaii, adultery opportunities were organized on a grand scale. "*Ume* was a pastime that was very popular with all Hawaiians. It was an adulterous sport," states one account. A large enclosure was built in town, or very close by. At night a huge bonfire was kindled in the enclosure and the participants gathered and seated themselves in a circle. A man acting as major-domo called the people to order, whereupon another, carrying a long wand trimmed with bird feathers, entered the circle singing a "gay and lascivious" song. As he made his rounds of the circle, he would tap men and women alternately. These would pair up and retreat into the shadows. Other pairs were arranged by the playing of a game similar to our quoits or horseshoes.[18]

Since the aristocracy deemed it beneath their dignity to engage in the sport of *ume,* they contrived their own version, called *kilu,* which could be played only by people of a certain recognized rank. Even the king and queen would participate in this activity, and, in theory, all were supposed to be equal once admitted to the hall. The game was played with great regard for dignity, as was appropriate for those of high station. The men sat at one end of the hall, the women at the other; the space between the players was covered with mats. Five or more players of each sex were chosen at a time, and these sat on the floor facing one another across the matted area, each person with a conical block of heavy wood propped up in front. Each player also had a dish made from a coconut shell, which was scooted, rotary fashion, across the mats. If the dish succeeded in hitting the block in front of another at the opposite side, the sender was entitled to a kiss (probably of noses, though we are not told), a forfeit that was usually demanded immediately. Ten hits and ten kisses entitled a player to the ultimate pleasure,

though, being aristocrats, couples did not leave the hall while the game
was in progress but met later that evening. One has to be an adult in
order to commit adultery—and know how to count to ten.

In theory, even the lowest-ranked aristocratic male was entitled to
capture the queen or high chiefess in this game, but in reality, such
rights were often abandoned by the victor in favor of some land or other
possessions. It was not always wise in such circumstances for men to
claim the women as prize.[19] Even in conditions of extreme license, tyranny did not abdicate its privileged position.

If the concept of vice no longer subsumes actions that involve gambling, prostitution, exhibitionism-voyeurism, and compulsive adultery,
then by what legitimacy, if any, are such forms included together in
the same chapter? They all arise from the fixation of the libido on some
preadult level of development. When a person who otherwise acts generally as an adult returns to such a fixation for satisfaction, "regression"
is an appropriate description of the behavior. Here not only is libido
a source of sexual energy and a means for its satisfaction; more particularly, libidinal energy is used as *a mode of attachment.*

The child, as it develops, forms a multitude of attachments to the
parent, or parents, who nurture it. Traditionally, the mother has been
the primary nurturing person and, therefore, the primary object of attachment. The fact that the mother, over a period of years, remains the
primary object of attachment does not mean that the nature of this attachment stays the same. Old attachments to the mother (or substitute
mother, or both parents) are continually being replaced with attachments of a different order as the child develops. Psychic strain and psychic disorder result when the child refuses, for whatever reason, to give
up an attachment that was appropriate to a certain stage of development
but no longer serves a useful purpose in the new stages. Commitments
to ancient, no-longer-useful modes of attachment are "fixations."

The stages of the development of the libido—oral, anal, genital—
indicate the primary modes of attachment at each stage of psychic development, but they give us only a small part of the picture. The child
in the oral stage is attached to its mother through the mouth, but the
child also takes pleasure in and develops attachment from being
touched, touching, being sung to, singing, being seen, seeing, and
smelling. All the senses give libidinal satisfaction and create attachments. And as the psyche develops, not only does the child have to give
up some oral satisfaction for a new anal satisfaction, but, equally important, the modes of seeing, hearing, touching, and smelling also change,

and the modes of attachment to the nurturing parent change with those transformations. Besides being fixated in the oral stage or the anal stage, a person may also be fixated in a certain infantile or childish stage of hearing or smelling or touching or seeing. A person who walks around all day with a portable radio glued to his ear cannot liberate himself from a fixation on a certain stage of hearing. What he hears on that radio is not just the music and the commercials; he also stays in touch with a nurturing parent at the point at which he is fixated. What may be noise to us is mother's milk to him.

The same is true of seeing. At all stages of development, seeing is an important mode of libidinal satisfaction and psychic attachment. It is too simplistic to say that in the oral stage we enjoy seeing the breasts; in the anal stage, the buttocks; and in the genital stage, the genitals. There is, however, an intimate and complex relationship between the stages of libidinal development and the modes of visual attachment, although no one has yet worked it out. Failure to give up and transform early modes of visual attachment results in fixations at those points. The newsstands of our present Western societies seem to cry out that the culture, at least the male part, is experiencing a massive fixation on visual modes of attachment. I want to emphasize here that people are drawn to pictorial nakedness as much by the return to an ancient mode of attachment as by the actual sexual response to the pictures.

Where psychoanalytic theory has been inadequate, up to this point, is in giving us some conception of how the symbolic return to ancient times is made. Gambling, for instance, clearly seems to be related to anal fixations. That money and anality are associated is not a recent idea, but why money? How is the symbolic transition from anality to money or gambling made? If a person is anally fixated, why does he not spend most of his time in the bathroom; how is it that the dice table draws him with an ineluctable force? People who are orally fixated would spend their time, one would assume, drinking warm milk with sugar in it. Instead, many get their oral satisfaction from alcoholic drinks that are bitter-tasting and, on the superficial level, seem a long way from mother's milk. We do not know how this symbolic transformation to alcohol is made, or why it is made. We do not know why some people with oral fixations eat too much while others become anorexic, why some become alcoholics and others develop ulcers. Our lack of a theoretical structure makes it impossible to say how the symbolic forms of gambling, prostitution, exhibitionism-voyeurism, and adultery relate to fixations in the modes of attachment.

What does seem true is that, as the kinship system broke down, old modes of attachment and reassurance were rendered inoperable, and the psyche sought compensation in regression. Just as today the psychologically unprepared young person—a person not yet ready to leave family attachments—goes off to college and ends up with too much alcohol, drugs, or sex, so did complex society find itself psychologically overextended and reach out for regressive behavior in an attempt to restore balance. In certain ways, it appears that every society since the breakdown of the kinship system has been in a similar circumstance.

Slowly and painfully, society has been attempting over thousands of years to construct new forms of attachment and reassurance that would compensate us for our kinship paradise lost. "Vice," "decadence," and regression are always available when that process fails in its purpose.

IV

THE KINSHIP SYSTEM,
THE STATE, AND
THE BEGINNINGS
OF TYRANNY

21

From Kinship to the State;
from Band Society to Complex Society

The great revolutionary political accomplishment of complex societies was the creation of a form of social cohesion other than kinship. When we consider that the first complex societies on the face of the earth probably originated in the Near East between 10,000 and 8000 B.C., this means that for the previous million or two million years—for however long humans had lived in societies—the only form of political cohesion, the only force that kept human society together, was kinship politics.

It is difficult to imagine how immense a change this transition to nonkinship forms was. It has taken Western Europe more than three hundred years of enormous social and political turmoil—from the Puritan Revolution of 1640 until the end of World War II—to complete the revolution that has brought the final triumph of the bourgeoisie, capitalism, and democracy. Western Europe was the birthplace of modern democracy, and yet it was not until the death of Franco in 1975 that *every* country in Western Europe was simultaneously democratic in form. How much greater a human task to transform an institution that had served humankind for a million years.

Kinship in the psychological, not the social, sense is the feeling of closeness to certain people that results from being related to them. This closeness usually includes affection, although hostility and ambivalence also have their share. That the original feelings of kinship are directed toward mother, father, and siblings, and then radiate out to cousins, uncles, aunts, grandparents, and in-laws, seems clear enough. Kinship is the sum total of all the feelings and actions that pertain to those to whom one is related.

The relationships of husband and wife and of parents and children are the primary ones, but other, more extended kinship feelings can have great importance. The relationship of cousin to cousin, for example, has had much more importance in periods of history other than our own. Our "nuclear family," and the all-encompassing manner in which it encloses the individual, is the end product of a long process of development within the family. Our present situation, with extended kinship relations having such comparatively little significance, is unique in the history of the world.

Today we distinguish between family and politics, but our capacity to make that distinction is an inheritance from the complex world. In the primitive and band societies that preceded complex society, no such distinction was made: all politics was family politics.

Kinship has always been important for human society, but the nature of kinship, its relationship to other modes in society, and particularly, for our purposes, its connection with politics, have all undergone numberless vicissitudes over the course of history. The alterations in kinship relationships were crucial to the revolutionary changes from band to primitive society and from primitive to complex society.

The plan of this chapter is to break the chronological sequence by starting with primitive society as a fixed point, then moving backward to band society and forward to complex society.

PRIMITIVE SOCIETY AND KINSHIP SYSTEM

The revolutionary change in human relationships that marked the beginnings of primitive society was the replacement of kinship by a kinship system. Whereas band society was totally a kinship society, primitive society took those kinship associations and welded them into a structured system. Kinship feelings, though powerful, can be vague, amorphous, and flexible. Such feelings organized into a kinship system became rigid, inflexible, and structured.

This contrast between kinship and kinship system can be illustrated with examples from our present situation. My brother-in-law is clearly my kin, and I am ready to be affectionate toward him as an extension of my feelings toward my wife (if he is her brother) or toward my sister (if he is her husband). If my brother-in-law and I care about each other, we may extend aid—financial or otherwise—to each other, aid that we would not give to any "stranger." If we like each other as friends, we will both want to enhance the friendship because of the kinship bond.

When we regard each other, we are both aware that we are kin. But the kinship feeling and action are loose, flexible, and unstructured. There is no law dictating how we must treat each other. There are not even strong social sanctions prescribing particular actions in regard to each other: one would never be refused admittance to a club, for example, because one had refused to lend one's brother-in-law money when he was in financial straits. Ultimately, our relationship depends upon how we feel about each other, and upon how the woman (wife or sister) who links us together feels—that is, upon the general psychological dynamics of the situation. Between me and my brother-in-law there is kinship, but there is no kinship system.

The relationship between my wife and me not only includes intense feelings of kinship but also falls within the kinship system, because there are many elements in it that are inflexible and structured. The law governs many aspects of the status husband and wife have vis-à-vis each other, dictating whom one can marry (when it prohibits certain marriages as incest), how many people one can marry at one time, how old one has to be to marry, what kind of financial support is required, when and how one can divorce, who inherits, and so on. In addition to the force of the law, there are strong social sanctions (albeit fast disappearing) which dictate the behavior of husband and wife and social censure for failure to observe them. Only recently, for example, has a divorced politician been able to run for high office in this country.

In the modern world, the kinship system has become so narrow that it includes only wives, husbands, and their children. Everybody else—uncles, aunts, cousins, in-laws of all kinds, even siblings—pertains to one's feelings of kinship but is outside of a structured system.

The primitive world was all kinship system. There were no brothers-in-law, only sister's husband and wife's brother, but even these designations are not sufficient. It is important to know whether it is the older sister's husband or the younger sister's husband, the wife's younger brother or the wife's older brother. In many primitive societies the older brother might make the marriage contract for his younger sister; this put the new husband and the wife's older brother into a particular relationship. I might owe my wife's older brother a certain kind of service; my younger sister's husband might owe me the same kind of service. If such is the custom of the society, performance of these services does not depend upon personal option. Whether we like each other or not, a particular relationship is dictated by custom, and custom is as powerful in primitive society as the law is with us. Some primitive peo-

ple disobeyed custom; most did not. Some modern people break the
law, but most do not. Brothers-in-law, in the primitive world, were not
only part of the feelings of kinship, but were enmeshed in a structured
kinship system as well.

The same was true for cousins. For us, mother's sister's son and
mother's sister's daughter and mother's brother's son and mother's
brother's daughter and father's sister's son and father's sister's daughter
and father's brother's son and father's brother's daughter are all cousins. In primitive society, there might be a different relationship with
each of these eight different categories of cousins. A mother's brother's
daughter might be the most desirable wife one could take, whereas to
marry a father's brother's daughter might be forbidden as incest.

Kinship relationships that we hardly pay any attention to were politically significant in some primitive societies. The murder of my third
cousin may have placed me under obligation to avenge that homicide.
If my second cousin once removed committed murder, I may have been
obligated to pay part of the compensation to the survivors of the murdered man.

For primitive society, the kinship system was so pervasive that it
is impossible to describe it without talking about the kinship system.
Evans-Pritchard writes of the Nuer on the White Nile: "The kinship
system derives from the family, being, through marriage, built up of
a series of families, and it has among the Nuer . . . an almost limitless
extension, at any rate in the sense that everyone can in one way or another and in some degree be placed in a kinship category by everybody
else and addressed by them by a kinship term which in common usage
is a family relationship term. The whole society is, in this sense, one
great family."[1]

It was not, however, one great family in the same way that in certain
small European villages almost everybody was related to everyone else.
The Nuer were one great family in a highly structured, highly inflexible system. It was not only kinship—the sense of family—but the kinship system that bound them together. It was precisely the structure
that created primitive society, that differentiated primitive societies
from the band societies that preceded them. The first great political revolution resulted from the creation of a *structured* family—the kinship
system.

The kinship system completely dominated all forms of social action
in primitive society. Whereas we have an economic system, a political

system, a legal system, a family system, an educational system, and a religious system, in primitive society there was only the kinship system. We may distinguish, in such societies, among economic, political, legal, and religious actions, but all such actions were taken under kinship-system auspices. Almost everything we know as politics fell under the authority of the kinship system.

A society that has no strong kinship system—and in this regard, band and modern societies are alike—does not distinguish between degrees of closeness of those related on the father's side and those on the mother's side. If our society prohibits marriage between first cousins, it forbids such connection with all eight categories of cousins. It does not say it is permissible to marry mother's brother's children but not father's brother's children. That kind of distinction is precisely the kind made by the vast majority of primitive societies. This unilateral kinship, which emphasizes for political and other purposes the precedence of kinship relations through only one parent, seems to be the essence of a kinship system.

In most kinship systems, clan or lineage status comes from either father or mother. If from the father, the situation is described as patrilineal. That means that father's brothers, father's sisters, father's brothers' sons, and father's brothers' daughters all have the same social place in the world. Father's sisters' children, however, are not of the same lineage and clan, even though father's sisters are, because these sisters are married to men of other clans and the children take their father's clan and lineage. These "cousins," as we would call them, are already different from the "cousins" who are of the same lineage and clan. Usually under such a patrilineal system, marriage with father's brother's daughter is prohibited as incestuous, because she is of the same clan as oneself, but mother's brother's daughter is of a different clan and therefore marriageable.

Under a patrilineal system, one's mother, her brothers, her sisters, her brother's children, but not necessarily her sister's children are all of different clans and lineages than one's own. As the system ramifies, as it extends to more distant relationships, it gets more and more complicated, as is attested by the several hundred thousand pages that have been written to explain it in all its variety. Compared with kinship, the kinship system is enormously complex, and possibly that complexity was precisely one of the things people wanted from it. One thing that happens after people liberate themselves from the stifling influence of family domination is that they become enamored of systems. That a system of families should become the very first infatuation is an inevitable irony in the process.

Kinship systems usually maintain an inflexible custom concerning residence after marriage. Residence with the husband's family is termed "patrilocal," with the wife's family "matrilocal," with both families in some sort of organized alteration "ambilocal," with an uncle "avunculocal." Patrilineal societies are not necessarily patrilocal; there are patrilineal-matrilocal societies as well as matrilineal-patrilocal societies. What is almost universal in all kinship-system societies is that after-marriage residence is not left to individual option: in a patrilocal society *all* married couples live with the husbands' families. Such rigidity is inherent in the structured nature of a kinship system.

The inflexibility of the system binds people into situations of great psychological stress. In a patrilocal system, the husband lives with his family and the wife lives with "strangers." The tensions involved in such a situation differ markedly from those of a matrilocal world, where the wife lives among her relatives while the husband lives with "strangers." Whatever the tensions, the only option of the married couple is to live with them. The kinship system is not sympathetic to choice.

All politics—that which treats of the society as a society, that which goes beyond immediate family concerns—are in the primitive world kinship politics. An essential function of any and every political system is to define a person's place in the social world. The complex manner by which a kinship system accomplishes this can be illustrated by the Nuer.[2] What Evans-Pritchard, but not the Nuer themselves, calls a "minimal lineage" consists of a man, all his sons, all their sons, and all the sons of their sons: four generations. The youngest members of this minimal lineage have the relationship that we would call second cousins: they share a common great-grandfather. It matters not, for Nuer purposes, whether the original father is still alive, because this minimal lineage can still maintain its existence. At some point, however, as the generations move on, the original point of reference for the lineage (that is, the great-grandfather for the youngest) changes and the whole minimal-lineage structure is reshuffled. Every Nuer belongs to one such minimal lineage, and his place in the world is defined by that "citizenship."

In this system, if we reckon back six generations instead of four, so that the youngest members, who share a great-great-great-grandfather, are now all fourth cousins, then we get what Evans-

Pritchard calls a "minor lineage." Every Nuer is also a member of such a minor lineage and his place in the world is defined by such membership.

We may then do the same for eight generations and get a "major lineage," and the same for ten generations and get a "maximal lineage." Several maximal lineages are then grouped together, under a real or fictional common ancestor, into a clan.

Every Nuer, then, is simultaneously a member of a minimal lineage, a minor lineage, a major lineage, a maximal lineage, and a clan. It does not stop there, however. There is also a system of villages and tribal sections that culminate as full tribes. This system is distinct from the lineage system, but it is intimately related to the system of lineages because every village, tribal section, and tribe has a predominant lineage of that division that enjoys a position of particular prestige.

As far as sentiment is concerned, the Nuer system of place in the world does not stop at these tribal boundaries. All Nuer have a common sense of themselves as Nuer. They all share a homogeneous culture, a common language, the absence of lower incisors, and (for men) six cuts on the brow. They also share a sense of themselves as Nuer, as opposed to other peoples. Should two Nuer meet outside of Nuer country, they immediately establish a situation of friendly relations.

Thus, a Nuer's place in the political world is established by a very complicated set of coordinates. This leads to certain ambiguities and contradictions. Concerning some political action, my minimal lineage may be in opposition to, may be antagonistic to, the closest (in regard to kinship) other minimal lineage. Five days from now, however, my minimal lineage may join with this other minimal lineage, and we may establish ourselves along the lines of a minor lineage in order to operate against another minor lineage concerning another political action. At some point, all the various lineages of a clan, who have opposed one another on various occasions, may join together as one clan group in order to fight another clan. Tribal politics, which cuts across clan politics, provides additional complexities.

Despite the great intricacy of the situation, one thing remains constant: all political forms of feeling and action are kinship forms, family forms. The language of family, the feeling of family, the necessity of common ancestor, the sense of belonging to one group and being thereby in opposition to another—all this dominates the system. The one great thing that keeps society together, the one great form of political cohesion, is the kinship system. For the Nuer, nonkinship forms of politics do not exist. All the various ways of defining place in the political world are kinship ways.

The state system, on the other hand, is erected with the creation of nonkinship forms of social cohesion. The state is an outgrowth of kinship society, a transformation of that society, and it carries with it the marks of its origins, but this does not mean that state forms are just another version of kinship forms. State forms are qualitatively different. The authority of the king and the authority of the kinship system are two very different things. So important is this nonkinship aspect of state society that, in my view, it defines the state: *the state is that form of human society in which nonkinship forms of social cohesion are as important as, or more important than, kinship forms.*

In complex societies kinship and nonkinship forms are of equal importance, whereas in the modern state, nonkinship forms are more important than kinship forms. Implicit in this definition is the concept that kinship forms of social cohesion continue to exist within state society.

The perseverance of kinship forms of social cohesion becomes apparent when we examine the state system under which we currently live, with its foundation in nationalism. One wonders, for instance, to what extent modern notions of "national honor" and what is needed to preserve it differ from the kinship conception of revenge required for injury done a kinsman. If the worst jingoistic expressions of patriotism frighten us, it is in part because we recognize how much our Nuer past still rules our lives.

Before beginning to examine by what means primitive society was transformed into state society, it is helpful to look back at the origins of the kinship system itself.

BAND SOCIETY TO PRIMITIVE SOCIETY

The general hypothesis governing this section, a hypothesis for which there is no proof, asserts that before primitive society there existed a form of human society of small autonomous groups, each group operating as an extended family. These groups were held together primarily through bonds of kinship, but the bonds were unstructured, flexible, and informal—not organized into a kinship system. Feelings, not rules about feelings, kept the bands together. Since they were essentially extended families, it is hard to know whether it is correct even to use the word "society" in connection with them. This form of social grouping ended with the transformation of kinship into a kinship system, and the creation of primitive society. It is my belief that the universal human impulse toward individuation, toward separation from one's immediate family, the inclination to live a life larger than that offered by the family experience, provided the force that drove this revolutionary process and put an end to band society. This bold assertion cannot tell us, however, why certain peoples took that step and others did not, or why some peoples took it earlier than others.

The only available data that would tend to support or contradict the hypothesis concerning the existence of a band stage come from a group of very simple societies, approximately two dozen, that survived into the nineteenth or twentieth century and were described by observers sufficiently to give an idea of the varieties of social life that existed there. All shared two attributes. First, they were hunters and gatherers, practicing neither agriculture nor the domestication of animals; they ate what nature provided for them and did nothing to increase the available food supply. Second, the basic social group was a small company of people traveling together, a group that maintained relations with other groups but preserved its own distinctiveness and its own size. In some cultures, the groups ranged from 30 to 60 people; in others, from 50 to a maximum of 150.

The absence of agriculture and of the domestication of animals is not absolutely correlated with band society. Although the concept of the "Neolithic Revolution" (the beginnings of agriculture and the domestication of animals) has placed all hunters and gatherers in paleolithic times,[3] an age, supposedly, of both technological and social simplicity, we have considerable hard data indicating that many "paleolithic" peoples lived not in bands but in kinship-system societies:

All societies at the band level of integration are foragers of wild food. Not all wild-food foragers are at the band level, however. Along the northwest coast of North America were large populations of maritime peoples whose environment was so remarkably bountiful that they lived in complex communities at the level of chiefdoms. In California were other societies who lived in such natural abundance that their societies transcended the band level. The paleolithic era thus may well have had some forms of society in addition to bands.[4]

Abundance was not the only prerequisite for hunters and gatherers living at the primitive level. All the native peoples of Australia lacked agriculture and animal domestication; some lived in areas of abundance, which allowed for dense and sedentary settlements; others lived in arid places, which could tolerate only a sparse population.[5] Even those in the desert areas, however, lived a complex social life, under a complicated kinship system; not one of them was a band society as the term is used here.[6]

The great revolutions of human history, the very first of which was this development from band to primitive society, cannot be adequately explained solely by changes in technology. People transformed kinship societies into kinship-system societies without changing the tools they used or the environment in which they lived. There is a formidable human drive to develop. Any theory of social development that pays no attention to that drive will fail in its purpose.

One of the first people to make a systematic study of very simple societies was Julian Steward, who divided them analytically into two categories: patrilineal bands and composite bands.[7] Steward's patrilineal bands lived under kinship systems that differed not at all from those of large groups living in primitive cultures. Even though they were hunters and gatherers, in our terms they represent the primitive stage of society.

Steward's composite bands, on the contrary, lacked rules regulating whom one could or should marry; they had no explicit customs in regard to residence after marriage. They represented "more of an expedient agglomeration than a structured society."[8] Kinship held them together, but they lacked a kinship system. Such a band was, in essence, one large family.

Steward's analysis of composite bands has been criticized by Elman Service,[9] who seeks to demonstrate that such bands do not represent the traditional state of these societies but reflect a condition of social dissolution, decomposition, and degeneration brought on by contact with European and American cultures. It was catastrophic losses of population resulting from new diseases and other, subtler subversions of the traditional culture that produced composite bands, Service argues, not the normal process of social development.

Even if we grant Service's argument without reservation, there still may be some important truths to be learned from the existence of these "degenerate" bands, these societies without a formal, structured kinship system. First, such societies work. The band does not dissolve after one or two generations. Some, in fact, went on in adverse circumstances for more than a hundred years. Thus we learn that social life, or at least extended family life, is possible without a structured kinship system.

This does not establish that there was such a stage in the natural development of society, but it does help demonstrate the possibility.

Second, Service does not deal with the possibility that these composite bands are not only decomposed and degenerate, but that they are also *regressed*—not merely fallen apart, but fallen back to a previous stage of orientation. If the ordinary course of development was from band society to primitive society, from kinship forms of social cohesion to kinship-system forms, and if certain societies had taken that step only recently so that their hold on the new form was tentative and vulnerable, it is not inconceivable that they would respond to a cultural shock by letting go of the new forms of cohesion and returning to old patterns. The new social order of advanced complex societies was fragile; even the great archaic civilization of Egypt was victim to two major periods of dissolution and disunity; why, then, could not the same thing have been true of early primitive societies?

We also know, from African history, that when the centralized state of advanced complex societies was dissolved, society was not destroyed but instead regressed to the form that preceded the centralized state: to chieftainship, in which kinship politics played a larger role. Could it not be that Steward's composite bands, even though the result of a cultural trauma, reveal to us a traditional and authentic stage of society?

If this argument concerning regression is accurate, technological considerations could play a crucial role in the process. Except in circumstances of great abundance, hunting-and-gathering societies cannot live a settled life and are forced to travel in small groups. Under ordinary conditions, only agriculture or the domestication of animals makes settled life and large social groups possible. It may be that small unsettled groups of hunters and gatherers, even when they have reached the stage of primitive society (structured kinship system), are more vulnerable to culture shock. It may be that their hold on the new stage of development is more tentative and fragile than the grasp of a large settled community, which has had the opportunity to generate many forms of kinship-system cohesion. The smallness of the group may itself place a limit on the extent to which the kinship system can ripen and mature. We have no way of knowing, but it is also possible that, previous to contact with Western culture, some of these small groups spent hundreds of years alternating between band and primitive society. When we observe a group of people suffering a trauma of social contact, we tend to feel that things were very stable before that meeting, yet exactly the opposite may have been true.

The invention of the kinship system and the inauguration of primitive society—as remarkable and as important for humanity as anything that has ever happened—are not the subjects of this book, and there will be no further discussion of that great transition here. However, a penetrating psychocultural analysis of that revolution could teach us an enormous amount about ourselves and the political world that shapes our lives.

FROM PRIMITIVE SOCIETY TO THE STATE

Central to any society is the definition and locus of *political authority.* Authority has its origins in the family; political authority results from the transformation of family hierarchical relationships. Every great revolution in social life involves a transformation of the forms of political control and dominance.

The developmental sequences—band society to primitive society to complex society, and kinship to kinship system to state—reveal a dialectical movement in regard to political power. Authority within the family, and within band societies, which operate on a kinship basis, is personal: mother, father, aunt, uncle, older brother, older sister, husband. Within such a system, there are no abstract loci of power. A person both has, and is, authority. Once a kinship system is erected and primitive society comes into being, however, political authority is no longer concentrated in a select group of individuals but is spread through the community as a whole. All those who have studied primitive society firsthand are agreed that they can find no center, or centers, of political control. Having themselves been raised in a society where political power resides in individuals, those who describe primitive societies sometimes talk as if there were no political power at all, which is clearly not the case. Authority, within primitive society, is communal rather than individualistic and personal.

When the state develops, power returns, dialectically, to the individual basis from which it started. The king becomes the main instrument in the destruction of the kinship system and the erection of the state. The sense of communal power gives way to "the cult of personality," and the character of the king carries the burden of the polity.

In turn, as the state develops, as the king begins to rule larger and larger areas, as an individual's contact with this new polity becomes increasingly bureaucratic, as the tax collector and not the king begins to stand for the state, political power becomes for most people depersonalized again, but this time the sense of community is lacking. Then, in many instances, political authority becomes equated with dominance and political tyranny becomes a crucial form of social cohesion. The state, which began as a liberator from the kinship system, becomes an instrument of oppression.

In primitive society, before chieftainships began to develop, political authority was diffuse, indistinct, informal, elastic, accommodating, and malleable.

Within the hill or valley area occupied by a maximal lineage there was no institutionalized political authority. . . . Within a lineage area individual family heads who combined wealth with wisdom could become respected leaders of opinion, both political and legal, but they had no formally recognized authority. There were also men who obtained authority within limited spheres, as, for example, rain-making and war, but such authority was not institutionalized and did not survive a man's period of active success within that sphere. Outside the clan there was no political authority, though there were rudimentary mechanisms for settling clan disputes, as, for example, by the intervention of the elders of a neutral clan with which one of the disputing sides had a joking relationship.[10]

In all human situations there are natural leaders, but natural leadership and institutionalized political authority are different.

Among the Nuer, the closest thing to permanent political authority was the institution of leopard-skin chiefs, who arbitrated certain social disputes. But these, Evans-Pritchard tells us, never received more respect than any other person, and were never referred to as people of importance.[11] Having no power to enforce their decisions, they were simply mediators: "Only if both parties want the affair settled can the chief intervene successfully."[12]

This lack of a centralized, coercive political power allowed people in primitive society to move on and move out when they found themselves unhappy with their circumstances. In our present state system, citizenship is not voluntary; one may leave the state one lives in, if that state permits, but only with the compliance of another state. Among the Nuer, if a whole community fought with its neighbor and was discontent with the outcome, it had the option of moving to a different section or different tribe and taking up residence there.[13]

An individual had the same option.

Thus Nuer have always felt themselves free to wander as they pleased, and if a man is unhappy, his family sick, his herds declining, his garden exhausted, his relations with some of his neighbors uncongenial, or merely if he is restless, he moves to a different part of the country and resides with some kinsmen. It is seldom that a man goes alone, for brothers are a corporate group, and, especially if they are sons of one mother, stick together. So, frequently as a result of quarrels, a group of brothers will often leave a village and settle elsewhere. Nuer say that they usually make for the home of a married sister, where they are certain to be well received.[14]

The Baganda were also extremely mobile, but changes in residence occurred in Buganda society only when someone switched allegiance to another *chief*. Whereas in state society people move from one localized political-power center to another, the Nuer moved from one diffused authority position to another.

There were certain ill-defined positions of political authority within primitive society. The heads of kinship structures, such as lineage heads and clan headmen, usually had authority roughly equivalent to that of a Nuer leopard-skin chief; although an individual of great personal power might temporarily raise such a position to a place of unusual authority, that heightened authority would disappear at his death.

Lineage headmen and clan leaders dealt with people politically only on a *face-to-face* basis.[15] Their weak authority might extend over people with whom they did not come into contact, but only if a kinship relationship existed between the headman and the others. So important is this face-to-face and kinship relationship that we can define the very beginnings of complex society as occurring when a person begins to rule others who are not in that situation: *a chief is a political leader who rules over people with whom he does not come into contact and over people with whom he has no kinship relationship.*

If four clans, for instance, each with its own clan headman, are joined together to form a tribe and that tribe has no tribal leader, we are still in a primitive situation, even should one of these clan headmen have a certain ritual precedence over the other three, as often happens. As long as this *primus inter pares* headman does not rule people from other clans, he is not yet a chief within the definition used here. When that headman, by whatever process, becomes more than a first-among-equals and proceeds to exert real political authority over people from the other clans—people with whom he has no kinship relationship and people whom he does not meet on a face-to-face basis—then he becomes a tribal chief engaged in the process of transforming a kinship system into a state system.

Size has much to do with this whole process. A population of twenty-five thousand people will have from three to eight thousand male adults. No person of political authority can deal on a direct basis with so many people. The leader of a political entity of such size would certainly be designated a "chief." What happens in primitive society as the political units defined by the kinship system get larger and larger is that the units split up into smaller units with several localized centers of kinship politics replacing the larger one. In primitive society, there is a limit to how large the polity can grow, set by the psychological powers of face-to-face contact and kinship relations.

The beginning of complex society—the beginning of chieftain-ships—requires a new order of political cohesion. The concept that a person may rule over people with whom he does not come into contact and with whom he has no kinship relations represents a radical break with the past, because it contradicts all the experience of power within the nuclear or extended family. In the family, all power is held by people one knows and to whom one is related; no stranger takes your goods or sends you off to war. And although primitive society creates a world beyond the extended family, in that world of kinship-system politics people are still not ruled by nonkin. In primitive society, except in war-fare—where foreigners are the enemy—no unrelated person holds the power of life or death over another.

With the state, all that changes, and we find the beginnings of politi-cal tyranny in complex society. Primitive society can provide many examples of people's cruelty to one another—as can the family situa-tion—but the expressions "political tyranny" and "political oppression" do not describe what goes on in those circumstances. When the kinship system is broken, when people begin to rule over people whom they don't know and are not related to, then the equality of political life in primitive society is destroyed; freedom is taken away from some people; social class becomes a weapon of dominance. This suggests that people can tyrannize over others only after they first make them into strangers, that people would much rather enslave strangers than their own rela-tives. If the world is entirely composed of relations, there is little room for political oppression. The psychological power that breaks the kin-ship system may be the same power that creates tyranny.

Even in primitive society, all are not equal. Some people have more prestige; some lines of descent have more honor; firstborn children may be more highly regarded than others. Such inequality is not meant to oppress. In many cases, those with more prestige have to take greater care of others, have to give more. To create a line of descent with more honor is to create honor, is to announce that all human beings are not ordinary. It is similar to the creation of the hero; it is the endowment of some human beings with godlike qualities. From this small fissure in the pattern of equality have developed the great chasms of inequality and oppression that are the despair of political life. The Nuer leopard-skin chief, who has no capacity to oppress, whose main function is to make social life easier, *can come only from certain lineages.*[16] A man who does not, no matter how wise and forceful he may be, is not allowed to become such a chief.

Similarly, in every Nuer tribe, one clan holds a superior status.[17] These "aristocratic lineages" have a self-consciousness about their superior place in the world: "We found it easy to obtain from any adult member of an aristocratic lineage an account of the other maximal and major lineages of his clan and a long list of ancestors, some nine or ten at least, giving a consistent length from the founder of the clan; whereas we found that we could not elicit the same information from members of clans which had no tribal associations."[18] Nothing in Evans-Pritchard's data, however, indicates that these prestige lineage members had more wealth, more cattle, more wives, more say in tribal decisions, or more capacity to oppress others. They, and their honor, were their own excuse for being.

"How can it be explained," asked Evans-Pritchard, "that among a people so democratic in sentiment and so ready to express it in violence a clan is given superior status in each tribe?" His answer, though tautological, is of interest. "As there are no tribal chiefs and councils, or any other form of tribal government, we have to seek elsewhere for the organizing principle within the structure which gives it conceptual consistency and a certain measure of active cohesion, and we find it in aristocratic status. . . . In the absence of a chief or king, who might symbolize a tribe, its unity is expressed in the idiom of lineage and clan affiliation."[19] None of this explains why the idiom of unity is *inequality*—that some lineages are somehow better than others. Because there is no chief or king, some clearly superior social entity must take their place if society is to be held together, says Evans-Pritchard. Without inequality, we are told, there can be no society. This contention should not be lightly accepted or rejected.

What is so important about the "aristocratic status" of certain lineages is that it provided the foundation out of which chieftainship and kingship grew. A headman of an aristocratic lineage, a man with exceptional personal power in politics and warfare, is a perfect candidate to become a chief—a man who rules over people from other lineages and clans. In most advanced complex societies (Buganda was an exception), the king was always chosen from a royal clan. It is a reasonable assumption that the ancestors of these royal, monarchical clans were the prestige lineages of primitive society.

To explain this necessity of inequality, it may be helpful to go back to the beginnings of authority in the family. The family situation may be loving, nurturing, and benevolent—but it is never equal. In writing of the equality in primitive society, we must make it clear that we are talking only of adult males. Between men and women there was no equality; between parents and children, there was hierarchy. And for many primitive people, the superior power of the father was extended to the situation of the sons, who were not considered equal to each other but were ranked in terms of who would take the father's place. The Dinka were a neighboring tribe of the Nuer, at the same stage of political development. They understood the existence of prestige lineages in family terms:

The Dinka may explain that certain subtribes of a tribe, considered together, are the eldest "son," others together the middle "son" and others the youngest "son," so that the relationships of the subtribes are conceived on the model of the three brothers. Among the Dinka, the eldest son of a family usually takes over the management of his family when his father dies, and, representing his father and his agnatic ancestors, he is thought to have the greatest share of the totemic spirit of his descent group, the *yath*. When a tribe is conceived of on this pattern, one subtribe is spoken of as the "subtribe of the totem" (*wun yath*) and its function, ideally, is to look after the tribe as an eldest son looks after his deceased father's family, making peace between the other "sons" when they quarrel.[20]

True, it is a vision of benevolence, but it is a situation of hierarchy. Nurturing and benevolence require a giver and a taker, between whom there can be reciprocity but no equality. The necessity of inequality is a legacy society has inherited from the family. Social authority, being a transformation of familial authority, cannot escape—indeed, at its beginnings, sees no reason to escape—the hierarchical nature of its antecedent. And yet this does not explain why, as the state develops and kinship modes of cohesion grow weaker, oppression and tyranny grow apace, with people inventing degrees of hierarchy and dominance unknown in a kinship society. No kinship society, for example, was capable of conceiving, or executing, an act of genocide; only the state has such a capacity. The normal state can commit acts that only a psychotic family would allow itself.

Though all this is so, we can also observe in complex societies a process parallel to that of accelerating oppression: cultural forms expanding with explosive force, leaving some people free to live a life fuller, deeper, more expansive than human life had ever been lived. To trace the path of social and cultural development requires double vision. That journey has been both wonderfully life-enhancing and woefully costly of human happiness. To deny either thrust is to lose half the truth.

22

The Transformation
of the Kinship System

It is difficult for us to imagine how a society can work with no law, no courts, no official judges, no police, and no centralized political power to enforce civil peace. We immediately wonder what happens to thieves, rapists, and murderers, and what keeps everybody from doing as he pleases in regard to the property and person of others. Projecting backward from our own social situation, we may assume that life in such a society would conform to Hobbes's hypothesis: nasty, brutish, and short. What we imagine is *our* society without law and police, but ours is a society that has abandoned the powerful control of the kinship system, and without police power and law, our society would indeed degenerate into an anarchic state.

Unlike our modern society, primitive society had a powerful kinship system and a conception of self-help in matters of justice, both of which united in keeping society functioning in an orderly manner. Although statistics are lacking, nothing we know of primitive society indicates a higher level of crime than in societies at other stages of social development.

Family feelings on the one hand, and courts and law on the other, do not seem to mix well. We find something particularly distressing and/or intriguing about lawsuits between members of the same family. A family, we feel, should be able to settle its problems without recourse to "strangers." Family matters should be settled by discussion, not by law and coercion. Primitive society, conceived of as one large family, felt no need for a superstructure of law, judges, and police to dictate terms of peace between family members: "A Nuer only associates with people whose behavior to him is on a kinship pattern."[1] For him it is

immoral to commit adultery with the wives of men from his own village, but not with the wives of members of other villages.[2] His relationship to those he meets on a face-to-face, daily basis is controlled by an
unwritten sanction that is as powerful as any law. Despite that sanction,
some do commit adultery within their own village, but, then, our legal
system and police do not put an end to crime, either.

The reality of aggressive behavior in primitive society does not always conform to the ideal of the family peacefully resolving its problems, and such society is rife with feud and mechanisms of self-help.
The kin should, but in many cases do not, solve their problems and conflicts, and no social form exists that can force a decision. Evans-
Pritchard relates: "Within a village differences between persons are
discussed by the elders of the village and agreement is generally and
easily reached and compensation paid, or promised, for all are related
by kinship and common interests. Disputes between members of nearby
villages, between which there are many social contacts and ties, can also
be settled by agreement, but less easily. . . ."[3] Such is the theory, but
in reality: "I lived in intimacy for a year with Nuer and never heard
a case brought before an individual or a tribunal of any kind, and, furthermore, I reached the conclusion that it is very rare for a man to obtain redress except by force or threat of force."[4]

Within primitive society, there are no crimes against society or
against the state; all crimes are personal, and it is the duty of the injured
person and his close kin to repair the loss, either by receiving compensation (peacefully or forcefully) or by injuring the perpetrator of the
crime. If, for instance, someone kills my brother, it is the job of myself,
my remaining brothers, and whatever kin we can enlist to find the culprit and make him pay compensation, or to injure him or one of his
kin if he refuses. Justice results only from self-help: "What chiefly
makes people pay compensation is fear that the injured man and his
kin may take to violence. It follows that a member of a strong lineage
is in a different position from that of a member of a weak lineage."[5]
A member of a strong lineage may do injury to another and pay nothing, because there is no power that can force him.

Without law, a man is only as strong and as safe as his spear and
his kin, and Nuer from early childhood are taught to settle all disputes
by fighting.[6] Close kin can be defined as those who fight for one another
in all circumstances. Fighting was not continuous, but almost every
year every adult Nuer would engage in some kind of combat in which

killing occurred, either against the neighboring Dinka or with another Nuer tribe, or in some more localized personal dispute. It was not nasty, brutish, and short, but neither was it a Garden of Eden.

When the state replaces primitive society, it becomes the task of the state to prosecute and punish the thief, the rapist, and the murderer; and although the criminal may pay monetary compensation to the injured or the survivors, he or she must also pay recompense to the state—in money, in time spent in prison, in his or her very life. In Buganda a transitional point was reached in regard to punishment for homicide: the dead person's kin were not allowed to take their private justice, but had to bring the culprit before the *kabaka*. If found guilty, the murderer was not killed by the state but was turned over by the *kabaka* to the dead person's kin to render whatever punishment they had in their heart to give.[7] The kin were allowed their revenge, but justice had become the prerogative of the *kabaka*.

The systematization of the ways in which aggression is to be expressed plays an enormously important role in kinship-system politics. The questions of who fights whom, when, and how are crucial to the determination of place in the world and to the location of political authority. "The simplest definition," writes Evans-Pritchard of the Nuer, "states that a tribe is the largest community which considers that disputes between its members should be settled by arbitration and that it ought to combine against other communities of the same kind and against foreigners. In these two respects there is no larger political group than the tribe and all smaller political groups are sections of it."[8]

We already know that this concept of peaceful settlement by arbitration is an ideal, observed as much in the breach as in the actuality. We should not be surprised to discover, however, that primitive society may be held together in part by an ideal that is rarely realized. The same is true of our society and of all societies.

All societies define their limits: everyone on this side is "us"; everyone on that side is "them." We may fight more among "us" than with "them," but it seems to be important that we are able to differentiate. Among the Dinka, "The tribe is thus the political unit for defence in the dry-season pastures. . . . It is also, in their theory, the largest group of people among whom it would be possible and desirable to settle cases of homicide by the payment of compensation in cattle, rather than by the self-help and feud which were not only inevitable, but principles of honor, where members of another tribe had killed one's kinsmen.

The tribe, then, marks the limits of the possible recognition of any convention that disputes should be settled peacefully. . . ."⁹ "Us" are those
who share that ideal.

What happens when the ideal does not work, when there is fighting
within the tribe because compensation cannot be agreed upon, is that
"us" begin to fight among ourselves, which necessitates smaller and
smaller definitions of "us." Those who fight with me when we fight
among ourselves are clearly closer to me—more my kin—than those
who fight with me only in tribal matters against "them." All these dis-
criminations are essential to define a person's place in the political
world.

This kind of differentiation between various kinds of fighting has
led observers of primitive society to distinguish between "warfare" and
"feud."

There are in Lugbara sixty or more groups called *suru* which average some
4,000 people occupying a territory of on the average twenty-five square miles.
I call them Tribes. The tribe is the largest unit within which it is said that disputes should ultimately be settled by discussion. Fighting may break out within
the tribe but it should give way to discussion and there are institutionalized
means to achieve this. Fighting between tribes cannot so be settled—or at least
there is no machinery to ensure such settlement—and there may be a permanent state of hostility between them. For this reason I refer to inter-party fighting within the tribe as feud and to that between tribes as warfare. . . .¹⁰

People in primitive society may make the same kind of distinction between different kinds of fighting. Among the Nuer, when tribes fought
one another, certain conventions prevailed: "Women and children were
not molested, huts and byres were not destroyed, and captives not
taken."¹¹ When the Nuer fought the Dinka, however, no limits were set
on aggression. Among the Dinka themselves, when fighting took place
among members of the same tribe, clubs were permissible but spears
were not. When tribes fought one another, no restrictions applied.¹²

One purpose of any society is clearly to provide civil peace within
a certain population. All societies can live with a reasonable number
of criminals or violators of custom, and primitive society could continue
with some amount of internal feud and self-help, but no society lasts
where every man's hand is raised against the next. What we learn from
primitive society, operating within kinship forms of cohesion, is that
the size of the population in which civil peace can prevail is limited, and

that, even within that limited area, individual and kinship force (self-help) plays a large role. The Lugbara comprised almost 250,000 people, but civil peace prevailed only over sections of about 4,000 souls. The Dinka numbered almost 1,000,000 in recent times, but the areas of civil peace were as small as among the Lugbara. There was no means within primitive society, within kinship-system politics, to create a large area of political authority that would maintain civil peace over, let us say, 25,000 people.

With the state, all that changes. The *kabaka* of Buganda ruled 1,000,000 people. Once the form of the state was created, there was no limit to the size to which centralized societies could grow; some single states today have more people in them than live in the whole of Africa. Once state mechanisms of control and state psychological means of cohesion were perfected, the geographical possibilities of the state became enormous, as witness the Roman and British empires. Whether this growth of the capacity of the state is good, bad, or ambiguous for human happiness, compared with the limitations of primitive society, it represents an extraordinary achievement.

The state puts an end to self-help in matters of punishment, compensation, and revenge. The state becomes the sole dealer in retributive justice. This is what Max Weber meant when he defined the state as maintaining a monopoly of legitimate force in society[13]—an individual and his kin are no longer part of the system of the enforcement of justice. Vigilante-ism in all forms, as instanced by the "private justice" of fascist gangs, is a regression back to kinship forms of self-help and revenge, which is why it can so seriously threaten the civil order of the state.

In Buganda there was a complicated system of law courts, with appeals possible to higher and higher courts. At the apex of this system stood the *katikiro* and the *kabaka,* both of whom represented—at least in theory, and most times in reality—the whole kingdom, not just a single faction. Each, therefore, was capable of judging cases impartially, especially when he had no particular private interest in the matter. On a day-to-day basis, justice did not fare too well: bribery of judges was common, social and political power played their role, family connections made a large difference. But the system of justice in kinship societies did not work very well, either. What had been created in Buganda was an ideal of justice that was radically different from what had previously existed, as well as a machinery for the purpose of implementing the new ideal. This new conception implied that justice could exist among people who were not related to one another, and was itself based on the political ideal that people who were not related could live together in a situation of civil peace.

Psychologically considered, it is freer, more open, more expansive, more advanced, more developed, more mature to be able to live in civil peace with people to whom one is not related, and not to regard all nonrelated people as enemies. Despite the costs—psychological and moral—and despite heightened anxiety, human sacrifice, and political tyranny, the movement from kinship to nonkinship forms of social cohesion was a great developmental step forward, one that had to be taken. We may wish that things had been different, that people had been less conflicted, that such a great advance could have been made with much less cost, but we must keep in mind that the course was necessary.

A million Dinka, living in a kinship society, are continually at feud and war with one another. A million people organized into one state can live in civil peace without fighting one another. But not, it seems, even today, without tyrannizing over others, and this raises the question of what connection exists between the abandonment of kinship and the beginnings of tyranny against social class. Is class tyranny a replacement for the hostility kin used to act out against one another? Can family strife cease only when the kin organize aggression against "others"?

Freud has said in *Civilization and Its Discontents* that people live together in a state of peace only by projecting their hostilities toward one another outward onto some foreign population.[14] The aggression that would tear society apart is directed at outside enemies, and this unification through warfare helps keep society stable. The insight can be further elaborated. Societies, as societies, express aggression not only toward other societies but toward people within the societies themselves (poor people, black people, Jews, slaves). Institutionalized aggression against a group of men within society I call "class tyranny."*

Warfare and tyranny against class are two distinct things. It is important to note that warfare was ever-present in primitive society, but class tyranny had almost no place. It began in earnest in early complex societies, came to full flowering in advanced complex societies, and has been with us ever since. One cannot find, however, the beginnings of

---

*I distinguish between tyranny against women, which is found within primitive society, and tyranny against men, which is not. This last form I refer to as "class tyranny" or "political tyranny." See the chapter "On Tyranny" for a discussion of the three forms of tyranny (against children, women, social class).

warfare; it seems to be as inseparable from the human condition as speech or religion or sexuality. Though there is no prewarfare human situation, we do find a pre–class-tyranny condition in primitive and, of course, band society. If tyranny against social class began in complex society, its existence there cannot be explained by some immutable aspect of "human nature." If such tyranny began in complex society, it must be related to everything else that was happening at this revolutionary time.

What we can observe in advanced complex societies is that one form of social aggression—the constant feuding and self-help of kinship societies—has been given up, and two new forms—human sacrifice and political tyranny—have arisen. It seems reasonable to conclude that there is a trade-off here—that one has been given up *because* the others have been taken up, and that the others have been taken up *because* the one has been abandoned. The kin will cease feuding only so long as they can combine together to oppress a group of victims. In the beginning, class tyranny and the state were inseparable.

Freud's proposition that social aggression outward is a displacement of social aggression inward also suggests that this outward aggression will carry with it the seeds of its origin. In a part of the mind, those who are oppressed will be considered kin by the oppressors, since they carry the burden of abandoned kinship aggression. Aggression and affection among kin is one paradigm of ambivalence, and all tyranny includes a strange mixture of love and hatred.[15]

Even warfare has an element of affection, which results from the fact that it, too, is a projection outward of feelings of aggression originally directed at the immediate family and the kin. Nobody has any psychological interest in killing someone who is a complete stranger. If the person one kills in warfare does not, in some way, remind one of kin toward whom one has strong feelings of affection and hatred, then why bother to kill him?

The Dinka and the Nuer were intermittently, but continually, at war with one another and themselves. Lugbara tribes fought one another. As soon as primitive peoples reach the boundaries of the kinship relation, they fight those beyond that boundary. It is possible to imagine a different response. To expect peaceful and friendly intercourse would be asking too much of the human psyche, but people intent on preserving relations with kin only could refuse to have *any* dealings with those who were nonkin. They could even refuse to fight with those whom they did not know in a family way. Primitive society might have con-

sisted of groups of kinship-system tribes who refused to have anything
to do with one another. That it did not indicates that kinship relationships were not sufficient for the political life of primitive society, whose
members needed nonkin, if only so they could raid them, kill them, take
from them their cattle, their women, and their children.

In the capturing, the ambivalence is revealed. Nuer loved their cattle
almost more than anything in the world. Cattle captured from the
Dinka were integrated into a man's herd and loved as much as his own
cattle. Dinka women captured in raids became wives, not slaves, of their
Nuer captors (although not of full status). Dinka children captured by
the Nuer were integrated, by adoption and other methods, into the
Nuer kinship system, since it was impossible for anyone in the society
to be nonkin and since there was no slave category. In other words,
the Nuer raided the Dinka because they were not kin and then proceeded to make kin out of the spoils of the raids. After the Athenians,
in the Peloponnesian War, destroyed the island of Melos, killing off
all the adult males, the great Athenian political leader Alcibiades
adopted one of the young girls who survived the slaughter. Hatred very
rarely walks alone.

Warfare, then, as opposed to feud, plays a unique role in primitive
society: it is the fundamental form of contact with nonkin. Warfare is
the nonkinship form of politics in a kinship society. It provides, therefore, the perfect instrument for the building of the state. When complex
society has ripened to the point where a true state is possible, nothing
provides a better catalyst for this transformation than the unification
of several chieftaincies under one king for the purpose of making war
on other polities. The histories of early complex societies tell of many
occasions when such war confederacies were only temporary and
quickly dissolved once the war was over, but when statehood and monarchy are ideas whose time has come, warfare is the perfect midwife.
Many states in traditional Africa, for instance, were built by strong military leaders who succeeded in permanently dominating several chieftaincies and welded them into a unified polity.[16]

Warfare by itself can never create a state. Only when society has
developed to the point where nonkinship forms of social cohesion are
possible can warfare aid in state making. Nuer tribes fought one another
and the Dinka for centuries without its occurring to anyone to change
the basis of society radically. Some people have argued that military
conquest is the *primary* mechanism of state creation,[17] but no Nuer becomes a Baganda merely by fighting with others.

The forms of warfare depend upon the forms of political life, and warfare develops as society develops. In the earliest stage of warfare, killing and raiding are the only aims of the fighting. Whether the warriors are cannibals who want flesh to eat, or head-hunters who need the crania of others for religious and magical purposes, or simply killers and booty collectors like the Nuer, this kind of fighting results in no conquest of land or people. In the second stage of warfare, the enemy may be driven from the land and the country occupied by the conquerors, who want more or better pastures or fields. Primitive peoples are capable of both these kinds of warfare because neither involves any transformation of the kinship system.

The third stage of warfare, which involves conquest of another people, is an entirely different matter. To conquer a land and let the defeated continue to live on it, no matter in what condition of servitude, requires a notion that people who are nonkin can live together in the same society. Even to become master over a class of nonkin slaves requires a notion of political action that was alien to primitive peoples. Traditional Africa provides many examples of conquest states— Rwanda in East Africa, for instance—where a militaristic people moved into an area, conquered its people, and established themselves as a caste of rulers. To imagine, however, that the Tutsi conquerors of Rwanda were a simple, primitive people like the Nuer, with no conception of nonkinship politics before they set out, is badly to underestimate the revolutionary implications of nonkinship forms of social cohesion. Before a Nuer tribe could pick itself up, move on, conquer an alien people, and settle down to rule over them in a state, a profound change would have to occur *within* Nuer society. The Tutsi conquest of Rwanda was the final act of a revolutionary drama, not its only act.

The great developmental question is: what makes the Baganda and the Tutsi undertake such a process in the first place? One wonders why any person leaves the cozy, intimately hostile, familiar world of kinship for the cold, competitive, unfamiliar world of nonkinship politics. Obviously, what is cozy and familiar is not sufficient to satisfy human needs. Something drives us. The same something drives the development of society. We cannot understand the creation of the state unless we understand the human drive to transcend kinship.

23

"He Who Never Travels Praises His Mother's Cooking"

John Papa Ii was raised in traditional Hawaiian society. When he was still prepubescent, he was sent from home, under his uncles' protection, to serve the Crown Prince Liholiho, the son and future successor of Kamehameha I:

Once when the parents of the boy brought up the subject of his going to court, they warned him of the things he might encounter in the place where his older brother Maoloha had died for committing a misdeed. "Therefore make yourself wise," said they. The young boy said, "How strange for you to take me to the royal court to stay where my older brother died. Perhaps the same fate will befall me there."

His mother answered, "Yes, that may be true, if you do not heed all we taught you. Your brother died because he did not observe all we had taught him. Your uncles who are now in the royal court do not go about as they please, but heed the instructions they receive from their elders. So do we teach you. Because we have nothing to give to those in whose house we live, your father and I have agreed not to keep you to ourselves though you were born to us, a son from our loins. We know that you are capable of taking care of yourself if you heed our teachings. These you practiced before us, therefore I am letting Papa [his uncle] . . . place you with any chief he chooses. To him you must be obedient. Thus did your uncles become seekers of the welfare of their chiefs' homes from the time they were poor until they became prosperous. They bore with patience the poverty and the many troubles that rested upon them. So must you, if you heed our teachings. . . ."

The boy knew by the words of his mother that she was determined to make him a member of the court. He made no comments, feeling it best to comply.[2]

His mother said, "So you have come? Your uncle Kaleiheana has been here and gone. He came to take you back to the chief, to the place we have trained you for, to observe, to be obedient, and to take care. You do not belong to us, though we begot you. You must become the servant of the chief, Liholiho, and all the chiefs whom your uncles serve. Do as you did before them and your chief. Since you have agreed to do as I wish and as your father has taught you, you have been summoned. We know that you will be mindful of all we have taught you."

As the boy talked with his mother, he forgot the pleasures in which he had been so interested. Before he left her he asked, "What must I do when I long for you and for my father, now that we are separating? Perhaps we shall never live together again."

His mother said, "Do not think of us. The chief alone must be your father and your mother. From him shall come your vegetable food, your meat, your tapa coverings, and malos."

The boy asked, "May I not come and see you sometimes when you are as near as you are now?"

"It will be all right to do so at the proper time," she replied, "but it would be much better for you to remain with the chief with no thought of us, whether we are as near as we are now or far away."

While they talked, the sun passed to the opposite side of Mount Kaala, and his mother said, "Night has come for you."

"*Homai ka ihu* (embrace me; literally, give the nose)," replied the boy. Thus ended their living together, and the boy stood up and went to the residence of the chief.[3]

As the boy drew near the Hale o Lono, he saw two crossed lama sticks outside the entrance gate. He knew that the tapa covering he wore must be removed before entering, and this he did although he was not yet near the houses. Then he walked to the steward's house just outside the enclosure and found Liholiho there waiting for him. When he was recognized by the occupants of the house and was told to enter, he went in and sat by the edge of the fireplace. He bundled his tapa and just sat as a stranger. The chief and people of the house treated him kindly.

Night had fallen . . . and the burning Kukui-nut candles furnished the light there. After they had finished eating in the men's house, which was the one he had entered, the chief and the others stood up and went to the Hale a Lono. The boy departed with them, imitating their way of walking, just as his parents had told him to do. Thus began his knowledge of life in the royal court.[4]

We have no evidence from Hawaii and Tahiti that would indicate just how prevalent was the custom of sending small children away from home to be raised by others. In Buganda, the practice was general. In the middle of the twentieth century, when the practice was already dying out, 48 percent of all children in one Buganda school said they had spent an average of two years away from home, in the households of others—most of them at the ages of three to five.[5]

Many Buganda situations resembled that of John Papa Ii: a young boy would be sent to relatives with strong political connections in order to promote his way in the Buganda political world. If the powerful relation had influence at the royal court, the boy would join the group of court pages, who were the pool from which the future politicos of the state were drawn. The kinship connection might be a provincial governor, or someone serving such a governor, in which case the young boy would serve his political apprenticeship at one of the ten provincial capitals. If the boy was the son of a poor *mukopi* (peasant) but showed some intellectual promise, he could be sent to some subgovernor's or sub-subgovernor's house where he had a kinship connection.

Although the political bureaucracy in Buganda was large, it was limited, and these political apprenticeships did not account for the extraordinarily large number of young people who were sent from home. Many children were sent to live with grandparents, to be raised by them. Sometimes the grandparents seized the initiative, asking to take an offspring from their son because they desired "to have a child about the place."[6] In other cases, the parents were intent on sending a child away. In such circumstances, the first choice fell to the grandmother, who was perceived as loving the child the most. If neither grandmother was inclined to burden her old age, another female relative, preferably father's or mother's sister, was chosen for the honor. And if no one seemed to want the child, and the parents were intent on separating from it, they could drop it off secretly at the house of one grandmother and she was obliged to take the child in.[7] Under mutually agreed-upon circumstances, the child could also be sent to the father's brother.[8] The mother's brother sometimes claimed a child; he was traditionally responsible for making the marriage arrangements for his sister and, in return, was entitled to take certain of her children unless money or other compensation was paid him.[9] Various mechanisms were clearly available to accomplish the same goal, that the child be raised by people other than its parents.

In all these circumstances, there is no hint that lack of financial means to support the child played the slightest role. Even in the story that John Papa Ii tells, when his mother announces that the parents have "nothing to give to those in whose house we live," she is referring to political connection, not to food and drink.

These family separations, as opposed to political apprenticeships, applied to both boys and girls, though in what proportion we do not know. They could be of a temporary nature, with the child returning to its own family after two, three, or four years, or they could become permanent.[10] The temporary separations usually occurred when the children were between the ages of three and seven.[11]

Aside from the clear political advantage to those who were sent to seats of power, several explanations were given by the Baganda themselves for their sending their children to be raised by others. In the case of the father's brother's taking the child, it was claimed that he would be stricter than the father, who would incline to indulgence.[12] Another explanation, suggesting that the mother sent the child away so that she could devote her full attention to a new baby,[13] might help explain the fact that children were separated so young. A vaguer explanation offered that the children were sent from home to " 'learn their relatives'; or as a sign of respect paid by young parents to older kinsfolk."[14] None of these explanations seems to carry any more than a superficial truth. Something much more complex was going on.

These arbitrary, painful, aggressive separations were not the first for the Buganda child. The traditional mode of weaning from the breast seemed to be designed to be as traumatic as possible. No effort was made to wean the child gradually; the breast was suddenly withdrawn one day, usually when the child was two or three, and if the child insisted on sucking, chili powder was put on the nipple to make it unpalatable. Some children refused to be put off by this evil-tasting barrier and persisted in sucking. The mother would then smear on something even worse and tell the child that it was feces, which would make it sick.[15]

After this abrupt weaning, the child was physically removed from the mother's house for two days and taken to one of the grandmothers. This enabled the baby to "forget the breast." Sometimes the child was permanently separated from the mother at the time of weaning, to stay with the grandparents. Before departing, however, the child was allowed to spend the third night after weaning with its mother.[16]

In the attempt to understand these forms of child rearing, it would be a mistake to reduce them solely to their aggressive dimension. Undoubtedly, parents were aggressive toward the children, on whom such experiences took a large psychological toll. There are more humane ways to wean a child, and societies at all stages of development have found gentler ways of breaking the child of this oral attachment. Yet the Baganda would have claimed that they were doing it all for the good of the child, and in a way they were. They clearly felt that the infantile attachment to the mother should be violently broken, probably so that the child could develop a more separated and individuated ego. Like most things that go on between the authority of parents and the helplessness of children, there was a large mixture of aggression *and* concern in the process.

The motives for sending the child away from home to be raised by others were equally ambiguous. Some parents in our society send their postpubescent children to boarding school to be raised by others during the crucial adolescent years. In our mother country, England, the process starts, for some, when the child is seven or eight. The stated reasons for this behavior are similar to those given by the Baganda: to help the child do better in the world. Particularly in the case of boarding schools for adolescents, there is the stated notion that at such a crucial time others can discipline the child better than the parents. Common to both the Buganda and the modern situation is the desire of the parents that *other* people should raise their children.

In ancient Buganda there were no schools; there was no reading and writing to be taught. The very first thing the Christian missionaries did there was to teach reading to anyone who was interested. These informal schools provided the lever that eventually moved the whole country. In our society, we rely on the school system to break the bonds of family attachment and train the child in the process of living in the larger society. Most children in our society return home each day after school, a gentler mode than the Buganda or the boarding-school method, but even so the first day at school can become a memorable trauma. We can imagine the shock to a five-year-old child sent away from home for three years.

For us, the socialization process is not easy, even though we live in a culture with a history of several thousand years of nonkinship society. The Baganda had no such tradition; they were in the midst of the process of transforming the kinship system. That this transformation was accompanied by a certain amount of seemingly unnecessary violence is not surprising. Periods of great revolutionary change are never easy on the people whose task it is to carry them out. It is easy enough for us, the beneficiaries of that revolution, to feel that it should have been done in a more humane manner. But it is very difficult to establish just how much violence was necessary to bring about such a transformation.

Though people did not live in the Buganda world without attachments, for many the patron-client relationship replaced the attachment to close kin that had been the foundation of kinship society. A young man, during his adolescence or early manhood, would attach himself to a patron with political power. It could be the relative to whom he had originally been sent, or the person of political power whom that relative served. Such attachment could result even from a chance meeting if an older person with power found a young man attractive and intelligent and invited the youth to become one of his men.

In terms of its own goals, the system worked. It did produce young adults of more ambition, more freedom, and more independence than was possible in kinship societies. Young men were not required to live in their fathers' villages or in the villages of their spouses, unheard-of in a kinship society. A young adult could set up his own home and arrange a marriage without his father's permission or approval.[17] "Unlike his counterpart in most patrilineal societies of East Africa, he acquired rights over land through his political rather than his kinship affiliations. He often secured a wife in the same way, that is to say from his patron rather than through the economic contributions of his paternal relatives. He was thus foot-loose as compared with the young man of other Bantu societies whose fortunes were completely dependent on the elders of a local patrilineage."[18]

What we are describing here is a social process remarkably similar to the psychological process in the individual that Margaret Mahler has brilliantly illuminated and called "separation and individuation." Members of complex societies were thoroughly and pervasively engaged in a massive process of socially separating and individuating. New, stable forms that combined individuation and security had not yet been created; it was a time of transition. According to Mahler's work on the individual, anxiety is an inevitable first result of separation, and anger comes soon after. The anxiety caused by the separation and individuation in complex society, and the violence that resulted when the process did not work smoothly, were both at fever pitch. Human sacrifice and political tyranny were the costs paid for individuation. Christianity triumphed in these societies because it provided a more humane, more loving mode of leaving one's parents. The love of Christ was more reliable than the approval of the *kabaka,* who might take one's life tomorrow. The Christian sense of community replaced the feelings of close kinship that had been abandoned.

In Buganda, one result of these constant separations from families was that the society exhibited an extraordinary mobility, both as to social position and as to place. The vast majority of people, even in sophisticated Buganda, were peasant farmers. Many people—we don't know what percentage—still lived on clan lands and held their property under clan auspices. The clans were subdivided into lineages, sublineages, and sub-sublineages, and many people spent their entire lives on the lands of one of these kinship-system divisions. Other farmers—possibly a majority of the peasant class—broke away from the kinship lands and became clients of a person of political authority, who provided them with land to live on. The patron might very well be a relative of the client, but this would be a kinship, not a kinship-system, form of action, similar to a powerful political boss in a twentieth-century democracy seeing to it that his nephews have gainful employment on the public payroll.

People of authority within the political hierarchy were constantly being shifted about by changes in their fortunes or in the general political situation. Three to five changes of position and residence in a lifetime was the average for a person in the political bureaucracy.[19] These transfers would result in changes of residence for a substantial number of people. When, for instance, a subgovernor of a province was promoted to the governorship of another province, many of "his men" would move with him—not only his subordinate officials, but also many simple landholders who either were related to him or felt some feeling of attachment or considered that they would do better to follow their patron to his place of enhanced prestige. In the new bailiwick they would be assigned lands on which to live. Very few people of the middle and upper strata of society died in the same villages in which they had been born.

Even more remarkable in this regard is the fact that individual peasants were free to change their patrons whenever they liked. There was always another person of political authority ready to give them land and take them under his protection. Both the wealth and prestige of a headman were increased if he added new peasant-clients to his domain and decreased if they left.[20] If the population of a village decreased noticeably, the headman might be deposed by his political superior.[21] When a peasant-client found the demands of the headman too exacting, or when he quarreled with his neighbors, he could find himself another village headman and move on. He merely went to the new headman, asked if he might become his man, made a token gift of a cock, and was presented with a new holding. Provided he gave tribute of beer and food, as well as certain days of labor and military service, he was entitled to stay on the land as long as he wished and pass its possession on to his children.[22] As a result of changing masters or of following a master to a new residence, many peasant lives contained as much movement as those of upper-class families.[23] The option to move on clearly lessened the possibilities of tyrannical behavior on the part of the patron.

In Buganda, we are told, it was not uncommon for a person to change his clan affiliation if this would help him prosper in his political career. Certain clans had greater prestige and power in certain areas, and for a person intent on "making it," there was an advantage in belonging to the most prestigious clan.[24] Such mobility indicates just how far the kinship system had eroded in the rise of state politics.

Though the kinship system was disintegrating, kinship continued to play a very important role in Buganda politics, even on the highest level. The sons of the *kabaka,* the royal princes, took the clan of their mothers, since there was no royal clan in Buganda. The *kabaka* had a multitude of wives; all clans could be represented among his offspring. Each clan, in fact, endeavored to provide the *kabaka* with as many wives as possible. The prestige of the clan was enhanced by the royal connection; a royal prince who attained any influence would distribute power to the members of his mother's (and his) clan. And when the *kabaka* died, and the new monarch was chosen from among his sons, the clan connections of the princes played a significant role. If a prince had to fight for the throne, his clan relatives, especially his mother's brothers, were the backbone of his support. When political jockeying, not fighting, was to decide the choice, clan members who had political influence at high levels brought it to bear in the interest of the selection of their clansman. When the new *kabaka* began to distribute the multitude of political plums that were his to give away, his fellow clansmen received a significant share.

In any highly competitive political situation, allies are needed in order to succeed: no one can go it alone. In a society that was just liberating itself from the kinship system, a society in which feelings of kinship still ran very strong, natural allies in the competitive struggle would be those who shared the same clan status.

These kinship affiliations asserted their power at all levels of the political hierarchy, and there was a substantial interpenetration between kinship-system politics and state politics. It sometimes happened that the *kabaka* would appoint a clan official to a political office, such as a subgovernorship. The appointee would leave his clan land to take up

his new post, but the chances were that he would take many of his clansmen with him, and that together they would establish a new clan
center.[25]

The Muganda left his home in early youth to get experience and a powerful
patron, but once established in life he tended to attract his relatives to live with
him, forming a loosely organized kinship group which became the dominant
core of the village in the case of a man of authority. . . . Thus the Muganda
was apparently as anxious to live with his relatives as are members of societies
with villages based on corporate patrilineages but his life cycle was different.
He was forced to become independent of his parents in early life, often with
the help of his father's or mother's brothers. . . . When he had acquired a post
he built up a residential group both within his enclosure and near it.[26]

Success in the harsh, competitive world of Buganda politics required
breaking from family, but once success was achieved, the family was
gathered about. The bigger the man had become, the more family he
could attract. The transformation of the kinship system, like the great
process of individuation to which it is intimately related, is never completed. It is an unending process, dialectical in its nature. We are still
in the midst of it.

24

The Kabaka and the Clans

The King was the state in advanced complex society, and the state was built at the expense of the kinship system. The fundamental political conflict in such societies was thus between an ascendant monarchy and a declining kinship system; state building was the process of kingship triumphing over kinship.

Whenever a state is erected within a tribal society, the primary resistance it will have to overcome arises from the kinship system. Kwame Nkrumah, the founder of the state of Ghana, declared that his primary problem was to "combat not only tribalism but the African tradition that man's first duty is to his family."[1] In advanced complex society, without any of the various modern forms of political cohesion, only the power of the monarchy allowed the kinship system to be transcended.

The historical information that confirms and expands these general propositions comes primarily from Buganda. Similar data for Polynesia are too sparse.

Fundamental to any society is the form of land ownership, since, immediately or ultimately, everyone lives off the land. No one in a kinship society owns land in the same manner as it is held in a modern society, in which the possessor is free to sell it, give it away, or bequeath it as he or she sees fit. In primitive society, the kin have as much to say as the individual cultivator in regard to what happens to the property. No one in primitive society is free to sell his land to an outsider. No Nuer sells land, or even its use, to Arab traders, European explorers, or to a Dinka. A man may pass his land to his brothers, or sons, or nephews—as the custom of the kin allows—but he cannot separate it out of the kinship system. In that sense, the kin own the land and people have the use of it. The absence of individual ownership is commensurate with the communal nature of primitive society.

No individual in Buganda owned outright the land he lived on. The *kabaka* and the clans were the only possessors, and people cultivated land at their sufferance. Three types of landholding existed: *bataka* land—clan land cultivated by clan members; *saza* land—land controlled by the ten provincial governors and their political subordinates, with the *kabaka* the ultimate owner; *batongole* land, given by the *kabaka* to individual *mutongole* to use. These *batongole* fiefs were scattered throughout the ten provinces.[2]

Use of *bataka* land differed in no way from land use in a primitive society. All transfers, including inheritance, had to be approved by the kin. Since only thirty-five to forty clans existed in Buganda, each clan was too large to operate on the face-to-face level required of a kinship system, but the clans were subdivided into small groups. In 1911 Roscoe could still count 526 separate clan centers;[3] each served one to two thousand people, such size being compatible with kinship-system forms of land tenure. The *bataka* form of landholding prevailed where the *kabaka*'s power was least active:

The power of kinship heads tended to be greatest in the areas furthest away from the King and least in the areas where the control of the King was greatest. In the latter areas, most of the estates of the King and the royal relatives were situated, and it was here that most of the grants to the chiefs and other palace functionaries were made. In these areas, the clan heads were limited to single villages or to the tops of the hills. Farther away from the palace the people lived more or less under the direct control of their kinship heads who combined the political duties imposed upon them with the traditional control over land exercised by a clan or lineage.[4]

Saza-land tenure was inseparable from political office. The ten provinces of traditional Buganda each had a governor responsible to the *kabaka,* maintaining control over all land in his province that did not belong to the clans and was not *batongole* land. The control of *saza* land was hierarchically organized from the top downward: from the *saza* governor to subgovernors to sub-subgovernors, each of whom had clients who cultivated the soil. At the beginning of the Buganda state, each governorship was the property of a particular clan, and as the power of the *kabaka* expanded, he succeeded in wresting the ownership of most of these governorships—and the land use they subsumed—from the clan hierarchies.

Batongole land was taken by the *kabaka* from conquered territory, clan land, or *saza* land, and given to his own personal representative. If the land grant was large enough, the *mutongole* would invite his kin or other peasants to take up residence on it. These fiefs were granted to people who had rendered the *kabaka* particular service, perhaps in war, or to anyone the king might wish to honor. Many *batongole* fiefs were given to people whose function was to inform the monarch of what went on in the province, warning him of conspiracies, seeing that provincial governors did not overstep their authority, hold back taxes, or grow too powerful. Control of this land lay directly with the *kabaka,* and when a *mutongole* died, it was the king who decided who should succeed to the fiefdom. Many times a son succeeded to his father's *batongole* status, but only at the *kabaka*'s pleasure.

As we have seen, an individual peasant was free to move about from one form of land authority to another. Dissatisfied with the situation on his own clan land, he could become a client of a *mutongole* or *saza* patron; he was even free to move to other *bataka* land, to a clan or lineage not his own.[5] All three forms of landholding patrons were anxious to obtain as many cultivators as they could. "But his security of tenure and freedom from molestation and petty irritants were greater if his chief were a clansman. This feeling sometimes gave rise to wholesale movement of larger sections of the population as clansmen followed a successful member of their clan in his progression from bigger to bigger chieftainships."[6] Such movements, though based upon feelings of kinship, were destructive to the kinship system, because the power of the clans and their control over land were thereby weakened. People followed their kinsman, but his movement was determined by his success or failure in the political hierarchy.

All changes of land tenure contributed to the general erosion of clan power. Sometimes the *kabaka* would turn a clan headman off *bataka* land and give it to someone appointed by him.[7] He was not supposed to transfer *bataka* land from the control of one kinship corporation to another, and "whenever he dared to do so, the group of people that had been deprived of their rightful chief and given another not belonging to their clan would lodge a complaint about it in the Native Council or Lukiko and have one of their fellow clansmen appointed as their chief in that particular village."[8] The formality of the procedure of redress suggests that frequent attempts were made by the *kabaka*. It is doubtful that all of them failed.

When the *kabaka* was not happy with a particular clan headman, he could depose him, but the normal procedure called for the clan to nominate one of its members as successor, though the candidate would then have to be approved by the *kabaka*.[9] The clan would continue to hold the office, but no personal or political opposition to the throne was tolerated.

The *kabaka*'s control over *batongole* land was absolute. No matter how many generations of one family had been buried in a particular soil, the king was still free to turn the chiefs out.[10] It was in the interest of his authoritarian rule to convert as much land into *batongole* status as possible, although the amount of such land could be increased only at the expense of the other forms of land tenure. These conversions, a form of tyranny exercised by the *kabaka*, must have provoked feelings of anger in those who were forced to agree to a diminished status for themselves, thereby lessening their power. An elaborate ritual evolved to handle the tension that such exchanges provoked:

If one of the lower chiefs or even a peasant was granted by the king himself a holding or an estate for his permanent personal occupation, the grantee brought one cow to the King and was then given a special messenger by the King. The messenger would then take the grantee to his chiefs starting from the highest to the lowest. Each of these chiefs would add his own messenger, all of whom would be present when the King's messenger planted the bark-cloth tree. Any one of the messengers or all of them together, would be witness to the permanent claims to that piece of land by the grantee.[11]

We know almost nothing about how those within the kinship system felt about these invasions of its power, because almost all the oral history we have centers on the throne and its interests. Even when Mutesa decreed that the forms of inheritance on all lands, including *bataka* land, should be changed from succession by brother to inheritance by sons,[12] we are not told what, if any, resistance the clan leaders mounted to this radical transformation. In the twentieth century, the clans began to write their own histories, but even these do not bring us close to the feelings of those engaged in this great struggle with the *kabaka*.

In the Hawaiian Islands, some data we do have indicate that Kamehameha I, in the process of building his empire, had recourse to the Babylonian system of breaking people's loyalty to their homelands: he transplanted large numbers of people from one island to another, a process the Hawaiians referred to as "scrambling." On Oahu there were two hills, Pu'u-o-Hawaii and Pu'u-o-Maui, upon which were buried the peoples from the islands of Hawaii and Maui who had been made into émigrés by the sovereign.[13] The power that is strong enough to crack the kinship system can easily get accustomed to moving people about as if they were objects. Tyranny requires a tyrant.

The building of this centralized, authoritarian power at the expense of the kinship system can be traced in detail for Buganda. Originally, all ten *saza* governorships "belonged to" individual clans, which meant that the incumbent had to be a member of the particular clan. For instance, each man who filled the office of the governor of the province of Kyadondo was called *kago* and had to be a member of the Colobus Monkey Clan.[14]

It is probable that these *saza* provinces originated in two ways. One was by conquest, and for this we do have data. In the reign of Katerega, the fourteenth *kabaka* according to oral tradition, the king sent out his General Balamaga to conquer the province of Gomba from the neighboring state of Bunyoro. Successful in the attempt, Balamaga was appointed as the *kitunzi*—governor of the province. The office was hereditary in his clan for 150 years.

Other *saza* governorships came into being at the beginning of the Buganda state. In traditional Africa the expansion of state societies like Buganda often results from the subjugation of neighboring chieftainships and their subsequent incorporation into the centralized state. It is a reasonable assumption that some *saza* provinces in Buganda were originally small states, ruled by chiefs, and that the chieftainships belonged to one particular royal clan in each small state. When the state was conquered by the *kabaka,* the chieftaincy would be maintained but made subordinate to the authority of the *kabaka.* Since the original chieftainship resided in one particular clan, the subsequent governorship would continue in the same group.

At the beginning of this kind of arrangement, those in the conquered state probably retained a significant degree of autonomy in regard to the choice of their chief, now reduced to governor. As the power of the *kabaka* expanded, however, he established a veto power over these incumbencies. With time, the fact that the office of *kago,* governor of Kyadondo, belonged to the Colobus Monkey Clan did not mean that the elders of the clan were free to depose the *kago* without consulting the *kabaka,* or that they could appoint a successor *kago* without the permission of the sovereign. The king's power developed to the extent that, if he quarreled with the incumbent *kago,* he could depose him. He would then ask the clan to select a successor more to his liking.[15]

This power of approval and veto turned out to be not enough for the *kabaka*s, who desired full authority over these most important political posts. Kabaka Mawanda, the twenty-first monarch, reigning in the early eighteenth century, "was a fearless warrior and not a respecter of persons. His reign was dominated by wars of aggression against his neighbors and inevitably he befriended brave men like himself rather than the traditional chiefs, many of whom were very old men. He inaugurated his reign by dismissing Kago, the county chief of Kyadondo of the Colobus Monkey clan who had held this chief hereditarily for five generations. The process of dismissal and installation of men of his own choice was repeated in Kyaggwe, Singo and Bulemezi. Mawanda thereby created a class of chiefs characteristically known as the *king's men* in the sense that their political futures depended on royal pleasure."[16]

The final result of this process was that at the time of Mwanga's reign, only two or three (sources disagree) out of ten *saza* governorships were still hereditary in the clans.[17] Why these few were able to hold out against the pressure of the *kabaka,* we are not told. What had begun as a working compromise between the two political principles of kinship system and statehood ended with the almost total victory of authoritarian monarchy.

Despite this political process, the values of the kinship system maintained deep roots in Buganda society. We even know of several instances when the *kabaka* permitted an office that he could freely appoint to revert to being the property of a certain clan. The *saza* governorship *katambala* was given back to the Sheep Clan by Kabaka Mutebi after years of depending on the king's sufferance only.[18] In advanced complex societies, kinship forms of social cohesion were still as important as nonkinship forms.

In Tahiti, where the development of statehood was considerably behind that in Buganda, the hold of the kinship system on the land was so powerful that the king's authority was severely limited, even in the case of rebellion: "For treason, rebellion, or withholding supplies, individuals were liable to banishment, and confiscation of property. The king had the prerogative of nominating his successor, but could not appropriate the lands of the exile to his own use."[19] We are not told, but we may assume that the successor had to come from the same family as the banished headman, because the monarch was not yet powerful enough to appoint whomever he wished.

Buganda history does provide a few tantalizingly brief views of what the conflicts and tensions between the *kabaka* and the royal-clan chieftains must have been like at the beginnings of the state. "Kagwa . . . mentions 23 clan authorities (*bataka*) who avoided meeting the Kabaka because they had formerly been independent on their own lands and hence did not care to see the man who had been their equal and had then 'turned them into peasants (*bakopi*).' These men wore special brass rings and head-crests and were represented at the capital by their sons or deputies until the breach was apparently healed by Mutesa I at the end of the nineteenth century."[20]

Kagwa gives a detailed description of one of these *"Kabaka*[s] in miniature."* Mugalula of the Grasshopper Clan called himself a *kabaka* and would never meet the king of Buganda. He maintained a small court with ritual forms similar to those of the Buganda ruler. His throne, made of copper, was covered with lion and leopard skins. People from various clans had the ritual of performing certain functions for him: holding his throne, grazing his cattle, drumming his drums, holding his copper spears. He performed a new-moon ceremony, as did the *kabaka* of Buganda.[21]

One reasonable hypothesis would be that before the formation of the Buganda state, there were several small kingdoms of more or less equal power, neighbors to one another, sharing the same cultural patterns, each with its own ruling *kabaka*. Exactly this situation existed in Busoga, next land to Buganda, until the English came to dominate the area. At some point in Buganda, one of these small states, probably under the leadership of a psychologically powerful monarch, may have begun to dominate and conquer the surrounding states, reducing their *kabaka*s to *bakopi*. What is remarkable is that these twenty-three miniature *kabaka*s maintained their ritual existence for four or five hundred years—from the beginnings of the state until the reign of Mutesa.

Though they were on the losing side of the struggle for political dominance, the clans nevertheless were powerful enough to humble the great Mutesa, even in his ripe years. The *kabaka* had gonorrhea, and from 1876 until his death in 1884 he was bedridden. By 1879, when the medical efforts of Père Lourdel, Reverend Mackay, and certain Zanzibari Arabs had failed to make him better, the conservative forces in the country took advantage of Mutesa's weakness and launched a major attack on his violation of clan rights. Allied for this purpose were the queen mother (a defender of traditional values), the clan hierarchy (threatened by Mutesa's increasing absolutism), the priests of the traditional gods (resentful of Mutesa's flirtations with Islam and Christianity), and the older members of the political hierarchy (unsympathetic to Mutesa's "modernizing" tendencies). A natural alliance existed between the priests of the traditional gods and the clans, "since it was on clan lands that the shrines of the gods were established, and it was the clan heads who supplied the priests to look after the shrines: thus the god Mukasa's shrine was maintained by the Sesse clans, Kibuka's by the Sheep clan and Nende's by the Mushroom Clan."[22]

Previous to the great confrontation of 1879, Mutesa had committed certain specific transgressions of clan rights. First, he had attacked and dismissed the incumbent *mugema,* provincial governor of Busiro. The office of *mugema* had been held by the Monkey Clan since the beginning of time, since Kabaka Kimera, the third *kabaka* on the list of kings. The governorship of Busiro included the task of guarding the royal tombs, which were located in that province:

Mutesa declared to his assembled chiefs that, ever since the Mugema had brought Kabaka Kimera from Bunyoro he had been loaded with honor in Buganda; he had been called the father of the Kabaka and accorded a higher rank than the other clan heads. Despite this, however, when Mutesa had recently questioned him he had discovered that the Mugema did not even know the whereabouts of the royal tombs, and had tried to excuse himself by saying that it had been no part of a Mugema's duties to attend the Kabaka's funeral. He must therefore be dismissed and his work taken away from the Monkey Clan, which had failed in its duty. Mutesa's favourite, Tebukoza, who was of the Pangolin clan, was then awarded the Mugema's administrative duties in Busiro, with the title of Kyambalango ("Wearer of the Leopard Skin"—the royal livery). He took the land at the Mugema's old headquarters and the Mugema was relegated to the position of an ordinary clan head.[23]

Mutesa's second transgression was to appoint Sekamwa to the office of *kimbugwe,* a post responsible for the guardianship of the king's umbilical cord. Sekamwa was a member of the Oribi Antelope Clan, and no one of that affiliation had ever held the office of *kimbugwe* before.[24]

Mutesa's third transgression was to arrest and put in the stocks Kabazzi, who was the head of the Genet Clan and was connected with the cult of the god Mukasa in the Sesse Islands. Kabazzi was guilty of giving girls to an Arab instead of offering them first to the *kabaka.* Even so, no king had ever dared touch the head of the Genet Clan before.[25]

The conservative allies expostulated with Mutesa that his neglect of the ancient gods had brought on his illness, that he had been getting worse since he demonstrated an interest in and a tolerance for Christianity, and that the only solution for his ills was to call Mukasa, the god of the lake, to his palace. Mutesa agreed, either because he could not resist the political pressure of such a powerful alliance or because he felt the god might help him. The strength of the conservative opposition is demonstrated by the reports which reached the English missionaries at the capital that Mutesa was to be killed or deposed if he refused to obey the commands of the god's oracle.[26]

The priests of the god Mukasa were clear about what was needed in order to cure Mutesa's illness: (1) the office of *mugema* must be restored to the Monkey Clan; (2) the head of the Genet Clan was to be released from confinement; (3) the office of *kimbugwe* must return to the Pangolin Clan.[27] Mutesa, having called the god, had no choice but to comply with his instructions, and the king even went further on his own when he announced, to the distress of the Christian missionaries, that the Baganda would now return to "the religion of their fathers."[28] We may doubt whether, Mutesa being well, the clans would have begun this contest. It ended with their temporary victory over the *kabaka,* but it was the last triumph of the clans. Christianity and Islam, not clanship, were destined to bring the *kabaka* down.

It is an open question whether the *kabaka*'s seizure of prerogatives and political power from the clans should be described as a tyranny or merely as factionalism. If two factions of the aristocratic class struggle with each other for political power and the privilege of impoverishing the peasantry—as they did in England in the fifteenth century—the punishments they mete out to each other are the result of factionalism, not of tyranny. The peasantry suffers the tyranny, no matter which faction triumphs. We do not know enough of the relationship of the clan hierarchy to clan members to decide whether that hierarchy should be described as a faction struggling with the *kabaka* for the privilege of oppressing the *bakopi* (plural of *mukopi,* peasant) or whether the clans, leaders, and members together, were a real corporate group who were gradually being made to feel the *kabaka*'s tyranny, as he took from them, one by one, the privileges that had been theirs for centuries. I am inclined toward the latter explanation, an interpretation that is reinforced by the *kabaka*'s persecutions of particular clans, some of which suffered a form of political genocide.

These persecutions resulted from the same view of the world that has fueled all persecutions: a people, as a whole, are considered guilty of a crime committed by one or several of them. This view is directly opposed to the legal-rational concept that only the actual perpetrator may be prosecuted for a crime. To hold the whole kin responsible is a value of kinship society that survives with great strength even today. The world will never be safe from the enormities of persecution and genocide until this particular value of kinship society is finally transcended. Religious wars, nationalism, Nazism are the grim shadows of kinship society that darken our lives. "High treason in all its forms was always punishable with death. And whenever a chief was convicted of this crime he would be killed and all his people or clan would be exterminated, not as accomplices, but simply because they happened to belong to one and the same clan with the offender."[29]

We have no record of the persecution of the clans in the early history of Buganda; it seems to have begun about the same time that the *kabaka*s started to take away their political power. Kabaka Kagulu, having reigned for many years in an acceptable manner, turned tyrant. He arrested and executed his brother, ordered that when people were brought into his presence they should be forced to kneel on needles, killed many, and even ordered the execution of the *mugema,* governor of Busiro. Following this latter act, the country rose in revolt, killed the king, and set his brother, Kikulwe, on the throne.[30] The tyrant Kagulu had been a member of the Elephant Clan (because his mother was), and the new *kabaka* reasoned that the only way he could wipe the slate clean of the outrageous acts committed by his brother was to persecute the whole clan. It was decreed that no royal prince born of a mother who was a member of the Elephant Clan could ever assume the throne.[31] The persecution grew in severity; three successive *kabaka*s felt the need to maintain the harassment, so that members of the Elephant Clan began to deny their membership and claimed instead that they belonged to the Civet Cat Clan.[32]

Escape from persecution by refuge in another clan was a general practice: the Bushbuck Clan hid in the Monkey Clan; the Leopard Clan, having been persecuted by Kabaka Katerega because it claimed its members were of the royal family, formed an entirely new clan, the Genet. This hapless clan was almost completely destroyed by Kabaka

Kamanya, Mutesa's grandfather, and "it was not until the 1920's after the establishment of the Pax Britannica that members of the clan revealed their true identity."[33]

It seems that almost any excuse could be used by the *kabaka* to set the mechanism of "collective responsibility and punishment" into motion. Some members of the Lungfish Clan had conspired and killed Kabaka Junju. King Semakokiro decided to hold the whole clan responsible and sent many raiding expeditions to kill and despoil its members.[34] Sometimes, as happens in all intensely political societies, the wheel of fortune would lift a clan up as well as carry it downward. The Grasshopper Clan had been subject to severe persecution, its members forced to seek asylum in many other clans, when one of their children was chosen as the *kabaka*. He re-collected the clan and gave high office to many of its members.[35]

Although these persecutions undoubtedly helped establish the psychological hegemony of the *kabaka* over the clans and, therefore, served his purposes in the struggle for political power, one cannot help feel that pleasure in cruelty—persecution and genocide for their own sakes—had much to do with it. An almost universal human need of those in power, it seems, is to have a victim. Lacking Jews, the clans would serve. We are inclined to regard the pursuit of cruelty as something irrational, whereas the pursuit of political power appears to us utterly rational. This latter proposition is worth questioning. The *kabaka* persecuting the clans to satisfy a desire for revenge is behaving irrationally, but the *kabaka* dominating the clans and taking away their powers one by one is only doing his job as *kabaka*. How many people in the history of the world have sought political power without pleasure in the exercise of cruelty, or at least pleasure in the exercise of dominance, playing a substantial role in their ambitions? There have been a few. No *kabaka* was among them.

Despite all the evidence of hostility between the *kabaka* and the clans, certain harmonious relationships did exist between the two factions—harmonious and benevolent, but not equal. The hierarchical nature of human society is a reflection of the hierarchical nature of the human family. The most loving of parents are not on the same level as their children. The most loving husband, in a male-dominant society, has power over his wife. The most benevolent *kabaka* was hierarchically superior to the clans.

The mode of ritual reconciliation in Buganda lovingly demonstrated the inferior position of the clans, who would participate as clans in all the rites that surrounded the *kabaka.* Every ritual office connected with the monarchy was filled by a member of a particular clan. The Colobus Monkey Clan supplied the king with his chief butler, called *bumba,* and with the man who was in charge of the monarch's drinking water, *kalinda.* The latter was put to death when the *kabaka* died. After a new sovereign was crowned, he always sent the son of the head of the Colobus Monkey Clan to the god Mukasa to announce to the deity the coronation of the king. The Otter Clan supplied the attendant who was in charge of the royal tobacco.[36]

Similarly, the ceremonies in connection with the inauguration of a new *kabaka* were intended to demonstrate that the clans acquiesced in the power of the monarch. New kings were sent to be "endowed with magic strength and long life, at the clan center of the Lung-fish Clan. At a subsequent stage in the proceedings they travelled around the county to various clan centers, such as the *Butaka* of the Mushroom and Wild-cat Clans where they were ritually given wives provided by the clan in question."[37] Some clans were "honored" in providing some of the human sacrifices without which no coronation ceremony was complete.

In some bourgeois families not so very long ago, one child would bring the father's slippers, another child his pipe, and a third his newspaper. In many bourgeois families today, even when both husband and wife work, the wife makes dinner and has the honor of serving it to her husband.

None of these hierarchical oppositions—father-children; husband-wife; *kabaka*-clans—is quite like master and slave. The wife and the children are supposed to participate in, identify with, swell with pride about, the power of the husband. The ordinary clan member was supposed to, and most did, take pleasure in what a powerful and terrible ruler the state provided. They created his power by acquiescing in it. Fearing to become adult themselves, they huddled under his authority. He recognized his role as father, not slaveowner, by providing them with ritual participation in his power. He was *ssaabataka:* chief of all the clans.[38]

Such trade-offs between those who rule and those who are ruled have been the despair of revolutionaries from Tiberius Gracchus to Lenin. The international socialist movement was destroyed by the First World War when the working-class members in each country decided to fight the war—to ally themselves with their "capitalist oppressors" rather than with their "proletarian brothers" in other countries. And in the second century B.C., Tiberius Gracchus, with very little success, urged the common people to live on their own power instead of living vicariously through the power of others: "You boast that you are Lords of the World, but you do not possess a foot of land which you can call your own."[39] Too few are willing to take control of their own lives.

That judgment, however, like all such judgments, is too severe, especially in regard to the Baganda, who were capable of making the revolution in personal and social values that transformed the kinship system. Without the charismatic power of the *kabaka,* and Baganda identification with it, the kinship system would have continued supreme, and a certain kind of separation from the family and individuation of the self would not have happened. If the Baganda felt obliged to huddle close under the power of the *kabaka,* it was because they were on a very dangerous journey. And if the *kabaka* himself panicked every so often under the burden of leading such an expedition, that, too, could be expected.

The complexity of political life in Buganda, with its intricate mixture of kinship and state politics, is best illustrated by the office of *mugema,* who was head of the Monkey Clan and governor of the province of Busiro. The office remained hereditary in clan possession down to the establishment of the English protectorate:

The *Mugema* had three spheres of authority. He was head of his clan . . . and in this capacity he ruled over the affairs of the Grey monkey clan which had eleven major lineage centres, four in Buddu, two in Kyaddando, two in Kyaggwe, and one in Mawokuta, Busujju and Ssingo respectively. The head of the clan presided over discussions of the clan council which was composed of all major lineage heads in the clan and this body settled succession and similar disputes, enforced the rules of clan exogamy and incest, and collected boys and girls from the clan to be sent to serve at the Kabaka's palace. The *Mugema* was in charge of the clan centre (*butaka*) on Bbira hill, where there was a shrine containing the jaw-bone of Katumba, the first *Mugema.* He presumably took charge of the important death ceremonies of clan members and the periodic legitimacy rites for groups of clan babies as well as clan fertility ceremonies.

Secondly the *Mugema* played a key part in the national rituals of Buganda. Katumba, the first ancestor, had been given the chieftainship of *Mugema* and the title of "father of the Kabaka" on account of services he had rendered to Prince Kimera, then in exile in Bunyoro, who became the third Kabaka of Buganda. The Mugema's person was sacred. He was the leading figure in the installation ceremony of each new king and the burial of his predecessors. Besides this, he was in charge of the shrines (*amasiro*) erected to dead kings of which there were 29 in Busiro. For this reason he was known as the Chief Minister (*omukulu*) of the dead kings.

Lastly the *Mugema* was the king's governor over Busiro and in this capacity kept order in the county, presided over the collection of the royal tax and the raising of the military levy of the county and also over its judicial court. Like all other chiefs or office-holders he was in direct charge of his own personal domain, in this instance Bbira, the *butaka* hill of the Grey monkey clan.[40]

The power of the *mugema* did not pass away despite all the radical changes that occurred in the hundred years following Speke's arrival. Even though the *mugema* ceased to be the governor of Busiro, up to the middle of this century *kabaka*s had to deal with the antagonism of the *mugema* toward their centralized government.[41] "The clan head," the Baganda say, "is a cockroach and does not die in the smoke."[42]

The persistence of kinship forms of social cohesion was remarkable. In the 1920s, the *bataka* party, organized to promote clan interests, became an important political faction in state politics. Within the last twenty years, the Lungfish Clan decided to honor the memory of their ancestor Kabaka Suna II (1824–56), Mutesa's father, by erecting a large conical shrine near the capital city, to serve as the ritual headquarters of the clan and as an attraction for tourists. Among the dedication ceremonies was a procession of a large number of twins. Not since the beginning of the century had there been such a ritual parading of twins, an important rite of the traditional religion.[43]

When the kinship system is transcended, kinship does not disappear but is transformed into a new shape. When people are separated and individuated, they do not cease to be members of a family. The great forces—the monarchy, the state system, and the modern religions—that arose in Buganda to challenge and struggle against the kinship system were themselves metamorphosed forms of kinship. It is a philosophical nicety to decide exactly how far this transformation process had to proceed before the new forms can be denoted as "nonkinship." Though I define the state in this work as built upon nonkinship forms of social cohesion, from another point of view nonkinship forms of social cohesion do not exist. Or, at least, all forms of social cohesion have kinship forms as their ancestor. This does not mean, however, that between fundamental and advanced forms there is no difference, that all are alike. But it is an open question whether the force that holds any society together can accurately be described as "nonkinship."

The monarchy, the hammer that broke the kinship system, was itself born of family feelings. First, the king is undeniably considered a father to his people—benevolent, tyrannical, or both. Second, the legitimate successor to the king is *always* a close relative of his. Even in second-century Rome, when emperors were succeeded by people who were not related to them, the successor was adopted by the emperor during the latter's lifetime. The problem of legitimate succession was the rock on which many monarchical systems cracked, and it has been observed that monarchy could not be stabilized until there was monogamy and primogeniture—until there was no question about who was the legitimate successor to the king. It is possible to have a king without a family, but it is impossible to have kingship (a king followed by a king) without a royal family. Third, throughout the history of kingship, dynastic marriages have played a significant role in the construction of monarchical power. The great Hapsburg hegemony over Europe in the early sixteenth century resulted from a series of fortuitous marriages—and deaths. In ancient Tahiti, ambitious dynastic marriages were important in the building of centralized power and served well the Pomare family, who ultimately provided the founder of the centralized Tahitian state.[44] Monarchy destroys the kinship system, but the king's kin are crucial for kingship.

This same kind of dialectical irony operated in the case of the modern religions as well. What made the Christian and Muslim converts in Buganda powerful enough to overthrow the *kabaka* and assume political hegemony was the firmness with which they cohered. They lived together and were willing to die together. They cared for one another in the very way that clansmen used to care for one another in primitive society, not in the flexible, loose, competitive manner that had developed as the kinship system started to disintegrate. "Mutesa had been able to set man against man and use individual greed and ambition to break up potentially dangerous cliques of chiefs. Mwanga soon discovered that the Muslims and Christians operated as well defined military and political blocs, each bloc kept firmly intact by the strength of shared religious belief."[45] Much of what kept the religionists together was new—conscious ideology, modernization, individualism—but at its core was the stuff of kinship: intense ties to those who are the same as you, equally intense antagonism toward those who are not identical in belief.

What we can observe here is a dialectical process—an ascending alternation between the poles of individualism and community—a spiral staircase that keeps rising as it keeps coming round to the same few cardinal points. Nothing has been more important in the development of our political life than this creative conflict between individualism and community. Neither individuality nor the sense of community by itself is adequate for human needs. Each is enormously creative; each enormously lacking. The individuation of complex society negated the communal sense of primitive society. The sense of statehood, the feeling of nationalism, and the intense emotions of religious community then negated that individualism. But these negations were part of a dialectical process, so that the negation also included the incorporation of what had gone before. The Buganda Christians and Muslims did not return to the kinship system after the experience of individuation. They returned to an emphasis on community that incorporated the previous experience of individualism.

We are still on that staircase today. We have reached the end of one of the world's greatest eras of individualism. What was at its beginning a progressive force has ceased to serve humankind. We cry out for the restoration of the sense of community. We long to live, once again, in a society that consciously moral people could love. We have grown lonely and frightened out there all by ourselves. Our task is to insist that the next turn will keep us ascending: that individuation, and the freedom it carries with it, are not to be rejected, but negated in a dialectical sense—incorporated and carried with us to enhance the restoration of the communal ideal.

25

On Tyranny

Women, children, commoners, and degraded classes are the objects of tyranny. Men in primitive societies exercised their tyrannical inclinations against children and women only, since it was a classless society. Advanced complex society was the first stage of society that practiced all the forms of tyrannical behavior.

There are mild and harsh tyrannies and all grades in between. The degree of the severity of oppression differed greatly from one complex society to another, just as the degree of tyranny against children and women varied from one primitive society to another.

There appears to be an intricate and intimate relationship between the forms of oppression. It seems clear that the subjugation of women and that of children have a related cause; it seems equally clear that hierarchical relationships within the family are the paradigm for social inequality.

Certain differences in the modes of tyranny are apparent. Male children, no matter how subjugated by their fathers, will someday become fathers; female children will become mothers capable of oppressing their own children; but women never become men and slaves almost never become masters. The wives and children of the aristocracy are oppressed in a very different way from people of the lower class.

The construction of a theory of tyranny over children, women, and class that would see the whole process in developmental perspective and delineate the intricate relationships of the three modes of oppression is a task toward which people have only recently begun to devote their efforts.[1]

Tyranny is an abuse of hierarchy. Between parents and small children, equality is neither possible nor desirable. Social action in a society of any degree of complexity requires leadership positions, which are hierarchical by nature. There is nothing in the nature of hierarchy that inevitably causes it to degenerate into tyranny, although that has overwhelmingly been the case in all societies since the primitive.

Political oppression is easier when there is a racial or cultural distinction between the masters and the oppressed. Tyranny will be harsher in a state established through conquest of one people by another than in a state where all share the same language, culture, and history. But such differences are not necessary for tyranny. The ancient Hawaiians created their own pariah class; the Buganda *bakopi* were racially indistinguishable from the political elite.

The forms of tyranny, once established, have remained remarkably unvaried over thousands of years. Capitalist enterprise, with landless free workers laboring in productive units not owned by themselves, was the first radically new form of tyranny since complex society. With that exception, it was all there from the beginning.

THE DAY-TO-DAY FORMS OF OPPRESSION

"A poor peasant was coming in the opposite direction, carrying some sweet potatoes on his head, doubtless a day's food. At a signal from the Kadu Lubare (head wife), the youngster in charge swaggered up to him, and ordered him to stand and deliver. The man, not liking to lose his dinner, demurred, whereupon the urchin began to lay his stick across the back of this insolent slave who dared to refuse his potatoes to his superiors. . . . I had seen a similar party a few days previously meet a little girl, and quietly strip her of her clothing and leave her to go her way without a single rag. It is the custom that the great and powerful have *carte blanche* to seize people on the road, and take whatever they are carrying."[2]

"I have seen a considerable chief at Woahoo [Oahu] sit in his canoe alongside, without an article for sale himself, and watch a poor fellow that had perhaps paddled from the opposite side of the island with all his family, and perhaps all their worldly property and substance; such as two or three pigs, a few plantains, pieces of cloth, and some breadfruits; and after selling their little cargo, and getting for it a few bits of iron and some little trinkets, things (the iron in particular) that are unestimable to them; that greedy and tyrannical chief hath jumped out of his canoe into the water, swam to the poor man, and demanded of him every article which he had. . . ."[3]

Ellis relates of Tahiti that generosity and liberality in giving were considered the greatest virtues in a king, but despite that, when the court lacked provisions to feed its many followers and hangers-on, the monarch sent his servants to despoil the neighboring farmers. They were not reluctant to seize every article of food that was in evidence, including pigs. If a canoe was tied up at a dock, they would load their plunder into it and ride merrily back to their master. The farmer knew enough to maintain silence.[4]

In Buganda, it was customary for women to nurse children for three years and, in many cases, to refrain from sexual intercourse during that period. When a favorite wife of the *kabaka* gave birth, a wife whose sexual services the king was reluctant to dispense with, the man who held the post of *mugema* was responsible for securing a substitute nurse for the child. He had the highways watched, and when a woman with an infant of the same age and sex of the king's child appeared, she was seized. She became a foster mother to the king's child, nursed it while she fed her own child on cow's milk, stayed with the royal child for three years, and was finally reunited with her husband. It was considered an honor to be a foster mother to a prince, who always remembered her nurturing kindly and many times raised his surrogate mother's husband to important office.[5]

The differential treatment of commoners and aristocracy is illustrated by hundreds of instances. On Hawaii, during a spear exercise practiced by a commoner and the son of a chief, the former accidentally wounded the young noble, not very seriously. The unfortunate man was seized, his eyes put out, and then, two days later, he was executed.[6] In Tonga, rape was a crime only if the woman was of a clearly superior rank to the man.[7] Hawaiian bailiffs, called *konohiki,* who managed land areas for their lords, usually reserved for their own exclusive consumption the most plentiful kind of fish in a region. Anyone could catch as much of other kinds as they liked.[8] And in Buganda, "Peasants did not care to live long in the capital, because food was scarce and because the danger of being seized and put to death was great; they only went there when they were obliged to do so to perform some work, and they returned to the country as soon as they were free to do so."[9] The memory of these harsh tyrannies was long-lived. As late as the 1960s:

Elderly Baganda will sometimes volunteer to act out scenes as they remember them at a great lord's court. In such a piece of play-acting, the imaginary peasant or subordinate creeps along the verandah of the lord's house, waiting at the door to be spoken to or even to be noticed. He kneels to greet his superior and agrees with whatever the latter may say. The man acting the lord pays him little attention, or else returns his greetings in a summary fashion. He barks out the most peremptory orders to fetch or carry. The scene is done with such gusto that it is difficult not to imagine that the actors admire the authoritarian behavior of the lord. The flattery of the peasant is usually overacted, and the audience is obviously amused at the inferior's attempt to pander to the great man by giving him obsequious praise.[10]

The many steps on the tyranny ladder made it possible in certain instances to lay off one's own victimization on others. Kabaka Suna II, returning across the river Katonga to his capital from Busiro, where he had had the jawbones of the former *kabaka*s decorated, ordered his soldiers to execute all those who were still on the other side of the river. Included among these unfortunates was a high-ranking official, the *mukwenda.* Another official intervened, deflected the spear meant for the *mukwenda,* and pleaded with the monarch for the latter's life. Suna agreed, provided the *mukwenda* would bring sixty victims to the *kabaka* to redeem his life. Returning to his place of residence and power, the *mukwenda* made a huge feast, inviting hundreds of guests. Fifty cows were necessary to feed the crowd. As they feasted and reveled, sixty of the *mukwenda*'s guests were seized, bound, and sent off to the *kabaka,* who had them executed to praise his father's memory.[11]

The hierarchical-tyrannical nature of social relationships in advanced complex societies was constantly asserted and emphasized by the forms of address between subordinate and superior people. In Buganda, a socially inferior person meeting one of higher rank bent forward and placed his hands on his knees. If he was carrying a stick, he would lean far forward, using the stick for support. If the discrepancy in ranks was very great, the subordinate person knelt down and grasped the legs of his superior, addressing him as "master" or "sir."[12] "No inferior might take a thing from a superior, or pass it to him with one hand; he was obliged to hold out both hands, or to take the object in one hand and stretch out the other hand so as to touch the arm in which the object was held."[13] The word *mukopi* (plural *bakopi*) has been translated "peasant," but it really meant any person who had no particular social distinction. Most *bakopi* were peasants, but a fisherman or a barkcloth maker was also a *mukopi* to anyone of superior status.[14] In Bunyoro, a person of higher rank was addressed as "my master," or "sir, our master," or "father." He, in turn, responded with "my child." The inferior person represented himself as "your slave or servant," or "your child."[15] In Tonga, obeisance was made to one's hereditary chief by kneeling down in front of him and placing his feet on the top of one's head.[16] As in feudal Europe, everybody, every minute of the day, knew where his position was on the tyranny ladder.

In Polynesia, great distinctions were made in matters of dress, with particular articles of clothing or decoration reserved for certain statuses only. Archery on Tahiti,[17] and a certain billiardslike game on Tonga,[18] were played only by aristocrats. Tongan chiefs had a monopoly on freshwater wells for bathing.[19] And on this island, the practice had already begun of what in our society we call "playing a customer's game." In the game of dart throwing, where distance won, the chief's dart could be turned over three times after it landed, adding an honorary distance to the actual throw.[20] For Hawaiians, even marriage celebrations were subject to severe class distinctions. The aristocracy got married with full-day feasts to which relatives and friends were invited. For common people there was no celebration; such a marriage, as the saying had it, "was just a pebble to pelt a rat."[21]

Equal justice under law was an unstated ideal in Buganda society, but, as in more developed cultures, being rich was better than being poor in matters of justice as well as in other things. Court cases were expensive, which prevented people of limited means from embarking on them. Mutesa heard cases without a fee, and was generally regarded as giving fair decisions, but no *mukopi* ever brought a suit that reached such exalted heights. Poor men did not sue rich men, except in those rare cases when a chief would champion the cause of one of his subordinates; otherwise they would be despoiled, or even killed, if they brought such a case to court.[22] All of this confirmed the Zulu proverb which stated that "The voice of the poor is not audible."[23]

Though Buganda was a mobile and reasonably open society in which there were many cases of poor men of ability rising to high station, in general it was the sons of officeholders who received advantageous political appointments.[24] Buganda was a bureaucratic state, and bureaucrats do not expect their sons to start on the same rung of the ladder as everyone else.

Slavery was a fact, but not an important institution, in complex societies. There was no large agricultural or industrial slave population.

The surplus value produced in society was drawn off from individual peasants by means of taxation, forced labor, and tribute. Those who worked the soil were not owned by anyone. A war state, like Buganda, produced a certain number of slaves, mostly women and children. Most of these became household workers who could also be sent to do agricultural work. The children of slaves remained in that category,* so that the institution perpetuated itself even without fresh spoils from raiding. Slaves were not badly treated, but they were liable to sale to Arab slave-traders, who would subject them to the worst forms of bondage.

The Hawaiian lower-caste people were called *kauwa,* which has been translated "slaves," but they seem to have been more of a pariah class than anything else. In addition to providing certain human sacrifices, these *kauwa* were "set apart from the rest and treated like filthy beasts. They could not associate with other men. They were called 'corpses,' that is, foul-smelling things. They were not allowed to marry outside their own class." After the abolition of the tabu in Hawaii and the spread of Christianity, the restrictions on these human outcasts were gradually lifted, although for many generations it was considered an abomination for any respectable person to marry someone whose ancestors had been *kauwa* in the old days.[25]

TAXATION AND FORCED LABOR

Although the mythic imagination feels the necessity of explaining when death came into the world, we know that it has been coeval with life. But taxes have been inevitable only since complex society. Primitive peoples knew only the necessity of death.

Taxes in ancient Buganda were of three kinds: payments in connection with forced labor, direct taxes, and market dues.

Here is Roscoe on the subject of forced-labor payments:

Every person called to do any state-work had to pay the overseer a sum of cowry-shells; during King Suna's reign the amount demanded was ten cowry-shells, in later times this was augmented to one hundred. If the work-

---

*C. T. Wilson and Felkin, *Ugunda,* p. 186, support this view, although John Rowe (in a personal communication) asserts that the opposite was true, citing as support for his position the fact that no permanent slave class existed.

man had not the sum to hand, he was required to give something else, such as a barkcloth, or an equivalent in food or beer. Until this had been paid, no workman was allowed to begin his work, but unless he made a start within a given time, he was fined. If he was unable to obtain the amount by barter, or to borrow it, and still delayed making a start, his wife, or some other member of his family, would be taken as hostage, until he should bring the necessary sum; the woman or child thus taken would be required to work for the chief during the time of detention. This custom held good with all State-labour. . . ."[26]

As for direct taxes, the *kabaka*, the *katikiro*, and the *kimbugwe* fixed the date on which they were to be collected. Announcement was made in the general council (Lukiko), and a special tax collector was appointed for each district. Taxes were based on the number of houses, the exact amount being settled with the head of each subdistrict, and were paid in cowry shells, barkcloths, iron hoes, and cattle. It could take two months for the full collection. The *kabaka* took half the taxes. The rest was divided among the *katikiro*, the *kimbugwe*, the king's mother, and the governor of the province, the latter portion to be shared with his subgovernors.[27]

Market dues of 10 percent were charged on all merchandise at the regular market places that existed, under supervision of the political authorities, throughout the country in the later period of the state. Those who sought to avoid the dues by selling their wares privately, outside the market place, were heavily fined and had their goods confiscated if they were caught.

In addition to the direct payment of taxes, individuals were subject to forced labor on public roads, the buildings and enclosures of the *kabaka*, and the headquarters of local governors and subgovernors.[28] We hear nothing of forced labor on the land in Buganda, although direct confiscation of goods was also a recourse for the hungry overlord.

Household servants in large numbers were needed to support the royal bureaucracy. Either the wars of plunder did not provide a sufficient number, or else there was a desire to have Baganda boys and girls, because "from time to time the king would send out special messengers to collect boys and girls for the royal enclosure; and each chief would have to supply a number according to the population of his district. The messengers made a census of the population in a particular district; they obtained their information chiefly by getting one person to tell about another; and finally they settled with the District-Chief, who was to contribute a child and who was to be spared. The boys and girls were then taken to the King; he retained as many as he wanted, and sent the others to his Mother, to the Queen, and to the *Katikiro* and *Kimbugwe.*"[29]

Between the *kabaka* and the high-ranking members of the political hierarchy, and among the latter and their subordinates, there was a system of tribute giving that cannot be described as "taxation." The chiefs brought "presents" of food and animals and firewood to the royal court,[30] and it is a reasonable assumption that subgovernors did the same with governors. We may imagine that those in a subordinate position were not free to omit this gift giving, an expected tribute that had survived from the very beginnings of complex societies, when chieftainships first appeared. In early chieftainships, there was no taxation, but those below brought gifts to the chief, and he in turn distributed gifts to his supporters. It was more like family and less like a state. Even in families, certain gifts *must* be given.

All taxation is not necessarily part of the tyranny system. Our taxes, for instance, provide fire and police protection, garbage collection, and protection from foreign enemies. In the welfare state, taxation is the mode by which income is redistributed from richer to poorer people. For complex societies, exactly the opposite was true. Taxes and forced labor were the means by which much of the economic surplus was drawn off from the people who created it and placed in the hands of those who held political power. Complex society was the first human society in which some who did not work could still eat.

The evidence from Polynesia indicates hardly any direct taxation of the kind existing in Buganda. There the mode was forced labor on a regular basis, consisting mainly of agricultural work on the lord's land, or the land of his agent, the *konohiki,* or on the king's land. So onerous were these labor demands that one nineteenth-century observer in Hawaii estimated that the average Hawaiian yeoman was able to retain only a third of the product of his labors, with the remaining two-thirds going to the various ranks of chiefs.[31] During the early days of the monarchy, in the first third of the nineteenth century, the areas of land that belonged to the lord and were worked by his tenants were called *po-a-lima* (fifth-day) patches, because the peasants worked them on Fridays.[32] Friday they worked for the landlord and Tuesday they worked for the king. In 1840 this tax was reduced to thirty-six days each year for king and lord together.[33]

The *konohiki,* the lord's representative, held the direct tyrannical position in the Polynesian system. Since land could be held only by performing work for the *konohiki,* failure to do so, for whatever reason, resulted in expulsion from land that a peasant might have spent years cultivating:

Lands were given by the *konohiki* in the days of Kaikeoewa (governor of Kauai, 1825–1839) and have been held till 1849 when claimant was elected superintendent of schools and became freed from the *konohiki* work. The result was that the *konohiki* took away his lands and gave them to another tenant. Kowelo was left destitute of food.[34]

Konohiki took away numbers 3 and 4 on the grounds that claimant was getting old and his labor on the *konohiki* days of little worth.[35]

In our society we have utility companies that turn off old people's source of heat and light when they can no longer pay their bills. Like the *konohiki,* they have their orders. Any society that separates itself too much from feelings of kinship is subject to this kind of cruelty.

Polynesian society, in general, was less advanced in the direction of statehood than Buganda, and this must have contributed to the relative absence of direct taxation. It also accounted for the much greater importance of tribute, that flexible, informal, seemingly voluntary mode of taxation. Here, once again, Mariner gives us the clearest sense of what life was really like. He describes tribute giving on Tonga, a relatively centralized state:

The tribute generally consists of yams, mats, gnatoo, dried fish, live birds, etc.; and is levied upon every man's property in proportion as he can spare. The quantity is sometimes determined by the chiefs of each district, though generally by the will of each individual, who will always take care to send quite as much as he can well afford, lest the superior chief should be offended with him, and deprive him of all that he has. This tribute is paid twice a year; once at the ceremony of *Inachi,* or offering of the first fruits of the season to the gods, in or about the beginning of October; and again, at some other time of the year, when the tributary chief may think proper, and is generally done when some article is in great plenty. The tribute levied at the time of the *Inachi* is general and absolute; that which is paid on the other occasion comes more in the form of a present, but is so established by old custom, that, if it were omitted, it would amount to little less than an act of rebellion. It may here with propriety be observed, that the practice of making presents to superior chiefs is very general and frequent. The higher class of chiefs generally make a present to the king, of hogs or yams, about once a fortnight: these chiefs, about the same time, receive presents from those below them, and these last from others, and so on, down to the common people. The principle on which all this is grounded is of course fear, but it is termed respect (*ofa*).[36]

When the state is in the formative stage and this combination of fear and respect has not yet been internalized by enough people, those underlings who wish to say no to the state simply stop sending tribute. It is, as Mariner says, an act of rebellion. The central authority has no alternative but to resort to arms to subdue the wayward province. The first European visitors to spend any length of time on Tahiti were a small group of Spanish friars who had no success in converting the Tahitians. At that period, Vehiatua was the most powerful prince on Tahiti, having succeeded, more or less, in welding the whole of the lesser peninsula into one kingdom. The diary of Máximo Rodríguez tells of how a group of Tahitians refused to send the expected gifts of food to Vehiatua, who then banished them from the lands they occupied. At such a point, a pitched battle between the rebellious forces and the central government was the only mode of resolution.[37] It is a reasonable assumption that this kind of tax rebellion was frequent in every emerging state and that superior force was necessary for the survival of such fragile politics. Fear alone, however, would not suffice. Only when those conquered willingly accepted the concept of the state could the state have any permanence. Vehiatua's kingdom, for instance, did not survive his death.

THE ETHOS OF SUBORDINATION

It is not surprising to discover that these societies were self-conscious and outspoken on the questions of tyranny and the hierarchical nature of power. People in all three cultures were fiercely aware of who was up, who down, who took orders, and who gave orders. In Buganda, not only did individual offices have names, but there were names for the rank order of particular offices. The ranks were: *mumyuka, ssaabaddu, ssaabagabo, ssaabawali, musaale, mutuba.* If a provincial governor had five subgovernors under him, they were ranked in order of importance. The most important subgovernor was *mumyuka,* the next *ssaabaddu,* and so on. The queen mother of the *kabaka,* a personage of political power, had several chiefs under her. Each of these was ranked: *mumyuka, ssaabaddu, ssaabagabo. . . .*[38] The Hawaiian concern for genealogical rank was almost obsessional. No marriage could be concluded among aristocrats without determining which partner outranked the other. To be the firstborn of a high-ranking title was much more important than to be the last-born. Who ranked whom was legally and authoritatively determined by the Aha Alii (councils of the nobles, or Alii), who were guided by experts in the specific genealogical lines involved.[39]

From Hawaii, Tahiti, and Buganda one receives the impression that the ethics of rank, and the day-to-day workings of the status system, were more important to the people who ran the societies than religious ritual and the gods. They were status-intoxicated. "An elderly informant living in Kisozi today admitted that some of the Mukamba's personal headmen ruled over very few people but he added, quite in conformity with the Ganda *ethos,* that 'a man always likes to have some people under him, even if they are few.' "[40] At some point, clearly, this status pyramid had to rest on the ground; some people did not rule anyone.

The cruelty implicit in the kind of political power invented by complex societies was openly acknowledged. Kinyaro of the Monkey Clan gave one of his daughters in marriage to the *kabaka* and, as part of the ceremony, advised the newly crowned monarch: "Whosoever despises your honor, kill him, for all the peasants are like sorghum—whosoever mows it down, owns it."[41] The Hawaiians said it succinctly: "A chief is a shark that travels on land."[42]

Considerations of rank order even interfered with the efforts of the Christian missionaries on Tahiti. As late as 1826, Reverend Orsmond ran into intense opposition because he received a few common people into communion ahead of the royal family. Some of the missionaries were asked straight out "whether the message of the British God was to the toutous as well as to the kings and chiefs?"[43]

Efforts at amelioration of the worst abuses in the tyranny system brought immediate resistance from those who owned the power. As late as 1840, Hawaiian chiefs complained that only the traditional modes could preserve order: "If we can not take away their lands, what will they care for us? They will be as rich as we."[44] British rule in Buganda went on so long it was subject to certain ironies of history. In the beginning, the most enlightened branch of English imperial government was enamored of the policy of native self-rule, which left local authority in the hands of strong chiefs: the British would deal with the chiefs and the chiefs would deal with everyone else. In primitive societies, this did not work very well. The English could not find any chiefs and had to create them, insisting they had been there all along. Buganda, now part of Uganda, was a showcase of self-rule; the chiefs knew what it felt like to be a chief, and the common people knew how to take orders. Over the years, things changed—in Britain. After the Second World War, a Labour government was elected. The Colonial Office decided that democracy, not native hierarchy, was to be the British mission in Africa. "Chiefs who had been taught in the early years of British Administration to tour districts and to advise on welfare and educational matters were told in 1949 to regard themselves as neutral chairmen, engaged in finding out what their councils wanted. An older Ganda statesman thought this nonsense and said: 'Ideas do not come up from the bottom. Orders come down from the top.' "[45]

The system of subordination, hierarchy, and tyranny was reflected in proverbs, some instructive, some ironic, some resigned to the nature of things. The Baganda said, "The king is the lake." A lake does not discriminate whom it drowns: those who are only occasional travelers are equally vulnerable. Just so, the king's taxes fell on everybody.[46] "Never mind if the taro at the bottom burns," said the Hawaiians, "but watch out that that at the top is not under-cooked"—meaning simply that the wishes of the common people can be ignored, but the high chiefs had better be taken care of.[47]

Hawaiian folk wisdom even came close to the Greek idea of hubris—that one should not strive for too much because disaster will result. In Hawaii, it was the tyranny of the aristocracy one had to fear, not the jealousy of the gods as in Greece: "Stay among the clumps of grasses and do not elevate yourself."[48] "It is a stone that is high up that can roll down but a stone that is down cannot roll."[49]

Here, too, the common people took their pitiful revenge on the nobility, by declaring proverbially that what matters is the people, that without the support of the commoners, a chief has no prestige: "It is the tail that makes the kite fly."[50] Even so, it was better to be a kite than a tail.

Along with the invention of aristocracy and of a high culture came the polarity of the sophisticated courtier and the country bumpkin, a situation fraught with possibilities for comic invention (as in Shakespeare) or tragic overtones (as in the attempted seduction of Zerlina in Mozart's *Don Giovanni*). In most East African kingdoms, country folk coming to court were subject to mockery and abuse. Those in Hawaii who lived on the windward side of an island, considered the back side, were called *kua-aina,* back-country folk, a term of deprecation.[51] "The courtiers of Hawaii, like those of medieval Europe and the city folk of all times, have regarded the farmers as country louts."[52] The situation was ripe for sexual tyranny:

If an insolent courtier were to see that a country clown had a beautiful woman for a wife he would say to her, "You come along with me," and the country clown would be too spiritless to make any resistance. Or one of the women about court, meeting a handsome young countryman whom she fancied, would turn his head with flattery and try to win him to herself, saying, "Why does such a fine fellow as you condescend to live with such a fright of a creature as that wife of yours? You'd better come along with me."[53]

Undoubtedly, as in all such cases then and now, the chosen one was thrown away when no longer needed. We begin to see how, once the adult-male equality of primitive society was broken, the forms of oppression that developed are remarkably familiar to us. Not only is tyranny an evil, it is also dull, unimaginative, and deadly repetitive in its forms. Nothing brings us closer to the people of complex society, nothing makes us react so strongly that it-is-just-like-us, than the abuse common people suffered at the hands of those who lorded it over them.

FAIRY TALE AND HIERARCHY

The atmosphere of fairy tale and popular story, the world over, is permeated with the spirit of hierarchy. The story of doomed love that cuts across class lines, for instance, has never lost its power. Many stories are concerned with the revenge that those who have been oppressed take on their oppressors. Children get even, or triumph over, their parents ("Hansel and Gretel"), or their step-parents ("Cinderella"). The youngest child, who is traditionally ill-treated, ends up with the plums of life ("The Three Little Pigs"). It is rare that women obtain revenge on men, and it never happens that commoners settle the score with the aristocracy. Some common people in the tales may have more virtue than some lords or ladies, but in general, virtue belongs with the ruling class and power always resides there.

In ancient Tahiti, all these forms of tale which reflect on hierarchical disparities are found, not in a crude archaic form, but full-flowered. They lack nothing, except a change in locale, to be admitted into the Grimms' collection. Henry tells a long, flowing tale of brothers who go to another island in search of a princess that one of them shall marry. They are deceived by the princess's maid into believing that she is the royal person they seek. After many trials and adventures, after the youngest brother is abandoned to die in the sea, the false maid is revealed, and the youngest brother is saved, then discovers and wins the heart of the true princess. The end of the tale allows the younger brother his revenge on his brothers, but the false commoner must pay the ultimate penalty for crossing class lines:

The elder brothers arrived and were astonished and conscience-smitten to see the younger brother, whom they thought they had left dead in the open ocean, safe and well. Yet they still sought by various contrivances to get rid of their rival. But they utterly failed, and at last their sisters advised them to remain content as servants to their younger brother, who had won the fair princess and who would be appointed king over North Tahiti by their parents. To this they agreed, and domestic harmony in the family soon followed. Amid auspicious circumstance and in due time the marriage of the happy young pair took place.

Hina-te-pipiro, the heartless maid, became a prey to shame and chagrin, and at last, after a painful interview with her mistress, she died uttering her own dirge:

> The waves of the sea do not, do not at night sleep, sleep,
> Which propelled me. I must leave
> My princely suitors in retribution, I am dead!

And this was the last of Hina-te-pipiro, whom they quietly buried beneath the drooping boughs of a toa tree in North Tahiti.[54]

And in the stories of class-crossed lovers, there was sorrow aplenty: "The princess was soon to marry a young prince who was heir to one of the neighboring kingdoms, and though she had no deep-seated affection for him she had been brought up to feel that such a union would be most suitable and proper. But now when the eyes of the fair young damsel and the elegant mountaineer met for the first time and they bashfully exchanged the friendly greeting (may you live), they at once felt a kindred attachment to each other, which they could not shake off."[55]

We may each imagine our own tragic ending to the tale.

SEXUAL AND FAMILIAL TYRANNY

As part of the tribute paid by chiefs to the king, or included with the return gifts made by the sovereign to his subordinates, and usually part of the tribute that dominated foreign rulers sent to their overlords, was an item of nonmaterial wealth: women. So many cattle, so many iron hoes, so many barkcloths, so many cowry shells, so many women. The *kabaka* had three to five hundred wives. With numbers like that, it seems clear that the issue is ownership, not sexual pleasure or variety. Some women did object. In Buganda, when a roundup of young women to be sent to serve the *kabaka* and other subordinate chiefs was made, the mothers who did not want their daughters to go scarified them on a prominent place on their faces, thereby disqualifying them as wives for the *kabaka*.[56]

None of this seems to exist in Polynesia, either the giving of women as tribute, or large harems for kings. In East Africa, it was a prevalent mode, either because of the advanced nature of the kingship, or as a result of influence from the Near East, which dealt in women and harems, or because of basic cultural differences that are beyond our current knowledge.

The man, like this Bunyoro prince, who has the power to take a woman away from another man exercises a double tyranny: "When he heard of or saw some maid who attracted him, he sent for her, and few parents could refuse their daughters to a prince. It mattered little whether the girl he desired was already betrothed or not, he simply demanded her, and a gift to the man to whom she was betrothed, in addition to the regular marriage fee to the parents, would remove all difficulty."[57]

In Buganda, when a peasant discovered that his chief was making love to his wife, he feared for his own life and immediately made plans to leave the district at night. If his wife would not join him, he left her behind.[58] And in Rwanda, the most tyrannical of societies, fathers exercised a fierce despotism over their sons, which continued even after the sons were married. To punish his son, a father would take the son's wife to his bed and refuse the husband access to her for a period of time. There was no incest prohibition against such acts.[59] In Freud's fable of the origins of society, as given in *Totem and Taboo*, the father monopolizes all the women in the band until the sons rise up and kill him.

In both Rwanda and in Freud's fable, the wishes of the women involved play no part in the drama.

The authoritarian mode of paternal power was so severe in Buganda and other East African kingdoms that the most exaggerated conceptions of the Victorian father seem the appropriate analogy. "In the past the Ganda father expected deference and often abject humility from his wife and children and from the other members of his household. . . . A wife . . . knelt to greet [her husband] on his return from a walk or an expedition and was prepared to bring him water to wash his feet. He had the best of the food, which was prepared to his special liking and kept waiting at his wish. Some say that the wife did not normally eat with her husband. . . . She was a minor at law in that she was under the control of her father, her brother, or her husband as regards the conduct of court cases."[60]

When children spoke to their father, they knelt down, crouching at the door of his room and speaking in a high-pitched, squeaky voice that was an indication of respect.[61] In Bunyoro, a man, no matter of what age, did not sit on a chair or stool in his father's presence, but squatted on the floor. He was forbidden to marry any girl not approved by his father. He never wore any of his father's clothes or used his spear. He could not even begin to smoke or shave without presenting his father with a gift.[62]

It is startling to discover that in authoritarian Rwanda the correspondence with Victorian family and sexual mores went so far that "it was very improper for a wife to manifest pleasure or to be other than purely passive during love-play and intercourse."[63] It recalls instructions to Victorian women not to move during sexual congress and is a reminder that the nineteenth century in Western Europe was a great age for the repression of women, children, working-class people, and sexuality, and the time supreme of the authoritarian father. Clearly, we are dealing with a pattern of cultural forms that brings together several diverse attitudes. Why and when it happens—in nineteenth-century Europe or in complex East Africa—and why it then changes into something else are unanswered theoretical questions of the highest importance.

Bunyoro inheritance patterns may illuminate the institution of primogeniture, a practice that violates ideas of equality and has proved oppressive to many younger children. The Bunyoro heir was never the eldest son, but only one heir was named. His function was to replace the father and preserve his authoritarian power. The heir was said to "become" his father; his sisters' husbands, after his installation, addressed him as "father-in-law." For his brothers, he replaced the father's authority, though admittedly not with the same degree of harshness.[64]

What seems to be at work here is the need to preserve a certain conception of power, one that we would describe as authoritarian and tyrannical, but that the society felt it necessary to maintain. Having several heirs for the father would obviously dilute that authority from the psychological point of view, just as having several successors to a king divides and dilutes royal omnipotence. There seems to have been a need to actualize in the real world a view of omnipotence. People felt better because *someone* was omnipotent, even though, and possibly because, they were required to humble themselves before that awesome power.

God is omnipotent. He could have made the world any way he wanted. The tyrannical, authoritarian Calvin said God made up the world in such a way that only a small number of people would be saved; the rest were doomed to damnation. People believed in Calvin's God, just as people in Buganda believed in authoritarian fathers and a tyrannical *kabaka;* the future lay with Calvin. For years people willingly—and unwillingly—suffered under the tyranny of Calvin's God until a more ameliorative concept enlightened Protestantism. It is to be wondered whether that detour into religious tyranny was necessary in order to make the modern world possible.

In complex societies, the hierarchical and tyrannical modes that determined political and family life were consciously recognized as the same pattern. Paternal autocracy was legitimized by political tyranny; political oppression was legitimized by family tyranny. "What is remarkable in this instance is the exactness of the parallel between the child-father, subject-chief and subject-king relationships, so that there is a single authority pattern throughout the society. Unusual also is the fact that the Baganda themselves recognize the parallels so clearly and express them by saying, for instance, that the father is like the Kabaka or that the father's authority depends on that of the Kabaka. . . ."[65] When the British deported the *kabaka* in the 1960s, the Baganda expressed fear that familial authority would collapse.[66] In Bunyoro the view was the same; people insisted that the father ruled the household as the *mukama* ruled the whole country.[67]

A seeming contradiction, a strange irony, suffuses the entire cultural situation. People are in the process of liberating themselves from the narrow confines of the kinship system. They are striking a blow for individual freedom by placing themselves under the fierce authority of father and *kabaka*. It is not only analogous to, but much the same process that Michael Walzer delineates in *The Revolution of the Saints*. The Puritans, Walzer says, the spearhead of a revolutionary drive that would eventually put an end to authoritarian kingship, placed themselves, in their private and public lives, under an authoritarian regime much more severe than the royal absolutism they were destroying. That new regime regulated almost every aspect of public and private life and allowed for practically no individual options. The final result of this whole process, Walzer points out, was not the permanent establishment of a Puritan theocratic state, but the creation of the liberal society in which we are still living. Puritanism was, in this regard, a transitional phenomenon. It was the mechanism by which the old regime was toppled. This achievement of a positive result by way of a tyrannical detour may have come about because, at least at the beginning, people became Puritans through *voluntary* action, not through the commandment of the state.

Authoritarian fathers and *kabaka*s cannot be described as transitional phenomena, but it does seem accurate to describe their existence as resulting from, and making possible, the overthrow of the kinship system. The Puritans, having killed the king, created the dictatorship of Oliver Cromwell. The Baganda, having half killed the kinship system, created the autocratic power of monarch and father. The male child in our society, whose psychological separation from the mother is deeply problematic, may attach himself to male authority figures in a pathological manner. The political forms of such attachment are authoritarian, nationalistic, and warlike. The long, long history of tyrannical kings and authoritarian fathers would indicate that the scar that resulted from the separation from the kinship system has never quite healed. Democratic forms—nonauthoritarian ways of people living together in society—are possible only when a people educates itself and its children to stop grieving for the loss of the kinship system. As long as we are in mourning for a kinship-system paradise lost, just so long will authoritarian males rule the world.

I speak here of kinship system, not of kinship. We never transcend the need for kinship; in fact, at this moment, our society suffers from the failure of those in it to treat one another caringly, as kin; but the failure to transcend the kinship system can make democracy impossible, and in many parts of the world it is doing just that.

THE GOLDEN CHILD

There was a singular practice on the island of Tahiti that appears so contrary to the ordinary forms of hierarchy and tyranny—indeed, seems so perfectly designed to signify direct opposition to those concepts—that it makes me wonder whether understanding it might not provide a key element in unraveling the whole question of subordination and oppression. With certain high-status titles, including that of *arii de hoi* (king), when the eldest son was born the father immediately gave over his titles and his honors to the child. The father, of course, retained political and military power, but sacredness passed to the infant child. If he was a king, the father would vacate the throne in favor of the infant and act as regent to the monarch.[68] Political life was unaffected, but the world of ritual, myth, and sacred power obviously recognized some strange truth here.

Vancouver tells of the meeting of the aged grandfather with the small child Otoo (the future Pomare II, the first king of united Tahiti), who had succeeded to his father's titles and honors:

It was shortly announced that *Otoo* was approaching. On this occasion, it became necessary that the grandfather should pay homage to his grandson. A pig and a plantain leaf were instantly procured, the good old man stripped to the waist, and when *Otoo* appeared in front of the marquee, the aged parent, whose limbs were tottering with the decline of life, met his grandson, and on his knees acknowledged his own inferiority, by presenting this token of submission; which, so far as could be discovered, seemed offered with a mixture of profound respect, and parental regard. The ceremony seemed to have little effect on the young monarch, who appeared to notice the humiliating situation of his grandsire with the most perfect indifference and unconcern.[69]

"And when they were come into the house, they saw the young child with Mary his mother, and fell down, and worshipped him: and when they had opened their treasures, they presented unto him gifts; gold, and frankincense, and myrrh."[70] How many delightful portrayals of the gifts of the Magi play lovingly on the obliviousness of the young child to the great commotion all round—just as with the King Otoo.

We must remember also that in the great universal myth of the birth of the hero, of which King Oedipus is only one example, the birth of the son (always the first) presages the death of the father.

Why this great reversal? Why, in a world dominated by hierarchy and tyranny, do fathers, grandfathers, and kings humble themselves before an infant boy? Why, in societies in which infanticide is a common practice, in which fathers every day kill their newborn children, do the myths tell that the son's birth will bring the father's death?

There are times when the argument that all aggression—against children, women, and class—is defensive seems undeniable. Fearing something that probably is, in most cases, totally irrational, the psyche defends itself by attacking. The existence of the child is somehow threatening to the parents. In the rational mind, this seems too absurd to be taken seriously, yet the myth is there and has come from somewhere. The infanticidal myth of abandoning the infant hero on the mountainside because he will bring his father's death, and the exaltation of the Christ child share one crucial aspect: in both, the infant has enormous power. Christ is the infant Oedipus grown benign.

If people kill their newborn infants because they are afraid of them—and the chapter on infanticide has shown how pervasive that practice was—and tyrannize over their children, when they are suffered to live, out of the same kind of fear, then the golden child is a vision of bliss, a sense of how wonderful the world might be if we could cease fearing and start loving one another. In order for that to happen, the child has to be transformed magically into a source of benevolence. The King Herod orders a slaughter of newborn infants in Judea in order to forestall the terrible consequences that one of these shall bring to the world. We know that the child is promised not as a destroyer but as a savior.

It is probably true that fear, anxiety, and panic are not the sole causes of human tyranny, but it does seem true that tyranny begins to be ameliorated only when fear, anxiety, and panic begin to lessen. Only when these begin to disappear, or at least become manageable, will tyranny cease to be the mode by which humans live together in society. Not only did the breakdown of the kinship system make tyranny possible—since there were now strangers living in the same society—but, perhaps, it also made tyranny necessary. The fear and anxiety caused by separation from the kin could only be handled, it seems, by the invention of class oppression.

PRIMITIVE EQUALITY, TYRANNY, DEMOCRACY

It accomplishes nothing to argue that there should have been a better, more moral way to get from the primitive to our present situation, without all the tyranny: no one seems to have found that way. Every society that has left the kinship system behind has invented, and fully exercised, political forms of tyranny.

No matter what great intellectual, moral, and artistic advances were made by ancient Israel, ancient Greece, the Chinese Empire, the prophet Mohammed, twelfth-century Europe, or Renaissance Italy, none of these cultures had any intention of eliminating tyranny over children, women, and social class. It is only with the emergence of democratic political forms that the eradication of the various forms of oppression has become an ideal and a possibility of society.

In the history of the world, there have been only three fundamental ways for people to come together in society: primitive equality (for adult males); tyranny (monarchical, aristocratic, and capitalistic); democracy (political, economic, sexual equality). The last form is a fragile infant on the world stage—political equality is found in a few places; sexual equality is a current battleground in even fewer places; economic equality a mere dream of a handful of prophets. From the first breakdown of the kinship system until the beginnings of democratic life, political and economic tyranny have been the mode of the world. And on most of the earth today, that mode continues.

Somehow, in many parts of the world, somewhere deep within primitive society, the forms developed that allowed primitive society to transcend itself and be transformed into complex society. That developmental advance was perhaps morally ambiguous: it brought us both freedom from the kinship system and the tyranny of the *kabaka*. Somehow, in only one part of the world—in Western Europe—deep within tyrannical society, the forms developed that made democratic life possible. That developmental advance was no longer ambiguous; it was both morally and developmentally progressive. This would indicate that, somewhere in the tyrannical stage, the moral and the developmental became inseparably linked together. After that juncture, all developmental advance was destined to be a moral advance. And the next devel-

opmental steps for society—the realization of economic and sexual
equality—will clearly be morally liberating.

The great linkage of the moral and the developmental could never
have occurred within the limitations of primitive society. The existence
of this intricate and ambiguous situation may permit us, in retrospect,
to welcome the advent of complex society—a welcome albeit seasoned
with sadness.

V

THE STATE AS
A WORK OF ART

26

Chieftainship

"Rather than dating the effacement of the individual from the institution of a despotic authority, we must, on the contrary, see in this institution the first step made towards individualism. Chiefs are, in fact, the first personalities who emerge from the social mass. Their exceptional situation, putting them beyond the level of others, gives them a distinct physiognomy and accordingly confers individuality upon them. In dominating society, they are no longer forced to follow all of its movements. Of course, it is from the group that they derive their power, but once power is organized, it becomes autonomous and makes them capable of personal activity. A source of initiative is thus opened which had not existed before then. There is, hereafter, someone who can produce new things and even, in certain measure, deny collective usages. Equilibrium has been broken."[1] Thus writes Emile Durkheim on the emergence of individual leadership out of the kinship collectivity.

Durkheim's perception remains descriptive, not analytical. He does not address the question of *why* individual leadership emerged out of the collective mass, or *how* it emerged. The creation of the state was one significant product of the process of evolving individual political leadership. The why and how of individualism are the why and how of the state.

It is my position that we cannot understand the whole process of the breakdown and transformation of the kinship system, the erection of chieftainship, and the eventual creation of monarchy and the state without postulating a powerful human drive to separate and individuate from the mother, from the parents, from the kin. The word "instinct" when applied to human beings creates more problems than it solves,

but the concept of "drive" is useful and necessary if we are to understand how human beings and human societies work and develop from
one stage to another. A powerful, universal human inclination, or drive,
toward individuation is one of the great sources of energy that propel
human society through its developmental process.

"Powerful" and "universal" do not signify "irresistible." Even the
most potent drives may be resisted, suppressed, repressed, and nothing
signifies that the most powerful drives are inevitably slated for fulfillment. Nothing indicates that the Nuer, left to themselves, would not
stay in a kinship-system society for a million years. Our understanding
of human society is not yet sharp enough to explain why the Nuer remained encompassed by the kinship system whereas the Baganda were
free enough to create the state. One thing, however, seems clear: the
Nuer stayed Nuer by repressing the drive toward individuation, and
the Baganda developed the state by responding to its call. Over and over
again, the literature reveals that primitive societies were deeply antagonistic to any strong manifestation of individuality: "Although the Kaingáng respect power they cannot tolerate any kind of intensification of
it; for such intensification is felt by them to be disruptive. Through their
insistence on the primary importance of the other person and their failure to reward achievement, the Kaingáng have suppressed processes
that encourage the concentration of power in the hands of outstanding
individuals."[2] What a far cry from advanced complex societies, in
which it was the authoritarian power of the king that held society together, and the society delighted in every manifestation of individual
expression—in sport, in art, in theatrical performance, in sexuality, in
politics, in living.

In the beginning, both in the individual psyche and in the social
system, the drive toward separation and individuation has no moral
thrust. The power to remain individuated is the primary power sought.
Individuation is achieved at cost to others; separation is attained through
disregard of the existence and feelings of other people; the kind of conscience that would make cowards of us all gave very little trouble to
the makers of the first kingdoms. If tyranny was an inevitable part of
the developmental process at the beginning, that was because tyranny
served the interests of separation and individuation. Since we value both
individuation and morality, we would prefer that it had been otherwise,
but if we are to understand the tragic nature of human history, we must
pay attention to these facts. Those who created advanced complex societies wanted a certain kind of power. If acting morally, with concern

for others, gave them that power, they embraced morality, as when Kamehameha forgave the man who had attacked him with the canoe paddle. If embracing tyranny gave them the power to individuate, then tyranny it was. That we have come to a different place—that the stages of social development have brought us to the point where moral advance is the primary energy that drives the social developmental process—does not mean that it was so at the beginning.

The progressive process that goes from clan headman to centralized monarch, which I shall briefly outline in this chapter, is a process of increasing the power of the person at the head of society. As we move from headman to chief to king, the person at the top of the political system increasingly rules more people, increasingly begins to give orders rather than ask for advice or consensus, and is increasingly potent enough to enforce his commands over the resistance of others. Individuals with enormous political power are the end result of the whole journey.

It would be a mistake to imagine that all this happens without the consent of the governed. If members of a society did not want this kind of authoritarian power to evolve, as those in primitive society did not, the whole process would have been stillborn. There is only one king in a centralized monarchy, but there may be hundreds of governors and subgovernors and thousands of petty officials attached to power, and hundreds of thousands who, unable to separate and individuate themselves, identify with a monarch who seems capable of omnipotence. The lowliest person on the ladder wants that kind of power to exist in the world—for others if not for himself. Years after the *kabaka* of Buganda had been transformed into a quiescent constitutional monarch, the Baganda could express a nostalgic longing for the old days, when people trembled when the *kabaka* spoke and hundreds died in a single swoop. Just as middle-class people today watch television romances of the glittering past of the high aristocracy and inwardly imagine that, had they lived then, they would have been lords, not peasants, just so the twentieth-century Muganda, longing for the old days of the *kabaka*'s omnipotence, inwardly assumed he would have been an executioner, not a victim.

In reality the *kabaka* had the power, but in fantasy everyone could be a *kabaka;* so today in fantasy everyone can be a movie star, a great quarterback, a rock singer, or a Nobel Prize winner. And lest we tend to denigrate the importance of that kind of fantasy participation, it should be noted that twentieth-century fascism would have been impos-

sible without it. The posing, posturing, pouting Il Duce was living out
many people's fantasy of sexual and aggressive omnipotence.

The drive to separate and individuate, the drive to create powerful
individuals, is as potent as any force that drives the development of society. By itself it cannot explain the whole process that has transformed
human beings from hunters and gatherers to twentieth-century post-
industrial beings, but it is a fundamental constituent of that process. In
the first monarchies, in the first states, the first omnipotent human beings walked the earth, not in mythic fantasy but in reality. The kind
of power those first kings wielded had never before been experienced.
It was created not only to oppress human beings but also to exalt them.
And it all began with the appearance of the first lowly chief.

Precise definitions are essential to describe the developmental progress from clan headman to authoritarian king. No single word in all
of anthropological literature has been as misused as the designation
"chief." As an example (my italics):

Throughout this region a *chief* was . . . known as *Ntemi*—he who cuts short
discussion by giving judgement. Almost everywhere, and even if he only ruled
a thousand subjects, the *chief* could be described as a "divine *king*," the possessor of special insignia, and of royal fire from which all fire in the *king*dom must
be kindled. Everywhere the *king*'s death and burial was the subject of special
rites. In principle the *king* could not die a natural death; he must be buried in
a completely special way and usually to the accompaniment of human sacrifice.
All this . . . the typical *chieftainship* of West Tanganyika region shared with
the *chieftainship* of the Interlacustrine region.[3]

Such confusion of chiefs and kings inclines one to imitate Alice, throw
up one's hands in despair, and announce that they are all just a pack
of cards. It is possible, however, to discriminate precisely between chiefs
and kings.

As earlier defined, a chief is a person who rules over people to whom
he is not related and/or people he does not meet on a face-to-face basis.
*A king, then, is a person who rules over people who rule other people to
whom they are not related and/or do not meet on a face-to-face basis.* It
would be simple to say that a king is a person who rules over chiefs,
but I think it is of value to keep the word "chief" for an independent
ruler who has no authority above him. The powerful subordinates of
a king can be designated "governors" or "king's lieutenants" without
confusion. Maquet has said much the same thing: "In traditional Africa

government was always monarchical. There was a chief or king at the head of every political network. Where the number of subjects and density of the population allowed the monarch to rule directly, we call the political unit a chiefdom. It is called a kingdom when the sovereign has to delegate his power to officials who exercise it in his name."[4]

Clearly, a chiefdom is a simpler society than a kingdom, and much simpler than a complex kingdom, in which the monarch has hundreds of lieutenants and governors. The development from chieftainship to kingship was not undertaken lightly, and many cultures were capable of moving from primitive society to chieftainship society but incapable of taking the step into kingship. Again, why any particular society stops at any particular point in development is one of the great unanswered questions.

Primitive society had certain politically superior people who did not really rule anyone but did exercise a certain kind of nonauthoritarian, flexible, kinship-type authority. I call them "clan headmen" or "village headmen."

The process here goes from headman to chieftainship to simple kingdom to complex kingdom. After each major step there is a transitional state; many societies, for example, cannot accurately be described as chieftainships or simple kingdoms, but as transitional between the two. The complete process goes thus: headman—transition —chieftainship—transition—simple kingdom—transition—complex kingdom.

CLAN AND VILLAGE HEADMAN

"The members of each clan lived on their own particular part of the mountain, and had their own head-man who was responsible for all affairs concerning the clan and its relations with other clans. He claimed no rights as ruler over the clan, for he was its Father, not its king. His power was greatest in connection with the land, and it was to him that all disputes concerning the boundaries of cultivated plots or of clan land were brought. These, however, were not frequent, for unclaimed land was so plentiful that quarrels on this account were few. . . . The father of the clan demanded no payment of taxes or rents, but he expected to receive a pot of beer each year after the harvest was over."[5] Flexible. Easy. Unstructured. Familylike; Roscoe uses the word "Father." Actually the headman was more like an uncle than a father. There were no taxes, no tribute, no forced labor. Certainly, there was no oppression and no social tyranny. A headman might come only from a certain lineage in the clan. Many times he was simply the oldest living member of that lineage. If he was a clan head, he presided—not ruled—only over people to whom he was related; if a village head, only over people he met on a daily basis. Nothing about such a leadership role was in conflict with kinship and kinship-system values. Society being one large family, he was simply the head of the family.

In one important sense, the role was structured and pointed toward more complex forms of leadership: it was a permanent, not an *ad hoc,* office. In many primitive societies, leaders were selected to direct one particular function, such as a hunting expedition or a raiding party, and then dismissed. A clan or village headman, on the contrary, occupied a permanent office. Fathers are fathers and not committee chairmen. Under ordinary circumstances, the headman was changed only at death, just as a family does not get a new head until the death of the father. The belief in a permanent leadership position, no matter how benignly and lightly exercised the leadership might have been at the start, provided the opening for an elaborate development of political leadership.

THE TRANSITION FROM HEADMAN TO CHIEF

All transitional states of society have something atonal, asymmetrical, off-balance about them. As one reads about them, these societies sometimes seem made up, not authentic. The Anuak are a Nilotic people in the Sudan. They were divided into two kinds of political structure. One was a type of kingship; the other, leadership by village headmen who were on the way to developing into chiefs, though the process was frustrated by the fact that the society was enormously ambivalent about this development and, therefore, most of its political energy went into deposing the headmen-chiefs and replacing them with others. "For in spite of the great outward respect paid to a village headman his power is subject to popular control and if he loses the support of a large section of his community he may be overthrown by a revolution, usually a bloodless one, and expelled from the village. This form of ostracism is known as *agem.*"[6]

On the one hand, the villagers treated him like a chief: he could be a headman only if his father had held that position; they brought him gifts of food and hoed his land for him; he could raid a member of the village and take his goods; he maintained a system of spies to keep him informed of plots against him; he was expected to provide some of the poorer members with the material wealth to secure a bride. And on the other, they rose up and threw him out with an enthusiasm matched by our own treatment of incumbent presidents during the 1970s.

When one of these headmen-chiefs was deposed, there was always an excuse: he failed to distribute his food to the villagers; he refused to use his wealth to assist the poor; he slaughtered a cow and invited only a few to join him for dinner. "After all what did we make him headman for except to eat from him?"[7] No headman, however, was wealthy enough to live up to the demands for redistribution. What the people really wanted was to have a chieflike headman, and then throw him from office and set another in his place. They were both attracted to and repelled by an intensification of power. They created it but would not have it.

CHIEFTAINSHIP

Chieftainships are still primarily kinship-system societies. Any accurate description would perforce devote more space to kinship-system functions than to the area of chiefly politics. According to our definition of the state as a society in which nonkinship forms of social cohesion are as important as kinship forms, a chieftainship is not yet a state.

The power of chiefs seems to grow naturally from the aristocratic lineages of primitive society, the heads of these noble lineages usually becoming the clan and village headmen. Most chieftainships seem to have begun their political life in this way, and then, by an undocumented historical process, some of these leaders manage to establish a rule over a clan or village in which their kinsmen do not reside. The chief continues as leader of his own clan or village, still more or less as a headman. But over the stranger clan, he is now a chief. His clan, then, becomes the royal clan of the chieftainship; the successor to his office as clan headman also succeeds to the whole chieftainship. Succession to the chieftainship is determined by the rules that govern the kin group from which the chief comes. Kinship-system notions of power continue to dominate the polity.

In such a society, lineage headmen, clan headmen, and village headmen—all representatives of the kinship system—continue in the same relatively powerless leadership roles that existed in primitive society. Now, however, the headmen are responsible to the chief, and often a new headman has to be approved by him. Whatever ruling the chief does is done through the various headmen, who become the crucial intermediaries between the people and the nonkinship political power. The centralized power of the chieftainship, if it expands, grows at the expense of the headmen. In Busambira, a very small chiefdom in the country of Busoga, northeast of Buganda, many of the village headmanships were in the hands of the sons of the chief.[8] Such centralization at the expense of the kinship system moves a chieftainship in the direction of monarchy, since it substitutes king's lieutenants for kinship-system headmen as the functionaries directly under the central political power.

The power of a chief is absolutely different from that of any headman, and many symbolic forms and rituals are invented to underscore the radical nature of that power, even in the simplest of chiefdoms. In the chieftainship of Busambira in Busoga, the ruler had "no staff of chiefs interposed between himself and the village and sub-village headmen. He or his *katikiro* dealt directly with the headman...."[9] The political unit was very small (in 1948, the population of the territory was 3,894),[10] and there were no territorial subdivisions under governors. There was simply the chief and twelve villages under him. As simple as this political structure was, the symbolic dimension of the chief's power went quite deep. *Kisambira,* as the chief was called, could trace his descent from Igaga, a legendary first ancestor. *Kisambira* was considered to be the ultimate owner of all the land in the chiefdom and his position was partly sacred. "He held in his possession the ancestral stools, spears, drums and other symbolic paraphernalia of rulership and was looked upon as the chief link between the people and the royal ancestors and other supernatural forces."[11] He was much more of an individual than any headman had ever been.

Similarly, among the Alur, a Nilotic people who lived considerably north of Buganda, "belief in the supernatural efficacy of a chief's person finds general expression in the fear and reverence professed for him, and the restraining influence which the mere presence of a chief or a chief's son is said to have in stopping fighting...."[12] All Alur chiefs had to be expert rainmakers, and this magical capacity contributed greatly to the awe in which the chiefs were held. Chiefs had the capacity to break certain rules and tabus that no ordinary person enjoyed:

This building of ancestor shrines . . . in contravention of the normal rules of eligibility is consistent with their capacity in a number of other contexts to rise above the fears and ritual restrictions which constrain the ordinary Alur individual. . . . He demonstrates symbolically the superior force of his character, which enables him to flout the rules which restrict others in the kinship status, without fear of the normal supernatural consequences.[13]

These "normal supernatural consequences" are, after all, a human invention, albeit an unconscious one. People invent tabu and the automatic punishments that are supposed to be meted out when the tabu is broken—and then they invent powerful individuals (chiefs and kings) whose job it is, in part, to break the tabu in order to demonstrate how really potent they are. Every ordinary person is in fantasy a tabu breaker, and the fantasy is partly satisfied by identification with the chief, who is a tabu breaker in reality. The chief is relatively unrestrained—the first hero to walk the earth.

The kind of political power that we associate with monarchies and the state, Weber's monopoly of legitimate force, was only feebly developed in chieftainships. Kinship-system self-help in matters of justice still held a large role in the social system, although Alur chiefs, for example, forcibly restricted the areas in which it could operate.[14] In contrast to the neighboring Lendu, a primitive people who had no superior power that could prevent the fighting that frequently broke out over compensation, Alur chiefs did step in and terminate feuds. An Alur chief could call in neighboring chiefs to help suppress civil contention in his chiefdom; he also had call on the warriors of his own royal lineage to take police action. To discourage personal violence, the chief could levy his own fine of a sheep or a goat, which was added to the compensation an offender had to pay the victim.[15]

In addition to the power to break tabu, to make rain, to preserve peace, and to contain sacredness within themselves, the first chiefs also had the power to make war in a more serious, more organized fashion. Controlling a larger population than any headman, a chief could bring more warriors to bear in any particular battle. Among the Alur, warfare became more destructive with the rise of the chiefs. Chiefless communities did not burn and plunder one another after battle, whereas a chief felt entitled to such actions when putting down a clan that had failed to keep the peace.[16] In early chieftaincies, the world discovered for the first time that the concentration and heightening of power is both an exhilarating and a dangerous thing.

THE TRANSITION FROM CHIEFTAINSHIP
TO SIMPLE MONARCHY

The simplest monarchy resulted from the unification of two chiefdoms into a single polity in which one former chief reigned as king. In such simple circumstances, the new king would probably continue as chief in his own district; it is unlikely that he would feel so exalted that he would require a governor for his own people. Unification of two chiefdoms might result from conquest, in which case the chief of the conquered district might be demoted to governor and owe obeisance to the king, or the chief might be deposed and a governor appointed from the conquered people. In rare cases, the new king might designate one of his own people to act as governor over the defeated chiefdom.

The unification of two chiefdoms into a simple monarchy did not have to be accomplished by violence. In many chiefdoms, it happened that neighboring chiefs stood in close relationship to one another: father and son, brothers, uncle and nephew. If one such chief died without an heir, the elders of the chiefdom might invite the related chief to assume rule over both polities, especially if he had an unusual reputation for military, magical, or moral power. The new king would have the task of designating a governor over the leaderless chiefdom. In such peaceful circumstances, this would be done only with the consent of the governed.

Simple kingdoms were also formed by the domination of a chiefdom over a primitive society, which was devoid of chiefs. Again, a kingdom could be secured by conquest, the more organized military forces of a chief moving into a district where only headmen presided. The permanency of the conquest depended primarily on the efficacy of the arrangements in regard to the governorship of the new province.

There were also peaceful mechanisms by which these unions could be accomplished. We have historical data from the Alur indicating that sometimes a people without a chief would ask a neighboring chief to send one of his sons to be chief over them.[17] Once the fledgling chiefdom was established, there was clearly a bond between the two chiefdoms, and a peaceful unification was ultimately possible.

The situation of a simple kingdom was inherently unstable. The energy that drove the developmental process—the heightening power of the individual chief—also produced the instability in the rivalry for power between the king and his governors. No monarchy, even the simplest, exists unless the office of governor is established, the governor being the king's designated power in the district. The political problem was not one of having people obey the governor: in most cases they had become accustomed to rendering obedience to a chief, and the governor merely stood in his place. The crucial issue was what kept the governor contented and subordinate to the king. In many cases, the answer was "nothing," and the monarchy dissolved.

A large kingdom is inherently more stable than a simple monarchy. If a king has ten provincial governors and one, two, or even three of them raise the banner of revolt, he still has seven, eight, or nine provinces to call upon to put down the rebellion. A king with one or two governors, should they refuse to obey his commands, must fight on an equal basis. It was many times easier to let the rebellious governor go and return to being a chief.

The rivalries between a king and his sons and among the sons—rivalries that continued to produce tension and instability in complex monarchies—could prove disastrous to simple kingdoms. Among the Alur, there are five recorded cases in which younger sons were chosen to succeed their fathers as head of the chieftainship of Ukuru, whereupon the eldest sons seceded from the district to found chieftainships of their own.[18] In the Ukimbu region of what is now Tanzania, an area where there was constant oscillation between chiefdom and small monarchy, the tensions between the ruler and his sons produced many fissures in the body politic.[19] In this same Ukimbu region, the councilors of the chief-kings played a crucial role. They were constantly deposing unsuccessful or unpopular rulers. "Usually the first indication a chief (-king) had of deposition was to hear the sound of the ghost-horn being played for his successor."[20]

Once the conception of a powerful, individuated person had been invented, once the kind of centralized political power implicit in monarchy was realized in the world, nothing signified that such power would, or could, remain the monopoly of only one person in each polity. Especially at the beginning, when individuated power for its own sake was the energy propelling the process of development, the mechanisms—such feelings as loyalty, honor, justice, order, nationalism, and religious purpose—that we recognize as helping people in a subordinate position assent to the dominance of a king were practically nonexistent. Postchiefdom, early-kingdom societies, making do with raw ambition, were torn by rivalries for power. Such intense factionalism did not nec-

essarily lead to larger and larger kingdoms as the more successful triumphed over the weaker. In as many cases, the attempts at early kingdoms dissolved back into the chieftainships out of which they had come.
A chief, needing no governors, dealing only with clan headmen, had
to face far fewer challenges to his authority once his power had been
established.

In all socially unstable circumstances, like those of transition from
chiefdoms to simple kingdoms, personality plays a crucial role. Marshall
Sahlins has described the cyclical process of the "big-man" in Melanesia. Certain figures of outstanding psychological power arose in the society, and the society permitted and encouraged this. One of these
"big-men" would start to build a political power base that dominated
the whole district. For a while it would look as if he were on the way
toward the erection of a strong kingdom. Then, inevitably, either
through the defection of his followers, or their outright rebellion, or
the death of the chief-king, the whole structure would dissolve, only
to be built up again by the next big-man.[21] Like the towers of blocks
children build in nursery school, their purpose seemed to be both to
stand tall and to be knocked over.

SIMPLE KINGDOMS

The inherent instability of the earliest kingdoms was overcome by several means: the establishment of a kingdom by military conquest; the
transformation of the king from a power into a superpower; the creation
of a nonaristocratic power structure that served to foster equilibrium;
and the invention of stabilizing forms that honored the polity more than
the man.

In the traditional society of Ukimbu in what is now Tanzania, almost fifty simple kingdoms existed in a relatively stable political environment during the nineteenth century. Many of these kingdoms were
established by the process of fission within an established monarchy.
Most of the original kingdoms, however, were brought into being as
a result of military conquest.[22] There is a stability inherent in a conquest
state; the king and his governor do not face each other in circumstance
of near equality, and revolt is unlikely when the king possesses a clearly
superior military force. A king, conquering a neighboring chiefdom,
may choose to demote that chief into a governor responsible to the king;
or he may depose the reigning chief and ask the elders of the conquered

chiefdom to select another of their members to act as governor. It is far easier for the monarch to overawe his subjects in such a circumstance than it is in a case where two chiefdoms of more or less equality combine into one kingdom. Stability is greater where the hierarchical lines are clearly drawn.

If the psychological gulf that separated the king from his "aristocratic" subjects was widened to the point that even the most intrepid "nobleman" trembled to violate the tabu of the sovereign, the chances of the monarchy's abiding were enormously increased. When the king alone had the awesome power to demand and command human sacrifice, for example, it was less likely that just any aristocrat felt strong enough to challenge and assume such potency. In all stable early monarchies, we find a fully developed symbolic system that emphasized the superhuman capacities of the king. This is not to say that symbolic power systems were consciously erected in order to strengthen the political staying power of the sovereign: such potency and omnipotency were desired for their own sakes. Political power was part, not the exclusive aim, of the whole process of producing superhuman individuals.

Many of the traditional kingdoms in western Tanzania were extremely small, some no larger than a thousand people and capable of being ruled by one man with the help of his close family.[23] Despite the limited nature of these polities, the symbolic potency of the king was fully developed. No one could gather honey until the king gave the word for the season to begin. A portion of every animal killed in a hunt had to be brought to the monarch. No hunter was allowed to kill an elephant, whose ivory was a royal monopoly, or a lion, the royal animal. The king had a special cadre whose task was to search for iron ore. He maintained a monopoly of trade in cloth, which he distributed to his subjects. When arms were introduced into the area, no one but the sovereign and his immediate lieutenants could deal in such merchandise.[24] Only the monarch possessed certain royal insignia. From his fire every new fire in the kingdom was kindled.[25] When he died, he was buried in a manner that suggested he still lived: seated on a stool, and holding a staff in his hand, he was wrapped in a white calico shroud. At least one boy and one girl, and sometimes several of each sex, were killed as part of the funeral rites.[26]

These kingdoms were far from being the magnificent centralized monarchies of Buganda, Bunyoro, or Hawaii, yet the sovereign was already a "divine" ruler. The forms of omnipotence that we generally associate with "divinity" were, in the beginning, more the prerogative of real though exalted humans than they were of supernatural beings.

Terror alone can never hold society together for very long. Fear of the omnipotent power of the king was not sufficient to stabilize a monarchical system; forms of stability and social coherence had to be developed as well. Threats to the throne came from other aristocratic members of society who felt powerful enough to challenge the monarch. Early kings soon learned that one important counter to this political threat was the elevation of commoners to positions of dependency on, and loyalty to, the throne. A commoner client or *katikiro* cannot attain royal station, cannot challenge the king's basic authority. Such a person is a perfect ally for the monarch in any power struggle with disaffected nobles.

Bulamogi was one of the largest states in Busoga; its population in 1948 was about forty-nine thousand, and the traditional kingdom in the nineteenth century may have had, at the most, seventy-five thousand inhabitants. The king who ruled Bulamogi had a large staff of administrators, household officials, and territorial governors. He had a *katikiro,* a commoner, who was in charge of the royal palace. A number of provinces were included in the kingdom, each of which was administered by a royal prince *and* a commoner governor appointed by the king:[27]

The administrative staff through which the ruler in each of the kingdoms governed was recruited neither through patrilineal kinship in commoner lineages nor through membership in the royal group. The ruler's leading lieutenants—the prime minister and the chiefs of territorial divisions—were commoners bound to the ruler by personal loyalty. . . . Throughout the kingdom there were princes—junior members of the royal group—in control of villages or groups of villages, and these persons were a potential threat to the paramount authority of the ruler. . . . The institution of clientship, through which commoners of administrative and military ability were raised by the ruler to positions of authority and thus were bound to him as personal followers, provided an administrative staff which could be trusted with power. Not sharing the inherited rank of the princes, they were not potential usurpers. At times of succession, the client under the previous ruler participated along with members of the royal clan in choosing a new ruler and thus exercised a disinterested and stabilizing influence upon the ambitious princes.[28]

All these mechanisms for manipulating the balance of power, however, would have failed of their purpose without the simultaneous creation of a sense of social coherence, a sense—to give it a not-quite-appropriate name, of nationhood. This was sorely needed to replace the cohesiveness of the kinship system that was breaking down, and it was provided by the king. In a kinship-system society, the ancestors of the lineage or the clan play a crucial symbolic role in creating a sense of social cohesion. People belong to one another and to the group, in large part, because they all have the same ancestors. Ancestors enable the feeling of family to be broadly extended. The celebration of George Washington's birthday is a ritual relic of ancestor worship that we continue to nurture in the interest of political cohesion. The stability of early monarchies was enhanced by making the king's ancestors everybody's ancestors:

In the structure of the state, the principle of ascribed rank set one patrilineal descent group—that of the ruler—above all others. Princes were, by birth, assigned higher status and an in-born fitness to rule. Like commoner lineages, the princes had a corporate authority structure and corporate economic and religious interests, but unlike commoner lineages, the royal group's unit of reference in authority, property and religion extended beyond its own members to the state as a whole. The authority of the ruler, as representative of the royal group, extended over members of all clans; the royal ancestors were in a sense "national" ancestors and the royal group, through the ruler, had interests in all the land of the state and its products. The royal group was thus more than a *primus inter pares* among patrilineal descent groups; it was the structural manifestation and the symbolic embodiment of the unity of the whole state.[29]

All of these mechanisms—state creation through conquest, elevation of the monarch to superpower status, use of commoner administrators, and the erection of non-kinship-system forms of social cohesion—came to full ripeness in complex centralized kingdoms. These forms of action and ritual were the basic building blocks not only for simple monarchies but also for the much more complex polities that succeeded them.

THE TRANSITION FROM SIMPLE TO COMPLEX KINGDOMS

Historical evidence seems to show that once simple kingdoms had been stabilized, three courses of action were possible. First, the politics within one small kingdom or within an entire district or country could remain relatively stable over a long period of time. Such, apparently, was the case in Busoga, where approximately fifteen small to middling kingdoms, the populations of which ran from four to fifty thousand, maintained their existence over several hundred years without dominance by one or two states over the others, and without serious regressions back into chieftainships.[30]

Second, periodic eruptions could occur when first one small kingdom and then another *attempted*—under the leadership of a particularly charismatic king—to dominate its neighbors and merge several small kingdoms into a complex centralized state. In this particular circumstance, such attempts universally failed. The complex states proved temporary and collapsed either at the death of the founder or soon thereafter, since permanent mechanisms of large-state control were not erected. After the breakdown of these temporary states, each smaller polity reverted to its small-kingdom status. This description exactly fits the political conditions of both the lesser and greater peninsulas of ancient Tahiti, during the period that preceded contact with the outside world.[31] And conditions remained the same on Tahiti until Pomare II, with Christian guns and Christian religion, conquered the whole island.

All these stillborn attempts to create a centralized monarchy seem to have been brought about by military conquest. The charismatic kings who made such attempts were all unusual military leaders.

The third possible scenario available to stable simple monarchies was the circumstance when one particular state in an area succeeded in the drive to reduce its neighbors and erect a permanent centralized kingdom. Both Hawaii and Buganda are representative of this kind of state building. This has usually taken place over a reasonably long period of time (the Buganda state was three to four hundred years in the making) and has required several charismatic kings with superlative military powers. With the arrival of firearms, permanent state building like Kamehameha's Hawaiian kingdom was accomplished in one generation. It is doubtful whether these results could have been produced with traditional weapons, for it was the presence of guns that allowed for a concentration of military power in the hands of one state. It is a question, for example, whether a unified Tahitian state would ever have been erected with traditional modes of killing.

Historical information indicates that every complex centralized monarchy was built on a foundation of military conquest. Small kingdoms were erected as the result of peaceful expansion, amalgamation, the consent of the governed, but for the centralized state this seems never to have been the case.

Aylward Shorter has given us a case study of an area in western

Tanzania dominated by small kingdoms, which produced in the nineteenth century clear-cut examples of both eruptive, impermanent state erection and also of the solid building of a centralized monarchy. Shorter calls all those who ruled there "chiefs," but, by the definitions used here, most of them were simple kings. There were between fifty and a hundred different polities in this one area.[32]

Mirambo was a military genius who used the new weapons of firearms to construct a large empire:

His only organization was military. When he conquered a chiefdom, he often killed the ruler who had resisted him, but he usually agreed to replace him by another member of his chiefly lineage. This chief became his client and Mirambo relied on his gratitude and on his fear of reprisals to keep him loyal. If there was a rebellion, Mirambo struck with lightning swiftness to punish the rebel and to replace him by yet another of his house. Mirambo, therefore, left no permanent organization when he died and his "empire" began to disintegrate within a few days of his death in 1884.[33]

Nyungu-ya-Mawe, a king in the same general area of Tanzania, was a contemporary of Mirambo's. He could not compare to that conqueror in military skill, but he did manage to overwhelm thirty-two out of thirty-eight small kingdoms in Ukimbo, and many others in neighboring districts, so that eventually he ruled an area of almost twenty thousand not very densely populated square miles.[34]

Nyungu was a remarkable statesman who knew what was required to build a permanent state. He did not rule through the conquered kings but established his own corps of *vatwaale*, six or seven military governors who owed loyalty to him alone. The conquered kings, if not killed during the conquest, were reduced to ritual functionaries and were often not replaced when they died. Thus Nyungu broke the power of the small kings and built a hierarchical, secular, nonkinship state. Insubordination from any of his *vatwaale* was severely punished. One governor did have the temerity to re-join the political and ritual functions that Nyungu had sundered by performing some ritual office in one of the small kingdoms he governed. Nyungu had him executed and replaced by another ambitious military commander. Nyungu was the only one in the new kingdom who was allowed to exercise both political and sacred power.[35] In essence, he had made himself into a *kabaka*.

And it worked. Unlike Mirambo's personal achievement, Nyungu's state survived his death through two of his successors, both of whom happened to be women. Europeans, however, had invented a greater power than Nyungu could imagine. The Germans dismantled his state ten years after he died.[36]

Though we are forced to admire Nyungu's achievement, especially in contrast to the firefly Mirambo, he was nevertheless, like Alexander, Caesar, and Napoleon before him, a civilized killer. The brute force that seems to have been essential to the erection of complex centralized kingdoms must be related to the pervasive, assumed tyranny in those societies. Maybe there was so much oppression in this last stage of complex society because the people who created that stage were so good at the tyrannical mode.

Nyungu, Kamehameha, Pomare II, Finow I, Alexander, Caesar, Ivan the Terrible, and William the Conqueror were all of a piece: annihilators of people and builders of states. They were not merely sadists killing for its own sake; nor were they gangsters or pirates seeking only wealth and the unlimited power to take whatever they wanted; nor were they complete megalomaniacs in whose psyches rampant ambition had driven out all other considerations. Their fierce individualism operated, to a significant degree, under the banner of an ideal: the creation of a large permanent state. Theirs was not a paltry ambition. However, from another point of view, they *were* sadists and pirates and megalomaniacs, and tyranny stalked all the great states they built.

In this brave new world of politics that replaced the kinship system, these were the individuals who created the centralized state—magnificent heroes with only a rudimentary conception of morality. It was their energy that drove society through that particular stage of development. They were the idea whose time had come. They invented a mode of politics that has served, and disserved, humankind for thousands of years.

27

Kingship: The Dream of Omnipotence

The *kabaka* of Buganda and the king of Bunyoro each took as his queen a half-sister born of the same father but a different mother. The *kabaka* was permitted to marry his full sister, but in Bunyoro this connection was forbidden, even for the king.[1] In Dahomey, the report was that "brothers, sisters, and cousins indulge in the greatest possible freedom stopping only short of actual sexual contact, and, should they be members of the royal sib, not stopping at that point."[2]

Royal incest between brothers and sisters was characteristic of most advanced complex societies and found its fullest elaboration in the Hawaiian Islands. Here, a suitable marriage partner for a great noble was his half-sister; the children of such a marriage were designated *niau-pio* chiefs.[3] The highest intensity of marriage was achieved when two *niau-pio* children from different families married each other, and then the male and female offspring of their union married. The children of this last, superincestuous *pio* marriage carried the highest possible tabu; they were "gods, a fire, a blaze, a raging heat, only at night is it possible for such children to speak with men. . . ."[4] Kamehameha III, who reigned from 1825 to 1854 and was a nephew of the first Kamehameha, was the last great noble of Hawaii to marry his full sister.[5]

"Omnipotence" is a pale word to describe fully the ideal of kingship in complex societies. It does not give enough of the dreamlike, poetic sense of living without bounds or restrictions, of living in a world in which there are no laws of incest or morality or gravity, no shadow between the wish and the deed, no temperance, no measure, no "reality principle," a world where one is all mouth and can fly at will. Every woman in the world—save one—is food for the sexual appetite; the death of every man is subject to the nod of the head. Nothing is forbidden. Tumultuous tantrums are followed by cascades of generosity. Nothing seems to matter except that what is done is done on a scale of which mere humans are incapable. The houses of the king in Tahiti were called "the clouds of heaven"; his canoe was "the rainbow"; lightning, not torches, illuminated his residence; and when he passed through a province on the shoulders of his bearers, the people announced that he was flying from one district to another.[6] To marry one's sister was only natural to such an almighty person.

The world, however, would not be subjugated and periodically this dream of omnipotence soured. Other people's wills provided the rude awakening. Kings were overthrown by sons, brothers, or governors. And barring such events, death became the last compromiser. The history of the first great monarchies and the tensions within these societies are found deep within this dream of omnipotence and within the ambivalence about that dream.

The irrational sources of this kind of political leadership—and, to some degree, of all political leadership—are revealed by the insistence, in most cases, that any physical imperfection barred a person from becoming king. This was true in Buganda, Bunyoro, and Ankole, as well as in the smaller East African states of Buhaya and Buzinza.[7] If human beings created kingship for rational reasons only—that is, to erect a strong and efficient state—they would have preferred an exceptionally talented leader with a crooked nose to a handsome mediocrity, but such was not the case. For that matter, how many bad-looking men have been elected president of the United States in this century? In Dahomey, "at the demise of the late king . . . the eldest son's right of primogeniture was disallowed, because one of his toes from some accident overlapped the other; and his next brother . . . who, with respect to form, is certainly 'a marvelous proper man,' was elected in his stead."[8] As late in history as the Byzantine Empire, an incumbent emperor would cut off the nose of a potential rival for the throne, since the physical disability disqualified the victim. People do not want to be led politically except by those who partake of perfection.

License is implicit in omnipotence. The two great licenses are the sexual and the aggressive, and early kings were expected to exercise both. Sexual license has been so integral to the concept of kingship that, many times in history, almost psychotic sexual behavior has been tolerated, and even encouraged, in monarchs who inclined in that direction.

It is not surprising to discover that the Caligulas and Henry VIIIs of the world had predecessors in advanced complex societies. Kabaka Kamanya, grandfather of Mutesa, would demand presents from the wives of his chief subordinates whenever they went to war, and would insist that he was the substitute for their absent husbands. "He also used to uncover his men and look at their genitals. If he saw a small man, he would scornfully comment on his size that he would never find women to love him. He would then give him about ten women to take to wife. To a huge man he would give about twenty women and again scornfully comment on his size, that he would never find enough women at Mpumudde to satisfy him."[9] We may easily detect repressed homosexual inclinations in such behavior, but what is significant for this argument is that the *kabaka*, being the *kabaka*, was free to follow his proclivities no matter where they led him, no matter what degree of humiliation of others (men and women) they entailed. People did not throw him from office for such offense. Kamanya died a natural death and was succeeded by his son.

As important as sexual indulgence was for early kings, the completely uninhibited expression of aggressive inclinations was of far greater significance. A king was a king because he could kill at will. Among Tswana peoples in South Africa, the monarch, at his installation, was given a spear, an axe, and a club, and told that now he had "the power to kill or let live."[10] When King Liholiho of Hawaii arrived on the island of Kauai, he was greeted: "Here comes the son of our land; he alone has the right to gouge out our eyes."[11] Buganda proverbs were replete with praise names for the *kabaka* that emphasized his destructive capacity: " '*Mufumbyaganda—nantabulira—busenya,*' which means that he is like a cook who has plenty of firewood; he uses it as extravagantly as he wishes without caring for those whose job it is to bring firewood. In the same way the *Kabaka* can kill people as he wishes, without mercy to the parents."[12] David Livingstone wrote in his journal in 1872, "Some foolish speculations resemble the idea of a Muganda, who said last night that if Mtésa did not kill people now and then, his subjects would suppose that he was dead!"[13] People in early states obviously took the same kind of pride in their kings that our military commanders take in their sacred "firepower." The existence of such explosive possibilities gives people reason to live, though they may, in both cases, provide the means of destruction. Reverend Felkin, one of the early Buganda missionaries, comments how Mutesa's illness had softened the cruelties of his early reign and how his chiefs missed that destructive presence. "Ah, if Mtesa were well, there would be plenty of executions."[14]

Our own primary acquaintanceship with the idea of omnipotence comes from the attributes of the Hebrew-Christian God, Jahweh. Many students of early kingship use words like "divine" or "godlike" to help us comprehend the nature of these monarchs. From a cultural-historical point of view, such an approach is backward. The God Jahweh was a highly elaborated and sublimated symbolic form, one of the foundations of which was the omnipotent kingship of complex and archaic societies. Jahweh was so powerful (I do not speak here of the moral dimension, but of pure power as such) because he was *kinglike*. Our God has an absolute control over life and death because the ideal of early kings was that they have such power. If God holds the ultimate dominion over death, if it is he who giveth and taketh away, his predecessors in this terrible office were the omnipotent monarchs of the complex societies which preceded the archaic civilizations of the Near East.

So almighty were the kings of complex societies that they constantly exercised a prerogative that even Jahweh was not sure belonged to any creature, human or divine—the right to take human life in religious ritual. Human sacrifice was the ultimate certification of the power of early kings. On the island of Tahiti, ritual homicide *made* kingship. The heir to the throne, from birth on, was the subject of a multitude of rituals: circumcision, presentation to the various districts of the kingdom, coming of age. At each occasion, one or several human victims were killed for the greater glory of the prince royal.[15] "In fact, so powerful a sanction was human sacrifice, and so apparently *necessary* was it to chiefly authority, that some chiefs, upon being urged by Europeans to give up the practice, exclaimed, 'If we do there will be no Chiefs.' "[16] It is impossible, given a form as complicated as human sacrifice, to find a single cause for its existence in complex society. It undoubtedly served many functions, but certain things seem to be true: the society was intoxicated with the idea that some humans could become omnipotent, and the exercise of ritual homicide reinforced that dream.

Such an extreme concentration of human potency would require equally exceptional rituals of obeisance from ordinary people. The kings of Hawaii, Buganda, and Tahiti always traveled on the shoulders of human bearers. In Hawaii, when the rulers walked abroad during certain tabu periods, people prostrated themselves as they passed, forcing their faces into the ground. Tahitians were compelled to uncover themselves to the waist whenever they were in the presence of the king.[17] In Buganda, when the *kabaka* sneezed, everyone sneezed; should he have a cold, everyone at court simulated the same; when the king went to his barber, each of the courtiers did likewise. "If any one receives a favor of the king he thanks him in a peculiar manner. He kneels down, and placing both hands together he sways his body backwards and forwards, his hands rising and falling on either side of his face, while he says *Nyanzig* (I thank), repeating the word and action some twenty or thirty times. He then suddenly falls flat on his face, and commences to beat the ground with his hands and cheeks, the head being rotated at each prostration, first one cheek and then the other touching the ground, the legs being vigorously kicked at the same time."[18]

Since the king was the state and only his omnipotence kept that nonkinship polity going, it is not surprising that the symbolic connection was made between the ruler's physical health and the strength of the state. The king of Rwanda was not allowed to bend his knees, lest the territory of the country shrink.[19] "Of the Swazi . . . we [are] specifically told that the national welfare is mystically related to the chief's own physical vigor, and will suffer if he becomes ill or is in mourning; his death, moreover, 'is considered to be a direct attack upon the nation. . . .' "[20] An old and feeble monarch was a terrible problem for a society dependent upon the symbols of absolute power. Such failing omnipotencers were poisoned or strangled in East African countries like Ankole and Bunyoro, and possibly elsewhere, too.[21]

In a democratic society, we have more sublimated ways to handle our panic and anger when we discover we are being ruled by those who cannot deliver omnipotence. First, we tell the Gallup Poll what a poor job our leaders are doing, and then we throw the incompetents out and bring in a new set who promise to reach the same summit of absolute power but by a different route. No one gets elected if he or she merely hints that the omnipotence to solve all problems may not exist. Our journey in the large, nonkinship world is more frightening than we consciously allow; unconsciously, we are insistently searching for all-powerful magical charms to keep us safe. Leadership without magic seems to threaten our existence.

One enormously important result of the omnipotence of kings was that, being able to do anything human beings take it into their heads to do, they could also be consciously moral in a more concentrated, more deliberate way than anyone had been before. As part of the accession rites of the new *kabaka,* the *mugema* announced: "I am your father, you are my child. Through all the ages, from your ancestor Kimera when he took possession of Buganda. My child, look with kindness upon all your people, from the highest to the lowest; be mindful of your land, deal justice among your people . . . treat your *bataka* [clans] with honor . . . all your men, the chiefs of the nation, treat them with honor."[22] Among the Tswana in South Africa the new chief was told "to look after his tribe properly and keep it at peace; to rule firmly but justly and impartially, and not to favor his own kin ('We look not at the person, but at his fault,' says the proverb); to attend constantly at his council-place, 'so that you may get to know your people, and they may get to know you'; to abandon his boyhood practices and youthful associates, and to listen to his advisers; to respect the persons and property of his subjects, and not to abduct their wives, seduce their daughters, or take cattle to enrich himself; to support orphans, old people, and cripples, and feed his people generously . . . to be long suffering and patient. . . ."[23]

The installation ceremonies that accompanied the coronation of Hawaiian kings were long and complicated, taking many days; they emphasized the benevolent, caring, protecting aspects of the monarch, who would bring rain, full crops, "blessing to the government, prosperity to the land."[24] Hawaiian kings had the power, once in office, to pronounce a sacred *kanawai* after a ferocious battle, in which the captives taken in the struggle were marched before the king and he decreed that they were now no longer slaves or potential ritual offerings and were free to go wherever they pleased. We have many recorded instances of the actual use of this royal prerogative.[25] An omnipotent monarch could enact such a decree, because no one would accuse him of acting morally out of weakness.

These paternal characteristics forcefully remind us of Jahweh. The complicated combination of omnipotent power, sporadic nurturing, ultimate morality, arbitrary personal justice, and formidable anger is an archetypal symbol of enormous importance. That it resonates with the experience of a small child vis-à-vis its father in an intensely patriarchal family seems more than likely. That such symbolic constructions became necessary precisely at the time that the kinship system was breaking down may be deeply related to the whole psychic process of separation and individuation from the mother, and the role of the father in that process.

Death is the great, irrevocable separation, and death is antithetical to the dream of omnipotence that denies the inevitability of separations. No matter how close the *kabaka* might come to wielding absolute power, that power was never sufficient to exercise dominion over death. It may be that people eventually turned from kings to gods for their sense of omnipotence in part because the gods did not die. The deceased monarch could do nothing about his circumstance, but those who were left behind could do their best to preserve his existence symbolically. One's king, one's father, one's mentor may be dead and in the grave, but psychologically one can still choose how much life they are to have. People in complex societies did their utmost to preserve the memory, the presence, the power of their dead rulers. The Tahitians knew something of the art of embalming, and the bodies of great men were preserved for a year or more. After the more ephemeral parts were drained from the body cavity, the remainder of the corpse was dried in the sun. The embalming process being completed, the body was placed in a sitting position, dressed in tapa cloth, with a cape over its shoulders and a turban on its head. The family brought flowers, dried food, and fresh fruit daily to the corpse. "It was addressed as a living being."[26]

The placenta and umbilical cord of Hawaiian kings were kept at a sacred place, a practice also observed in Buganda. The burial places of Hawaiian monarchs who had ruled especially well became famous centers of sacred interest.[27] Nothing, however, rivaled the continuity with dead kings that was maintained in Buganda. The tombs of the *kabaka*s "became in effect miniature reproductions of the royal capital. . . . The jaw-bone and the personal effects of the dead monarch were housed in a large conical hut of similar dimensions to the house of the reigning king. . . . The older surviving wives and officials of the late king took up their residence around it. As the widows died, their place was taken by fictitious widows, who were frequently women who imagined themselves to be possessed by the spirit of the dead king. As the real officials died, at least one or two of the most important posts, such as Katikiro and Kangawo, were filled up, usually by direct descendants of the original office-holders. In the course of time and of successive re-buildings, the size of the shrine . . . became reduced to one or two widows and a Katikiro. Nevertheless, even the oldest shrines remain, and still remain [1959], places of pilgrimage to pious . . . (princes): ceremonies of various kinds are performed there. . . ."[28] The tombs of the thirty *kabaka*s from Kintu, the founder of the kingdom, to Mutesa were known and preserved. Everything that mortals could do was done to make the *kabaka*s immortal.

THE DREAM OF CHILDHOOD

Two matters that relate to the first kings indicate that the drive for omnipotence had its origin in early childhood: they were inordinately
pampered in their day-to-day activities, and they were allowed the most
tumultuous of tantrums. The royal courts were full of personal servants
of the king who supervised his minutest needs. The king's food, the
king's tobacco, the king's milk, the king's chamber pot, the king's
staff—each was taken care of by a separate officer. Some kings were
watched over when they slept;[29] others were not allowed to feed themselves and had to be nurtured by servants. All this creates a desire to
understand the symbolic mechanism in the psyche that can transform
such infantilization into an honor. Even in sexual matters, the king, unlike an adult, had to make no exertion to satisfy his needs beyond lifting
a little finger and pronouncing, "I want." It is every infant's fantasy
of the completely complaisant mother.

The tantrum behavior of the twenty-one-month-old toddler was *de
rigueur* for kings in complex society. If one fails to get one's way, then
lay waste. When a high priest of Oro complained to Pomare I that an
uncle of Pomare's had committed adultery with the priest's wife, the
king promptly informed the adulterer that he was to be banished from
the kingdom. Pomare's parents and other relatives, sympathetic to their
kinsman, disagreed strongly with the verdict, whereupon the king got
so angry he extended the banishment to all of them, including his
mother and father. Tears in their eyes, the proscribed nobles set to work
to gather up their belongings. Visited by Máximo Rodríguez, who tells
the story, and advised by him that he would attempt to get Pomare to
rescind the decree, the relatives strongly urged Rodríguez not to attempt any reconciliation, since that would only make the king angrier
and possibly bring about an even stronger punishment. The Christian
went ahead, however, and he did ultimately succeed in reaching the
heart of the king; the decree of banishment was rescinded.[30]

Much of the blatant, sadistic cruelty in complex societies resulted
from the fact that the king was not only permitted to indulge in tantrum
behavior but was expected to do so. Vehiatua I, who died around 1770,
had succeeded in forging the smaller peninsula of Tahiti into a single
state. A former governor, Mae, rebelled against him, was defeated in
battle and brought before the king. The rebel's arms were pinioned be-

hind him, his scalp was cut off, his eyes pulled from his head, and his body mutilated in various other ways while he struggled with death and those around him mocked his sufferings. Finally, the head was cut from the body and the skull made into a drinking cup out of which Vehiatua could taste his revenge whenever he wished.[31] Such was the end of a man who dared to cross an omnipotent monarch.

This kind of tantrum behavior continued in the world as long as real monarchy existed. Henry II, king of England in the twelfth century, was significantly responsible for building the bureaucratic machinery that made a modern state possible. But when he did not get his way, he threw himself into rages, dashing himself to the ground and biting the carpet. He excused his behavior by equating himself with Jahweh: "By nature I am a son of wrath: why should I not rage? God Himself rages when He is wrathful."[32] Freud's explanation of how we manage to give up certain behavior by laying it off on God or the gods was cited earlier. The function of kings, it seems, was to have people in the world who did not have to give up anything. This childlike power they wielded unfortunately brought death to others.

THE PROMETHEAN STRUGGLE

As long as the gods remain omnipotent, people will never fully grow up. The Hebrew God, almighty and morally infallible, though bargained with by Abraham and upbraided on occasion by Moses, ultimately proved unchallengeable. The Hebrews never wrote tragedy. The corruption of the Greek gods—liars, adulterers, thieves, and tyrants—gave space for humankind to claim a higher morality than that of the divinities. The tragic form carried that confrontation. The omnipotence of early kings gave them the capacity to challenge directly the omnipotent claims of the gods, and the history of complex societies is replete with stories of challenge by the king of the magical claims of divinities. Though from one point of view this was merely a struggle between opposite claims of omnipotence, from another, everyone, including the king, knew the truth: the monarch was only human. His triumph over the all-powerful, all-consuming claims of the gods represented a human triumph; he, at least, was allowed to grow up. That the only grownup in the society also indulged himself in tantrums, infantile and indulgent behavior, is an ambiguity that I cannot adequately explain. Many holders of power in the business, professional, and political worlds still exhibit this same contradictory pattern of dominance.

The great Shaka, who took Zulu society from chieftainship to empire in one generation, conducted a monumental struggle against the
practitioners of divining witchcraft. The specialty of the latter was the
"smelling out" of the perpetrators of theft or murder or revolt against
the king. Many times those smelled-out were perfectly innocent, but
the psychological power of the diviners was so great that no one
had the capacity to dispute their findings. Shaka, determined to break
their hold on the imagination of the culture, arranged one night for his
hut to remain unguarded and then he himself proceeded to spill blood
on the walls and surrounding ground of the house. Such an outrage
to the king's domicile had to be immediately avenged. A great meeting
of thirty thousand citizens was held where the 152 diviners of the land
proceeded to smell out those who had committed the sacrilege. Intoxicated with their power, some of the diviners reached high and indicated
that close associates of Shaka were implicated in the crime. A whole
day was consumed in the collection of those presumed guilty, but none
was executed immediately. When the diviners were through with their
roundup, the witch hunt was turned against the witches: Shaka revealed
the truth and pronounced that the diviners were useless and venal, that
they should be executed instead of their intended victims. One after-
noon's slaughter put an end to the whole tribe of false prophets.[33]

Mutesa of Buganda carried on a running quarrel with the gods and
their priests. In part, Mutesa's "enlightened" stance resulted from his
contact with and partial conversion to Islam, as well as his general impulse toward "modernization" in all its forms. The traditional stance
in Buganda, however, also allowed that if the *kabaka* was vexed by one
of the gods, he could loot his temple and surrounding estate.[34]

Buganda society produced many *mandwa,* or mediums, who
claimed to be possessed by the spirit of a dead *kabaka* or some other
high official. Mutesa, knowing that such possession was fakery, arranged with a young subordinate that, when one of them died and a
mandwa pretended to be possessed of his spirit, the surviving person
would ask an agreed-upon set of questions. When the medium failed
to answer, the whole institution would be discredited. Though Mutesa
never had the opportunity to use this particular stratagem, in 1869 he
nevertheless is said to have ordered the *mandwa* arrested and despoiled
of their property.[35]

A person with the power to overthrow the gods was an individual
in a way that no one had been an individual before. We know that such

power was most times not exercised in a benevolent fashion, but a monarch who possessed it was in a position to do what Durkheim said a chief could do: "produce new things and even . . . deny collective usages."[36] And there is no question that some of the new things this leadership could bring moved the society in the direction of more rationality and a heightened sense of morality. It is one of the ambiguities of social development that omnipotent human beings led society in a direction that ultimately lessened the importance of omnipotence.

CHARISMATIC KINGSHIP
TRANSFORMS CUSTOM

Nalinya was the *kabaka*'s sister-wife. Her name meant "I will climb." In the old days, it was an accepted notion that if a woman climbed on a house while it was being built, the house would not last very long. One day at court, previous to the reign of Mutesa, when this question was being discussed, the then *kabaka* decided to test the proposition, but the court women were afraid to climb the house. The queen sister, who carried the name *lubaga* at that time, volunteered, and the *kabaka* accepted her offer. Ten years passed and the house was still standing, so the *kabaka* called a council of his chiefs, pointed out the falseness of the tabu, and bestowed the name *nalinya* on his sister in appreciation of the bravery she had exhibited. Afterward, all queen sisters of the *kabaka* were called both *lubaga* and *nalinya*.[37]

The tremendous changes that Mutesa made in the value system of Buganda society became possible largely because of the *kabaka*'s contacts with Islamic and Christian cultures. How far Mutesa would have moved in the direction of modernization if the society had remained isolated is an open question. What does seem true, however, is that Mutesa was able to make such changes because he was an omnipotent ruler. In modern society, we are used to having charismatic leaders appear on the scene every so often; complex societies were impossible without the constant presence of one. A singular quality of the charismatic leader, as Max Weber has said, is the capacity to make fundamental changes in the value system of society. The break away from kinship-system society was obviously too difficult to be made by ordinary political process. Nothing short of an ideal of omnipotence could turn a million years of human history.

At the time of Speke's visit in 1862, Mutesa was already talking disparagingly of the traditional priests and their ceremonies. He had previously abolished the custom whereby the *kabaka* was required to take all his meals in absolute seclusion.[38] In 1869, he gave orders that the jawbones, heads, and skeletons of the dead *kabakas*—which traditionally were buried separately, be exhumed and reburied, with all the bones of each king together. He also gave instructions that when he died he was to be buried intact and no human sacrifice was to be offered.[39] Then he announced that no one was to claim that the spirit of a dead king had entered into him, or announce to Mutesa's sons that the king's spirit had entered his head.[40] Mutesa even went so far as to change the traditional patterns of inheritance. Normally, a brother or another relative of the same generation was chosen as heir to a deceased person; Mutesa decreed that only sons should inherit.[41]

In a world of children, anyone willing to be adult seems all-powerful. It is only in the past three hundred years, in which the democratic ideal has arisen, that more than a handful have had the right to become adult. Democracy, by claiming that many have that power, becomes antithetical to the existing concept of omnipotence. To live without omnipotence existing somewhere is full of risk and frightening. The "fear of freedom" that many have talked of really is a fear deep within everyone's psyche that existence is not possible without omnipotence, that the full democratic life that puts an end to the dream of absolute power is itself merely a dream.

At one time, human beings struggled to liberate themselves from the confines of the kinship system. They accomplished this only by ascribing omnipotent power to a few human beings, thereby erecting a new prison of political tyranny. More recently, we have begun the liberation from that garrison existence, only to find that the dream of omnipotence provides the greatest hindrance to our human aspirations. In this fateful striving, it is important to know the great adversary with which we are struggling.

28

Kingship: The Failure of Omnipotence

When the king of Bunyoro died, it was customary to maintain a period of interregnum anarchy, during which the most forceful sons of the late king fought one another until only one was alive or only one was undefeated and unchallenged. The survivor of this mad Darwinian process was then installed, with a complexity of rites, as the new king. At the final purification ritual, the chief minister, *bamuroga,* went to one of the young princes who had not fought and announced that the people had chosen him to be the new king. Whether the boy believed the minister or not, he had no choice but to be taken and set upon the throne. The real king, and all the high chiefs, entered into his presence, bringing gifts of cows, offering their congratulations, and pledging fealty to him. After everyone had performed his duties, *bamuroga* turned to the real king and demanded: " 'Where is your gift to me?' " The king answered arrogantly that he had already given his present to the proper person. *Bamuroga* pushed him by the shoulder and demanded, " 'Go and bring my present.' " The real monarch called to his followers and left the enclosure in a state of anger, whereupon *bamuroga,* turning to the mock king, cautioned, " 'Let us flee; your brother has gone to bring an army.' " He then took the boy to a room in back of the throne and strangled him. "This completed the death ceremonies and the subsequent purifications, and the new king could take his seat upon the throne and begin his reign."[1]

Similarly, after the death of the king in the state of Ankole, the royal brothers fought and killed one another in order to seize possession of *bagyendanwa,* the sacred drum, which carried the kingship as its prize. Before that struggle began, a mock battle occurred in the royal kraal between common herdsmen, the winner being chosen as mock king to rule until the end of the interregnum anarchy. When the new king had finally defeated or killed his brothers and taken possession of the sacred drum, he returned to the royal kraal with his mother and sister and killed the mock king before being inaugurated as monarch.[2]

The Banyoro were so enchanted by the idea of the mock king that they felt the need to repeat a similar ritual each year. One particular clan had to provide the candidate to impersonate the dead king—that is, the father of the reigning monarch. The belief was that the deceased monarch was reincarnated in this man for the week in which he "reigned" in the old king's temple. During this time he was given great honor, the wives of the deceased sovereign for his pleasure, and lavish gifts of slaves and cattle from the reigning monarch. At the end of this temporary paradise, *bamuroga* took the mock king to the back of the temple and strangled him.[3]

It is not easy to discover what unconscious conflict is being played out here. The institution of mock king was far from universal in complex societies. The only evidence I have discovered is from the two states mentioned above, but I suspect there are other instances; the yearly mock king in Bunyoro is remarkably close to the Aztec victim who impersonates a god for a year and is then ritually sacrificed. In both Bunyoro and Ankole, the institution of mock king was closely connected with the interregnum civil war of succession among the royal princes, a type of warfare not general within complex societies. There seems to have been a close connection between such royal struggles and the institution of mock king.

What both cultural forms seem to be announcing is that kingship is a very fragile thing, that there is a strong element of make-believe in it, that it can only survive if we forcibly destroy the doubts within ourselves as to its efficacy. Not only is the mock king a false king, but he also mocks kingship; his is a charade, a burlesque of a king. He has to be killed, because he sticks out his tongue at the pretensions to omnipotence. Announcing that the emperor, all emperors, have no clothes, he is killed for his truth telling.

The Ankolean mock king was called *ekyibumbe,* a word that had a multitude of usages. In common speech, it meant a stupid or foolish person, one who was on the receiving end of jokes and tricks. It was also used to designate a "small, toothless baby, who must be taken away from the kraal upon the death of its father."[4] The mock king becomes equated, then, with a small infant, left to the mercy of its mother, with no hope that it can look forward to the normal help of its father in the struggle against engulfment by the mother. The new king, having killed his brothers in the war of succession, kills the *ekyibumbe,* symbolically announcing: We men are not small, toothless, helpless infants; we are strong, powerful killers, omnipotent kings. Thereby they killed within themselves doubts of their own pretensions. So pervasive were these doubts, it seems, that, at least in Bunyoro, the rite had to be renewed yearly.

Omnipotence of the monarch was the ideal, but so fragile was the belief in it that credence could vanish in an instant. This was especially true when the king died. In such circumstances many complex societies acted as if order and the power to maintain it had been lost forever. Panic and anarchy prevailed.

The death of the king was like a huge gap opening up in the middle of the world, a disruption of order that seemingly could not be healed. People behaved as they might if the end of the world had come: they went into masochistic frenzy, or gave themselves over to total sexual abandon, or permitted themselves unlimited aggressive license, or set the sons of the king the task of killing one another in the hope that one of them would inherit the omnipotent power that would restore order.

Masochistic frenzy was the mode in Tonga:

As the funeral was to take place today, brother Bowell went with Ambler to Bunghye to see the ceremony, and found four thousand persons sitting round the place where the *fiatooka* stands. A few moments after our arrival we heard a great shouting and blowing of conch-shells at a small distance; soon after about an hundred men appeared, armed with clubs and spears, and rushing into the area, began to cut and mangle themselves in a most dreadful manner: many struck their heads violently with their clubs; and the blows, which might be heard thirty or forty yards off, they repeated till the blood ran down in streams. Others who had spears, thrust them through their thighs, arms, and cheeks, all the while calling on the deceased in a most affecting manner. A native of Feejee, who had been a servant of the deceased, appeared quite frantic; he entered the area with fire in his hand, and having previously oiled his hair, set it on fire, and ran about with it all on flame. . . . Four of the foremost held stones which they used to knock out their teeth; those who blew the shells cut their heads with them in a shocking manner. . . . Another [man], who seemed to be a principal chief, acted as if quite bereft of his senses; he ran to every corner of the area, and at each station beat his head with a club till the blood flowed down his shoulders.[5]

The Hawaiians, a sexually unrepressed people, added sexual anarchy to masochistic frenzy. Archibald Campbell tells us that at the death of Kamehameha I's brother, people cut off their hair, went about naked, knocked out their front teeth, and set hot stones and burning calabashes to their faces. "At the same time, a general, I believe I may say an universal, public prostitution of the women took place. The queens, and the widow of the deceased, alone exempted."[6] When Kamehameha himself died, in 1819, so great was the mourning that no one was excluded from the sexual license: "This day all the men and women even to the royal family went to commit fornication one with another."[7] And with the close connection between eating tabus and sexuality in Hawaii, we are not surprised to find that, at such a time, "forbidden foods are devoured without scruple, especially by women. . . ."[8]

The triumph of masochism over license was the mode in some African states. When the mother of Shaka Zulu died, the king's prime minister pronounced the decree of mourning: "As the great Female Elephant with the small breasts—the ever ruling-spirit of Vegetation—had died, and as it was probable that the heavens and the earth would unite in bewailing her death, the sacrifice would be a great one: no cultivation should be allowed during the following year; no milk should be used, but as drawn from the cow it should be poured upon the earth; and all women who should be found with child (thereafter) during the year should, with their husbands, be put to death."[9] The death of the king of Rwanda likewise brought a period of sexual abstinence; even the bulls and the cows, the rams and the sheep were separated from one another.[10] During the civil war of succession in Bunyoro, all cultivation of the fields ceased; no one was allowed to do any work except to cook food and to bring firewood. The peasants maintained emergency pits or wells, six to eight feet deep and filled with grain, in order to stay nourished during these periods of interregnum.

All of this gives a remarkable demonstration of Freud's concept that, in the unconscious, the thing and its opposite are identical, that one can accomplish the same psychic work either by expressing something to excess or by repressing it to an inordinate degree. One can mourn the king and deal with the panic caused by his death by practicing either sexual abstinence or sexual excess.

Much more prevalent than sexual anarchy was the unlimited aggressive license that accompanied the interregnum anarchy. Even in Buganda, which had no general interregnum civil war and had brought the form of peaceful, orderly succession to a high degree, there was a short period after the death of the king was announced when a "wild state of disorder ensued, anarchy reigned, people tried to rob each other, and only chiefs with a strong force were safe, even the smaller chiefs being in danger from stronger chiefs, who did as they liked during the short interregnum."[11] The quick inauguration of a new king put an end to this license. Of the Suku people, near the Congo in Africa, we have exactly the same report,[12] and in Ankole this kind of anarchy continued throughout the whole war for the throne. The Hawaiians, finding that the breaking of sexual and eating tabus was not enough, accompanied the death of the king or great chief with the same kind of lawless aggressive behavior.[13] On Maui, when the queen was thought to be close to death, people took their personal effects into the missionaries' enclosure, hoping they would be safe there during the ensuing riots.[14]

At least three things seem to be active in the psyche at such times, causing these orgies of sexual excess and aggressive license. First, the stern punisher of disorder, the omnipotent tyrant father, is gone, and therefore no one can punish the children when they go against convention and law. Second, there is an intense feeling of panic that the protector of life has vanished, the end of the world has arrived, that nothing matters anymore, and that the only psychic solution is to regress to a time before one cared about or knew of the world's demands and realities. And, third, there is an attempt to incorporate the dead monarch by identifying with him, by behaving as he behaved—with complete sexual and aggressive license. For the moment, everyone becomes a *kabaka* and claims the right to kill or fornicate where he will.

Needless to say, none of these defenses works, the only real solution being the restoration of the monarchy. Some complex societies seemed intent on making that restoration as difficult and drawn out as possible. The three societies that are the main subject of this work did not engage in institutionalized interregnum civil war, but from East Africa there is evidence of it in Rwanda,[15] Bunyoro,[16] and Ankole.[17] In Bunyoro and Ankole the struggle was intense and ended only when the victorious brother had succeeded in killing off his rivals—either in open battle or by poisoning or assassination—or by forcing them to flee into exile. It was an insane way of choosing the head of a state, but it seemed necessary for the rekindling of the sense of omnipotence. Only he who had killed his brothers in the worst kind of guerrilla warfare was worthy to lead the country. If we can find the place deep within ourselves that responds to this mode of thought, and that regards such a system as a logical way to chose a king, we will understand better why our political life has brought us so much grief.

THE ROUTINIZATION OF OMNIPOTENCE

A society based wholly, or primarily, on the omnipotent power of the ruler is inherently unstable. Very few people in the world have the capacity to become a Mutesa or a Kamehameha. More often than not, no matter in what manner they are chosen, the successors of great charismatic kings are merely ordinary mortals. Far more important, a heightened state of charismatic omnipotence cannot be sustained. As omnipotence becomes routinized, as charisma becomes bureaucratized, more and more people feel they are entitled to partake of kingly power. Starting with the relatives of the king—his brothers, who had the same charismatic father; his uncles, who were the brothers of omnipotence; and his sons, who take on at birth his divine nature—and then extending to ordinary powerful nobles, usually the provincial governors, the king is challenged in his claims to be the sole representative of omnipotence. When we are young, we are taught that the history of the world consists primarily of events like the American Revolution, Napoleon's invasion of Russia, or the conquests of Alexander the Great: great charismatic moments. The sad truth is that most of what has gone on in the world has been a struggle between various factions of the aristocracy to see which of them would possess political power. The emperors of medieval Germany against the nobles of Saxony; the house of York versus the house of Lancaster; the czars and the boyars—all of these demonstrate how lacking in omnipotence monarchs really were. When the ideal of an omnipotent ruler became routinized, human society was left with the rule of political bosses—a rather paltry substitute. This was already the case in advanced complex societies.

The long-range instability of early monarchies indicates that advanced complex societies were essentially a transitional phenomenon, although there is not enough evidence to demonstrate it. It seems that when states had developed to the point that had been reached by Buganda, or even Hawaii, if left to themselves they either had to take another great leap forward into archaic civilization, or regress to chieftainships and simple monarchies; that somehow they could not stay as they were. We have no data that illustrate the transition from advanced complex to archaic societies. None of the great complex societies "discovered" in the eighteenth and nineteenth centuries were left to develop on their own, and the evidence concerning the beginnings of the archaic civilizations of Egypt, Mesopotamia, and China is archaeological, not historical. There is, therefore, no means available to test this hypothesis. We know that certain forms of society—primitive cultures, archaic civilizations, "Oriental monarchies"—could maintain themselves with essentially the same culture for thousands of years. My sense is that this was not possible for advanced complex societies: first, because the democratization (more accurately, aristocratization) of omnipotence undermined the authority of the kingship; second, because the kind of energy, the need for progress and change, and the capabilities that developed in these societies were explosive, making cultural revolution imminent.

The trouble for omnipotence begins where all troubles begin—in the family. The king does not live forever, and more than one of his sons feels entitled to take his omnipotent place. Polygamy enormously increases the number of possible contenders. Speke had been keen enough to observe that the competition between princes was "an endemic cause of instability and disorder throughout the area."[18] In southern Africa, Zulu folk wisdom declared that the monarch ruled with the aid of his brothers and uncles but also hated them because they coveted the throne.[19]

This typical competition of family members for the legacy of omnipotence can be illustrated by the constant rebellions in the small kingdoms of Busoga. Here the king would appoint one or several of his sons to be governors of provinces. Such a prince-governor, finding one of his brothers elected to the kingship after his father died, not only had his resentment to nurse but also possessed a power base in the province. Rebellion was almost inevitable. Sometimes the new sovereign succeeded in putting down the revolt and restoring the centralized state; with equal chance, the rebellious prince was successful in maintaining his independence, thereby fragmenting the polity. As we have seen in other societies, one solution to this inevitable conflict was the appointment of commoners to crucial subordinate posts, since the notion of royalty remained sacred enough to keep them from monarchical pretensions.[20] It undoubtedly helped the stability of the Buganda state that royal princes were never appointed to important political posts.

The history of the Zulu Empire presents us with fratricidal strife of a degree appropriate to a Jacobean tragedy. The great Shaka himself was stabbed to death by his half-brothers Dingane and Mhlangana. Not long after that, Dingane had Mhlangana assassinated, becoming sole ruler. Afraid for his own position, Dingane proceeded to "set about a systematic extermination of all that remained of his family and relatives, all his friends and former comrades, the great ones of the nation."[21] A few he let live, including an insignificant youth, Mpande, his half-brother. As Dingane's tyrannical mode intensified, Mpande's popularity increased to the point where, fearing for his life, he fled to neighboring Natal. Soon after, he returned with several thousand followers, reinforced by a group of Boers. Dingane was defeated in battle and fled to Swaziland, where he was killed by the local inhabitants. Three years after Mpande assumed the throne, he executed the last surviving brother of his generation. Fratricidal activity now shifted to the younger generation. Mpande's eldest son and the son of his favorite wife became bitter enemies. Since each was a formidable chief in his own right and commanded many followers, a great battle ensued. The eldest son triumphed in the struggle, killing his rival along with five other brothers, and succeeded to the throne on Mpande's death.[22]

This kind of history no longer reads like the heroic tale of omnipotent kings but like the paltry rivalry of aristocratic gangsters killing one another for the spoils. Once it had been demonstrated that a certain kind of psychological and political power was possible, once the great breakthrough had been made, once the constrictions the kinship system exercised on individual assertion had been smashed, then it became possible for a certain kind of human trash—those whose only "virtue" was a potent will-to-power—to become the leaders of society. In the Guatemalas and Chiles of the world, we still have not gone beyond that possibility.

Those societies, including Buganda, that did not provide for interregnum warfare were left with the problem of the new king's brothers. A drastic solution was to have them killed after the new sovereign took office. The Venda of southern Africa tried a compromise, killing at birth all the king's sons except the first three, "lest they be too many and cause strife about the chieftainship."[23] In Buganda, the killing of all the king's half-brothers except for one or two was a recent innovation. It seems clear that by the time of Mutesa's father, the practice was fully established.[24] Roscoe says that, in Mutesa's case, his mother made sure that the other princes were put to death.[25] The evidence is not complete, but indications are that one or two princes were spared in case they were needed to fill the kingly office. It is not clear why the practice started in Buganda. Possibly it was because in the past there had been interregnum civil war,[26] or because, as the omnipotence of kingship became routinized, the half-brothers felt free to challenge the chosen one's right to rule. In any event, the life of a royal prince in Buganda was precarious.

Closely related to fratricidal conflict is Oedipal strife between kings and their sons. As the separation and individuation process continued during the development of complex societies, as the primarily pre-Oedipal nature of kinship-system politics gave way to Oedipal concerns, violent conflicts between kings and princes became primary matter for the political process. And, as in the story of the ill-fated Oedipus, the fathers were often the original aggressors. Fearing Oedipal attack, they struck first. Both Shaka Zulu and his murderer and successor, Dingane, killed all their sons at birth to forestall the possibility of being ousted by them when they grew up. A Natal Nguni king, in the same area as the Zulu, put all but two of his sons to death, "lest perchance, they should . . . murder him."[27] The Buganda kings had a special sacrificial place called Benga to which a large number of royal princes were taken whenever the *kabaka* was warned by the gods that some of his sons were planning rebellion.[28] At times, undoubtedly, a conspiracy *was* being planned.

Those sons who were allowed to survive were equally willing to attack their fathers. In the country of Buhaya, south of Buganda, princes who had been appointed to rule over small villages proceeded to secede from the central state. This process kept the politics in continuous turmoil, and the "legends of Buhaya are full of tales of rebellious sons, avenging fathers, and fratricidal strife ending in the splitting of kingdoms."[29]

Sometimes the rebellion of a prince ended in a new, permanent arrangement. By the middle of the nineteenth century, the country of Toro was an important small neighboring kingdom of Buganda. It had not been established until 1830, when Kaboyo, son of the king of Bunyoro, revolted against his father, fled with a group of followers and many of the royal cattle, and established himself in Toro, at that time a province of Bunyoro. The father sent the expected expedition, but Kaboyo was able to defeat the forces sent to assassinate him. Beset by other rebels in his territory and by incursions by Buganda forces, the father sent Kaboyo a royal drum and other insignia as a symbol of reconciliation. Kaboyo "continued to send presents to his father until the latter's death and refused to be greeted with the royal salute until that time."[30] Toro remained as an independent state until Europeans conquered the whole area.

Once it was established that kingship was, in Aristotle's phrase, one of the goods that could be fought over; once, that is, the sacred, charismatic, omnipotent aspect of monarchy had become contaminated by raw power struggles among the royal family, then it was inevitable that any psychologically powerful aristocrat would feel free to challenge kingly authority. Eventually the governors under a king gave him more trouble and posed a greater threat to the stability of the state than did the royal princes. Princes, as in Buganda, could be kept out of political office, but no state could function without governors. Many governors, patterning themselves on the king, put on grand airs. Vancouver describes the entrance of a Hawaiian provincial governor, Tamaahmotoo, into a bay with "great pomp, attended by a numerous fleet of large canoes that could not contain less than a thousand persons, all paddling with some order." Kamehameha, who was with Vancouver at the time, described Tamaahmotoo as "the proudest man in the whole island."[31] Pomp was one thing, but chances were that such pride could only lead to confrontation with the king.

Kamehameha himself had begun his meteoric political career as a rebellious chief against the king on his native island of Hawaii,[32] and when he died, his son Liholiho was confronted with serious opposition from the subordinates of his father. One of these set about a conspiracy that would overthrow the royal power and massacre all the Europeans living in the islands.[33] This plot was unsuccessful, but Liholiho held his throne only by allowing the high-placed politicos to retain possession of land they had been granted by Kamehameha. Under traditional Hawaiian usage, all such land reverted to the new king when he assumed office, but it is unlikely that Liholiho could have retained the monarchy had he refused to compromise.[34]

Similarly, in Buganda, the reign of a great charismatic king—Mutesa in this case—had resulted not in the oppression of provincial governors, but in its exact opposite: the elevation of these subordinates to such a high level of psychological and political power that they felt themselves equal to the king. John Rowe explains why Mutesa, and then Mwanga, were not free to do whatever they willed in regard to the new religions:

To begin with, the two kings—even if they had wished to do so—were not in a position to grant the missionary demands. Both the declining Mutesa and, after 1884, the youthful and inexperienced Mwanga, had to take account of other powerful forces at court who saw the missionaries . . . as dangerous rivals. The senior chiefs were consciously wielding considerable new powers, acting as virtual lords over their estates almost unchecked by rival authority. They traded privately with Zanzibari "Arabs" and amassed personal wealth and armaments in a way that would have been unthinkable a decade earlier. . . .[35]

It was enormously difficult for the king in a complex society to control these miniature monarchs, especially when any distance separated them. In many cases, if the provincial governor was far enough away from the court, he just ignored the royal imperatives and ceased sending the regular tribute.[36] It became the practice in most advanced complex societies for the king to insist that the provincial governors spend most of their time at the royal court. Kamehameha "often summoned the chiefs to come and live with him, and he discouraged their living far away in the back country where they might gather men about them and some day take it into their heads to conspire against his rule. When he saw any chief collecting a number of retainers about him, he would summon the chief to him at Kawaihe or some such place; when the provisions ran short the hangers-on had to go back to the country, but the chief was always well provided. . . ."[37] Cook observed the same mechanism at work on Tonga, where, he says, the inclination to revolt was defused by having all the major governors reside at Tongatapu.[38] Likewise, in Buganda, the governors were required to spend most of their days at the royal court, absenting themselves only when it was necessary to conduct the affairs of their provinces—and doing so then only with the *kabaka*'s permission.[39]

What is crucially important here is that these provincial governors were not so overawed by the charismatic, omnipotent, divine nature of the monarchy that they were incapable of challenging it. They felt *entitled* to confront royal power and to incorporate all the attributes of that power into themselves. Omnipotence was no longer the exclusive prerogative of the sovereign. In becoming available to others, however, the mana of the kings degenerated. It was no longer what it had been; no more was the challenging of a king met with a supernatural lightning bolt; no longer was the monarch so sacred that his very disapproval could kill. In making themselves almost equal to him, the governors not only elevated themselves but also brought the king low. The king is dead; long live the aristocratic political boss.

This was, of course, *not* a sequential historical process. There was no age of omnipotent kings followed by an age of degraded sovereigns and powerful aristocratic governors. Both forms of leadership existed simultaneously. All-powerful monarchs were always being challenged by their brothers, their sons, and their governors. Two kinds of psychological and political power were being created at the same time: one, the sacred, divine, charismatic, omnipotent power of the king; the other, the raw power of the political boss. And for raw political power, the consent of the governed was no longer necessary. Common people fought and died in the battles of aristocratic struggles for power whether they assented or not. Common people were oppressed by nobles whether they admired and identified with them or not.

The charismatic king, despite his great indulgence in both sexual and aggressive tyranny, somehow still represented a moral, progressive force. His was the power that smashed the kinship system; he was the heroic figure who made everyone feel magically powerful. He had the vision to create large political entities with universal, not local, loyalties. It was he who could create the sense of nationhood that replaced the more limited sense of kinship.

The provincial political boss, on the contrary, was obeyed primarily through fear. His scope was narrow; his vision parochial; his interests self-serving. His time on this earth, unlike that of charismatic kings, is enduring. He still lords it over Central American states and international corporations, and still rules the bureaucratic socialism of the Soviet Union.

In reality, no one particular political ruler was all king or all boss: every actual lord was a combination of the two. Terror can never be the only form of social cohesion; any society that endures must elicit some consent from some of the governed. Such was the case in advanced complex societies and such is the case today.

What was, and remains, true of both the charismatic-omnipotent and the raw-political modes of power is that most people did not feel entitled to partake of either form. What set the aristocracy apart from common people was the assumption that they had the capacity to challenge the king and grab a piece of power for themselves. Common people were too closely tied to the bonds of the kinship system to liberate themselves and assume nonkinship forms of power. As such, they remained in a childlike position vis-à-vis those who held office. And the fear of adult responsibility still plagues our own democratic polity. Most people, and especially those of deprived economic standing, still do not feel that they are entitled to control their own lives. Political power is something that others possess. Childlike, they don't vote, and passively accept what comes.

Kingship, aristocracy, and a bureaucratic upper class (as existed in Buganda) were the fundamental political achievements of complex society. So enduring and so exclusive were these forms of rule that it was not until the eleventh and twelfth centuries in Europe that a new class of people appeared who felt entitled to take power, trained themselves to do so, and accomplished the fact. The bishops of the Church, including the bishop of Rome, and the new classes within the cities represented the first real challenge to monarchical and aristocratic power. It is to their success that we owe democratic society.

Advanced complex society, it seems, was a great transitional form of politics. Its central political form—the kingship that had smashed and transformed the kinship system—could not by itself solve its great political problems. Something more was needed before a truly stable society could be erected. The archaic civilizations of Egypt, Mesopotamia, and China maintained themselves—with vicissitudes but without fundamental changes—for thousands of years. Although the reasons why that should have been so are beyond the scope of this book, it would seem that the ideal of kingly benevolence, a deep longing for stability and order, and the beginnings of the rule of law clearly had something to do with it. It was necessary to move to a higher level of abstraction, to move from the particular person to the general quality—not this king and that king, but kingship; not this governor and that governor, but government; not this dictum and that dictum, but law. And this was a developmental step that advanced complex societies, in their characteristic mode, were incapable of taking. From complex societies, however, archaic civilizations were born—proof that they had done the work they were meant to do.

VI

RMS

PSYCHE AND SOCIETY

29

Toward a Theory of Social and Cultural Development

An assumption common to most psychoanalytic and psychological sociology, as well as to much social psychology, is that there is an intimate and crucial relationship between the psyche and society. The most insightful of these various theoretical approaches recognizes that the psyche and society are *mutually interdependent,* that we cannot understand one without comprehending the other, that each is the cause of the other. The psyche, though rooted in our animal biological nature, is not the given, with all social forms being variables. The human species has a symbol-making capacity and a symbol-making drive, and the symbols it creates take root in social forms. To understand the psyche without understanding the symbols it uses to do its work is a vain pursuit. Not to see that society carries, and modifies, the symbolic system that the psyche draws from is a form of psychological reductionism that does not bring insight. Between the self and society there is constant interplay, constant alternation of giving and receiving, constant modification resulting from the recognition of their mutual needs.

This two-way interdependence between society and the self, however, does not seem to me adequate to reveal the complex mechanism of social and cultural development. As a model, it seems to me incapable of explaining exactly how changes in society are communicated to the psyche, or how the developmental drive in the psyche is ultimately made manifest in social forms. The connecting links are missing.

The possibilities of theoretical insight become enormously enlarged if the family is added to this self-society dyad, especially if the child-rearing aspects of the family are emphasized. In the triad of family-self-society, there are six fundamental influences at work: the family and the self react on each other, as do the family and society, and as do society and the psyche:

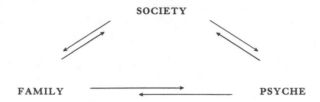

SOCIETY

FAMILY   PSYCHE

At least theoretically, if not actually, we can use this new model to begin to see how certain connections in a developmental system are made. If a society, for whatever reason, begins to break down the kinship system, it may decree that small children are to be sent away from home for three to five years. Parents, who would not on their own conceive or approve of such a form, now find themselves ejecting their small children from the house, because it is the custom, or everybody does it, or it is "good for the child." A child raised in such a situation has a different set of psychological parameters from a child raised in a kinship-system environment. He is a different kind of person, prepared for a different kind of citizenship in a different kind of society. As an adult, he sends his children away from home not only for the reasons enumerated above; he also does it because it was done to him. By introducing the child-rearing aspects of the family, we are able to see more clearly how changes in the value system of the culture produce changes in the psyche of the developing child.

　　None of this in itself explains where the initial impulses to change child-rearing practices come from. They may or may not originate in society. They may have their origin in the interaction of the family and the self, and then become established as a social form. Such questions of origins are enormously difficult to answer. What seems true, however, is that *all* impulse to change arises in either the psyche, the family, or society, or in the reactions of these three to the needs and realities of the others. I do not think that the theoretical approach from any particular corner of this fundamental triad is necessarily more valuable than that from the other two. The great questions about the nature of social development will ultimately be answered within the confines of this triadic structure, and the neglect of any one aspect—society, psyche, or family—must result in only partial solutions.

　　Though one may legitimately begin anywhere within this theoretical structure, I will begin with what interests me most: the role of the psyche in the creation and modification of social and cultural forms. Fundamental to such an approach is a theory of the psyche, a psychology; in my case, a psychoanalytic psychology. The theoretical structure left us by Freud, however, is grossly inadequate to our task. First, within Freud's theory of the psyche itself there are huge gaps—among others, the whole question of the pre-Oedipal development of the ego, the relationship of sexual and aggressive drives, the theory of narcissism, the psychology of women, the question of moral drives, and the implications for human history of the fact that all infant children, boys and girls, are nurtured almost exclusively by women. Second, in regard to the influence of the psyche on society, Freud's contribution is severely limited and exists only on the very highest level of generalization. His great gift to us in this regard was his insistence that such connection must be, and can be, looked at, his own perception being that there was no more important question in the world. To use in this endeavor to understand society only the work of Freud himself is to limit the discussion to the rather meager results that have accrued to us in the seventy years since the writing of *Totem and Taboo*.

A theory of society and social development adequate to our needs today must go beyond Freud's work. The insights of some of his followers can be applied to an understanding of society. I have found the work of Anna Freud and, most particularly, Margaret Mahler enormously useful in explaining the workings and tensions of complex societies.

HUMAN SACRIFICE AS A MECHANISM OF DEFENSE

Anna Freud's *The Ego and the Mechanisms of Defense* placed emphasis not on the theory of drives or development but upon certain given *mechanisms* in the psyche. Freud had already talked about certain psychic mechanisms, of which "the compulsion to repeat" is an example. This compulsion is independent of the drives of libido and aggression; it is unaffected by good nurturing or bad nurturing. If a child is nurtured well, it has a compulsion, when adult, to repeat that experience with its own child. The same thing happens with inadequate or poor nurturing. A psychic mechanism is a given of the psyche; there is no asking "why" it is there, though the question how it works is important. In regard to such mechanisms, the first theoretical task is purely empirical: to find and define them. Anna Freud did exactly that in regard to psychic defense mechanisms. Using her results, along with an understanding of other mechanisms in the psyche, we can come quite close to comprehending what function human sacrifice has served in political life. Ritual homicide could not exist if it did not satisfy some human needs. It would be helpful to know what those needs were—and are.

Anna Freud discusses at length the mechanism she designates "identification with the aggressor."[1] The ego, when faced with attack by someone in the world, attempts to defend itself against annihilation by identifying with the attacker. Instead of being an entity about to be destroyed, it becomes the destroyer. Certain phenomena, observed by many, of people in concentration-camp situations who take over the role of their executioners are explained by this psychic mechanism. Even in normal circumstances, it has enormous importance for all of us. Identifying with the aggressor is one fundamental way that children have to defend themselves against the aggression parents direct at them. Since the normal drives to identify with the parents are powerful, they combine with aggressor identification to incorporate the negative aspects of the parents within the self. Such incorporations play a profound role in the lives of most people.

Identifying with the aggressor can produce a healthy, assertive response to real-world dangers. It is of interest to consider how many people choose their life's work as a means of trying to deal with something they are afraid of, something that has threatened them.[2] In the story that follows, Ben is a young boy who had been to the hospital to have an operation, and Joe is his little brother.

When Ben came home from the hospital the following day, Joe could hardly contain himself: "Did the operation hurt? Were you scared?" Then he quickly added he did not want to see Ben's scar. Later that day he gathered an assortment of "operation tools" consisting of some paper, scotch tape, an empty medicine bottle, a needle, some thread, and a nail file which he placed in "Ben's hospital suitcase." Then he quickly donned his bathrobe, announced that he was a doctor, and sat inside the suitcase, which he said was his "hospital." . . .

For the next few days Joe played in his "hospital" as a surgeon operating on his "patients." . . . Occasionally, when he was bored with using toy animals, he recruited new patients from some of his more easily recruited playmates. After the third day of this activity, Joe mustered enough courage and asked to see Ben's scar . . . which by that time was no more than a 1 1/2 inch white line. Joe commented later that he thought the scar was "big" and "ugly." The next day brought a feverish return to full-time vigorous surgery on all the toy animals. . . .

By evening he entreated his family to call him "Dr. Joe" because of his decision to become a pediatric surgeon. He thought he might even study under the same surgeon who had operated on Ben so that he could become the "boss" of the whole hospital, because then he, Joe, could decide who was to become the "patient" and he could demand that all incisions be properly sewn together so that they would not "break open again."[3]

Most results of aggressor identification are not so delightful. There is an elaboration of the mechanism, not discussed by Anna Freud, which may be called "identification with the aggressor by making someone else the victim." Jay was a child with psychological difficulties, including fears that he would get his hands or himself caught in certain cracks. When Jay pointedly informed his therapist that his block buildings were rather tippy, the therapist responded by pointing out to Jay that maybe he felt himself to be lacking in strength, that he, too, was a little tippy. This interchange unleashed a spate of aggressive actions in Jay; he caught two persons' hands in the cracks of doors and attempted to pinion a child's head between two tables. "I interpreted that Jay was trying to make himself feel better by being in charge of this new trouble of frightening cracks, making other people afraid of cracks."[4]

Jay was subsequently menaced by a real-world danger and responded in a characteristic manner:

We soon learned one reason for Jay's newly heightened anxiety. He was threatened by a tonsillectomy because of tonsillar and associated middle-ear infection. His mother was determined to proceed with the operation, and announced the plan in the classroom, although the entire matter was news to the staff. Jay then wildly wielded a knife which had been used for cutting a face from a Halloween pumpkin. I interpreted to him that he was once more turning his own fear around by making other people afraid. The surgeon scaring Jay was now Jay frightening us with a knife.[5]

One cannot exaggerate the importance of this sort of aggressor identification for political life. All the great human sacrifices, witch hunts, persecutions, holocausts replicate Jay's surgical knife. If all human societies, up until today, have persevered in the necessity of having victims, it can only be that those who control societies are so deeply frightened that they can only feel better by seeing that others are brought down. From the horrors of Auschwitz to the sophisticated cruelty of cutting welfare payments, the same mechanism is at work though at different intensities of disorder: Someone must suffer or die so that I can breathe again. The *kabaka* of Buganda would have understood.

There is another mechanism available to the psyche, the comprehension of which will help our understanding of the "need" for human sacrifice in complex society. It may be called "beating on someone in order to combat the repressed within oneself." There is the cliché situation of the policeman who entraps and brutalizes homosexuals as a way of beating down his own homosexual inclinations. Most of the hostility of "straight" people and "straight" society against homosexuality is of this order. Homosexuality, from such a point of view, is a weakness that must be repressed at all costs. It is the fear of impotence among the "strong" that causes society to trample on those who are defenseless. "Teddy's reactions to another child's crying . . . were interesting to observe. He just could not bear to hear another child cry. This seemed somehow to stimulate his aggressive defensiveness; unprovoked, he would attack other children."[6] Much political action, especially in this period of cold war, proceeds from the part of the psyche that believes that offense is the best defense. From this point of view, much of human society has been a paranoid's paradise.

If one is an aristocrat living in a society whose highest members are in the process of liberating themselves from the kinship system, and if this liberation, as it must, produces a profound separation anxiety in each individual as well as in the aristocratic collectivity, inwardly an intense ambivalence about whether to make such advance will manifest itself. A part of the psyche of these new leaders of society will be anxious to plunge headlong back into the cozy ambience of kinship solidarity. The other part of the psyche will insist on marching forward into the sunrise of individualism and the state, and will hurl the usual invectives against the impulses of regression within the self: Impotent coward! Child! Woman! One solution to this sometimes unbearable anxiety and ambivalence is to catch a poor, weak peasant on the highway—a man who has not even begun to liberate himself from kinship attachments, a man who stands for all the cowardly, childish, womanish longings within oneself—and to cut his throat as an offering for the gods. Not only does one kill, thereby, the regressive passions within oneself; one also kills a representative of those—the kinship family—who are intent (so it seems) on drawing one back. Such an act of ritual homicide, which can accomplish so much, is irresistible.

The mechanism of identification with the aggressor by making someone else the victim is dependent upon a deeper psychic mechanism: the concept that, in certain situations of stress, one thing can substitute for another. The psyche assents to the idea that one person can die for another:

One of my most distant memories relates to my mother. She was very ill and had been in bed several weeks and a servant had told me she would die in a few days. I must have been about 4 or 5 years old. My most treasured possession was a little brown wooden horse, covered with "real hair." . . . A curious thought came into my head: I must give up my horse in order to make my mother better. It was more than I could do at once and cost me the greatest pain. I started by throwing the saddle and bridle into the fire, thinking that "when it's very ugly, I shall be able to keep it." I can't remember exactly what happened. But I know that in the general distress I ended up by smashing my horse to bits, and that on seeing my mother up, a few days later, I was convinced that it was my sacrifice that had mysteriously cured her and this conviction lasted for a long while.[7]

The hidden compulsion in the child was to kill itself so that the mother might live, revealing another mechanism of the psyche, which dictates, especially in matters of sacrifice, that a thing of lesser importance may be substituted for something much more valuable. Fingers may be sacrificed instead of the whole person, the horse was the *second* most-precious thing the child could have offered to the gods of fate. Though this is a moving story of voluntary self-sacrifice, the underlying psychic mechanism—that one person can die in place of another—can easily serve the tyrannical purposes of frightened persons who hold political power.

These various mechanisms of the psyche can tell us why sacrifice of others comes so easily to human society, but in themselves they cannot answer the question of why ritual homicide was a characteristic form of aggression in advanced complex societies and disappeared when that stage of society ceased. Related to this is the mystery of why, the road being so difficult, any society would set out on the journey away from the kinship system in the first place. We cannot answer these questions until we confront the formidable need for separation and individuation, and we cannot do that without regarding the work of Margaret Mahler.

SEPARATION AND INDIVIDUATION

There is no psychoanalytic work after Freud, in my view, that is as helpful as Mahler's in understanding the nature of human society, especially in developmental perspective. She herself has never made the connection between individual developmental patterns and society as a whole, but it is not difficult to do so on the basis of her work.

Mahler's intent is to describe the development of the sense of self in the psyche. Her notion of the "sense of self" is broader than Freud's idea of the ego, which Freud defines as that which is not libido or aggressive drive or the superego (conscience). Mahler's sense of self includes, for example, libidinal drives.

The sense of self, according to Mahler, goes through three fundamental stages in the first thirty months of the child's life: autism (birth to four weeks), symbiosis (one to six months), and separation and individuation (six to thirty months). A lack of differentiation characterizes the beginning of the autistic stage. Psychologically, the child does not know the difference between itself and its mother, its mouth and the breast, its clothing and its skin, its impulses and others' ministrations. Such differentiations are slowly learned during the autistic stage so that, when the child reaches the stage of symbiosis, it has an awareness of the difference between itself and the mother. In the symbiotic stage, however, it cannot conceive of existence apart from the mother. The child exists and the mother exists, but neither, in the child's view, can maintain life without the other.

During the third stage, the child does not become independent of the mother, but it does separate from her, and thereby individuates itself. It learns, essentially, that its existence is a separate thing from the mother's existence, that both child and mother are separate persons. Such, at least, is the ideal developmental pattern. Needless to say, for most people the central question is how close they come to the ideal achievement as they traverse this rather treacherous course.

In each of the three stages—autism, symbiosis, separation and individuation—there can be a relatively normal or a relatively pathological resolution of the problems the stage presents. Severe dislocation of the developmental process in the autistic phase produces what Mahler calls "autistic psychosis." In the symbiotic stage such dislocation produces "symbiotic psychosis." Disruptions in the separation-individuation stage, for the child who has more or less successfully managed the two previous phases, produce neurosis of greater or lesser intensity, depending upon the severity of the dislocations.

Understanding the separation-individuation phase in all its complexity can be of enormous help in comprehending certain problems of social development, especially those raised by the existence of complex societies. The first thing to be observed is that the stage itself is of tremendous length, occupying twenty-four of the first thirty months of a child's life. Clearly, many crucial problems are dealt with during this time.

Though the response of the parents to the child's thrust for separation is of great significance, the parents do not initiate the process. The child—every child—without being educated to the task, embarks on this great journey. Whether it is called an instinct, a drive, a need, or a universal human inclination, what is important is that separation and individuation are necessary to a healthy human condition and can be denied the child only at the cost of psychotic disorder. Since the understanding of social development is the ultimate aim of this discussion, it is worth pointing out that no society—primitive, complex, or more advanced—no people as a whole, has been fixed in the symbiotic stage. Some experience of separation-individuation is germane to all cultures.

As universal as the child's move toward separation-individuation is, however, the response of the society and of the parents, particularly the mother, to this impulse is crucially important. The child may be encouraged, or discouraged, or encouraged and discouraged, or encouraged up to a point and then violently discouraged, or discouraged at first and then forced to take certain steps. Any combination of human responses is imaginable and possible. The stage of society, as well as the particular society, make a significant difference to the pattern of the response. To use only one example, in a society where all children are nursed for four years, a child will spend the whole of the separation-individuation stage nursing and will have a profoundly different experience from that of a child in a society prescribing that he be weaned at six to twelve months.

Within the boundaries of behavior set by society, there is always room for personal option in response to the child's quest. "On the other hand, as we learned rather late in our study, the emotional growth of the mother in her parenthood, her emotional willingness to let go of the toddler—to give him, as the mother bird does, a gentle push, an encouragement toward independence—is enormously helpful. It may even be a *sine qua non* of normal (healthy) individuation."[8]

The fundamental dynamic of the whole separation-individuation process from the child's point of view is ambivalence. On the one hand, the biopsychological process is pushing the child to separate and to take pleasure in its individuation; but on the other hand, that separation produces intense anxiety. The child does not fully conceive that it can make it on its own. Without its mother, it feels, it is bound to crash. Yet refusal to proceed is not a real option. There is no solution until the whole process is over. From a larger point of view, of course, the process is never over. We carry the drive, the anxiety, and the ambivalence with us our whole lives. For the thirty-month-old child, however, a certain fundamental if temporary resolution of intense separation anxiety is possible.

Mahler proceeds to describe the separation-individuation stage in detail, breaking it down into four substages: differentiation (six to ten months); practicing (ten to eighteen months); rapprochement crisis (eighteen to twenty-one months); and consolidation of individuality (twenty-two to thirty months).

In the differentiation substage, certain motor actions, facial expressions, communicating sounds, and capacities to respond to particular play activities give indication that the child is beginning to regard itself as separate from the mother. These capacities for individuated action come to full flowering in the practicing substage:

During these precious 6 to 8 months (from the age of 10 or 12 months to 16 or 18 months), the world is the junior toddler's oyster. Libidinal cathexis shifts substantially into the service of the rapidly growing autonomous ego and its functions, and the child seems intoxicated with his own faculties and with the greatness of his world. Narcissism is at its peak! The child's first upright independent steps mark the onset of the practicing period par excellence, with substantial widening of his world and of reality testing. . . . The chief characteristic of this practicing period is the child's great narcissistic investment in his own functions, his own body, as well as in the objects and objectives of his expanding "reality." . . . Substitute familiar adults within the setup of our nursery are easily accepted (in contrast to what occurs during the next subphase of separation-individuation).

. . . exhilarated by his own abilities, continually delighted with the discoveries he makes of his expanding world, and quasi-enamored with the world and his own grandeur and omnipotence. We might consider the possibility that the elation of this subphase has to do not only with the exercise of the ego apparatuses, but also with the elated escape from fusion with, from engulfment by, mother.[9]

Mahler quotes Phyllis Greenacre, who described the child in this stage as having a "love affair with the world,"[10] a remark that immediately brings to mind the exhilarating, life-enhancing, adventuresome, open-ended human activities of complex societies. It seems likely, in fact, that all times of particular exhilaration—either in the personal life of one individual or in the larger area of cultural life (such as fifth-century-B.C. Athens or Elizabethan England)—hark back to this very first period of intense pleasurable exploration of the world.

The child's capacity to walk without help takes on enormous significance: "Walking seems to have great symbolic meaning for both mother and toddler: it is as if the walking toddler has proved by his attainment of independent upright locomotion that he has already graduated into the world of independent human beings."[11] It is of interest to note that, in both Hawaii and Buganda, royalty had a particular, unique way of walking, a sort of prideful showing off, as if to call intense attention to the fact that the monarch was walking. Such a performance seems to recollect the child's demonstration to its mother of its new motor capacities.

After this intense period of exhilarating individuation, the child has its first experience with fate, with *moira,* the first punishment for its hubris, the first tragic recognition that life is not going to be one round of exhilarating adventure after another. The child begins to question whether the whole process of separation is a good thing or not: "Increased separation anxiety can be observed: at first this consists mainly of fear of object loss, which is to be inferred from many of the child's behaviors. The relative lack of concern about the mother's presence that was characteristic of the practicing subphase is now replaced by seemingly constant concern with the mother's whereabouts, as well as by active approach behavior. As the toddler's *awareness* of separation grows—stimulated by his maturationally acquired ability to move away physically from his mother and by his cognitive growth—he seems to have an increased need, a wish for mother to share with him every one of his new skills and experiences, as well as a great need for the object's love."[12] The child is now face to face with one of the great ambiguities of human existence: separation, which is a necessary and life-enhancing experience, results in an intensity of separation anxiety.

The child is now squarely in the middle of the third substage, which

Mahler unfortunately calls the rapprochement stage, though at times she refers to it more accurately as "the rapprochement crisis." It is the critical pivot of the whole separation-individuation process, critical because it also offers the possibilities of regression, of *undoing* what has been accomplished:

In this third subphase, that of rapprochement, while individuation proceeds very rapidly and the child exercises it to the limit, he also becomes more and more aware of his separateness and employs all kinds of mechanisms in order to resist and undo his actual separateness from mother. . . . The child can no longer maintain his delusion of parental omnipotence, which he still at times expects will restore the symbiotic status quo. . . .

The junior toddler gradually realizes that his love objects (his parents) are separate individuals and with their own personal interests. He must gradually and painfully give up the delusion of his own grandeur, often by way of dramatic fights with mother—less so, it seemed to us, with father. This is the crossroads that we term the "rapprochement crisis."[13]

At this crucial juncture, the child must look for direction from its parents. The parents, in turn, are not free agents, but are under the dominion of the value system of the society in which they live. People in our present society who wish a child to become successful have no choice in the rapprochement crisis except to bar the doors to regression and sternly announce to the child, "Forward march!" Primitive, complex, and archaic cultures may have responded very differently, and each in its own way, to this crisis, and, as we shall see, the way in which they responded might be the very thing that kept them primitive, complex, or archaic.

As separation anxiety grows, the child entertains the idea of regression to the symbiotic stage as a mode of lessening anxiety. But this impulse, in turn, leads to a fear of re-engulfment by the mother, so that the child becomes trapped between two conflicting anxieties.[14] This unavoidable intense ambivalence leads to a great frequency of temper tantrums in almost all eighteen-month-old children. "We saw many signs of greater vulnerability, of impotent rage, and helplessness."[15] The tantrum child also directs intense anger at itself, furious that it is experiencing desires to stay engulfed by the mother. The king in complex societies, who is the leader of the movement of separation from the kinship system, is expected, as we have seen, to indulge in tantrum behavior. He, too, is struggling against the fear of re-engulfment.

At around the same eighteen-month point, the child experiences a return of the anxiety reaction to strangers that is typical of most children at seven to nine months but lifts during the practicing substage.[16]

In the traditional family situation, the child attempts to solve his fear of re-engulfment by the mother by turning to the *father*. Already, during the practicing substage, the child's expansiveness toward the world had brought the father more completely into its world view.[17] In the rapprochement crisis, the child's relationship to the father becomes a significant element in the whole psychic situation:

We believe a stable image of a father or of another substitute of the mother, beyond the eighteen-month mark and even earlier, is beneficial and *perhaps a necessary prerequisite to neutralize and to counteract the toddler's age-characteristic oversensitivity to the threat of re-engulfment by the mother.* . . .

We tend to think of the father too one-sidedly as the castrating figure, a kind of bad mother image in the preoedipal period. Loewald, to our knowledge, was the first to emphasize that, "against the threat of the maternal engulfment, the paternal position is not another threat or danger, but a support of powerful force." If there is a relative lack of support on the part of either parent . . . a re-engulfment of the ego into the whirlpool of the primary undifferentiated symbiotic stage becomes a true threat.[18]

We begin to understand why it is the king who leads the attack on the kinship system and becomes the bulwark against the fear of re-engulfment by it. For the small child, the mother is an omnipotent being—an all-powerful, all-providing, all-protecting, all-loving, all-hating entity. As the child begins to separate and individuate from the mother it begins to recognize that she is not a divinity but a person. This is frightening news, because the child thinks it must now stand completely on its own. The panic of having to live without omnipotent support drives the child back toward the symbiotic stage, but here again the fear of re-engulfment, the fear of losing all the gains of individuation, keeps the average child from total retreat. One solution appropriate for this stage of development, something Mahler does not discuss, is to transfer the old omnipotence from the mother to the father. He now becomes the all-powerful provider of life's necessities, and since he is not the mother, he does not present the same threat of symbiotic re-engulfment. In the father, the child seeks to discover what we all long for: omnipotent support without the threat of symbiotic regression. That is why all kings, especially those in advanced complex societies, where the separation from the mother-kinship system is so recent, assume an omnipotent stance. And that is why most supreme divinities, especially in advanced religions, are fathers.

In the midst of this trade-off, however, something sinister occurs. This, again, is an extension of her ideas that Mahler does not make. The father, the king, the noble, all recognize that they now hold a tyrannical power backed by the ultimate threat: Do as we say, or you will be thrown back into the maelstrom, sucked into re-engulfment, drowned in symbiosis; it is we, and only we, who stand between you and annihilation of your individuality; mothers will eat you if you leave our protection. It is no wonder that male tyranny over women and men, once established, held and holds such dominion over human life.

Once the father begins to play a crucial role in the resolution of the rapprochement crisis, Mahler tells us, boys and girls begin to react differently to their circumstances. Up until this point, Mahler describes no significant difference in the developmental pattern of the sexes. Now, everything changes. The mother, who stands for the threat of re-engulfment, is female, and girls are destined to grow up female. The father, the bulwark against regression into symbiosis, is male, and boys are destined to grow up male. In the traditional family, therefore, boys can disengage themselves more fully from the mother than can girls, who must solve the problem of re-engulfment with less reliance on the father.[19] A boy and his mother can start to go their own ways, whereas a girl and her mother must work out their problems, or fail to, within the same area of identification. In my view, the male bonding that ultimately brings us tyranny against children, women, and deprived classes has its genesis at this moment. Fearing the mother's power to re-engulf not only their individuality but also their unique maleness, fathers and sons join together in the attempt to make females harmless through degradation. The society that males create reveals this intention.

These bald statements, of course, are only part of the truth. Even within the traditional modes of child rearing, more humane treatment and more humane resolutions are possible. The *degree* to which the child is treated lovingly and the *degree* to which the child is caringly guided along this tortuous path of separation and individuation makes an enormous difference. The fact that we have reached the point in history where many people—though certainly not enough—are willing to live in a society where there is no tyranny, a situation that never existed in the past, indicates that something remarkable is going on in our child-rearing experience.

To return to Mahler's exposition, the fourth substage of the separation-individuation process is called "consolidation of individuality," and is characterized by an acceptance of separation, a great diminution of the rapprochement struggle, an ability to handle and not be panicked by the threat of re-engulfment, and a significant lessening of the need for omnipotence. All reasonably healthy children make great strides during this substage, although for most children there remain unresolved problems from the rapprochement crisis that reappear at all subsequent crises in the life of the psyche. In my view, the psychological problems engendered by the separation-individuation process are the most important encountered by the majority of individuals attempting to lead an orderly personal life. Psychological difficulties engendered by the Oedipus complex, which Freud enthroned as the primary source of neurotic disorders, are far less important. Freud said that the signs of psychological health were the capacities to love and to work. It is a reasonable proposition, worth examination, that our troubles in working and loving have much more to do with ambivalence about separation-individuation than with the Oedipus complex, that the nature of any particular child's Oedipal situation will be enormously influenced by how that child came through the separation-individuation process which preceded it.

All these problems of psychological development have a profound influence on society. Let's look again at primitive, complex, and archaic societies. All three pass through autistic and symbiotic psychological stages; none is fixated at those points. None can be characterized as psychotic. Equally true, I feel, is that all three societies go through the first two subphases of the separation-individuation stage (though possibly with greater or lesser commitment to the work of those subphases). In the rapprochement-crisis substage, however, each particular society—primitive, complex, archaic—has a characteristically different response, which determines the whole course of that society's attitudes toward individuation, kinship, government, family arrangements, religion, life itself.

In primitive society, at the time of the rapprochement substage (eighteen to twenty-one months), most children are still nursing at the mother's breast and a goodly number are still sleeping with the mother.[20] At the very least, the society is making a statement about how much separation and individuation any child is supposed to achieve. During the rapprochement crisis itself, even in our society, the mother has the option of trying to undo the results of the previous substages.

The child's ambivalence about proceeding further is apparent, and the mother may take this as an excuse to encourage regression: "In this third subphase, that of rapprochement, while individuation proceeds very rapidly and the child exercises it to the limit, he also becomes more and more aware of his separateness and employs all kinds of mechanisms in order to resist and undo his actual separateness from the mother."[21] By the subtle mechanism of not giving the child what it needs, the mother may sabotage the drive toward individuation, especially in this third subphase, when the child itself is so ambivalent: "The less emotionally available the mother is at the time of rapprochement, the more insistently and even desperately does the toddler attempt to woo her. In some cases, this process drains so much of the child's available developmental energy that, as a result, not enough energy, not enough libido, and not enough constructive (neutralized) aggression are left for the evolution of the many ascending functions of the ego."[22]

I am suggesting, but cannot at this point support with data, that this kind of *arrest* and *undoing* are exactly what goes on in primitive societies. During the rapprochement crisis, primitive society closes in on the whole separation-individuation process; it emphasizes separation anxiety, indulges a quasi-symbiotic relationship with the mother by means of a long breast-feeding period and the extended sleeping arrangements of mother and child, represses individuation and individuality, and maintains the kinship system as the social form that certifies a nonindividuated political life. The refusal to proceed fully with the separation-individuation process eventually leads to an underdeveloped Oedipal phase, thus maintaining the pre-Oedipal nature of primitive society: its lack of fully developed anthropomorphic gods; its use of shame and the absence of guilt; its vague relationship to conscience; its failure to develop advanced political forms.

There is a crucial correlation between the xenophobia exhibited by most primitive peoples and the stranger anxiety that Mahler observed as recurring during the rapprochement crisis: "There was a recurrence in many children of stranger reactions. As in the earlier stranger reactions (at 7 to 9 months) we could observe a mixture of anxiety, interest, and curiosity. Now there was often a self-conscious turning away from the stranger, as if the stranger at this point constituted a threat to the already toppling delusion or illusion of exclusive union with the mother."[23] Faced with this conflict and ambivalence, primitive society excluded the stranger and sought reunion with the mother. Not completely, for sure, because no society returns to the symbiotic stage, but primitive society did work out a significant compromise, which gave weight to the desire to regress and left the drive toward individuation severely handicapped. At what variance complex society was in regard to the matter of strangers can be read in practically every journal of the first explorers to visit them; how radically different was the reception in complex societies, which could not have been more curious, from that in the primitive world, where people remained frightened and hostile. Mahler's rapprochement crisis is the great turning point not only for individuals in our society but for the history of society itself.

Complex society remains precisely in the middle of the rapprochement crisis. It will not compromise with individuation as primitive society does, but it cannot quite work the crisis out and move on freely to the fourth stage, the consolidation of individuality. In certain matters, such as the maintenance of the "love affair with the world" and the resolution of stranger anxiety, complex society does resolve rapprochement problems. But in other regards it is the very picture of the twenty-month-old child wracked with separation anxiety, ambivalence, and aggressive thrashing about in the attempt to resolve the crisis.

Complex society preserves a tremendous fear of re-engulfment, sending its children away from home as the only means it knows to avoid such swallowing up. In the ritual of human sacrifice, it kills in order to prevent regression. It creates a tyrannical father in the king, who preserves the temper-tantrum behavior of the rapprochement phase, and who is strong enough to kill the mother should *she* seek re-engulfment. In my view, the child trapped in the rapprochement crisis projects onto the mother its own desires to regress to symbiosis. *She* then becomes the one who wants it; *she* then becomes the *cause* of regression; and killing her, in the child's unconscious, is one way of solving the unbearable tensions of ambivalence. True, only psychotic people, once they have grown, carry out that fantasy, but there was once a stage of human society, not psychotic, but threatened by re-engulfment by the kinship system, and it ritually slaughtered its own people by the thousands.

Complex society, unlike primitive society, refused to regress; it preserved the gains made during the practicing subphase; it maintained the achievements of separation and individuation. But it did all this at enormous aggressive cost, and it never succeeded, in its characteristic form, in liberating itself from the rapprochement crisis. It was a transitional form of society, a great bridge from the primitive to the archaic.

Archaic civilization, the successor of complex society, achieved the stability characterized by Mahler's fourth substage: consolidation of individuality, and the beginnings of emotional object constancy. Though certain modes of kinship-system behavior undoubtedly remained important in archaic society, the raucous struggle against re-engulfment by the kinship system seemed to be over. Differentiation was possible without the incessant use of certain kinds of aggression; human sacrifice was abandoned. Highly elaborated religious rituals pertaining both to the gods and to sacred kingship gave a sense of community independent of the individual personality of the king, which replaced kinship cathexes. The father-king was no longer required to be the terror of the world. The softening of kingship and an adequate resolution of the whole separation-individuation process left the psyche free to move on to Oedipal concerns and the formation of the superego, which terminates the Oedipal crisis. Archaic civilization was the first stage of human society that can unquestionably be characterized as moving beyond the pre-Oedipal. With concepts of justice, law, and the beneficent ruler as their ideals, archaic civilizations became the first societies in which a great discrepancy developed between ideal and actual behavior. A profound psychological stability had been achieved after the revolutionary fervor of complex societies. Great human gains were consolidated. In the West, thousand-year histories were written before the revolutionary hammers of Greece, Rome, and Israel announced the end of the archaic.

The development of the psyche is the paradigm for the development of culture and society. Society may choose to resist, perhaps permanently, the drive toward development, but once advance is resolved upon, society is not free to take any direction or any steps it wants. No primitive society develops into an archaic or a classical civilization. Every primitive society that embarks on a developmental journey becomes a complex society. The logic within this advance is not primarily economic, or scientific, or even rational, although these qualities are a part of that process; it is primarily a psychological logic. The stages in development from primitive to chieftainship to early monarchies to complex monarchies to archaic civilization are projections and magnifications onto society as a whole of stages in the development of the psyche. The journey of the psyche through the various phases in the process of separation and individuation is recapitulated in social development.

The fact that every primitive society differs from every other and that every complex society has its own individuality does not contradict the existence of certain developmental laws, any more than the fact that every individual in the world differs from every other individual means that we can have no science of medicine or psychology. All theory—medical, psychological, or sociological—demands an abstraction from the particular-individualistic to the general.

At any stage of development, society may renounce any further fundamental change, and such a situation is not necessarily unstable. Nothing we know of the Nuer, for instance, would indicate that they could not remain in the primitive stage for a million years or more if left to themselves. Certain stages of society are inherently more stable than others. Both primitive society and archaic civilization seem much more anchored than complex society, which I have described as "transitional." Here again, the psychic connection seems crucial. Certain psychic stages are more transitional, more critical, less adaptable to permanent compromise than others. Archaic civilization, corresponding to a reasonable resolution of the whole separation-individuation process, and primitive society, analogous to a stable compromise with developmental drives, are both capable of going on much longer than the raucous, overheated complex society, which lives its psychic life within the roar of the rapprochement crisis.

Although a subject for another study, it also seems that certain later stages in social development would follow the same kind of pattern. A society that takes as its paradigm the latency period—one of the most gentle of psychological stages—must produce a different aspect than a society working out Oedipal problems, since the Oedipal period in the individual is full of upheaval. Continuous revolution is as impossible as a continuous Oedipus complex; both the psyche and society, in such a stage, come rather quickly to the point where they yearn for resolution of the turmoil.

I am not postulating an identity between psychic and social stages. A paradigm is not the thing itself. Society is not psyche, although society, especially through its dictates about child rearing, crucially determines what kind of psyche its members shall have. Also, the psyche provides the limits of society and accounts for the fact that society develops in stages. The reason social development shows radical, revolutionary breaks and is not one long, continuous advance is that the development of the psyche proceeds in such a manner. Periodic turmoil and upheaval, not continuous motion, is the mode of psychic development.

Understanding the psyche and comprehending society are not the same thing. The six-way relationships among psyche-society-family produce an enormously complicated mechanism. Our theoretical understanding of the psyche is much further developed than our comprehension of the way society works, in great part because social development is more complicated than psychic development. The connections made here, if valid, are no more than the bare beginnings of a theory.

30

Drives, Needs,
and Symbolic Transformation

Insight may be enhanced or diminished by the use of particular words to describe phenomena. It makes a difference what name we give to those biopsychological impulses that are universal to all people. Freud used the German word *Trieb,* whose closest English translation is "drive," although many translations of Freud into English, including that of James Strachey in the Standard Edition, use the word "instinct." Freud himself, on a few occasions, made use of the German word *Instink.*[1] The decision about which word to use is dependent upon the overtones, the elaborations of meaning, that proceed from the word, and these may change with time. In our present circumstances, the word "instinct," in regard to human beings, seems unserviceable. It conjures up too many associations of birds building complicated nests or beavers constructing dams, and human action is not like that, even by analogy. It also seems to slam the door too boldly in the face of cultural and symbolic forms. "Instinct" describes a more complete, inflexible prescription for action than what we find in the human situation. It is much easier to think of a drive being modified, for instance, by cultural circumstances than it is to imagine an instinct being transformed by anything. In regard to sexual and aggressive matters, "drive" appears to be a much more accurate word than "instinct." "Drive" allows for the kind of complexity, ambiguity, and elaboration that is necessary to describe how human beings really feel and work.

The risk in not using the word "instinct," the danger in concentrating too much on social influence and symbolic transformations, is that we get too far away from the biological foundation of our psychology, and it is especially important that we do not do this when thinking

about developmental issues. At birth, we carry a given number of physiological "time capsules." We are programmed to smile at four weeks,
walk at fifteen months, turn pubescent at twelve years, become gray-
haired at forty-five, and die of cancer at seventy-five. The program may
be modified to a limited extent by circumstance. An autistic child may
never smile; a symbiotically psychotic child may not walk until five
years; chemicals and cigarettes may bring the cancer earlier—but none
of this contradicts the fact that, under normal circumstances, many future biophysiological necessities arrive with us at birth.

The same kind of programming—subject, however, to much greater
modification by actual circumstance—determines our psychological development. We begin the separation-individuation process at six
months and enter the rapprochement crisis at eighteen months; we
move from one libidinal stage to another in accordance with psychological time; we enter the Oedipal phase at one time and leave it at another.
The psychological "time capsules" that we carry with us from birth
determine the *limits* of our developmental journey. All of this is not
to say that we lack freedom. We are free, but only within limits.

It is of value to speak of "drives" instead of "instincts," provided
we do not forget that drives have a biophysiological foundation. Drives
by themselves, however, produce nothing. What is a sex drive without
a person to encourage it, direct it, satisfy it? Drives are integrated into
the human psyche only with the assistance of other human beings.
Without modification, without finding a local habitation and a name,
a drive can only create disorder. Once a drive has been domesticated
or humanized, however, it no longer looks like a drive. Sex is a drive,
many would agree, but what of love? It feels more accurate to describe
love as a "need" rather than a drive. In the human psyche, drives do
not stay drives. Drives—whether aggressive, sexual, or developmental—must be satisfied, sublimated, elaborated, and transformed. When
that happens, they are no longer drives but needs. The sex drive is transformed into a need for love; the aggressive drive is sublimated into a
need for order; the drive toward individuation is transformed into the
great pleasures of ego activity.

When thinking about society, this distinction between drives and
needs is significant. Let us take music, for example. No society has ever
been discovered that had no music. Human beings and music are inseparable. This universal human inclination may be described as an instinct
for music or a drive for music, though neither of these words seems
to have the right connotation. That human beings have a need for music

seems quite accurate. This need for music may, indeed, have originally been transformed from the sex drive, but it is not necessary to make that connection in order to understand society. If music is a universal human need, then society is obliged to make provision for its satisfaction, although needs may be repressed more easily than drives. And there are other human needs similar to music. Every society we know of also has had some form of dance, poetry, storytelling, history, and the decoration either of objects or self, or both, and these needs may be as important as expressing aggression and satisfying sexual impulses.

It is difficult to see how a universal human sexual drive, more or less the same in all people, can produce the vast multitude of arrangements that society has invented in regard to marriage, courtship, divorce, child rearing, premarital and postmarital sexual activity, and so on. Sexual drives, however, are transformed into needs based upon those drives, and these acts of transformation enormously increase the possibilities for modes of satisfaction. Needs are much more various than the drives from which they come. Human society is so complex because it deals fundamentally with human needs, not with drives. The kind of social-psychological analysis that seeks to equate social forms with drives brings very little insight.

Even drives, as autonomous as they may be, require *other people* to fulfill them. There may be a drive to satisfy hunger, but pleasure in eating implies the existence of another person. Originally, all drives and needs are satisfied (or not) within the family. Adequate satisfaction results in the development of a broader need for others—into a need for society itself. Here again, the transforming word "need" seems more accurate than the raw biological terms "instinct" and "drive." It does not ring true to say that we have an instinct for society or a drive for society, but the need for society seems undeniable.

Certain human needs are in direct contradiction to other needs: to express aggression and to satisfy eros; to stay secure and to grow up; to enjoy a deep sense of community and to exalt individuality. These contradictions are at the center of all great social conflict. Every human society, no matter how stable, has some form of inner conflict, because some human needs can be satisfied only by repressing others. To postulate universal human needs is by no means to postulate their necessary satisfaction. Puritan society repressed the human needs for music, dance, and self-adornment in order to encourage the nonnarcissistic elements in human sexuality. Medieval Christianity repressed the needs for sexual satisfaction, marriage, and children to enhance the needs of ego organization and development. The Nuer stayed Nuer by repressing the need for full separation and individuation. That which is repressed may be contained but not eliminated; it never goes away. Human society changes and develops by bringing back the energy of what has been repressed and using that energy to transform social forms. The great growth of individualism in the last three hundred years, for example, has been achieved only by the repression of the human need for community, and this age of individualism will cease only when the energy in the repressed need for community becomes viable again. Such is the dialectical nature of the relationship of needs and repression.

SYMBOLIC TRANSFORMATION

A human need as powerful as sex or aggression, a need that can be denied the psyche only at the cost of severe psychic disorder, is the need to create symbols and live in a symbolic world. In Cassirer's terms, it defines the species: *animal symbolicum.*[2] We are a symbol-making animal. Freudian psychoanalysis, to its detriment, has recoiled from this enormously important human instinct-drive-need, almost as if it fears a kind of Jungian re-engulfment, a mystical transformation, should it confront this necessity. Only dreams and dream-work, in most psychoanalytic theory, touch on the world of symbols; ego-id-superego live in a "scientific" landscape, where the perception is lost that they themselves are symbols, not things.

Psychic health depends directly upon the symbol-making capacity. In the pre-Oedipal stage, the child can solve fundamental problems with the mother only by separating the actual mother from a symbolic mother. Various "incorporations" of the mother at various stages of development are accomplished, clearly, not by eating the real mother but by complicated symbolic psychic work. The idea of mother—the symbol—must be disassociated from the actuality of the mother in order for psychic development to proceed. Failure to make that distinction results in pathology.

In the Oedipal stage, similarly, problems are resolved only by elevating the whole experience to a higher level of abstraction. Boys must learn to deal with fatherhood, not just their own particular father; girls must learn to deal with motherhood in the same manner. It is not the male child's task to contemplate killing his real, actual father and sleeping with his actual mother; such psychic work is impossible. The whole experience is played out on a symbolic level, where there is no real blood. He kills "The Father," and sleeps with "The Mother." When the Oedipal stage is completed, he has incorporated "The Father" within himself. In all this, if he had to deal only with his actual father, with a real name and a real face, the task would become impossible.

Once we observe that the child has the capacity—the necessity—to symbolize the two most important "objects" in its world, mother and father, we can see that the whole family situation can be generalized and symbolized even further. Society is the result of that capacity and necessity. Social action, in great part, is the attempt to work out family psychological problems on a higher level of abstraction. The ability to move to this higher level is a measure of psychic health. Without society, the burden of human pathology might be unbearable.

Included within the symbol-making capacity is the faculty to create symbolic transformations, and nothing is more important for cultural and social development. The state, as an example, has been defined in this book as that form of society in which nonkinship forms of social cohesion are as important as kinship forms; but from another point of view, there are no nonkinship forms of social cohesion. All forms of social cohesion are based upon kinship and are descended from kinship. The force that holds the state together in our supermodern, post-industrial society is still intimately connected with the cohesion of the kin. Patriotism, the sense of nationhood, love of country are important forms of social cohesion even in the most modern of twentieth-century societies; and yet all of these feelings are a direct transformation of the conceptions of kinship. State forms of social cohesion are kinship forms and *not* kinship forms. They are symbolic transformations of kinship, but a thing and its symbolic transformation are not identical. Certain fundamental tensions within the state arise because what holds it together is both kinship and not kinship at the same time.

Similarly, kingship is a symbolic transformation of certain relationships within the family, but the king is *not* one's father, however like one's father he may behave. A king is a father symbolically transformed, and the severe tensions within kingship result, in large part, from the fact that the king is simultaneously a father and not a father.

Such transformations are essential to all development, social or personal, and such symbolic metamorphoses are necessary to the giving up of certain primitive modes of action. Human sacrifice is abandoned only when animal sacrifice is put in its place. The killing is still there;

the blood is still present; the ritual exaltation remains—but a man is not killed. Human sacrifice, a symbolic activity in the first place, lends itself to further symbolic transformations.

The one great cause for optimism when regarding human society is that there seems to be no end to the possibilities of transformation. Every great social form, including the giant states of the modern world, is the product of many symbolic transformations. Every state, no matter how sophisticated or complicated, has its ultimate origins in complex society and carries, even in advanced form, the marks of its origins. No state, or the tensions within it, can be understood without recognizing that the state form of politics has never resolved the problem that it owes its origin to the breakdown and transformation of the kinship system. The most modern state still lays claim to kinship loyalties, even when it refuses to reward all its members with kinship equality. A further transformed sense of kinship, emphasizing equality and eros, still seems to be the only answer to tyranny.

It is an attribute of symbols and symbolic forms that they gain in power as they encompass more and more stages of psychological development. The most powerful symbols refer not merely to one psychic stage, and therefore to one psychic conflict, but to many such stages. The snake, for instance, has been a potent symbol for an extraordinary number of peoples. Psychoanalytic thought, with its emphasis on genital and Oedipal matters and its neglect of pregenital symbolism, has emphasized the phallic aspect of snake symbolism to the exclusion of all other interpretations. The snake clearly has oral and anal points of reference as well. Oral because it kills with its mouth; it literally bites one to death. When Clytemnestra, in the *Oresteia* of Aeschylus, recounts that she gave birth to a snake (the symbol for her son and portended killer, Orestes) and put it to her breasts to suckle,[3] the oral-aggressive aspects of the imagery are clear. And anal because the snake so closely resembles the feces that leave our body and that, we imagine, are alive and can wiggle. The great power in the symbolic image of the snake is that it can touch all these psychic points at the same time.[4]

In a similar way, every great symbolic form—religious, political, or artistic—operates on an Oedipal and pre-Oedipal level simultaneously. The story of Christ and his Father is one great attempt to reconcile problems of an Oedipal nature, but the Christ story also functions powerfully on a pre-Oedipal level. Human sacrifice, the cannibalism of the Eucharist, the various Mother Marys, all touch fundamental pre-Oedipal concerns. The story of King Oedipus himself is a great deal more than an Oedipal tale. Oedipus learns that as a child he was subject to his father's and mother's infanticidal inclinations, though miraculously saved. When, in the final horror, Oedipus charges into the palace to destroy his mother, we cannot give any simple answer for why he does so. We cannot say that he does it because she has become his mother-wife, or simply because he wishes to be avenged for the intended infanticide, or to free himself from the terrible infantile seduction by his mother that makes separation impossible. He does it for all these reasons. And when he ends by putting his eyes out with the brooch from her dress, to pronounce that act "self-castration" is to miss all the other symbolic aspects of this grievous tale.

The same kind of complex symbolism operates on a social level. The king in advanced complex societies is simultaneously the great omnipotent Oedipal father and the tantrum-crazed infant. Mother Russia is governed by a tyrannical, patriarchal czar. The modern state requires us to obey male authority figures and also to participate with them in excesses of pre-Oedipal paranoid anxieties.

No great symbol in the world ever expresses only one thing. Symbols that facilitate personal and social development are required to resolve a multitude of conflicts.

DIALECTICAL DEVELOPMENT

Social and cultural development progresses in a dialectical manner, not from some abstruse metaphysical cause. The first great developmental experience of the psyche—the full course of the separation-individuation process—assumes precisely this dialectical mode. The separation-individuation experience provides a paradigm for all other developmental sequences, both personal and social.

"Dialectical," as used here, implies a notion of progress, of development, which proceeds in the manner thesis-antithesis-synthesis. Antithesis is a negation of the thesis, but this negation is in turn negated by the synthesis. The negation of the negation produces a new thesis from which the whole process can begin again. Crucially important is the concept that the synthesis includes within it both the thesis and the antithesis, as well as something more than either of them separately. The synthesis does not destroy what had existed before, but *transforms* it into something new.

Mahler's description of the separation-individuation process outlines the dialectical nature of that journey. The child and its mother in symbiotic state are the thesis. As the child begins to separate in the differentiation and practicing substages, it takes an antithetical stance toward symbiosis. This antithesis cannot develop indefinitely, and the time comes to create a synthesis, which will include the child and its mother in a close but not symbiotic relationship. If this is done success-fully, the new synthesis of mother and child will incorporate all the ad-vances of individuation and separation that have been achieved in the antithetical phase. The last substage—consolidation of individuality and the beginnings of object constancy—represents a new thesis, a place of reasonable stability from which all future development will take leave.

For the psyche, every great critical developmental experience as-sumes this form, including the Oedipal stage and the troubles of adoles-cence. A more or less stable situation is disrupted by psychological earthquakes and tidal waves. Aggression, needed to crack the stable the-sis, accelerates at a rapid pace. A time of irrationality and turmoil marks the period of antithesis, and finally a new synthesis is carved out, one that now incorporates all the developmental advances made during the period of upheaval. One reason it is so difficult to be human is that we know no easier way to grow up.

This same dialectical pattern may be observed in matters of ritual, especially in those rites of passage that have been elaborated in the work of Arnold van Gennep.[5] Van Gennep demonstrates that all rites of pas-sage (birth, initiation, marriage, death) go through three fundamental stages: *"rites of separation, transition rites,* and *rites of incorporation."*[6] The dialectical nature of this process, and its close adherence to Mah-ler's substages, seems clear—a stable situation is ended by an act of sepa-ration, and after a period of upheaval, a new stable synthesis is erected.

All social development follows this same pattern. The movement from primitive to complex to archaic societies is a dialectical process of thesis, antithesis, synthesis. Complex society was the antithesis that cracked the stable thesis of primitive society, raised the level of violence and aggression, and finally gave way to a new, stable form of human society that no longer had need of the exaggerated aggressive behavior of the complex world, no longer presented the aspect of a frenzied, frag-ile culture. The primitive world had been permanently and irrevocably transformed. This drama was played out on an immense social stage, replicating the dialectical pattern laid down in the individual psyche.

All developmental advance produces tension. The disjointed antithetical stage, without which no progress occurs, is inherently a situation of heightened anxiety. Old forms of stability and security and relative freedom from anxiety are destroyed; the new stage of synthesis cannot be instituted overnight, cannot be established until the antithetical stage has run its course. A society in the midst of a first negation can never offer its members a deep sense of calm and order. The stage of antithesis in the dialectical movement is always transitional. The tension one senses in the cultures of advanced complex societies would indicate that, although many positive things were being accomplished, their work was primarily negative—the destruction and transformation of primitive society and its basis in the kinship system.

Such conflict does not pertain only to early societies. The heightening of anxiety as a result of developmental advance is responsible for tensions in democratic society. Democracy is possible only as a result of a further weakening of the ties of kinship, including dependence on the father-king. Democracy is the least dependent upon fundamental kinship ties of any political system ever invented, and as a result it generates an unusual share of anxiety, paranoia, and the need to express aggression outward, toward the world. Some have remarked on the intimate relationship of imperialism to democratic society. The first great democracy in the world, ancient Athens, developed into a tyrannical imperialist oppressor of other Greek states; England, in the nineteenth century, gave birth both to one of the very first modern democratic states and also to imperialist splendor; the United States in the last thirty-five years has demonstrated, at the least, that there is nothing incompatible between democracy and imperialism.

The fragility that all sensitive observers of our democratic life are aware of, the sense that for many people democratic politics is almost an intolerable burden, the feeling that democratic society is always struggling against the desire to plunge headlong back into the kinship paradise of *ein Volk, ein Reich, ein Führer,* all result from the fact that people find it enormously difficult to live without kinship-system supports, or at least without an omnipotent ruler who will reassure us and assuage our anxieties. The "fear of freedom" is a separation anxiety caused by the loosening of the bonds of kinship.

Without kinship, we have, it seems, only our own individualism to fall back upon. There is a fundamental tension between individualism on the one hand, and kinship or the sense of community (which is itself a transformation of kinship) on the other. A society that represses expressions of individuality as far as possible, remains primitive; a society that represses the sense of community to the degree that our present society does is in danger of breakdown. We owe the modern world, its greatness and also its potential for world destruction, to the apotheosis of separation and individuation and the deliberate exclusion of other fundamental human needs. Fearing a re-engulfment by old kinship ties, we have crippled the sense of community so badly that we no longer know whether we can revive it fast enough or effectively enough to make the future possible. In the United States, we have almost reached the point where we can enjoy the sense of belonging to a community only when we are engaged in fighting a "common enemy," either in cold or hot war.

The enormous push for individualism in the West that began in the twelfth century and came to full flower in the Reformation—a movement that has given us capitalism, liberalism, democracy, and the reign of science and technology—was an antithetical negation of conglomerate medieval Christian society. In its exaggerated form, it created an ideal of the individuated person capable of living with almost no sense of community, almost no sense of obligation to those who share his or her society—a pathological individualism. The next great developmental advance, the next movement of the dialectic, will surely negate this negation and produce a new synthesis, which will restore the sense of community without making us regress to medieval times, or give up all the legitimate gains of freedom that three centuries of intense individualism have brought us.

Such speculation might be pure wish fulfillment were it not for the fact that all of us have been there before. Mahler's last stage of the separation-individuation process is the consolidation of individuality and the beginnings of object constancy. "Object constancy" is the psychoanalytic, "scientific" way of describing the capacity to love someone.

DEVELOPMENTAL STAGES AND RADICAL LEAPS

Implicit in the concept that social development progresses in definite stages—primitive, complex, archaic; feudalist, capitalist, socialist—is the presumption that change from one fundamental stage to another requires a quantum leap, a radical transformation of the value system, a revolution in culture and society. Development within stages is by no means precluded; such changes are, in fact, necessary to move the society to the point where such quantum leaps are possible. Clearly, late capitalism is a different thing from early capitalism, just as advanced complex societies differ from the early complex societies of chiefdoms, but there is a certain symbolic coherence that compels us to call both, early and late, "capitalism," and to name both chieftainships and advanced monarchies "complex society." We observe the same phenomenon in art. Early and late Romanesque sculpture both deserve the name "Romanesque." At some point, however, with a revolutionary leap forward, Romanesque is transformed into Gothic; there has been a radical break with the past. At the time of the birth of the new form, transitional constructs may exist, like the sculpture on the west face of Chartres cathedral, which can, and does, provide either the last pages of a book on Romanesque sculpture or the first pages of one on the Gothic. Similarly, there is a question whether Aztec society at the time of the Spanish conquest should be described as a late complex or an early archaic society.

These quantum leaps from one fundamental stage to another take a degree of energy that is not necessary for the more gradual evolution within stages. Any basic stage of society allows for change, but only within a fundamental set of values and world views. Primitive society can change from hunting and gathering to agriculture, or from a pastoral existence to an agricultural one, or it can move from matrilineal to patrilineal lineages, or invent the concept of age sets, or make changes in its religion—it can do all this and, provided it does not transform the kinship system, still remain a primitive society. Once it starts to tamper with the kinship basis of its polity, however, a revolution in values is under way. Something that has enormous power holds a fundamental social form together; it is almost impossible to crack it. We know from history, however, that such fundamental forms of cohesion have been transformed many times. Somewhere, an energy must exist that is in opposition to the concept of stasis and is capable of overcoming the resistance to fundamental change. It will be of interest, a little later, to speculate on what that form of energy might be.

Also implicit in the concept of developmental stages is the assumption that there is a certain logic to their progression, and that it is impossible to skip a stage. Whether one talks of biological evolution or social development, the same iron logic applies. God does not, as Einstein remarked, play dice with the universe. Society does not go from primitive to archaic or from archaic to capitalist in a single step, any more than biological evolution progresses from reptiles to *Homo sapiens* without traversing the full course of mammalian evolution. In regard to social and cultural development, where the logic that dictates the particular order of developmental advance comes from is a question of the highest theoretical importance, one that I can only raise and merely begin to answer.

The one area, in addition to the biological and the social, that presents a clear case of development in definite stages is the development of the psyche. And here we find the same mechanisms at work: gradual change within stages leading to the unusual bursts of energy necessary to fuel the advance to a new stage; and, in many circumstances, an intensification of aggressive behavior at certain critical points along the developmental path. Latency, for example, is a six- or seven-year phase between the Oedipal stage and puberty. The ten-year-old child is by no means psychologically identical to the six-year-old child, but each can still be accurately described as in the latency stage. The leap to adolescence requires an enormous expenditure of psychic energy to break through the latency form and begin a period of turmoil and growth. A similar kind of critical expenditure of energy announces the end of adolescence and the beginnings of young adulthood. With the psyche, as with biological and social development, there is no skipping of stages. No one goes from latency to young adulthood without plowing through adolescence, no matter how pleasant such a change in the necessary order might be.

When we ask of psychological development the same question asked of social development—what determines the inevitable logic of progression from one stage to another?—we may come to see that nothing determines it except its own internal structure. The development of the psyche has an autonomy that the development of society does not demonstrate. True, social forces profoundly influence the development of the psyche. Adolescence, for instance, is by no means the same in all cultures: what happens to female adolescence in a culture that marries off girls at thirteen? A seventeen-year-old girl in such a society has had a far different psychological development from a girl of the same age in our own. This does not mean, however, that the basic psychological structure can be changed. Distortion is possible; repression is feasible; development may be cut short; but the basic structure remains. It is the same with biophysiological development. One may, by the use of psychological mechanisms, keep a child from walking; that does not mean that there has been a change in the fundamental biophysiological developmental pattern. It means only that this pattern is subject to distortion and inhibition by other than physiological means. Similarly, primitive society may severely repress the drives toward separation and individuation; that does not signify that these drives have ceased to exist in the psyches of the members of those societies, or that people in primitive society have a different psyche from people in more complex societies. A psyche in which fundamental human needs are repressed is still a psyche.

I want to postulate a primary autonomy for the structure of the psyche that determines its *potential* developmental progress, and I want to suggest that the structure of social development does not have the same autonomous existence. Its structure is dependent upon something that is not social, which is the psyche itself. This brings us back to the categorical statement made earlier: the development of the psyche is the paradigm for the development of society and culture.

One observation lends critical support to this basic hypothesis—the fact that particular modes of social aggression and sexual expression are characteristic of certain stages in the development of society. Cannibalism and human sacrifice, for instance, are not universally found in all stages of society, although they are crucially important in the stages where they are exercised. I can find no political or economic reasons why cannibalism and human sacrifice are taken up by society and then abandoned. We know, from the study of the psyche, that in various psychic stages certain modes of expressing aggression are characteristic. When the psyche successfully moves from a stage, it leaves behind that particular way of seeking aggressive satisfaction, although traces survive. Regarding the psyche, one does not ask why oral aggression is characteristic of the oral stage: it is in its nature to be so. Regarding society, on the other hand, we are compelled to ask why. Why does cannibalism cease to exist as a legitimate social form in all societies from the archaic forward? Why does human sacrifice begin in complex societies and cease when that stage of social development is surpassed?

Society borrows its stages, and the characteristics of those stages, from the psyche. As the psyche moves forward, transforming and abandoning modes of aggression, society progresses, in a similar but by no means identical manner. That these two developmental patterns are profoundly different, that understanding the psyche is just one of the beginnings, and by no means the ending, of comprehending society, that social and cultural development is more complex and more difficult to describe than psychic growth—all this, I hope, is made clear by this book. Ascribing a secondary, not a primary, autonomy to social life does not signify the reduction of society to the psyche.

STRUCTURE AND ENERGY

From a theoretical point of view, the problem of understanding the developmental process of society can be broken down into two separate areas: structure and energy. Although, within a system, structural and energy issues are always related to one another, each also has a certain autonomy. It is, for instance, possible to have the same structure fueled by different sources of energy. The heating system in a house may, for example, be changed from an oil-and-hot air system to gas-and-hot air, involving a complete change in the source of energy and a very small change in the structure; or else the oil may be kept and the structure changed from hot air to hot water. When thinking about society, especially in its relationship to the psyche, it is important to distinguish between structure and energy, between the shape social things take and the forces that drive social change.

In regard to the structural elements of social development, the first work is an empirical task, to describe the stages, informed by historical evidence. Primitive, complex, archaic, and feudalist, capitalist, socialist, are the outlines of two such empirical descriptions. No scientific proofs are possible in this task, because even such a seemingly simple empirical work is always determined by theoretical considerations. People's disagreements as to what the stages are usually result from differences in their basic view of history. People may also agree with one another about the existence of a certain sequence of stages—feudalism, capitalism, socialism—and yet find themselves in total disagreement about the reasons for the movement from one stage to another.

Once the theoretical distinction between structure and energy has been made, it quickly becomes apparent that it will not hold. Society, unlike a heating system, is not a dead thing; it is an organic entity with a life of its own. All social structures require a certain energy just to *maintain* themselves, and that energy differs from sources of energy that invite the possibility of radically *changing* the system. The energy that changes the system I call "developmental energy," and that which maintains the system I call "structural energy." This last is the only energy that functionalist and structuralist theories of society have been concerned with. Ignoring developmental energy, these theories have described society as if it never changes, certainly never takes revolutionary steps forward. Some of the proponents of functionalist and structuralist approaches may even write about society in a way that seems to indicate that they would rather not understand the mechanisms of social change. A. A. Radcliffe-Brown, for example, has stated: "To establish any probability for such conjectures [about historical change] we should need to have a knowledge of laws of social development which we certainly do not possess and *to which I do not think we shall ever attain.*"[7]

In the pursuit of survival, societies are forced to make changes, but these modifications are fueled by structural, not developmental, energy. The system of industrial production under which we live is dependent upon oil for its existence, and as that commodity gets scarcer, each industrial society modifies its behavior in ways that it would not have done had the oil remained plentiful. The energy required to make such changes is purely structural. The health of a society is determined, and its chances of survival are enhanced, by the degree to which it can call up structural energy in times of crisis.

Marx, in his analysis of capitalist society, attempted to demonstrate, in one grand theoretical construction, that considerations of both structural and developmental energy (though he did not use those terms) were leading to a collapse of the capitalist system. *Das Kapital* was a Promethean attempt to demonstrate that capitalist society, by the very nature of its structure and, therefore, the nature of its attempts at survival, was plunging headlong toward its own dissolution. The capitalist system has certainly demonstrated much more structural energy, or the capacity to survive, than Marx gave it credit for. The system may, in fact, change only in response to the insistent call of developmental drives, which, at this point in history, are inexorably intertwined with moral considerations that acutely perceive the aggressive basis of the system and demand a transformation and sublimation of that aggression.

Developmental energy, as cause, is the ultimate subject of this book, one of whose primary purposes is to think about and possibly come to recognize the energy that drives the whole human developmental process, that "force that through the green fuse drives the flower."[8] Why, in essence, does any primitive people embark on the journey that ultimately puts an end to primitive society?

When we look closely at primitive societies, there seems to be nothing in their economic, political, or social (kinship) systems that produces the kind of "internal contradictions," as Marx would have it, that

demand radical changes. In regard to economic viability, recent research has demonstrated the remarkable capacity of primitive cultures
to provide themselves with daily necessities. True, there were periods
of extreme drought or severe damage to herds by disease, but all societies have suffered from such disruptions in nature. The myth of primitive man's fighting a daily battle against the constant threat of starvation
and losing that struggle with great frequency no longer has any validity.
We have even discovered that the Bushmen of the Kalahari Desert in
Africa, the most hostile of environments, who were supposedly living
the most marginal of existences, spend at most 60 percent of their days
in the hunting and gathering of food. They can even afford the luxury
of having the men spend all their productive time in hunting, which
provides no more than 25 percent of the total caloric intake of the band.[9]
Such, and similar, information has led Marshall Sahlins to declare
half-ironically that hunters and gatherers were "the original affluent society."[10] It seems clear that the threat of starvation did not launch
human society on the path that eventually led to complex monarchies.

Similarly, in regard to matters touching on the social system and
politics, the unmistakable impression one gains from acquaintanceship
with the data on primitive societies is the profound *stability* of the systems. Nothing, for instance, that we know of the Nuer or of Australian
tribes indicates that, left alone, they would not stay essentially as they
are for a million years. No writer on the origins of the state that I know
of has suggested any irreconcilable contradictions in the politics or social life of primitive society that would force a developmental advance.
The most that is offered theoretically is that the possibilities of economic
surplus are seized upon by a few people who produce political oppression and the state. What in the nature of primitive society makes this
last development possible, how an egalitarian society provides the beginnings of tyranny, no one, to my knowledge, has truly explained. No
one has answered the great question of what there is in the nature of
the kinship system that could make the kinship system untenable.

Primitive society maintains itself only by repressing a profound
human drive to separate and individuate. It becomes thereby to a significant extent alien to the human condition. That this alienation can maintain itself in a more or less permanent state cannot be denied, but there
is nevertheless a profound contradiction within the kinship system produced by its denial of a basic drive. The situation is potentially explosive, though the explosion in most primitive societies never came. Why
it occurred when it did, why certain primitive cultures began the trans-

formation into complex society and others did not—such questions cannot as yet be answered.

What seems plausible is that the great contradiction, the severe tension, in primitive society was not economic, political, or social, but psychological. The energy that drives the whole history of the world is the force of the psyche struggling to fulfill its developmental destiny. That struggle is essentially an internal one against the energy of repression. The two great elements of developmental drive and repression, at eternal war with each other, dominate political life now as much as in the days when the first lonely chief emerged out of the kinship-system world. Our understanding of our present situation could be greatly enhanced if we would consider two questions about our society: What human drives and needs does it satisfy? And what needs and drives does it repress? We live at the intersection of those two questions.

Notes

Cherubino and the Countess
1 Based on a story in James Miti, "A Short History of Buganda, Bunyoro, Busoga, Toro and Ankole," trans. G. K. Rock, unpublished manuscript, n.d., copy in Columbia University Library, pp. 198–203.

An Introduction
1 Frankfort, Adventure
2 Reprinted in Bellah, Beyond Belief.
3 Fried, Evolution; Service, Primitive; Service, Origins; Claessen and Skalnick, Early State.

1 The Pearl of Africa
1 Low, Modern History, p. 13.
2 Kottack, "Ecological Variables," p. 355.
3 Rowe, "Revolution," pp. 30–31.

2 The Life and Times of Prime Minister Mukasa, Part I
1 Rowe, "Revolution," p. 139.
2 Stanley, Dark Continent, p. 386.
3 Ibid., p. 387.
4 Rowe, "Revolution," p. 140.

5 Stanley, Dark Continent, pp. 388–89.
6 Ibid., p. 392.
7 Rowe, "Revolution," p. 141.
8 Ibid., p. 142.
9 Ibid.
10 Ibid., p. 146.
11 Stanley, Dark Continent, pp. 390–93.

3 The Life and Times of Prime Minister Mukasa, Part II
1 Rowe, "Revolution," p. 148.
2 Ibid., p. 149.
3 Ibid., p. 151.
4 Ibid., p. 152.
5 Ibid., pp. 128–30.
6 Ibid., pp. 155–57.
7 Ibid., pp. 184–85.
8 Faupel, Holocaust, pp. 77–78.
9 Ibid., pp. 81–82.
10 Ibid., p. 128.

4 The Blood of the Martyrs, Part I: Mutesa
1 Vanzetti in Rodman, Modern Poetry, pp. 192–93.
2 Gray, "Mutesa," pp. 22–23.
3 Ibid., pp. 26–27.
4 Low, Modern History, pp. 21–22.

5 Oded, *Islam*, p. 66.
6 Gray, "Mutesa," p. 27.
7 Oded, *Islam*, p. 72.
8 Katumba and Welbourn, "Martyrs," p. 153.
9 Ibid., p. 154.
10 Mukasa, "Simuda Nyuma," pp. 19–20.
11 Ibid.
12 Katumba and Welbourn, "Martyrs," p. 151.
13 Mukasa, "Simuda Nyuma," pp. 22–23.
14 Rowe, "Revolution," p. 113.

5 *The Blood of the Martyrs, Part II: Mwanga*

1 Ashe, *Two Kings*, pp. 218–19.
2 Ibid., p. 219.
3 Thoonen, *Black Martyrs*, p. 182.
4 Ii, *History*, p. 24.
5 Ibid., pp. 24–26.
6 Thoonen, *Black Martyrs*, pp. 50–51.
7 E. W. Smith, *African Ideas*, p. 54.
8 Ellis, *Researches*, II:187–88.
9 Faupel, *Holocaust*, p. 205.
10 Tyerman and Bennet, *Journal*, II:176.
11 Ibid., p. 177.
12 Ashe, *Two Kings*, p. 225.
13 Ibid., p. 226.
14 Ellis, *Researches*, IV:390.
15 Dibble, *History*, p. 326.
16 Ibid.
17 Jarves, *History*, p. 140.
18 Miti, "Short History," p. 269.
19 Faupel, *Holocaust*, p. 194.
20 Matthew 10:37.
21 Ashe, *Chronicles*, p. 82.
22 Miti, "Short History," p. 274.
23 John Rowe, personal communication.
24 Alexander, *Hawaiian People*, pp. 189–90.

25 Faupel, *Holocaust*, pp. 195–96.
26 R. Oliver, *Missionary*, p. 185.
27 Daws, *Shoal*, p. 98.
28 D. A. Low in Harlow and Chilver, *History*, p. 116.
29 L. A. Fallers, "Despotism," p. 27.
30 Zimbe, "Buganda," p. 241.
31 D. Oliver, *Tahitian Society*, p. 1349.
32 Richards in L. A. Fallers, *King's Men*, p. 308.
33 Thoonen, *Black Martyrs*, p. 72.
34 Tyerman and Bennet, *Journal*, II:164–65.
35 Thoonen, *Black Martyrs*, pp. 210–11.
36 Sagan, *Lust*, p. 87.
37 Ibid., passim.
38 Ibid., pp. 89–95.

6 *The Life and Times of Prime Minister Mukasa, Part III*

1 Faupel, *Holocaust*, p. 111.
2 Ibid., p. 112.
3 Ibid.
4 Ibid., p. 114.
5 Ibid., pp. 123–24.
6 Ibid., p. 137.
7 Ibid., p. 140.
8 Ibid., p. 142.
9 Thoonen, *Black Martyrs*, p. 218.
10 Faupel, *Holocaust*, p. 183.
11 Ibid., p. 157.
12 Ibid.
13 Ibid., p. 162.
14 Ibid.
15 Ibid.
16 Ibid., p. 203.
17 Low, *1875–1900*, p. 8.
18 Kiwanuka, *History*, p. 207.
19 Ibid., p. 208.
20 Gray, "Three Kings," p. 25.
21 Ibid., p. 27.
22 Ibid., p. 36.
23 Ibid.

7 The Beauties of Tonga
1 All quotations in this chapter are from Mariner, *Account,* pp. 275–76.

8 The Enchanted Isles
1 Goldman, *Polynesian Society,* passim.
2 The basic historical data are found in D. Oliver, *Tahitian Society.*
3 For historical data, see Kuykendall, *Hawaiian Kingdom.*

9 The Arioi Society
1 D. Oliver, *Tahitian Society,* p. 919.
2 Ibid., p. 918.
3 Ibid., p. 923.
4 Ibid., pp. 923–24.
5 Ibid., p. 925.
6 Ibid.
7 Ibid., p. 914.
8 Ibid., p. 936.
9 Ibid. p. 937.
10 Ibid., p. 927.
11 Bligh, *Log,* I:391.
12 Ellis, *Researches,* I:232–33.
13 D. Oliver, *Tahitian Society,* p. 938.
14 Ibid., p. 939.
15 Forster, *Voyage,* p. 414.
16 Beaglehole, *Endeavour,* p. clxxxviii.
17 Rank, *Hero,* p. 20.
18 Oliver, *Tahitian Society,* pp. 939–40.

10 Finow, Father and Son
1 Mariner, *Account,* p. 71.
2 Ibid., pp. 71–72.
3 Ibid., p. 74.
4 Ibid.
5 Ibid.
6 Ibid., pp. 74–75.
7 Ibid., p. 77.

8 Ibid., p. 255.
9 Ibid., p. 129.
10 Homer, *Iliad,* bk. XXIV, lines 666–69.
11 Mariner, *Account,* p. 187.
12 Ibid., p. 125.
13 Ibid., p. 160.
14 Ibid., p. 161.
15 Ibid., pp. 161–62.
16 Ibid.
17 Ibid., p. 459.
18 Ibid.
19 Ibid., p. 460
20 Ibid., p. 113.
21 Ibid., p. 89.
22 Shakespeare, *Hamlet,* act I, scene v, line 171.
23 Mariner, *Account,* p. 89.
24 Ibid., pp. 300–1.
25 Ibid., pp. 267–68.
26 Ibid., p. 268.
27 Ibid., p. 275.
28 Ibid., p. 294.
29 Ibid.
30 Ibid., p. 260.

11 "The Taboos Are at an End. . . . The Gods Are a Lie"
1 Bryan, *Ancient,* p. 68.
2 Alexander, *Hawaiian People,* p. 174.
3 Ibid., p. 172.
4 Malo, *Antiquities,* p. 77
5 Sahlins, "Captain Cook," p. 24.
6 Vancouver, *Voyage,* III:53.
7 Ii, *History,* p. 35.
8 Daws, *Shoal,* p. 58.
9 Alexander, *History,* p. 49.
10 Sahlins, "Captain Cook," p. 24.
11 Jarves, *History,* p. 109.
12 Bryan, *Ancient,* p. 68.
13 Handy, *Revolution,* pp. 26–27.
14 Daws, *Shoal,* p. 58.
15 Campbell, *Voyage,* pp. 131–32.
16 Ferdon, *Tahiti,* p. 304.
17 Kamakau, *Chiefs,* p. 222.
18 Dibble, *History,* p. 124.

19 Kuykendall, *Hawaiian Kingdom,*
p. 67.

12 O Brave New World . . .
1 Emerson, *Literature,* p. 222.
2 Ibid., p. 234.
3 Cook, *Voyage,* III:146–47.
4 Beckwith, *Kepelino's,* p. 94.
5 Ibid.
6 Stanley, *Dark Continent,*
pp. 201–2.
7 Speke, *Journal,* p. 234.
8 Ibid., p. 224.
9 Ibid.
10 Handy, *Civilization,* p. 72.
11 Menzies, *Hawaii Nei,* p. 105.
12 Roscoe, *Baganda,* p. 442.
13 Handy and Handy, *Planters,*
pp. 25–26.
14 Goldman, *Society,* p. 177.
15 J. Wilson, *Voyage,* p. 207.
16 Bryan, *Ancient,* p. 43.
17 Gifford, *Tongan Society,* p. 155.
18 Henry, *Tahiti,* p. 154.
19 D. Oliver, *Tahitian Society,*
p. 865.
20 Best, *Maori,* I:92.
21 Kagwa, *Customs,* p. 163.
22 Maquet, *Inequality,* pp. 79–80.
23 Handy, *Religion,* pp. 303–4.
24 Ibid.
25 Rice, *Legends,* p. 26.
26 Tyerman and Bennet, *Journal,*
I:129.
27 Cook, *Voyage,* I:249.
28 Ibid.
29 Mariner, *Account,* p. 96.
30 Rowe, "Revolution," p. 39.
31 Stanley, *Dark Continent,* p. 396.
32 Ibid.
33 Handy and Pukui, *Family
System,* p. 113.
34 Handy, *Religion,* p. 294.
35 Cassirer, *Essay,* passim.
36 Ellis, *Researches,* III:122–23.
37 Marshall Sahlins, personal
communication.

38 Roscoe, *Baganda,* pp. 202–3.
39 Fornander, *Collection,* V:142n.
40 Ellis, *Researches,* I:150.

13 'Ban, 'Ban, Ca-Caliban
1 Harrison, *Mackay,* p. 182.
2 Roscoe, *Baganda,* pp. 334–35.
3 Harrison, *Mackay,* p. 182.
4 Henry, *Tahiti,* p. 186.
5 Malo, *Antiquities,* p. 166.
6 Gill, *Jottings,* pp. 124–27.
7 Ibid.
8 Ellis, *Researches,* II:128–29.
9 Ibid.
10 London Missionary Society,
Transactions (1806), p. 352.
11 Goldman, *Society,* passim.
12 Sahlins, *Stratification,* passim.
13 J. Wilson, *Voyage,* pp. 239–40.
14 Casati, *Equatoria,* II:50;
Harrison, *Mackay,* p. 182.
15 Roscoe, *Baganda,* pp. 210–11.
16 Ibid., p. 106.
17 Herskovits, *Dahomey,* II:31.
18 Roscoe, *Baganda,* p. 114.
19 Ibid., p. 112.
20 Thoonen, *Black Martyrs,* p. 53.
21 Henry, *Tahiti,* pp. 197–98.
22 Ibid.
23 Herskovits, *Dahomey,* I:100.
24 London Missionary Society,
Transactions (1804) p. 6.
25 Felkin, "Notes," p. 741.
26 Roscoe, *Baganda,* p. 322.
27 Henry, *Tahiti,* pp. 196–97.
28 Handy and Pukui, *Family
System,* pp. 204–5.
29 Menzies, *Hawaii,* p. 172.
30 Casati, *Equatoria,* II:33–34.
31 Ellis, *Journal,* pp. 201–2.
32 J. Wilson, *Voyage,* p. 167.
33 Kamakau, *Chiefs,* p. 194.
34 Handy, *Religion,* p. 194.
35 Ibid.
36 Ellis, *Researches,* I:310.
37 Sagan, *Cannibalism,* chap. 4.
38 Cook, *Voyage,* II:43–44.

39 Ellis, *Researches*, I:130.
40 London Missionary Society, *Transactions* (1806), p. 323.
41 Cook, *Voyage*, III:78.
42 Sagan, *Cannibalism*, chap. 3.
43 J. Conrad, *Darkness*, p. 493.
44 Froissart, *Chronicles*, p. 44.
45 Herskovits, *Dahomey*, II:53.
46 D. Oliver, *Tahitian Society*, p. 1059.
47 Sagan, "Religion," pp. 113–15.
48 Aeschylus, *Agamemnon*, line 151.
49 S. Freud, "Obsessive," p. 26.

14 . . . That Has Such People In't!

1 Ellis, *Researches*, I:199.
2 Beaglehole, *Resolution and Discovery*, p. 1154.
3 C. T. Wilson and Felkin, *Uganda*, p. 226.
4 Miti, "Short History," p. 1057.
5 Malo, *Antiquities*, p. 7.
6 Beckwith, *Kepelino's*, p. 80.
7 Handy, *Civilization*, p. 250.
8 Tyerman and Bennet, *Journal*, II:71.
9 Roscoe, *Baganda*, p. 42.
10 Ibid., p. 244.
11 Kagwa, *Customs*, p. 94.
12 K. Emory in Handy, *Civilization*, p. 242.
13 Dibble, *History*, p. 90.
14 K. Emory in Handy, *Civilization*, p. 242.
15 Dibble, *History*, p. 91.
16 Ibid., p. 92.
17 Fornander, *Collection*, VI:34.
18 Henry, *Tahiti*, pp. 236–38.
19 Ellis, *Researches*, III:43.
20 Kamakau, *People*, pp. 111–12.
21 Ibid., pp. 108–9.
22 Ibid., pp. 138–39.
23 Kagwa, *Customs*, p. 141.
24 Ibid., p. 142.
25 Ibid., p. 146.
26 Ellis, *Researches*, I:203.
27 Malo, *Antiquities*, p. 148.
28 Ibid., p. 224.
29 This quote and the entire story of the wrestling matches are taken from Ellis, *Researches*, I:204–8.
30 Goldman, *Society*, epigraph.
31 Maquet, *Inequality*, pp. 117–18.
32 Ibid.
33 Kagwa, *Customs*, passim.
34 Roscoe, *Baganda*, p. 136.
35 R. Oliver, "Royal Tombs," pp. 125–26.
36 Jarves, *History*, p. 104.
37 C. Ehrlich in Harlow and Chilver, *History*, p. 414.
38 Low, *Modern History*, p. 232.
39 Ibid., pp. 44–45.

15 Of Drums, of Cruelty, and Pissing on the King

1 Abraham, *Papers*, passim.
2 Fenichel, *Theory*, passim.
3 Casati, *Equatoria*, II:32–33.
4 This and other quotes about the prophet Kigemuzi are from Kagwa, *Kings*, pp. 118–19.
5 UPI, February 19, 1979.
6 Cunningham, *Uganda*, p. 61.
7 Fornander, *Collection*, V:138.
8 Kamakau, *Chiefs*, p. 46.
9 K. Oberg in Fortes and Evans-Pritchard, *Systems*, p. 151.
10 Fornander, *Collection*, IV:514.
11 Cook, *Voyage*, II:152.
12 Lindstrom, "Wisdom," p. 23.
13 Piaget, *Conception*, p. 38.
14 Ellis, *Researches*, II:423.
15 Vancouver, *Voyage*, I:121–22.
16 Ainsworth, *Infancy*, pp. 77–82.
17 Ibid., p. 82.
18 Roscoe, *Baganda*, p. 25.
19 Ibid., p. 28.
20 Ibid., p. 29.
21 Ibid., p. 30.
22 Kamakau, *People*, pp. 111–12.
23 Fornander, *Collection*, VI:100.

24 Beckwith, *Kepelino's,* p. 130.
25 Beckwith, *Mythology,* p. 84.
26 Roscoe, *Baganda,* pp. 27–28.
27 K. Oberg in Fortes and
    Evans-Pritchard, *Systems,*
    pp. 156–57.
28 Ibid., p. 151.
29 Best, *Maori,* I:79.
30 J. Wilson, *Voyage,* p. 361.
31 Roscoe, *Baganda,* p. 188.
32 Karugire, *Nkore,* p. 101.
33 Gill, *Myths,* p. 164.
34 D. Oliver, *Tahitian Society,*
    p. 1022.
35 Fornander, *Collection,* IV:166.
36 Kamakau, *Chiefs,* p. 91.
37 Kagwa, *Kings,* p. 117.
38 Grant, *Africa,* p. 230.
39 Speke, *Journal,* p. 312.
40 Long, *Africa,* p. 325.
41 L. A. Fallers, *King's Men,* p. 176.
42 A. Richards in ibid., p. 278.
43 Ibid., p. 263.
44 Ii, *History,* p. 59.
45 Kamakau, *Chiefs,* p. 232.
46 Mariner, *Account,* p. 63.
47 Roscoe, *Baganda,* p. 158.

16 Sing Muse: Of Bards, Jesters, Riddles, and the Birth of the Theatre

1 Ellis, *Researches,* IV:106–7.
2 Ibid., p. 462.
3 Ibid.
4 Ashe, *Two Kings,* p. 107.
5 D. Oliver, *Tahitian Society,*
   p. 864.
6 Kamakau, *Chiefs,* p. 111.
7 Ibid.
8 Ibid., p. 112.
9 Handy, *Civilization,* pp. 173–74.
10 Ibid., p. 174.
11 Ibid., pp. 177–78.
12 C. I. Wilson and Felkin,
    Uganda, p. 214.
13 Chadwick and Chadwick,
    Literature, p. 576.

14 Hommon, "Formation," p. 104.
15 Ellis, *Researches,* I:287.
16 Gifford, *Tongan Society,* p. 126.
17 Speke, *Journal,* p. 433.
18 Codere, "Power," p. 56.
19 Fornander, *Collection,* IV:594.
20 Ibid., p. 514.
21 Handy, *Civilization,* p. 219.
22 Kamakau, *Chiefs,* p. 54.
23 Cook, *Voyage,* I:254.
24 Vancouver, *Voyage,* III:77.
25 Gill, *Myths,* pp. 179–80.
26 Ibid., pp. 95–96.
27 Ibid., pp. 194–99.
28 Ibid., p. vi.
29 Emerson, *Literature,* p. 94.
30 D. Oliver, *Tahitian Society,*
    p. 340.
31 Emerson, *Literature,* p. 94.
32 Bligh, *Log,* I:426.
33 Beaglehole, *Resolution and
    Adventure,* p. 421.
34 Shakespeare, *Hamlet,* act II,
    scene ii, 575–78.
35 Beaglehole, *Resolution and
    Adventure,* p. 413.
36 Emerson, *Literature,* p. 93.
37 Ibid.
38 Ibid.
39 Ibid.
40 Corney, *Quest,* II:330.
41 D. Oliver, *Tahitian Society,*
    p. 342.
42 Beaglehole, *Resolution and
    Adventure,* pp. 842–43.

17 The Heroic Age

1 Zimbe, "Buganda," p. 231.
2 D. Oliver, *Tahitian Society,*
   p. 394.
3 Henry, *Tahiti,* pp. 304–5.
4 Mariner, *Account,* p. 80.
5 Ibid., p. 113.
6 Ritter, *Shaka,* p. 122.
7 Best, *Maori,* I:449.
8 Ibid., p. 378.
9 Mariner, *Account,* pp. 110–11.

10 Ibid., p. 185.
11 Ibid., p. 430.
12 Fornander, *Collection*, V:470.
13 Handy, *Revolution*, p. 25.
14 Kamakau, *Chiefs*, p. 182.
15 Stanley, *Dark Continent*, pp. 350–51
16 Ibid., pp. 351–58.
17 C. T. Wilson and Felkin, *Uganda*, pp. 220–21.
18 Fornander, *Collection*, IV:226.
19 This story of Liloa and all quotes for it come from Kamakau, *Chiefs*, pp. 2–7.
20 Williamson, *Systems*, III:203–4.
21 Roscoe, *Twenty-five Years*, pp. 219–20.

18 The Slaughter of the Innocents

1 Ellis, *Researches*, I:251–52.
2 Kamakau, *Chiefs*, p. 234.
3 Roscoe, *Baganda*, p. 54.
4 Bligh, *Voyage*, p. 79.
5 Ellis, *Researches*, I:257.
6 Ibid., pp. 257–58.
7 Ibid., p. 255.
8 Ibid., pp. 255–56.
9 Roscoe, *Baganda*, p. 54.
10 D. Oliver, *Tahitian Society*, p. 707.

19 Male Homosexuality and Male Bisexuality

1 Malinowski, *Sexual Life*, p. 584.
2 Mead, *Sex*, p. 214.
3 Faupel, *Holocaust*, p. 5.
4 Maquet, *Inequality*, p. 77.
5 Herskovits, *Dahomey*, p. 288.
6 Ibid., p. 289.
7 Maquet, *Inequality*, p. 77.
8 Kamakau, *Chiefs*, p. 234.
9 Beaglehole, *Resolution and Discovery*, p. 596.
10 Ibid., p. 624.
11 Ibid., p. 1226.
12 Malo, *Antiquities*, p. 256.

13 D. Oliver, *Tahitian Society*, p. 369.
14 Dover, *Homosexuality*, passim.
15 D. Oliver, *Tahitian Society*, p. 371.
16 Ibid., p. 370.

20 Gambling, Prostitution, Exhibitionism, and Adultery Games

1 Malinowski, *Sexual Life*, pp. 52–59.
2 Ii, *History*, p. 67.
3 Beckwith, *Mythology*, p. 111.
4 D. Oliver, *Tahitian Society*, p. 863.
5 Herskovits, *Dahomey*, p. 268n.
6 Maquet, *Inequality*, p. 78.
7 Schweinfurth, *Pasha*, pp. 87–88.
8 Genesis 3:11.
9 Beaglehole, *Resolution and Discovery*, p. 945.
10 Beaglehole, *Endeavour*, pp. 93–94.
11 Ibid., p. 93.
12 Beaglehole, *Resolution and Discovery*, p. 1063.
13 D. Oliver, *Tahitian Society*, p. 336.
14 Ibid., p. 339.
15 Ibid., pp. 368–69; Beaglehole, *Resolution and Adventure*, p. 1185.
16 Handy and Pukui, *Family System*, p. 101.
17 Bligh, *Log*, II:78.
18 Malo, *Antiquities*, p. 214.
19 Ibid., p. 217.

21 From Kinship to the State; from Band Society to Complex Society

1 Evans-Pritchard, *Kinship*, p. 178.
2 The general description of the Nuer which follows is taken from Evans-Pritchard, *Nuer*, passim.

3 Childe, *History,* passim.
4 Service, *Primitive,* p. 47.
5 Ibid., p. 49.
6 Spencer and Gillen, *Arunta,* passim.
7 Service, *Primitive,* pp. 46–98.
8 Service, *Primitive,* p. 47.
9 Ibid., pp. 72–98.
10 Richards, *Chiefs,* p. 284.
11 Evans-Pritchard, *Nuer,* p. 173.
12 Ibid., p. 174.
13 Ibid., p. 209.
14 Ibid., p. 210.
15 Ibid., p. 183; Lienhardt, *Divinity,* p. 8.
16 Evans-Pritchard, *Nuer,* p. 173.
17 Ibid., p. 235.
18 Ibid., p. 245.
19 Ibid., pp. 235–36.
20 Lienhardt, "Western Dinka," p. 120.

22 *The Transformation of the Kinship System*
1 Evans-Pritchard, *Nuer,* p. 183.
2 Ibid., p. 166.
3 Ibid., p. 169.
4 Ibid., p. 162.
5 Ibid., p. 169.
6 Ibid., p. 151.
7 Mair, *Government,* p. 59.
8 Fortes and Evans-Pritchard, *Systems,* p. 278.
9 Lienhardt, "Western Dinka," p. 118.
10 D. Tait in Middleton and Tait, *Tribes,* p. 207.
11 Evans-Pritchard, *Nuer,* p. 121.
12 Lienhardt, "Western Dinka," p. 116.
13 Gerth and Mills, *Weber,* p. 334.
14 S. Freud, *Civilization,* p. 61.
15 Sagan, *Cannibalism,* passim.
16 Shorter, *Chiefship,* passim; Schapera, *Government,* passim.
17 Oppenheimer, *State,* passim.

23 *"He Who Never Travels Praises His Mother's Cooking"*
1 Mukasa, "Simuda Nyuma," p. 53.
2 Ii, *History,* p. 22.
3 Ibid., p. 56.
4 Ibid., p. 58.
5 A. Richards in L. A. Fallers, *King's Men,* p. 260.
6 Mair, *African People,* p. 60.
7 Ainsworth, *Infancy,* p. 417.
8 Mair, *African People,* p. 60.
9 Ibid., pp. 61–62.
10 Richards, *Village,* pp. 19–20.
11 A. Richards in L. A. Fallers, *King's Men,* p. 260.
12 Mair, *African People,* p. 60.
13 Ainsworth, *Infancy,* p. 417.
14 Richards, *Village,* pp. 19–20.
15 Ainsworth, *Infancy,* p. 403.
16 Ibid., pp. 416–17.
17 Mair, *African People,* p. 69.
18 Richards, *Village,* p. 20.
19 Ibid., pp. 19–21.
20 M. C. Fallers, *Bantu,* pp. 35–36.
21 Mair, *African People,* pp. 158–59.
22 M. C. Fallers, *Bantu,* pp. 35–36.
23 Richards, *Village,* pp. 19–21.
24 Thoonen, *Black Martyrs,* p. 48.
25 M. C. Fallers, *Bantu,* p. 36.
26 Richards, *Village,* pp. 20–21.

24 *The Kabaka and the Clans*
1 Bozeman, *Conflict,* p. 25.
2 Roscoe and Kagwa, "Enquiry," passim.
3 Richards, "Mechanisms," p. 176.
4 Mukwaya, *Tenure,* p. 10.
5 L. A. Fallers, *King's Men,* p. 88.
6 Ibid., p. 89.
7 Roscoe and Kagwa, "Enquiry," p. 101.
8 Miti, "Short History," pp. 60–61.
9 Ibid.
10 Roscoe and Kagwa, "Enquiry," p. 19.

11 Mukwaya, *Tenure,* pp. 12–13.
12 Southwold, "Succession," p. 100.
13 Kelly, "Tenure," p. 78.
14 Kiwanuka, *History,* p. 110.
15 Roscoe and Kagwa, "Enquiry," p. 15.
16 Kiwanuka, *History,* p. 110.
17 Roscoe and Kagwa, "Enquiry" pp. 6–8; Cox, "Growth," p. 158.
18 Rowe, "Revolution," pp. 25–26.
19 D. Oliver, *Tahitian Society,* p. 1065.
20 Richards, *Chiefs,* p. 46.
21 Kagwa, "Clans," pp. 13–14.
22 Wright, *Buganda,* p. 4.
23 Ibid., pp. 4–5.
24 Ibid.
25 Ibid., pp. 5–6; Miti, "Short History," pp. 197–98.
26 Wright, *Buganda,* pp. 5–6.
27 Ibid.; Miti, "Short History," pp. 197–98.
28 Wright, *Buganda,* pp. 5–6.
29 Miti, "History," p. 61.
30 Kagwa, "Clans," pp. 29–30.
31 Ibid., p. 30.
32 Kiwanuka, *History,* p. 72.
33 Ibid., p. 55.
34 Miti, "History," pp. 38–39.
35 L. A. Fallers, *King's Men,* p. 172.
36 Roscoe, *Baganda,* pp. 142–44.
37 Richards, *Village,* p. 35.
38 L. A. Fallers, "Despotism," p. 19.
39 Cochrane, *Christianity,* p. 18.
40 Richards, *Village,* pp. 29–30.
41 L. A. Fallers, *King's Men,* p. 151.
42 Wright, *Buganda,* p. 4.
43 Ray, "Kingship," p. 67.
44 D. Oliver, *Tahitian Society,* pp. 1186–88.
45 Rowe, "Revolution," p. 188.

25 On Tyranny

1 Chodorow, *Mothering;* Dinnerstein, *Mermaid;* deMause, *Childhood.*
2 Ashe, *Two Kings,* pp. 65–66.
3 Hommon, "Formation," p. 154.
4 Ellis, *Researches,* III:128–29.
5 Roscoe, *Baganda,* p. 53.
6 Jarves, *History,* p. 87.
7 Mariner, *Account,* p. 364.
8 Handy, *Civilization,* p. 80.
9 Roscoe, *Baganda,* pp. 246–47.
10 A. Richards in L. A. Fallers, *King's Men,* pp. 270–71.
11 Kagwa, *Kings,* pp. 133–34.
12 Felkin, "Notes," p. 710.
13 Roscoe, *Baganda,* p. 44.
14 L. A. Fallers, *King's Men,* p. 68.
15 Beattie, *State,* p. 8.
16 Gifford, *Tongan Society,* p. 118.
17 D. Oliver, *Tahitian Society,* p. 785.
18 Gifford, *Tongan Society,* p. 117.
19 Ibid.
20 Ibid., p. 126.
21 Beckwith, *Kepelino's,* p. 166.
22 Harrison, *Mackay,* p. 188.
23 Schapera, *Government,* p. 60.
24 Roscoe, *Baganda,* pp. 12–13.
25 Beckwith, *Kepelino's,* pp. 143–44.
26 Roscoe, *Baganda,* pp. 241–42.
27 Ibid., pp. 244–45.
28 Ibid., pp. 241–43, 369.
29 Ibid., pp. 245–46.
30 Ibid., p. 206.
31 Hobbs, *Hawaii,* p. 11.
32 Handy and Handy, *Planters,* pp. 52–53.
33 Alexander, "Land Titles," p. 108.
34 Earle, "Hierarchies," p. 156.
35 Ibid, p. 157.
36 Mariner, *Account,* pp. 157n.–58n.
37 Corney, *Quest,* III:27.
38 M. C. Fallers, *Bantu,* pp. 63–64.
39 Handy and Pukui, *Family System,* pp. 196–97.
40 Richards, *Village,* p. 57.
41 Kagwa, *Customs,* p. 15.

42 Handy and Pukui, *Family Systems*, p. 199.

43 D. Oliver, *Tahitian Society*, pp. 789–90.

44 Kuykendall, *Hawaiian Kingdom*, p. 274.

45 Richards in L. A. Fallers, *King's Men*, p. 314.

46 Roscoe, *Baganda*, p. 490.

47 Handy and Pukui, *Family Systems*, p. 203.

48 Ibid., p. 195.

49 Ibid., p. 204.

50 Ibid., p. 203.

51 Hommon, "Formation," p. 72.

52 Handy and Handy, *Planters*, p. 19.

53 Malo, *Antiquities*, p. 67, trans. note.

54 Henry, *Tahiti*, p. 615.

55 Ibid., pp. 628–29.

56 Roscoe, *Baganda*, p. 81.

57 Roscoe, *Banyoro*, p. 170.

58 Roscoe, *Baganda*, pp. 263–64.

59 Maquet, *Inequality*, p. 43.

60 A. Richards in L. A. Fallers, *King's Men*, p. 259.

61 Ibid.

62 Beattie, *Bunyoro*, pp. 51–52.

63 Maquet, *Inequality*, p. 77.

64 Beattie, *Bunyoro*, p. 52.

65 Richards in L. A. Fallers, *King's Men*, p. 296.

66 Ibid.

67 Beattie, *Bunyoro*, p. 51.

68 Williamson, *Systems*, III:195.

69 Vancouver, *Voyage*, I:109.

70 Matthew 2:11.

26 Chieftainship

1 Durkheim, *Labor*, p. 195.

2 Henry, *Jungle*, p. 108.

3 R. Oliver in R. Oliver and Matthew, *History*, pp. 191–92.

4 Maquet, *Power*, p. 90.

5 Roscoe, *Bagesu*, p. 54.

6 Evans-Pritchard, *Anuak*, p. 43.

7 Ibid., p. 44.

8 L. A. Fallers, *Bureaucracy*, p. 138.

9 Ibid., p. 99.

10 Ibid.

11 Ibid., p. 138.

12 Southall, *Alur*, p. 91.

13 Ibid., p. 108.

14 Ibid., p. 144.

15 Ibid., pp. 198–99.

16 Ibid., p. 146.

17 Ibid., passim.

18 Ibid., p. 33.

19 Shorter, *Chiefship*, p. 151.

20 Ibid., p. 121.

21 Sahlins, "Poor Man," passim.

22 Shorter, *Chiefship*, p. 223.

23 R. Oliver in R. Oliver and Matthew, *History*, pp. 191–92.

24 Shorter, *Chiefship*, pp. 135–37.

25 R. Oliver in R. Oliver and Matthew, *History*, p. 191.

26 Shorter, *Chiefship*, p. 110.

27 L. A. Fallers, *Bureaucracy*, p. 99.

28 L. A. Fallers, *Inequality*, pp. 47–48.

29 L. A. Fallers, *Bureaucracy*, pp. 126–27.

30 Ibid., passim.

31 D. Oliver, *Tahitian Society*, p. 1232.

32 Shorter, "Embryo," pp. 49–50.

33 Ibid.

34 Ibid.

35 Ibid.

36 Ibid.

27 Kingship: The Dream of Omnipotence

1 Roscoe, *Baganda*, p. 84; Roscoe, *Twenty-five Years*, pp. 80–81; Roscoe, *Banyoro*, pp. 136–37.

2 Herskovits, *Dahomey*, I:153.

3 Malo, *Antiquities*, pp. 54–55.

4 Beckwith, *Kepelino's*, p. 195.

5 Handy, *Revolution*, p. 4.

6 Ellis, *Researches*, III:113–14.

7 Richards, *Chiefs*, pp. 37–38.

8 Herskovits, *Dahomey,* II:30.
9 Kagwa, *Kings,* p. 108.
10 Schapera, *Government,* pp. 102–3.
11 Kamakau, *Chiefs,* p. 252.
12 Mukasa, "Rule," p. 136.
13 Livingstone, *Journals,* p. 450.
14 Felkin, "Notes," p. 740.
15 Henry, *Tahiti,* p. 188.
16 D. Oliver, *Tahitian Society,*
   pp. 1059–60.
17 Ellis, *Researches,* III:105.
18 Felkin, "Notes," p. 711.
19 Maquet, *Inequality,* p. 125.
20 Schapera, *Government,*
   pp. 107–8.
21 Richards, *Chiefs,* pp. 37–38.
22 Mair, *African People,* pp. 180–81.
23 Schapera, *Government,* p. 138.
24 Malo, *Antiquities,* p. 176.
25 Kamakau, *People,* p. 17.
26 Henry, *Tahiti,* p. 296.
27 Kamakau, *People,* p. 3.
28 R. Oliver, "Royal Tombs,"
   pp. 125–26.
29 Malo, *Antiquities,* p. 59.
30 Corney, *Quest,* III:201–2.
31 D. Oliver, *Tahitian Society,*
   p. 1175.
32 Heer, *Medieval,* p. 349.
33 Ritter, *Shaka,* pp. 241 ff.
34 Roscoe, *Baganda,* p. 273.
35 Rowe, "Revolution," p. 70.
36 Durkheim, *Labor,* p. 195.
37 Mukasa, "Rule," p. 139.
38 Rowe, "Revolution," p. 68.
39 Cunningham, *Uganda,*
   pp. 226–28.
40 Roscoe and Kagwa, "Enquiry,"
   p. 52.
41 Kagwa, *Customs,* p. 110.

28 Kingship: The Failure of Omnipotence

1 Roscoe, *Soul,* pp. 202–3.
2 Oberg, "Ankole," pp. 158–59.
3 Roscoe, *Soul,* p. 200.
4 Oberg, "Ankole," pp. 158–59.

5 J. Wilson, *Voyage,* pp. 242–43.
6 Campbell, *Voyage,* pp. 98–99.
7 A. C. Conrad, *Marin,* p. 230.
8 Kelly, *Freycinet,* p. 78.
9 Ritter, *Shaka,* p. 313.
10 Maquet, *Inequality,* pp. 79–80.
11 Roscoe, *Baganda,* pp. 103–4.
12 I. Kopytoff in Gibbs, *Africa,*
   p. 460.
13 Kelly, *Freycinet,* p. 78.
14 Ellis, *Researches,* IV:177.
15 Maquet, *Inequality,* p. 125.
16 Roscoe, *Soul,* p. 140.
17 Oberg, "Ankole," pp. 158–59.
18 L. A. Fallers, *Bureaucracy,* p. 233.
19 Gluckman in Fortes and
   Evans-Pritchard, *Systems,* p. 35.
20 L. A. Fallers, *Bureaucracy,*
   pp. 134–36.
21 Schapera, *Government,*
   pp. 158–59.
22 Ibid.
23 Ibid., p. 171.
24 Richards, *Chiefs,* p. 47.
25 Roscoe, *Baganda,* p. 99.
26 Richards, *Chiefs,* p. 47.
27 Schapera, *Government,* p. 174.
28 Roscoe, *Baganda,* p. 336.
29 J. Fontaine and A. Richards in
   Richards, *Chiefs,* p. 178.
30 Richards, *Chiefs,* p. 132.
31 Vancouver, *Voyage,* III:35.
32 Alexander, *Hawaiian People,*
   pp. 118–19.
33 Kelly, *Freycinet,* p. 20.
34 Ibid., p. 111.
35 Rowe, "Introduction," p. xi.
36 Mariner, *Account,* p. 77n.
37 Kamakau, *Chiefs,* p. 178.
38 Cook, *Voyage,* I:411–12.
39 Roscoe, *Baganda,* pp. 237–38.

29 Toward a Theory of Social and Cultural Development

1 A. Freud, *Ego,* pp. 109 ff.
2 Rachel Sagan, personal
   communication.

3 Moore, "Surgery," pp. 537–38.

4 Kliman, "Nursery," p. 490.

5 Ibid., pp. 500–1.

6 Mahler, Pine, and Bergman, *Birth*, p. 97.

7 Piaget, *Conception*, p. 139.

8 Mahler, Pine, and Bergman, *Birth*, p. 79.

9 Ibid., p. 71.

10 Ibid., p. 70.

11 Ibid., p. 74.

12 Ibid., pp. 76–77.

13 Ibid., pp. 78–79.

14 Mahler, *Symbiosis*, p. 134.

15 Mahler, Pine, and Bergman, *Birth*, p. 93.

16 Ibid.

17 Ibid., p. 91.

18 Mahler, *Symbiosis*, pp. 141–45 (italics added).

19 Mahler, Pine, and Bergman, *Birth*, p. 102.

20 Whiting and Child, *Personality*, passim.

21 Mahler, Pine, and Bergman, *Birth*, p. 98.

22 Ibid., p. 80.

23 Ibid., p. 93.

30 Drives, Needs, and Symbolic Transformation

1 Strachey, "Introduction," pp. xxiv–xxv.

2 Cassirer, *Essay*, p. 26.

3 *The Libation Bearers*, lines 527–34.

4 Rachel Sagan, personal communication.

5 Van Gennep, *Rites*, passim.

6 Ibid., p. 11.

7 Radcliffe-Brown, *Structure*, p. 50.

8 D. Thomas, *Writings*, poem 2.

9 Elizabeth Marshall Thomas, personal communication.

10 Sahlins, *Economics*, chap. 1.

Bibliography

Abraham, K. 1927. *Selected Papers.* London: Hogarth Press.

Adams, H. 1947. *Memoirs of Arii Taimai e Marama of Eimeo.* New York: Scholar's Facsimiles and Reprints.

Aeschylus, 1959. *Agamemnon,* trans. Richmond Lattimore. Chicago: University of Chicago Press.

Ainsworth, M. 1967. *Infancy in Uganda.* Baltimore: Johns Hopkins Press.

Alexander, W. D. 1891. *A Brief History of the Hawaiian People.* New York: American Book Company.

Alexander, W. D. 1891. "A Brief History of Land Titles in the Hawaiian Kingdom." *Hawaiian Almanac and Annual,* pp. 105–24.

Ashe, R. P. 1890. *Two Kings of Uganda.* London: Sampson Low, Marston, Searle and Rivington.

Ashe, R. P. 1895. *Chronicles of Uganda.* New York: Randolph and Company.

Baker, S. 1875. *Ismailia.* New York: Harper and Brothers.

Beaglehole, J. C., ed. 1955. *The Journals of Captain James Cook on His Voyages of Discovery.* Volume I: *The Voyage of the Endeavour, 1768–1771.* Cambridge: Cambridge University Press.

Beaglehole, J. C., ed. 1961. *The Journals of Captain James Cook on His Voyages of Discovery.* Volume II: *The Voyage of the Resolution and Adventure, 1772–1775.* Cambridge: Cambridge University Press.

Beaglehole, J. C., ed. 1967. *The Journals of Captain Cook on His Voyages of Discovery.* Volume III. *The Voyage of the Resolution and Discovery, 1776–1780.* Cambridge: Cambridge University Press.

Beattie, J. 1960. *Bunyoro: An African Kingdom.* New York: Holt, Rinehart and Winston.

Beattie, J. 1971. *The Nyoro State.* Oxford: The Clarendon Press.

Beckwith, M. W., ed. 1932. *Kepelino's Traditions of Hawaii.* Honolulu: Bernice P. Bishop Museum, Bulletin 95.

Beckwith, M. 1940. *Hawaiian Mythology.* New Haven: Yale University Press.

Bellah, R. N. 1970. *Beyond Belief.* New York: Harper and Row.

Bendix, R. 1960. *Max Weber.* New York: Doubleday.

Best, E. 1924. *The Maori,* 2 vols. Wellington, N.Z.: Harry H. Tombs.

Bligh, W. 1792. *A Voyage to the South Sea . . .* London: George Nicol.

Bligh, W. N. d. *The Log of the Bounty,* 2 vols. London: Golden Cockerel Press.

Bovis, M. de. 1909. *État de la société taitienne à l'arrivée des Européens.* Papeete: The French Government.

Bozeman, A. 1976. *Conflict in Africa.* Princeton: Princeton University Press.

Bryan, E. H., Jr. 1938. *Ancient Hawaiian Life.* Honolulu: Advertiser Publishing Company.

Campbell, A. 1817. *A Voyage Round the World from 1806 to 1812.* New York: Van Winkle, Wiley and Company.

Casati, G. 1891. *Ten Years in Equatoria,* 2 vols. London: Frederick Warne and Company.

Cassirer, E. 1944. *An Essay on Man.* New Haven: Yale University Press.

Chadwick, H. M. 1912. *The Heroic Age.* Cambridge: Cambridge University Press.

Chadwick, H. M., and Chadwick, N. K. 1968. *The Growth of Literature.* Volume III. Cambridge: The University Press.

Childe, V. G. 1946. *What Happened in History.* Baltimore: Penguin Books.

Chodorow, N. 1978. *The Reproduction of Mothering.* Berkeley: University of California Press.

Claessen, Henri, and Skalnik, Peter, eds. 1978. *The Early State.* The Hague: Mouton Publishers.

Cochrane, C. N. 1977. *Christianity and Classical Culture.* New York: Oxford University Press.

Codere, H. 1962. "Power in Ruanda." *Anthropologica,* 2d ser. IV: 45–85.

Cohen, D. 1972. *The Traditional History of Busoga.* Oxford: The University Press.

Cohen, R., and Middleton, J., eds. 1970. *From Tribe to Nation in Africa.* Scranton, Pa.: Chandler Publishing Company.

Conrad, A. C., ed. 1973. *The Letters and Journal of Francisco de Paula Marín.* Honolulu: University Press of Hawaii.

Conrad, J. 1947. *The Heart of Darkness* in *The Portable Conrad.* New York: Viking Press.

Cook, J. 1784. *A Voyage to the Pacific Ocean . . . for Making Discoveries in the Northern Hemisphere,* 3 vols. London: W. and A. Strahan.

Corney, B. G., ed. 1915. *The Quest and Occupation of Tahiti by Emissaries of Spain.* Volume II. London: Cambridge University Press.

Corney, B. G., ed. 1919. *The Quest and Occupation of Tahiti by Emissaries of Spain.* Volume III. London: Cambridge University Press.

Cox, A. H. 1950. "The Growth and Expansion of Buganda." *Uganda Journal* XIV: 153–59.

Cunningham, J. F. 1905. *Uganda and Its Peoples.* London: Hutchinson and Company.

Danielsson, B. 1956. *Love in the South Seas.* London: George Allen.

Davidson, B. 1969. *A History of East and Central Africa.* Garden City: Doubleday.

Davies, J. 1961. *The History of the Tahitian Mission, 1799–1830.* Cambridge: Cambridge University Press.

Daws, G. 1968. *Shoal of Time.* New York: Macmillan.

deMause, L., ed. 1974. *The History of Childhood.* New York: Psychohistory Press.

Dibble, S. 1909. *A History of the Sandwich Islands.* Honolulu: Thomas G. Thrum.

Dinnerstein, D. 1977. *The Mermaid and the Minotaur.* New York: Harper and Row.

Dover, K. J. 1980. *Greek Homosexuality.* New York: Vintage Books.

Durkheim, E. 1933. *On the Division of Labor in Society.* New York: Macmillan and Co.

Earle, T. K. 1973. "Control Hierarchies in the Traditional Irrigation Economy of Halelea District, Kauai, Hawaii." Unpublished Ph.D. dissertation, University of Michigan.

Ellis, W. 1825. *Journal of a Tour Around Hawaii, the Largest of the Sandwich Islands.* Boston: Crocker and Brewster.

Ellis, W. 1969. *Polynesian Researches,* 4 vols. Rutland, Vt.: Charles E. Tuttle Company.

Emerson, N. B. 1965. *Unwritten Literature of Hawaii.* Rutland, Vt.: Charles E. Tuttle Company.

Emory, K. 1933. *Stone Remains in the Society Islands.* Honolulu: Bernice P. Bishop Museum, Bulletin 116.

Evans-Pritchard, E. E. 1940. "The Nuer of the Southern Sudan." In *African Political Systems,* ed. M. Fortes and E. E. Evans-Pritchard.

London: Oxford University Press.

Evans-Pritchard, E. E. 1940. *The Nuer.* Oxford: The University Press.

Evans-Pritchard, E. E. 1940. *The Political System of the Anuak of the Anglo-Egyptian Sudan.* London: Percy Lund, Humphries and Company.

Evans-Pritchard, E. E. 1951. *Kinship and Marriage Among the Nuer.* Oxford: Clarendon Press.

Evans-Pritchard, E. E. 1956. *Nuer Religion.* Oxford: Clarendon Press.

Fallers, L. A. 1959–60. "Despotism, Status Culture and Social Mobility in an African Kingdom." *Comparative Studies in Society and History* II:11–32.

Fallers, L. A., ed. 1964. *The King's Men.* London: Oxford University Press.

Fallers, L. A. 1965. *Bantu Bureaucracy.* Chicago: University of Chicago Press.

Fallers, L. A. 1973. *Inequality: Social Stratification Reconsidered.* Chicago: University of Chicago Press.

Fallers, M. C. 1960. *The Eastern Lacustrine Bantu.* London: International African Institute.

Faupel, J. F. 1962. *African Holocaust.* New York: P. J. Kenedy and Sons.

Felkin, R. 1886. "Notes on the Waganda Tribe." *Proceedings of The Royal Society of Edinburgh.* Volume XXXIII, pp. 699–770.

Fenichel, O. 1945. *The Psychoanalytic Theory of Neurosis.* New York: W. W. Norton.

Ferdon, E. N. 1981. *Early Tahiti as*

the Explorers Saw It, 1767–1797. Tucson: The University of Arizona Press.

Fornander, A. 1916. *Fornander Collection of Hawaiian Antiquities and Folk-Lore.* Volume IV. Honolulu: Bishop Museum Press.

Fornander, A. 1918–19. *Fornander Collection of Hawaiian Antiquities and Folk-Lore.* Volume V. Honolulu: Bishop Museum Press.

Fornander, A. 1919–20. *Fornander Collection of Antiquities and Folk-Lore.* Volume VI. Honolulu: Bishop Museum Press.

Fornander, A. 1969. *An Account of the Polynesian Race.* Rutland, Vt.: Charles E. Tuttle Company.

Forster, G. 1968. *A Voyage Round the World, in His Britannic Majesty's Sloop, Resolution . . .* Berlin: Akademie-Verlag.

Fortes, M., and Evans-Pritchard, E. E., eds. 1940. *African Political Systems.* London: Oxford University Press.

Frankfort, H., ed. 1946. *The Intellectual Adventure of Ancient Man.* Chicago: University of Chicago Press.

Freud, A. 1973. *The Ego and the Mechanisms of Defense.* New York: International Universities Press.

Freud, S. 1962. *Civilization and Its Discontents.* New York: W. W. Norton and Company.

Freud, S. 1963. "Obsessive Acts and Religious Practices." In *Character and Culture.* New York: Collier Books.

Fried, Morton H. 1967. *The Evolution of Political Society.* New York: Random House.

Froissart, 1968. *Chronicles,* trans. and ed. Geoffrey Brereton. Baltimore: Penguin Books.

Gennep, A. van. 1960. *The Rites of Passage.* Chicago: University of Chicago Press.

Gerth, H. H., and Mills, C. W. 1958. *From Max Weber.* New York: Oxford University Press.

Gibbs, J., ed. 1965. *Peoples of Africa.* New York: Holt, Rinehart and Winston.

Gifford, E. W. 1929. *Tongan Society.* Honolulu: Bernice P. Bishop Museum, Bulletin 61.

Gill, W. 1876. *Myths and Songs from the South Pacific.* London: Henry S. King and Company.

Gill, W. N.d. *Jottings from the Pacific.* New York: American Tract Society.

Goldman, I. 1970. *Ancient Polynesian Society.* Chicago: University of Chicago Press.

Golovin, V. M. 1974. *Chapters on Hawaii . . . from Voyage Around the World . . . 1817, 1818, and 1819.* Honolulu: University of Hawaii Press.

Grant, J. A. 1864. *A Walk Across Africa.* London: William Blackwood and Sons.

Gray, J. M. 1934. "Mutesa of Buganda." *Uganda Journal* I:22–50.

Gray, J. M. 1947. "Ahmed Bin Ibrahim—the First Arab to Reach Buganda." *Uganda Journal* XI: 80–97.

Gray, J. M. 1950. "The Year of the Three Kings of Buganda." *Uganda Journal* XIV:15–52.

Handy, E. 1927. *Polynesian Religion.* Honolulu: Bernice P. Bishop Museum, Bulletin 34.

Handy, E. S. C. 1931. *Cultural Revolution in Hawaii.* American Council, Institute of Pacific Relations.

Handy, E. S. C. 1933. *Ancient Hawaiian Civilization.* Honolulu: Kamehameha Schools.

Handy, E. S. C. 1971. *History and Culture in the Society Islands.* New York: Krause Reprint Company.

Handy, E. S. C., and Handy, E. G. 1972. *Native Planters in Old Hawaii.* Honolulu: Bernice P. Bishop Museum, Bulletin 233.

Handy, E., and Pukui, M. 1958. *The Polynesian Family System in Ka-U, Hawaii.* Wellington, N.Z.: The Polynesian Society.

Harlow, V., and Chilver, E. 1965. *History of East Africa.* Volume II. Oxford: The University Press.

Harrison, J. 1895. *A. A. Mackay.* New York: Armstrong and Son.

Hattersley, C. W. 1908. *The Baganda at Home.* London: Religious Tract Society.

Heer, F. 1963. *The Medieval World.* New York: Mentor Books.

Henry, J. 1941. *Jungle People.* Richmond: J. J. Augustin.

Henry, T. 1928. *Ancient Tahiti.* Honolulu: Bernice P. Bishop Museum.

Herskovits, M. 1938. *Dahomey,* 2 vols. New York: J. J. Augustin.

Hobbs, J. 1935. *Hawaii: A Pageant of the Soil.* Palo Alto: Stanford University Press.

Homer, 1951. *The Iliad,* trans. Richmond Lattimore. Chicago: The University of Chicago Press.

Hommon, R. J. 1976. "The Formation of Primitive States in Pre-Contact Hawaii." Unpublished Ph.D. dissertation, University of Arizona.

Huffman, R. 1970. *Nuer Customs and Folk-Lore.* London: Frank Cass and Company.

Ii, J. P. 1959. *Fragments of Hawaiian History.* Honolulu: Bishop Museum Press.

Jarves, J. J. 1847. *History of the Hawaiian Islands.* Honolulu: Charles Edwin Hitchcock.

Kagwa, Sir Apolo. 1969. *The Customs of the Baganda,* trans. Ernest Kalibala, ed. May Mandelbaum (Edel). New York: AMS Press.

Kagwa, Sir Apolo. 1971. *The Kings of Buganda,* trans. and ed. M. S. M. Kiwanuka. Nairobi: East African Publishing House.

Kagwa, Sir Apolo. N.d. "Ekitabo Kye Bika Bya Baganda: The Book of the Ganda Clans." Unpublished manuscript. Copy in Columbia University Library.

Kamakau, S. 1961. *Ruling Chiefs of Hawaii.* Honolulu: The Kamehameha Schools Press.

Kamakau, S. 1964. *Ka Po'e Kahiko: The People of Old.* Honolulu: Bernice P. Bishop Museum, Special Publication 51.

Karugire, S. 1971. *A History of the Kingdom of Nkore in Western Uganda.* Oxford: The University Press.

Katumba, A., and Welbourn, F. B. 1964. "Muslim Martyrs of Buganda." *Uganda Journal* XXVIII: 151–63.

Kelly, M. 1956. "Changes in Land Tenure in Hawaii, 1778–1850." Unpublished M.A. thesis, University of Hawaii.

Kelly, M., ed. 1978. *Louis Claude de Saulses de Freycinet: Hawaii in 1819.* Honolulu: Bernice P. Bishop Museum.

Kiwanuka, M. 1969. "The Evolution of Chiefship in Buganda c. 1400–1900." *Journal of Asian and African Studies* IV: 172–85.

Kiwanuka, M. 1972. *A History of Buganda.* New York: Africana Publishing Corporation.

Kliman, G. W. 1975. "Analyst in the Nursery." *The Psychoanalytic Study of the Child* 30:477–510.

Kottack, C. 1972. "Ecological Variables in the Origin and Evolution of African States: The Bugandan Example." *Comparative Studies in Society and History* XIV:351–80.

Kuykendall, R. S. 1947. *The Hawaiian Kingdom, 1778–1854.* Honolulu: University of Hawaii Press.

Lee, I. 1920. *Bligh's Second Voyage to the South Sea.* London: Longmans, Green and Company.

Lemarchand, R. 1970. *Rwanda and Burundi.* New York: Praeger.

Lewis, H. S. 1965. *A Galla Monarchy.* Madison: University of Wisconsin Press.

Lienhardt, G. 1958. "The Western Dinka." In *Tribes Without Rulers,* ed. J. Middleton and D. Tait. London: Routledge and Kegan Paul.

Lienhardt, G. 1961. *Divinity and Experience.* Oxford: Clarendon Press.

Lindstrom, Monty. 1981. "Achieving Wisdom: Knowledge and Politics on Tanna (Vanuatu)." Unpublished Ph.D. thesis. Department of Anthropology, University of California, Berkeley.

Livingstone, D. 1875. *The Last Journals of David Livingstone,* ed. Horace Waller. New York: Harper and Brothers.

London Missionary Society. 1804. *Transactions of the London Missionary Society.* Volume I: *1795–1802.* London: Bye and Law.

London Missionary Society. 1806. *Transactions of the London Missionary Society in the Years 1803, 1804, 1805, 1806.* London: N.p.

London Missionary Society. N.d. *Transactions of the London Missionary Society, 1818–1820.* London.

Long, C. Chaillé. 1877. *Central Africa.* New York: Harper and Brothers.

Low, D. A. 1968. "Converts and Martyrs in Buganda." In *Christianity in Tropical Africa,* ed. C. G. Baeta. Oxford: The University Press.

Low, D. A. 1971. *Buganda in Modern History.* Berkeley: University of California Press.

Low, D. A. N.d. *Religion and Society in Buganda 1875–1900.* London: Kegan Paul Trench Tribner and Company.

Low, D. A., and Pratt, R. C. 1960. *Buganda and British Overrule 1900–1955.* London: Oxford University Press.

Lowie, R. H. 1962. *The Origin of the State.* New York: Russell and Russell.

MacLeod, W. C. 1924. *The Origin of the State.* Philadelphia: N.p.

Mahler, M. 1968. *On Human Symbiosis and the Vicissitudes of Individuation.* New York: International Universities Press.

Mahler, M., Pine, F., and Bergman, A. 1975. *The Psychological Birth of the Human Infant.* New York: Basic Books.

Mair, L. P. 1934. *An African People in the Twentieth Century.* London: George Routledge and Sons.

Mair, L. P. 1961. "Clientship in East Africa." *Cahiers d'Etudes Africaines* II:315–25.

Mair, L. P. 1962. *Primitive Government.* Baltimore: Penguin Books.

Malinowski, B. N.d. *The Sexual Life*

of Savages. New York: Harcourt, Brace and World.

Malo, D. 1971. *Hawaiian Antiquities.* Honolulu: Bishop Museum Press.

Maquet, J. J. 1961. *The Premise of Inequality in Ruanda.* London: Oxford University Press.

Maquet, J. J. 1971. *Power and Society in Africa.* London: Weidenfeld and Nicolson.

Mariner, W. 1820. *An Account of the Natives of the Tonga Islands,* ed. John Martin. Boston: Charles Ewer.

Mead, M. 1950. *Sex and Temperament in Three Primitive Societies.* New York: Mentor Books.

Menzies, A. 1920. *Hawaii Nei, 128 Years Ago.* Honolulu: N.p.

Middleton, J., and Tait, D., eds. 1958. *Tribes Without Rulers.* London: Routledge and Kegan Paul.

Miti, James. N.d. "A Short History of Buganda, Bunyoro, Busoga, Toro and Ankole," trans. G. K. Rock. Unpublished manuscript. Copy in Columbia University Library.

Moore, W. T. 1975. "The Impact of Surgery on Boys." *The Psychoanalytic Study of the Child* 30:529–48.

Mukasa, H. 1946. "The Rule of the Kings of Buganda." *Uganda Journal* X:136–43.

Mukasa, H. N.d. "Simuda Nyuma (Ebiro by Mutesa)," trans. John Rowe. Unpublished manuscript. Copy in Columbia University Library.

Mukwaya, A. B. 1953. *Land Tenure in Buganda.* Kampala: The Eagle Press.

Nsimbi, M. B. 1956. "Village Life and Customs in Buganda." *Uganda Journal* XX:27–36.

Nyakatura, J. 1973. *Anatomy of an African Kingdom.* Garden City, N.Y.: Anchor Books.

Oberg, K. 1940. "The Kingdom of Ankole in Uganda." In *African Political Systems,* ed. M. Fortes and E. E. Evans-Pritchard. pp. 121–62. London: Oxford University Press.

Oded, A. 1974. *Islam in Uganda.* New York: John Wiley and Sons.

Oliver, D. 1974. *Ancient Tahitian Society.* Honolulu: University Press of Hawaii.

Oliver, R. 1959. "The Royal Tombs of Buganda." *Uganda Journal* XXIII:124–33.

Oliver, R. 1966. *The Missionary Factor in East Africa.* London: Longmans, Green and Company.

Oliver, R., and Matthew, G., eds. 1963. *History of East Africa.* Volume I. Oxford: The University Press.

Oppenheimer, F. 1926. *The State: Its History and Development Viewed Sociologically.* New York: Vanguard Press.

Piaget, J. 1929. *The Child's Conception of the World.* London: Kegan Paul, Trench, Trubner and Company.

Radcliffe-Brown, A. A. 1965. *Structure and Function in Primitive Society.* New York: The Free Press.

Radcliffe-Brown, A. A., and Forde, D., eds. 1950. *African Systems of Kinship and Marriage.* London: Oxford University Press.

Rank, O. 1969. *The Myth of the Birth of the Hero.* New York: Vintage Books.

Ray, B. 1977. "Death, Kingship, and

Royal Ancestors in Buganda." In *Religious Encounters with Death,* ed. F. Reynolds and E. Waugh. University Park: Pennsylvania State University Press.

Rice, W. H. 1971. *Hawaiian Legends.* New York: Kraus Reprint Company.

Richards, A. I. 1960. "Social Mechanisms for the Transfer of Political Rights in Some African Tribes." *Journal of the Royal Anthropological Institute* 90:175–90.

Richards, A. I., ed. 1960. *East African Chiefs.* London: Faber and Faber.

Richards, A. I. 1961. "African Kings and Their Royal Relatives." *Journal of the Royal Anthropological Institute* 91:135–50.

Richards, A. I. 1966. *The Changing Structure of a Ganda Village.* Nairobi: East African Publishing House.

Ritter, E. A. 1950. *Shaka Zulu.* New York: G. P. Putnam's Sons.

Rodman, S. 1938. *A New Anthology of Modern Poetry.* New York: The Modern Library.

Roscoe, J. 1907. "Kibuka, the War God of the Baganda." *Man* VII: 161–66.

Roscoe, J. 1922. *The Soul of Central Africa.* London: Cassell and Company.

Roscoe, J. 1923. *The Bakitara or Banyoro.* Cambridge: At the University Press.

Roscoe, J. 1924. *The Bagesu.* Cambridge: At the University Press.

Roscoe, J. 1965. *The Baganda.* London: Frank Cass and Company.

Roscoe, J. 1969. *Twenty-five Years in East Africa.* New York: Negro Universities Press.

Roscoe, J., and Kagwa, Apolo. N.d. "Enquiry into Native Land Ten-

ure in the Uganda Protectorate." Unpublished manuscript. Copy in Yale University Law Library of original in Oxford Library.

Rowe, J. 1964. "Mika Sematimba." *Uganda Journal* XXVIII:179–99.

Rowe, J. 1966. "Revolution in Buganda 1856–1900. Part One: The Reign of Kabaka Mukabya Mutesa 1856–1884." Unpublished Ph.D. thesis, University of Wisconsin.

Rowe, J. 1969. *Lugard at Kampala.* Kampala: Longmans of Uganda.

Rowe, J. 1970. "Introduction." In *Two Kings of Uganda,* by R. P. Ashe, 2d ed. London: Frank Cass.

Rowe, J. 1975. "The Patterns of Political Administration in Precolonial Buganda." In *African Themes: Northwestern University Studies in Honor of Gwendolen M. Carter,* ed. I. Abu-Lughod. Evanston: Northwestern University Press.

Rutter, O., ed. 1935. *The Journal of James Morrison.* London: Golden Cockerel Press.

Sagan, E. 1974. *Cannibalism: Human Aggression and Cultural Form.* New York: Harper and Row.

Sagan, E. 1979. *The Lust to Annihilate: A Psychoanalytic Study of Violence in Ancient Greek Culture.* New York: Psychohistory Press.

Sagan, E. 1979. "Religion and Magic: A Developmental View." In *Religious Change and Continuity,* ed. H. Johnson. San Francisco: Jossey-Bass.

Sahlins, M. 1958. *Social Stratification in Polynesia.* Seattle: University of Washington Press.

Sahlins, M. 1962–63. "Poor Man, Rich Man, Big-Man, Chief: Political Types in Melanesia and Polynesia." *Comparative Studies in Society and History* V:285–303.

Sahlins, M. 1972. *Stone Age Economics.* Chicago: Aldine Publishing Company.

Sahlins, M. N.d. "The Apotheosis of Captain Cook." Unpublished manuscript.

Schapera, I. 1956. *Government and Politics in Tribal Societies.* London: Watts.

Schmidt, P. 1974. "An Investigation of Early and Late Iron Age Cultures Through Oral Tradition and Archaeology . . ." Unpublished Ph.D. thesis, Northwestern University.

Schweinfurth, G. 1888. *Emin Pasha (Eduard Schnitzer) in Central Africa,* trans. Mrs. R. W. Felkin. London: George Philip and Son.

Service, E. R. 1962. *Primitive Social Organization.* New York: Random House.

Service, E. R. 1975. *Origins of the State and Civilization.* New York: W. W. Norton.

Shorter, A. 1972. *Chiefship in Western Tanzania.* Oxford: Clarendon Press.

Shorter, A. 1973. "Interlacustrine Chieftainship in Embryo?" *Tanzania Notes and Records,* no. 72, pp. 37–50.

Smith, E. W., ed. 1950. *African Ideas of God.* London: Edinburgh House Press.

Smith, M. G. 1960. *Government in Zazzau, 1800–1950.* London: Oxford University Press.

Southall, A. 1956. *Alur Society.* Cambridge: W. Heffer and Sons.

Southwold, M. 1965. "The Ganda of Uganda." In *Peoples of Africa,* ed. J. Gibbs. New York: Holt, Rinehart and Winston.

Southwold, M. 1966. "Succession to the Throne in Buganda." In *Succession to High Office,* ed. J. Goody. Cambridge: Cambridge University Press.

Speke, J. 1969. *Journal of the Discovery of the Source of the Nile.* New York: Dutton.

Spencer, B., and Gillen, F. J. 1927. *The Arunta.* London: The Macmillan Company.

Stanley, H. M. 1878. *Through the Dark Continent.* Volume I. New York: Harper and Brothers.

Strachey, J. 1966. "Editor's Introduction." In *The Standard Edition of the Complete Psychological Works of Sigmund Freud.* Volume I. London: The Hogarth Press

Taylor, J. V. 1958. *The Growth of the Church in Buganda.* London: SCM Press.

Thomas, D. 1946. *Selected Writings.* New York: New Directions.

Thomas, H. B., and Scott, R. 1935. *Uganda.* Oxford: The University Press.

Thoonen, J. 1941. *Black Martyrs.* London: Sheed and Ward.

Thornton, R. 1974. "The Kibuga, the Traditional Capital of the Buganda." Unpublished M.A. thesis, University of Chicago, Department of Anthropology.

Twaddle, M. 1972. "The Muslim Revolution in Buganda." *African Affairs,* no. 71, pp. 54–72.

Tyerman, D., and Bennet, G. 1822. *Journal of Voyages and Travels, Compiled by James Montgomery,* 2 vols. Boston: Crocker and Brewster.

United Press International. February 19, 1979. Dispatch from Berkeley, California, cited in *The*

Record (Hackensack, New Jersey).

Vancouver, G. 1967. *Voyage of Discovery to the North Pacific Ocean and Round the World,* 3 vols. New York: DaCapo Press.

Vansina, J. 1962. "A Comparison of African Kingdoms." *Africa* XXXII:324–35.

Vansina, J. 1966. *Kingdoms of the Savanna.* Madison: University of Wisconsin Press.

Walter, E. V. 1969. *Terror and Resistance.* Oxford: The University Press.

Walzer, M. 1969. *The Revolution of the Saints.* New York: Atheneum.

Westervelt, W. D. 1910. *Legends of Ma-ui, a Demi God.* Honolulu: The Hawaiian Gazette Company.

Whiting, J. W. M., and Child, I. S. 1953. *Child Training and Personality.* New Haven: Yale University Press.

Williamson, R. W. 1933. *Religious and Cosmic Beliefs of Central Polynesia.* Cambridge: Cambridge University Press.

Williamson, R. W. 1967. *The Social and Political Systems of Central Polynesia,* 3 vols. The Netherlands: Anthropological Publications.

Wilson, C. T., and Felkin, R. W. 1882. *Uganda and the Egyptian Soudan.* London: Sampson Low, Marstan, Searle, and Rivington.

Wilson, W. 1799. *A Missionary Voyage to the Southern Pacific Ocean.* London: T. Chapman.

Wright, M. 1971. *Buganda in the Heroic Age.* London: Oxford University Press.

Wrigley, C. C. 1959. "Kimera." *Uganda Journal* XXIII:38–43.

Zimbe, Bartolomayo Musoke. N.d. "Buganda and Kings, Being a Translation of 'Buganda Ne Kabaka,'" trans. Simon Musoke. Unpublished manuscript. Copy in Columbia University Library.

Index

abortion, 202
Abraham, Karl, 150
adaptability, in Buganda, 17
address, forms of, 280–1
adolescence, 48, 378
adultery, 218–20, 244
advanced complex societies, xx, 68;
    human sacrifice in, 132–3;
    orderliness and imagination in,
    99–101; plundering in, 74–5; power
    in, 14–15; schools and teachers in,
    104; as transitional phenomenon,
    336–7; see also complex societies;
    and individual societies
Aeschylus, 133, 175
Agamemnon (Aeschylus), 133
aggression, 248, 249, 379
aggressive drive, 368
aggressive license, 320–2, 334–5
aggressor, identification with the,
    350–3
Ahmed bin Ibrahim, 29–30
Ainsworth, Mary D. Salter, 157
alcoholic drinks, 16
Alur, 308–9, 310, 311
American missionaries, in Hawaiian
    Islands, 38, 39, 92–3
anarchy, interregnum, 331–9
ancestors, in early monarchies, 315
Anderson, William, 216, 217

animal sacrifice, 133, 371
Ankole, 7, 16, 185–6, 331–3, 335
anthropology, xviii
Anuak, 306
anxiety, 296; cruelty and, 165; human
    sacrifice and, 120–4; separation, 357,
    358; stranger, 362–3; see also fear
archaeology, xviii
archaic civilizations, xvii–xviii, 363–5;
    human sacrifice discontinued in,
    118–19
Arioi society, 69–77; application and
    initiation into, 73, 76; burial and
    funeral rites in, 73–4; infanticide
    in, 75–6; plundering associated
    with visits of, 74, 75; sexual
    violation in, 75; social class and, 73;
    as voluntary association, 72–4
aristocracy, 144–6, 342–3; dwarfs, fools,
    jesters and, 170–2; homosexuality
    among, 206; see also class tyranny
aristocratic lineages, in primitive
    societies, 240–1
Aristotle, 46
art, 141–2; erotic, 218
Ashanti, 169
Ashe, Robert, 25, 55–6
astrology, 137
astronomy, 137, 138
atheism, King Finow I's, 85

attachment, modes of, 220–2
Australian aborigines, 211–12
authority, 236; *see also* political
    authority
autistic stage, 354
Aztecs, 119, 129, 130, 332

Babylonia, 136
Baganda, the. *See* Buganda
Baganda missionaries, 44
Balamaga, 265
Balzac, Honoré de, 145
bananas, 8
bands (band society), 13, 232–6
Bantu language family, 5
Bantu peoples, 5, 257
Banyoro, the. *See* Bunyoro
bards, 166–8; *see also* poetry
bataka land, 262–4
batongole. See *mutongole*
batongole land, 262–4
Beaglehole, J. C., 76
Bellah, Robert, xix
Best, E., 188
betrayal, martyrdom and, 47, 48
Bible, the, 102
big-man, in Melanesia, 312
bisexuality, 205–6
Bligh, Capt. William, 75, 142–3, 180,
    197, 217, 219
Booboonoo, chief, 189
Borabora, 45–6
bowels, 155–7, 162
breakdown of kinship system, xx–xxi;
    in Buganda, 256–60; human
    sacrifice and, 121–2; modes of
    attachment and, 222; monarchy
    and, 274–5
Bruno and Bosa, story of, 46, 47
brutality. *See* cruelty
Buddu, 45, 100–1
Buganda (the Baganda), xv, xviii,
    3–26, 67, 135, 140, 174, 238; bananas
    as staple of, 8; bisexuality in, 205;
    under British rule, 147–9; changes
    in the value system of, 329–30;

chieftainships in, 265; child rearing
in, 10, 197, 254–6, 279; Christian
enthusiasm in, 44–5; Christianity
and, 19–21, 24–6, 29, 34–6, 40–1,
49–50; Christians in. *See*
Christians, in Buganda; clans, 6,
258–60, 262, 263, 267–74; cleanliness
of, 101; confrontation between
Suna and Kigemuzi, 151–4; cruelty
in, 162–4; eternal fire in, 110–11;
excretory functions in, 151–4;
executioners in, 112–13; forms of
address in, 280–1; hierarchy in,
286–8; history in, 5, 146–7;
household servants in, 283–4;
human sacrifice in, 112–13, 120–1,
124–6, 142; infanticide in, 200;
Islam and, 3, 4, 19–20, 24, 29–32, 35;
king in. See *kabaka*; kinship
system, 6, 256–60, 266; land
ownership in, 262–4; language in,
104–5; law and justice in, 247–8,
281; mediums in, 328; missionaries
in, 340–1; mobility in, 257–9, 263;
money in, 137; Muslims in, 275, 276
(see also Islam and *above);*
orderliness and imagination in,
99–101; patron-client relationship
in, 257–9; persecution of Christians
in, 24–6, 39–41, 43, 49–54;
persecutions of clans in, 270–1;
plundering in, 75; poetry in, 169;
political authority in, 258;
population of, 9; prime minister
(katikiro) in, 17–20; provinces of, 6;
provincial governors in, 13–18,
100–1, 258, 262–3, 265–6, 273–4, 286,
340–1; raising of boys in, 10;
religion in, 19–26, 29–38, 40–1,
44–5, 328–30, 340–1; religious wars
in, 4, 44; response to modern
society, 147–9; revolutionary
change in (1888–1900), 43–4; roads
in, 100–1; royal princes in, 11, 259,
337–9; *saza* governorships and, 262,
263, 265–6; sexual and familial

tyranny in, 291–5; slavery in, 14, 18, 19, 281–2; state system of politics in, 6; taxation and forced labor in, 137, 151–2, 282–5; tombs of kings in, 147; tyranny in, 269–70, 278–84, 291–5

Buhaya, 339

buildings, 101–3

Bulamogi, 314

Bulemezi, 105

Bunyoro (the Banyoro), 7, 8, 15, 126, 171, 281, 292–3, 319, 335; interregnum anarchy in, 331, 332; prostitution in, 213–14; succession of kings in, 331, 332

burial, in Arioi society, 73–4

Burundi, 7

Busambira, 308

Busiro, 268, 270, 273–4

Busoga, 8, 65, 142, 267, 314–16, 337

Buza, James, 41

Bwami, 51

calendars, 136, 137

Calvin, John, 293

Campbell, Archibald, 93, 334

cannibalism, 129–34, 379

canoes, 103

capitalism, 377, 381

Cassirer, Ernst, 110, 370

Catholicism, in Hawaii, 38–9

Catholics, in Buganda, 4, 24

celibacy, infanticide and, 75–7

centralized monarchies. *See* kingdoms

ceremonials, public, 122–3

Chadwick, H. Munro, 184

charismatic authority, 44

charismatic kingship, 329–30, 336

charity, Christian, 45–6

chiefs (chieftainships), xx, 7, 8, 301, 304–12; in Buganda, 265; definition of, 238, 304; gift-giving in, 284; kings distinguished from, 304–5; as kinship-system societies, 307, 308; in Polynesian societies, 63; power of, 307–9; transition from headmen

to, 306–7; transition to simple monarchy from, 310–12

childbirth, 199

child rearing, 252–6, 347, 349; in Buganda, 10, 197, 254–6, 279

children: mythic themes involving, 193–4; tyranny and, 291–5; *see also* child rearing; infanticide; infants; Oedipus complex; schools; separation and individuation

Christ. *See* Jesus Christ

Christian charity, 45–6

Christian enthusiasm, 44–6

Christianity, 33, 257; Buganda and, 19–21, 24–6, 29, 34–6, 40–1, 49–50; conversion to. *See* conversion to Christianity; human sacrifice and, 117–18; medieval, 369–70; in Tahiti, 36, 65; trial of pagan gods and, 41–2

Christian missionaries. *See* missionaries

Christians, in Buganda, 4, 38, 185, 275, 276; persecution of, 24–6, 39–41, 43, 49–54

Churchill, Winston, 8

circumcision, 31, 101

civil peace, 243, 246–7

clan headmen, 303, 305–8

clans (clan system), in Buganda, 6, 258–60, 262, 263, 267–74

classes. *See* social classes

class tyranny, 248, 279–82; taxation and forced labor as, 282–6

client-patron relationship, 257–9

Clytemnestra, 372

Colelallo, 120

Colobus Monkey Clan, 265

Colum, Padraic, 169

comedy, 179–80

community, sense of, 375–6; individualism and, 275–6

complex societies, xx–xxii; breakdown of the kinship system and, xx–xxi; human sacrifice in, xxii; rapprochement crisis and, 363; response to modern society, 147–8;

complex societies *(continued)*
    similarities among, xxi; stages of,
    xx; symbols and symbolic forms
    in, 110–11; taxation and forced labor
    in, 282–5; transition from simple
    kingdoms to, 315–18; wealth in, 13;
    see also advanced complex
    societies; kingdoms; *individual
    societies; and specific topics*
composite bands, 234, 235
conflict resolution: in primitive
    societies, 237, 243–6
conquest, 251; simple kingdoms
    brought into being by, 312–13,
    316–17
consent of the governed, 303, 310
control, 154; cruelty and, 165;
    repression and, 157–9
conversion to Christianity, 24–5, 40;
    attachment to old religions and,
    36–7; in Buganda, 36; in Tahiti, 65,
    94
conversion to Islam, 17, 24, 25, 40, 101
Cook, Capt. James, 66, 100, 107–8, 110,
    129, 155, 175, 180, 206, 216, 341; as
    sacrificial victim, 130
cosmogonic myths, 104
Cosmos, the, 128
cousins, 228, 229
creation myth, Tahitian, 138–40
crimes, xvi, 243–4
Cromwell, Oliver, 294
cruelty: in Buganda, 16, 112–13;
    excretory functions and, 150–1,
    162–3; psychological function of,
    164–5; *see also* tyranny
cultural development. *See* social and
    cultural development
custom, xvi; kinship system and, 227–8

Dahomey, 122, 124, 132, 205, 213, 319, 320
dance, 189; Arioi, 69–71; Polynesian,
    175
death of kings, 324–5, 331–5, 337–8
deception, in Buganda, 16
defecation, 151–4; *see also* excretory
    functions

defense mechanism, human sacrifice
    as, 349–53
democracy, 297–8, 330, 375; *see also*
    modern society
development. *See* psychological
    development; social and cultural
    development
developmental energy, 380–3
devil, 127
dialectical development, 373–6
Dingane, 338, 339
Dinka, 241, 245–7, 249, 250
disputes, settlement of, 237, 243–6
Dodds, E. R., xix
dreams, human sacrifice and, 123–4
drives, 367–9
drums, 150–1, 154, 157–8, 160–2
Durkheim, Emile, 301, 329
dwarfs, 170–2

eating: of sacrificed victims, 128–30;
    tabus, 90–4, 334
Edward II, king of England, 131
Egypt, ancient, xix–xx, 18, 101–3, 136
Ellis, Rev., 67, 111, 116–17, 140, 144, 156,
    166, 170, 196–8, 279
embalming, 325
emotions, 156
enemas, 159
energy: developmental, 380–3;
    structural, 380–1
England: fourteenth-century, 131–2; *see
    also* Great Britain
English missionaries, 70; in Buganda,
    4, 21, 25, 256; in Tahiti, 64
enthusiasm, 43; Christian, 44–6
epic poetry. *See* poetry
equality, 297
erotic art, 218
Evans-Pritchard, Edward, 228, 230–1,
    237, 240, 244, 245
evolutionary approach, xviii–xix; *see
    also* social and cultural
    development
excretory functions, 150–65; in
    Buganda, 151–4; control of, 157–9;
    cruelty and, 162–3; in Hawaii,

159–60; in Polynesian societies, 154–5

executioners, in Buganda, 112–13

Exesias, 98

exhibitionism, 215–17

fairy tales, 289–90

Falepapalangi, 103

family, the: authority in, 236, 239, 241; inequality in, 241; triad of the self, society, and, 347–9; tyranny in, 291–5; *see also* kinship

fathers: separation and individuation and, 359–60; sexual and familial tyranny of, 291–5

Faust legend, 127

fear, 296; of re-engulfment, 358–64; *see also* anxiety

Felkin, 282n

Felkin, Rev., 321–2

Fenichel, Otto, 150

fidelity, marital, 218–20

fighting, 244–6; *see also* warfare

Finow Fiji, 87

Finow I, king of Vavau, 59, 78–87, 89, 164; atheism of, 85; Capt. Cook and, 107–8; eloquence of, 82–3; Finow II and, 85–7; humanism of, 81–2; hunting birds and, 83–4; possessed by a former king, 85; Tootawi and, 84–5

Finow II, king of Vavau, 59–61, 80, 85–9; attempt to eliminate war, 87–9

fire, 110–11

fishing by torchlight, 111

fixations, 220–1

fono, 83

food tabus: Hawaiian, 90–4; in Tahiti, 93

fools, 170–2

forced labor, 282–3

Forster, Georg, 69, 76, 182

Frankfort, Henri, xix

fratricidal strife, succession of kings and, 331–3, 337–8

Frazer, J. G., 5

Freud, Anna, 349–50

Freud, Sigmund, 133–4, 248, 249, 291–2, 334, 349, 354, 364, 367, 370

Froissart, Jean, 131

funeral rites, Arioi, 73–4

gambling, 212–13, 221

genealogical rank, in Hawaii, 286–7

genealogy, 146, 169–70

Germany, Nazi, 116

gifts, 284; *see also* tributes

Gill, Rev. William, 175–6

gods: anthropomorphic, 132; eating of sacrificed victims by, 128–9; Greek, 327; kings and, 327–9; pagan, trial of, 41–2

golden child, 295–6

Goldman, Irving, 63, 119

Gomba, 265

gonorrhea, 20

Goodrich, Mr. (missionary), 42

Gordon, Gen., 31, 32

Great Britain, Buganda and, 147–9, 287–8

Greece, ancient, 167, 198, 205, 208, 327, 375

Greenacre, Phyllis, 357

guns, 11–12

Haapai, 80, 87

Habe, Mafi, 59–61

Hair (musical), 71

Hala Api Api, 86–7

Hamlet (Shakespeare), 85–6, 88

Hannington, Bishop, 49

harvest celebration: Hawaiian, 105–6; Makahiki, 143

Hauai, 63

Hawaii, 34, 42, 44, 46, 62, 63, 279; Catholicism in, 38–9; human sacrifice in, 114, 119, 125–6; infanticide in, 196; missionaries in, 38, 39; sports in, 143–4

Hawaiian Islands, 63, 66–8, 135–7; abolition of tabus in, 90–1; adultery in, 219–20; baby contests in, 218; children of liaisons with

Hawaiian Islands *(continued)*
 Cook's men, 110; cruelty in, 163–4;
 dance in, 175; excretory functions
 in, 159–60; forced labor in, 284–6;
 gambling in, 212; genealogical rank
 in, 286–7; harvest celebration in,
 105–6; heroic legends in, 189–90;
 hierarchy in, 286–9; homosexuality
 in, 206–7; interregnum period in,
 334, 335; kings of, 319, 321, 322, 324,
 325, 334, 357; knowledge about, 67;
 medicine in, 140–1, 158–9;
 missionaries in, 38, 39, 92–3;
 omnipotence of kings of, 321, 322,
 324, 325; pariah class in, 282; poetry
 and bards in, 166–70, 179; residence
 buildings in, 101; response to
 modern society, 147, 148; riddle
 contests in, 172–3; roads in, 102–3;
 surfing in, 98–9; theatre in, 179–81;
 transfer of people in, 265;
 transition from simple to complex
 kingdom in, 316; tyranny in, 278–9,
 281, 282; unification of, 66–7;
 vituperation contests in, 173–4; *see
 also individual islands and
 individual kings*
headmen, 303, 305–8
heirs, 292–3, 330
Henry, Teuira, 76
Henry II, king of England, 327
heroic age, 184–95; legends of, 187–91;
 themes of oral literatures of, 191–5
hierarchy: ethos of subordination and,
 286–9; in fairy tales and popular
 stories, 289–90; tyranny as abuse
 of, 277–8
Hihifo, 83–4, 88
Hinai, 168
historiography of Buganda, 5
history, sense of, 146–7
holua (sledding downhill), 143
Homer, 167; *Iliad,* 81, 82, 186, 189
homicide, ritual. *See* sacrifice, human
homosexuality, 204–10
Hoomanakii, 39
Huahine, 37, 180

human sacrifice. *See* sacrifice, human
humor, 142, 158; *see also* comedy;
 jesters
Hunnewell, Mr., 90
hunting-and-gathering societies. *See*
 bands

idealism: terrorism and, 47–8
identification with the aggressor, 350–3
idolatry, Catholicism as, 39
Ii, John Papa, 34, 35, 163–4, 252–5
Iliad (Homer), 81, 82, 186, 189
imaginative forms, explosion of,
 99–101
Imaikalani, king of Hawaii, 192
imperialism, democracy and, 375
inachi ceremony, 88
incest, 228, 229; royal, xxi, 319
India, 118
individualism, 301; community and,
 275–6; kinship and, 375–6
individuality, xvii, xxi
individuation. *See* separation and
 individuation
inequality: in the family, 241; in
 primitive societies, 239–41
infanticide, 193, 196–203; in Buganda,
 200; celibacy and, 75–7; female,
 198–200; motives for, 197–200; in
 Tahiti, 196–8, 200–3
infants: Hawaiian baby contests, 218;
 nursing, 279; weaning of, 255–6;
 see also child rearing; infanticide
instinct, 367–8
*Intellectual Adventure of Ancient Man,
 The* (Frankfort), xix
intellectuals, 104
interregnum anarchy (or civil war),
 331–9
irrigation, 101, 102
Islam: Buganda and, 3, 4, 19–20, 24,
 29–32, 35; conversion to, 17, 24, 25,
 40, 101

Jahweh, 322, 324
Jarves, James, 90
Jefferson, Henry, 209–10

jesters, 170–2
Jesus Christ, 116–18, 133, 193–4, 296, 372
Jews, 123
justice, 247–8; *see also* law

Kaahumanu, 91–2
kabaka (king), 6, 11, 14, 40, 107, 121, 122,
    147, 293, 303, 319, 357; accession
    rites, 323–4; clans and, 262, 263,
    267–74; death of, 335, 337–8; gods
    and, 328; killing of half-brothers of,
    338–9; land tenure system and,
    262–4; omnipotence of, 321–5;
    provincial governors and, 340–1;
    royal princes and, 11, 259; *saza*
    governorships in, 262, 263, 265–6;
    sexual and aggressive license of,
    321–2; succession of, 335, 337–8;
    tombs of, 325; tyranny of, 269 70;
    see also individual kings
Kabazzi, 268–9
Kaboyo, king of Toro, 339–40
Kaggwa, Andrew, 24, 53
kago, 265–6
Kagulu, Kabaka (king) of Buganda,
    270
Kagwa, Apolo, 5, 44, 185–6, 267
Kahu, 171
Kaingang, 302
Kakoloboto, 30
Ka-lani-opuu, king of Hawaii, 162
Kalaniopuu, king of Hawaii, 168
Kalema, king of Buganda, 55
Kalemba, xi–xiii, 34–5
Kamakau, 205–6
Kamanya, Kabaka (king) of Buganda,
    321
Kamehameha I, king of Hawaii, 66–7,
    90, 91, 147, 148, 189–91, 205, 264–5,
    334, 340, 341
Kamehameha III, king of Hawaii, 319
Kamrasi, king of Bunyoro, 171
Kanaloa-Kuaana, king of Hawaii, 154
Kapiolani, 42
Karague, 7
Karana-tua, 206
katikiro (prime minister), 17–20

Katinvuma clan, 164
Kauai, 66, 102, 111, 137, 155
Kauwa, 125–6
Kenya, 148–9
Kepakailiula, 155, 172–3
Kigemuzi, 151–4
Kihapi'ilani, king of Maui, 102
Kila, 162
kimbugwe, 268, 269
kingdoms, xv–xvii, 7; consent of the
    governed in, 303, 310; kinship and,
    274–5; simple, 310–18; *see also*
    complex societies; unification
kings (kingship): accession rites, 323–4;
    aggressive license of, 320–2;
    authoritarian and tyrannical nature
    of, 293, 294; in Buganda. See
    kabaka; charismatic, 329–30, 336;
    chiefs distinguished from, 304–5;
    death of, 324–5, 331–4; definition of,
    304; gods and, 327–9; Hawaiian,
    319, 321, 322, 324, 325, 334, 357;
    human sacrifice and, 132, 322;
    interregnum anarchy (or civil
    war), 331–9; marriage partners, 319;
    mock, ceremonies involving, 331–3;
    obeisance rituals, 322–3; Oedipal
    strife and, 339; omnipotence of.
    See omnipotence of kings;
    physical health of, 323; rebellion
    against, 337–41; sexual license of,
    320–1; sons of, 194–5; succession of,
    331–3; as symbolic transformation,
    371; in Tahiti, 266–7; tantrum
    behavior of, 320, 326–7, 358
kinship, 225–7; democracy and, 375;
    feelings of, 225–6; individualism
    and, 375–6; kinship system
    distinguished from, 226–7;
    monarchy and, 274–5; the state
    and, 232; unilateral, 229; *see also*
    clans; family, the; lineage
kinship system, xvi, 72, 73;
    authoritarian kinship and, 294;
    breakdown of. *See* breakdown of
    kinship system; Buganda, 6,
    256–60, 266; chieftainships and,

kinship system *(continued)*
   307, 308; kinship distinguished
   from, 226–7; monarchy and,
   261–76; Nuer, 228, 230–2, 250;
   origins of, 232–6; patrilineal,
   229–30; primitive societies and,
   226–32; the state and, 261; *see also*
   clans
Kinyaro, 287
Kitinda, 113
kitunzi, 265
Kiuebulaya, Apolo, 44
Kiwewa, king of Buganda, 55
Klein, Melanie, 162
Kluckhohn, Clyde, 68
Koki, 194–5
konohiki, 284–5
Kotzebue, Otto, 91, 93
Kukaea, 155
Kyandondo, 265

Laius, 76–7
laments, 176–9
land ownership, 148–9, 261–4
language: self-consciousness about,
   104–5; written, 136
latency, 378
latrines, 160–1
law, 243–4, 281
leaf of the coconut tree *(niau)*, 110
legends, heroic, 187–91
libido, 220–1
license: aggressive, 334–5; sexual, 320–1,
   334, 335
Liholiho, king of Hawaii, 67, 90–4,
   321, 340
Liloa, king of Hawaii, 192–3, 206–7
Linant, 163
lineage: aristocratic, 240–1; minimal,
   230; minor, 231; *see also* kinship
Livingstone, David, 321
Livinhac, Père, 34–6
Lourdel, Père, 26, 49, 53, 267
love, martyrdom and, 47–8
Luganda, 5, 104–5
Lugbara, 246, 247
Lumwemo Nakirindisa, 151–2

Lupeakawaiowainiha, 154
Luwedde, Princess, xi–xiii

Mackay, Alexander, 21–2, 24–6, 35, 38,
   51, 267
magic, xvii
Mahler, Margaret, 257, 349, 353–65,
   373–4, 376
Makahiki harvest celebration, 143
Makumbi, 16
Malinowski, Bronislaw, 204
Mamaeaputo, 103
mandwa (mediums), 328
Mangaia, 161; human sacrifice in,
   114–16; theatre in, 175–9
Mangareva, 194
Manihiki, 136
Mann, Thomas, 127
Maori, 104, 129, 160–1, 187–8
Mape, 144
Maquet, 205–6, 304–5
marae, 102
Mariner, William, 60–1, 63–4, 81, 85–9,
   108, 164, 187, 285–6
marionettes, Hawaiian, 179–81
marital fidelity, 218–20, 244
market dues, 283
Marquesas Islands, 128, 129
marriage, 227; dynastic, 275; residence
   after, 230; to sisters and half-sisters,
   319
martyrdom, 27–9; betrayal and, 47, 48;
   in Buganda, 48; love and hatred
   in, 47–8; morality and, 28; suicide
   and, 28–9; terrorism and, 47–8;
   tragedy and, 46–7
Marx, Karl, 381–2
masochism, 333–4
masturbation, 205
matrilocal system, 230
Maui, 63, 66, 101, 102, 335
Mawanda, Kabaka (king) of Buganda,
   266
Mbaga, 46
Mead, Margaret, 204, 208–9
medicine, 140–1, 158–9
Melanesia, 312

Mesopotamia, 102
Mhlangana, 338
military conquest. *See* conquest
minimal lineage, 230
minor lineage, 231
Mirambo, 109, 317
missionaries, 256; Baganda, 44; in
    Buganda, 340–1; English. *See*
    English missionaries; in Hawaii,
    38, 39, 92–3; in Society Islands,
    106–7; on Tahiti, 287
mock king, 331–3
modern society: human sacrifice and,
    127–8, 131, 134; response of complex
    societies to, 147–8; *see also*
    democracy
Moerenhout, 70–1, 76
monarchies. *See* kingdoms
monarchs. *See* kings
money, 137, 159, 221
morality: martyrdom and, 28
Morrison, James, 179
Moses, 193
mother: fear of re-engulfment by,
    358–64; as object of attachment,
    220, 221; separation from, 255;
    separation from the, 121–2 (*see also*
    separation and individuation); *see*
    also Oedipus complex
Mpande, 338
Mua, 162
mugema, 268, 270, 273–4, 279
Muggale, Princess, 51
Mugwanya, Stanislaus, 44
Mukajanga, 39, 43, 46, 50
Mukasa, Ham, 31, 32
Mukasa, Joseph, 24, 49–50, 53
Mukasa, Katikiro (prime minister),
    xi–xiii, 10–26, 50–6; assassinated, 55;
    cruelty and sadism of, 50–1;
    deception and cruelty of, 16–17; as
    kawuta, 12; Kiwewa and, 55; Joseph
    Mukasa and, 50; as *mutongole*,
    11–12; Mwanga and, 23–4; overthrow
    of Mwanga and, 54–5; persecution
    of Christians and, 51–4; as prime
    minister *(katikiro)*, 17–26; as

provincial governor *(pokino)*, 13–18;
    religion and, 20, 26, 41; sent into
    retirement, 55; as youth, 10–11
Mukwenda, 16
Muller, Max, 179
Mulumba, Matthias, 45, 52–3
music: Arioi, 69–71; *see also* songs
Muslims: in Buganda, 54, 55, 275, 276;
    see also Islam
Mutebi, Kabaka (king) of Buganda,
    266
Mutesa, Kabaka (king) of Buganda,
    xi, xiii, 3, 5, 9, 13–14, 19–23, 75, 108,
    142, 148, 205, 264, 275, 281; accession
    of, 10; changes in the value system
    and, 329–30; clans and, 267–9;
    cruelty of, 163; human sacrifice
    and, 124; illness and incapacity of,
    20–2, 321–2; omnipotence of, 329;
    religion and, 20, 24–5, 30–2, 35,
    328–30, 340–1
mutongole (batongole): land held by,
    262–4
mutongole (pl. *batongole*), 11–12
Mwafu, 51–2
Mwanga, Kabaka (king) of Buganda,
    4, 23–6, 148, 266, 275, 340–1;
    Muggale's affair with Bwami and,
    51; overthrow of, 54–5; persecution
    of Christians by, 39–41, 49–54
myths, 107; cosmogonic, 104; themes
    of, 191–5

naiu (leaf of the coconut tree), 110
nakedness, 215–17
Nalwanga, Sarah, 25
Namaka, 168
Namfumbambi, Alexandro, 33
navigation, 137–8
Nazi Germany, 116
needs, 368–70
New Zealand, 62; *see also* Maori
Njikiza Ngcolosi, 187
Nkrumah, Kwame, 261
Nott, Brother, 36
Nowfaho, 82
Ntwatwa, 18

Nuer, 215, 230–2, 243–6, 302, 365, 370; aristocratic lineages among, 240–1; conflict resolution among, 237, 244; fighting among, 244–6; kinship system, 228, 230–2, 250; leopard-skin chiefs, 237, 240; at war, 249, 250
nursing infants, 279
Nuu, 159–60
Nyungu-ya-Mawe, 317–18

Oahu, 63, 66, 265, 278–9
obeisance, rituals of, 322–3
object constancy, 376
Oedipus, king of Thebes, 76–7, 130, 167, 172, 193, 372–3
Oedipus complex (Oedipal stage or crisis), 129–30, 361, 364, 365; symbolic transformation and, 370–3
Oliver, Douglas, 213
Oliver, Roland, 147
omnipotence of kings, 132, 293, 303, 304, 313–14, 319–30, 333–43; accession rites and, 323–4; charismatic kingship and, 329–30; death and, 324–5; gods and, 327–9; human sacrifice and, 322; interregnum period and, 333–6; obeisance rituals and, 322–3; physical health and, 323; provincial governors and, 340–3; routinization of, 336–43; sexual and aggressive license and, 320–2; tantrum behavior and, 326–7
omnipotence of parents, separation and individuation and, 359–60
oppression. *See* tyranny
oral fixations, 220–1
oral tradition, 146–7
orderliness, in advanced complex societies, 99–101
Oresteia (Aeschylus), 372
Oro, 73, 74, 114
Orsmond, Reverend, 67, 71, 106, 107, 287

pages at Buganda royal court, 10–11, 163, 254

Pakuanui, 168
Palaha, 140, 159
panic, 165, 296
Papa, 104
Papara, 102
Parsons, Talcott, xix
Pasha, Emin, 55
patrilineal bands, 234
patrilineal systems, 229–30
patrilocal system, 230
patron-client relationship, 257–9
penis, 217–18
Phoenicia, 118
physical imperfection, as obstacle to kingship, 320
Piaget, Jean, 156
piety, 34, 36
Plains Indians, 204
poetry (songs; lays), 185; Hawaiian, 166–70, 179; warfare and, 186–7
poets. *See* bards
pokino (provincial governors), 13–18, 100–1, 258, 262–3, 265–6, 273–4, 286, 340–1
political authority, origin and basis of, 236–9
political power, 14–15, 236; in simple kingdoms, 313–14
political tyranny. *See* tyranny
politics, 226; kinship, 230
Polynesian peoples, 38, 62–3; canoes of, 103
Polynesian societies, 62–3, 111, 135–8, 140; bisexuality in, 205; categories of, 63; excretory functions in, 154–5; forced labor in, 284–6; human sacrifice in, 119; knowledge about, 67; sports in, 143–4; theatre in, 174, 179; tribute-giving in, 285–6; *see also individual societies*
Pomare I, king of Tahiti, 65, 93, 124, 326; birth of Pomare II and, 113–14
Pomare II, king of Tahiti, 45, 65, 94, 205, 295; birth of, 113–14
Pope, Alexander, 69
possession: of kings Finow I and II, 85–6

power, 132; political. *See* political
    power; symbolic, in simple
    kingdoms, 313; *see also*
    omnipotence of kings
pre-eminence of states, 7–8
pre-Oedipal stage, 370, 372
prestige, in primitive societies, 239–41
primitive societies, xvi–xx; age sets in,
    73; aristocratic lineages in, 240–1;
    associations in, 72–4; civil peace in,
    246–7; conflict resolution in, 237,
    243–6; crimes in, 243–4;
    developmental energy of, 381–3;
    development of, 364–5; fighting in,
    244–6; homosexuality in, 204;
    inequality in, 239–41; kinship
    system and, 226–32; land ownership
    in, 261–2; political authority in,
    237 9; prestige in, 239 41; rape in,
    75; separation and individuation in,
    361–3, 382–3; transition from band
    society to, 233–6; warfare in,
    248–51; *see also* tribal societies
primogeniture, 292
princes, royal, 331–3, 337–9; in
    Buganda, 11, 259
privies, 150, 153–4
Prometheus, 46–7
prostitution, 71, 213–15
Protestants: in Buganda, 24, 25; *see
    also* Christians
provincial governors, 340–3; in
    Buganda, 13–18, 100–1, 258, 262–3,
    265–6, 273–4, 286, 340–1
psychic mechanisms, 349–53; *see also*
    defense mechanisms
psychoanalytic theory, 349, 370, 372
psychological development: as
    dialectical, 373–4, 376; social and
    cultural development and, 347–9,
    364–6; stages in, 378–80; *see also*
    separation and individuation
public ceremonials, 122–3
public sphere, 74
Puheke, 140, 159
punishment, xvi
Puritans, 294

Radcliffe-Brown, A. A., 381
rage, terrorism and, 47–8
Raiatea, 128
raids, in Buganda, 12–13, 15, 18
Rangi, 104
Rank, Otto, 193
rank order, 286–9; *see also* hierarchy
rape, 75
rapprochement crisis, 358–63; in
    complex societies, 363; fathers and,
    359–60; in primitive societies,
    361–3
rebellion, 337–41
re-engulfment, fear of, 358–64
regression, 220–2; rapprochement crisis
    and, 358–63
religion, 105; abolition of tabus in
    Hawaii and, 92; attachment to old,
    conversion and, 36 7; Finow I
    and, 85; Mutesa and, 20, 24–5, 30–2,
    35, 328–30, 340–1; *see also*
    Christianity; gods; Islam
religious conversion: in Buganda, 48;
    see also conversion to Christianity;
    conversion to Islam
Religious Evolution (Bellah), xix
repression: control and, 157–9; of
    sexuality, 214–15
residence: changes in, in Buganda,
    258; after marriage, 230
riddles, 155, 172–4
ritual, 105–6
ritual homicide. *See* sacrifice, human
roads: in Buganda, 100–1; in Hawaiian
    Islands, 102–3
Rodriguez, Maximo, 286, 326
Rome, ancient, 198
Rongo, 114, 115
Roscoe, Rev. John, 5, 164, 194, 196,
    282–8, 305, 338
Rowe, John, 14*n*, 198*n*, 282*n*, 340–1
Ruggles, Mr. (missionary), 42
Rwanda, 7, 105, 125, 171, 189, 251, 323;
    homosexuality in, 205;
    interregnum period in, 334, 335;
    prostitution in, 213; Tutsi of. *See*
    Tutsi; tyranny in, 291, 292

sacrifice, animal, 133, 373
sacrifice, human, xxii, 27–8, 112–34,
       371–2, 379; anxiety and, 120–4; in
       Buganda, 112–13, 120–1, 124–6, 142;
       cannibalism and, 129–34; Christ as,
       117–18; as a defense mechanism,
       349; dreams and, 123–4; eating of
       victims of, 128–30; in Hawaii, 114,
       119, 125–6; high rank, people of,
       126; kings and, 132; in Mangaia,
       114–16; modern society and, 127–8,
       131, 134; omnipotence of kings and,
       322; social class and, 124–6; in
       Tahiti, 114, 115–17, 119, 123, 124,
       128–30, 322; in Tonga, 119–21; *see
       also* infanticide
Sahlins, Marshall, 119, 312, 382
Sappho, 97
saza land (or governorships), 262, 263,
       265–6
schools, 104, 256
science, 137–8, 140–1
Sebuta, chief, 36
seeing, 221
Sekamwa, 268
self, the: development of the sense of,
       354 (*see also* separation and
       individuation); interdependence
       between society and, 347–9
separation and individuation, 257,
       301–4, 353–66; ambivalence and,
       356, 361, 362; consolidation of
       individuality substage of, 361, 364,
       374; as dialectical, 373–4, 376;
       differentiation substage of, 356;
       disruptions in, 354–5; drive toward,
       368; fathers and, 359–60; fear of
       re-engulfment and, 358–64;
       omnipotence of parents and,
       359–60; practicing substage of,
       356–7; in primitive societies, 361–3,
       382–3; rapprochement crisis in,
       357–63; response of society and
       parents to, 355–6
separation anxiety, 357, 358
separation from the mother, 121–2, 255
servants: household, 283–4

Service, Elman, 234–5
sex (sexuality): in Arioi performances,
       70–2; nakedness and, 215–17;
       prostitution and, 213, 214;
       repression of, 214–15; vice and,
       211–12; *see also* bisexuality; erotic
       art; homosexuality
sex drive, 368, 369; *see also* libido
sexual abstinence, death of the king
       and, 334
sexual license, 320–1, 334, 335
sexual performances, public, 215–17;
       Arioi, 70–2
sexual tyranny, 291–5
Shaka Zulu, 328, 337–9
Shorter, Aylward, 316–17
simple kingdoms, 310–18
singing (singers), 142–3; *see also* bards
slavery, in Buganda, 14, 18, 19, 45,
       281–2
sledding downhill *(holua),* 143
snake: as symbol, 372
social and cultural development,
       xviii–xix, 371–83; as dialectical,
       373–6; stages and radical leaps in,
       376–80; structural and energy
       issues and, 380–3; symbolic
       transformations and, 371–3
social class(es): Arioi society and, 73;
       human sacrifice and, 124–6. *see
       also* aristocracy; class tyranny
Society Islands, 63, 69, 102, 106–7, 110,
       140; theatre in, 180; wrestling
       matches on, 143–4
songs, 142–3; *see also* bards
Speke, John Hanning, xv, xviii, 3, 75,
       100, 101, 163, 171, 337
Sphinx, riddle of the, 172
sports, 143–4
Ssebuggwawo, 51–2
Stanley, Henry Morton, xv, xviii, 20,
       100
state, the (state system), 247;
       definition, 274; definition of, 232;
       power and, 236–7; *see also*
       kingdoms
states, pre-eminence of, 7–8

Steward, Julian, xix, 234
stories, 289–90
Strachey, James, 367
stranger anxiety, 362–3
stratification, in Buganda, xv
structural energy, 380–1
subordination, ethos of, 286–9
substitution, as psychic mechanism,
    353
suffering, 117, 118
suicide: martyrdom and, 28–9;
    terrorism and, 48
Suku, 335
Sumeria, 118, 136, 137
Suna, Kabaka (king) of Buganda, 10,
    12, 20, 29–30, 108; confrontation
    between Kigemuzi and, 151–4
Suna II, Kabaka (king) of Buganda,
    274, 280
Suppliants (Aeschylus), 175
surfing, in Hawaii, 98–9
symbiotic stage, 354; regression to, 358
symbolic power, simple kingdoms
    and, 313
symbolic transformation, 370–3
symbols, 110–11

tabus: abolition of, in Hawaii, 90–1;
    chief's power to break, 308–9; in
    Hawaii, 38, 90–4, 334
Tahiti, 62, 63–5, 122, 174, 281, 286, 316;
    bards in, 167; Christianity in, 36,
    94; coronation ceremonies in, 161;
    creation myth, 138–40; discovery
    of, 64; eating tabus in, 93;
    embalming in, 325; golden child in,
    295–6; homosexuality in, 205,
    207–10; human sacrifice in, 114,
    116–17, 119, 123, 124, 128–30, 322;
    infanticide in, 196–8, 200–3; kings
    of, 322–3, 325–7; kinship system,
    266–7; missionaries on, 287;
    monarchy in, 275; nakedness in,
    216–17; political systems in 18th
    century, 64; prostitution in, 213–15;
    schools and teachers in, 104;
    temples *(marae)* on, 102; theatre in,

179, 181–3; unification of, 65;
    warfare in, 186–7
Tamaahmotoo, 340
Tannese, 156n
tantrum behavior, 320, 326–7
Tanzania, western, 312, 313, 317
tax collecting, 137, 151–2
taxes, 282–6
teachers, 104
Tebukoza, 18
Teriirere, Prince, 102
terrorism, 47–8
theatre (dramatic performances),
    174–83; Arioi, 69–72; comic, 179;
    Greek, 175, 176; Hawaiian, 179–80;
    laments, 176–9; in Munguiu, 175–9;
    Tahitian, 179, 181–3
Thebes, 172
thinking, 155–7
Tiberius Gracchus, 273
tombs of kings of Buganda, 325
Tonga, 59, 63–4, 103, 135, 175, 189, 216,
    279, 281, 341; human sacrifice in,
    119–21; masochistic frenzy in, 333–4;
    tribute-giving on, 285–6; warfare
    in, 187; *see also* Haapai;
    Tongatapu; Vavau
Tongatapu, 78–80, 83, 88
Toobo Nuha, chief, 78–80
Toobo Toa, 87–8
Toogoo Ahoo, king of Tongatapu,
    78–9, 86
Tooi Hala Fatai, 79–80
Tootawi, 84–5
Toro, 339–40
Toynbee, Arnold, 19, 94
tragedy: Greek, 175, 176; martyrdom
    and, 46–7
tribal societies, xv–xvi; *see also*
    primitive societies
tributes, 285–6, 291
Trojan Women, The, 82
Tswana, 321, 324
Tuitonga, 78, 80, 88
Tutsi, 145–6, 171, 189, 213, 251;
    homosexuality among, 205
Tuzinde, Mbaga, 43

Twa, 171
tyranny, 277–98; against class. *See* class
    tyranny; beginnings of, 239; in
    Buganda, 269, 278–84; class, 248;
    day-to-day forms of, 278–82;
    democracy and, 297–8; ethos of
    subordination and, 286–9;
    generational, xvi; in Hawaiian
    Islands, 278–9, 281, 282; sexual, xvi;
    sexual and familial, 291–5

Uganda, 4
Uganda Protectorate, 4, 147
Ukererere, 21–2
Ukimbo, 317
Ukimbu, 311, 312
Ukuru, 311
umbilical cords, 110
Umi, 192–3
unification: of Hawaiian Islands, 66–7;
    of Tahiti, 65; of two chiefdoms
    into a simple monarchy, 310–11
urination, 154; *see also* excretory
    functions
Usongora, 15–16

Vaitamana, 116
Vancouver, George, 90, 156–7, 175, 340
van Gennep, Arnold, 374
Vanzetti, Bartolomeo, 27–9
Vavau, 59–61, 78, 80, 81, 85, 87–8, 171,
    188–9; *see also* Finow I, king of
    Vavau; Finow II, king of Vavau
Vehiatua I, king of Tahiti, 286, 326–7
Venda, 338
vice, 211–12

village headmen, 305–8
vituperation contests: in Hawaii, 173–4
voluntary associations, 72–4

Wales, 182–3
walking, 356, 357
Wallis, Samuel, 64
Walzer, Michael, 294
war, xvii; chief's power to make, 309;
    Finow II's attempt to eliminate,
    87–9
warfare, 246, 248–51; Christian
    enthusiasm and rules of, 45; epic
    poetry and, 186–7; stages of, 251;
    Tongan, 79; tyranny against class
    and, 248–9; *see also* fighting
wealth: differences in, 13
weaning, 255–6
Weber, Max, 44, 247, 329
Wilson, C. T., 282n
Wilson, William, 120
wives: in Buganda, 45
women: Hawaiian tabus and, 90–4;
    rape of, 75; sexual and familial
    tyranny and, 291–5; as tribute, 291;
    wrestling, 144; *see also* marriage
Woolley, Leonard, 118n
wrestling, 143–4
writing, 136

xenophobia, 362–3

Zansanze, Princess, xi
Zanzibari Arabs, 20, 21, 29–30, 55, 101
Zimbe, Bartholome, 45, 185
Zulus, 187, 328, 337–8

A NOTE ON THE TYPE

This book was set in a digitized version of Janson, a recutting made direct from type cast from matrices long thought to have been made by the Dutchman Anton Janson, who was a practicing type founder in Leipzig during the years 1668–1687. However, it has been conclusively demonstrated that these types are actually the work of Nicholas Kis (1650–1702), a Hungarian, who most probably learned his trade from the master Dutch type founder Dirk Voskens. The type is an excellent example of the influential and sturdy Dutch types that prevailed in England up to the time William Caslon (1692–1766) developed his own incomparable designs from them.

Composed by The Haddon Craftsmen, Inc.,
Scranton, Pennsylvania.

Display typography by Trufont Typographers,
Hicksville, New York.

Printed and bound by Fairfield Graphics,
Fairfield, Pennsylvania.

Designed by Cecily Dunham.